Management of Competitiveness

Alexander Chursin • Yury Makarov

Management of Competitiveness

Theory and Practice

Springer

Alexander Chursin
People's Friendship University of Russia
Moscow
Russia

Yury Makarov
Federal Space Agency of Russia
Moscow
Russia

ISBN 978-3-319-16243-0 ISBN 978-3-319-16244-7 (eBook)
DOI 10.1007/978-3-319-16244-7

Library of Congress Control Number: 2015939909

Springer Cham Heidelberg New York Dordrecht London

Printed on acid-free paper

Springer International Publishing AG Switzerland is part of Springer Science+Business Media (www.springer.com)

Contents

About the Authors

Alexander Chursin Dr. hab. in Economics, Ph.D. in Engineering, is Director of the Institute of Applied Technical and Economic Research and Expertise in Peoples' Friendship University of Russia (PFUR), Head of the Department of Applied Economy Studies, Advisor of PFUR Rectorate, and Professor of the Department of Information and Computer Science at the Higher Qualification Commission of Russia. He is a member of the Scientific Council of Russian Academy of Sciences, Expert Council of the Russian Humanitarian Scientific Foundation, and is also a Professor at the Academy of Military Sciences.

Prof. Chursin has been working on executive positions in industry and scientific educational institutions for more than 50 years. He has led large projects of conversion of the defense industry of the USSR and the creation and development of innovative area within the CIS countries on the basis of developed with his participation "Interstate program of innovation cooperation of CIS member states for the period until 2020." He is an author of 23 inventions for which patents were obtained in the field of instrumentation and control system design. On the basis of the results of scientific activity, A. A. Chursin has published over 100 articles and 30 monographs. In recent years, he engaged in research problems of competitiveness management of production, organization, and ensuring the successful performance of domestic products in the world markets.

Prof. Chursin has been awarded many medals and orders of the USSR and Russia for high results in labor and scientific activities including the USSR Council of Ministers Award in the field of science and technology, Tsiolkovsky sign for personal creative contribution in the implementation of space programs and projects, and medal of the "Order of Merit for the Motherland of the II degree.

Yury Makarov Dr. hab. in Economics, Ph.D. in Engineering, is Chief of the Space Activity Strategic Department of the Federal Space Agency of Russia (Roscosmos) and Head of the Department of Competitiveness Management of Aerospace Companies of the Institute of Applied Technical and Economic Research and Expertise in the Peoples' Friendship University of Russia. He is an active member of an International Academy of Astronautics, Academy of Military Economy and Finance, Academy of Cosmonautics named K. E. Tsiolkovsky, and Academy of Engineering Sciences named A. M. Prokhorov, Presidium member of Federation of Cosmonautics of Russia, and a member of Council on Space of Russian Academy of Sciences.

Yury Makarov has been working in the field of space activity for 28 years. As the Head of Space Activity Strategic Department of Roscosmos, he directs the works related to the organization of business management concerning the development and creation of space facilities for socioeconomic and scientific purposes. Scientific and engineering results achieved under his supervision and direct assistance are widely adopted in different fields of Russian space activity and contribute considerably to organization and recognition of the Federal Space Program of Russia. Theoretical research in the sphere of space economy made it possible for Yury Makarov to develop practical approaches for techno-economic grounds of the creation and development of economically effective operation of organizations in terms of uncertainty, economic risks, and financial constraints. He is an author of over 200 scientific papers, including five monographs dedicated to the questions of organization of an effective management of industrial corporations.

Yury Makarov has a title of 1st Class State Advisor of the Russian Federation and has been awarded the Russian Order of Honor for his contribution to the design, development, and production of special equipment, labor achievements, and years of service and medal of the "Order of Merit for the Motherland" of the II degree.

Introduction

1

There is now a natural upsurge of interest in finding knowledge in the field of competitiveness management of production, services, firms, and industries among economists, businessmen, and managers of various levels. This monograph presents certain answers to specific considerations, such as the competitiveness management science advancement, the manner in which the basic economic laws in the process of manufacturing and marketing of products are linked and interrelated. The study shows what hypotheses, postulates, and laws provide the basis of the theory of competitiveness management and what mathematical methods and models within the framework of this theory can be used to perform a quantitative assessment of competitiveness and various economic entities. This monograph offers theoretical approaches for the construction of competitiveness management systems for both individual corporations and the whole industries. It suggests that it is possible to achieve considerable competitive advantages in the internal and external markets on the basis of development and application of innovative solutions.

The authors of this monograph have been dealing with this subject matter since the 1980s by means of tracing the theory of scientific and technological progress and defense-industrial sector of the USSR. The studies proceeded in analyzing new economic processes related to transition of the Russian Federation from the centralized planned system of economy to the market capitalist economy, development of globalization and internationalization of production and Research & Development, occurrence of economic and financial crises, looking for ways of economic recovery and enhancement of the national competitiveness on the basis of development, and commissioning of innovations in various spheres of business activities.

The analyses of development process of scientific and technological progress in the planned system of economy, creation, and implementation of innovative technologies in the market relations within an appreciable length of time clearly demonstrated that the said processes are governed by a human being and his mentality. The higher the mentality, the better the management based on economic laws and postulates when the market in the modern context serves as an index

A. Chursin, Y. Makarov, *Management of Competitiveness*,
DOI 10.1007/978-3-319-16244-7_1

(indicator) to choose direction for development and expansion of production of the most sought-after goods and services.

For the first time, the monograph offers inferential and mathematically proved law of competitiveness management and offers methods of competitiveness management in various competition environments; it also presents approaches to the evaluation of competitiveness of production, corporation, industry, and the state. The monograph identifies the basic problems of management and evaluation of competitiveness and presents original author's developments on competitiveness management in the high-technology industries, based on the use of specific techniques of evaluation of competitiveness of production, corporation, and an industry with application of economic-mathematical methods and models on the basis of specific System of Indicators.

The monograph presents step-by-step instructions to help the reader to evaluate competitiveness of production, corporation, and an industry with application of mathematical methods and models and makes it possible to have a quantitative assessment to form the basis for well-founded management decisions. Practical application of available recommendations for a specific corporation will contribute to creation of an integrated system of competitiveness management and enable considerable promotion of efficiency and profitability of production; it will give a chance to determine by what time the products should be upgraded and/or new products with high competitive advantages be made.

These are the issues and the problems of further development of the theory of competitiveness management this monograph is devoted to.

This monograph appeals to the middle and top management CEOs, working in the real sector of economy, as well as the scientists and experts in competitiveness management at various levels—production, corporation, industry, and national economy.

Formation of the Theory of Competitiveness Management

2

2.1 Genesis and Stages of Development of the Theory of Competitiveness Management Foundations

Nowadays the speculation about competitiveness is so extensive and intensive when scientific community expresses concern over potential influence of this discussion on acceptance of the large-scale governmental and corporate decisions engaging not only the industry and the market but also other major spheres of society. By virtue of the fact that this discussion is notable for its essential conceptual and terminological random nature, it is necessary to open a window on its purposes and to provide the key term being at the heart of debate—the very concept of "competitiveness."

The concept of competitiveness is a sophisticated category due to its application at various levels of generalization where it takes on various values and has various indicators of measurement. The most debatable issue is an interaction of factors to determine dynamics of competitive relations, with this in mind and as a natural result an opinion is advanced that it is impossible to specify how competitiveness is formed: is it additive, linear, or nonlinear, etc.? With reference to any object, subject, process, etc., it changes depending on the purposes, goals, and specific content of research studies; it is revealed from different perspectives depending on the target of research (factors of production, strategy, system, etc.) and the subject of competitiveness (person, enterprises, regions, country, integration associations, etc.).

There is much emphasis on competitiveness in the academic literature now; notwithstanding the foregoing, there are quite a number of ambiguous constructions concerning the very meaning of the term "competitiveness" and its most important determinants. The subject of competitiveness being the topic of discussion, without being a concept category of economy, is especially popular in such fields of research as international trade, economic strategy, global economy, economic geography, and applied economy.

A. Chursin, Y. Makarov, *Management of Competitiveness*,
DOI 10.1007/978-3-319-16244-7_2

With reference to an economic entity, market participant, economic process, etc., the meaning of "competitiveness" is interpreted in terms of the purposes, problems, and the content of the study. It is displayed from different perspectives, depending on the object of research (factors of manufacture, strategy, the system, etc.) and the subject of competitive relations (person, enterprise, region, country, integration associations, etc.).

Among those who contributed most of all in the development of "competitiveness concept," there were scientists who initially studied the "competition" concept. The founding fathers of the competitive theory are "Classical" economists (A. Smith and D. Rikardo), Marxist economists, German scientists (M. Weber, V. Zombart, J. Schumpeter), and American economists (A. Sloan, P. Druker, R. Solo).

"Classical" economists, first of all A. Smith in his work "An Inquiry into the Nature and Causes of the Wealth of Nations" (1776), have laid emphasis on major factors of competitiveness and the nations—the earth, the capital, natural resources, and labor power.

D. Rikardo in his work "On the Principles of Political Economy and Taxation" (1817) conceived a law of comparative advantage in competitiveness and the nations.

Economists of the Marxist school highlighted influence of the social and political environment on the economic development. First of all, it was "Das Kapital, Kritik der politischen Ökonomie"—"Capital: Critique of Political Economy" (1867), by Karl Marx.

German scientists have laid the basis for economic sociology: Max Weber in his "Economy and Society" (1922), V. Zombart in the "Bourgeois" (1924), and Joseph Alois Schumpeter who studied the business institute as a factor of competitiveness and in his work "Capitalism, Socialism and Democracy" (1942).

American economists A. Sloan and P. Druker developed the management concept as a key factor of competitiveness: "My Years with General Motors" (1963) by Alfred Sloan and "The Age of Discontinuity" (1969) by Peter Ferdinand Drucker.

Robert Merton Solow in his work "Technical Change and the Aggregate Production Function" (1957) investigated the role of education, technological innovations, and scholastic attainments as the major factors which have provided high level of competitiveness in the USA in 1948–1982.

Attempts to define competitiveness in general and in the context of various industries appear in the works of K. Fisher and S. Schoenberg, K. Ginger, K. Aginger, R. Flanagan, and some other authors who regard competitiveness as a converged concept, covering relative and multidimensional economic activities which are presented by variables of profitableness, productivity, and the output growth.

In the twentieth century in the sphere of competition and competitiveness the greatest prominence was achieved by the works of M. Porter which basically addressed nonmonetary factors of competitiveness. "An evident way to define non-monetary measurement of competitiveness would be the statement, that not non-monetary competitiveness is an ability of economy to sell products and to use diverse factors, other than the price,"—this idea formed the basis of the theory which had been put forward by Michael Eugene Porter. He set forth the fundamental determinants of competitiveness (competitive advantage) of a country or a model of "national rhombus" dealing with:

- Parameters of production;
- Parameters of demand;
- Parameters of related or supporting industries;
- Strategy of corporations, their structure, and factor of competition.

According to M. Porter competitiveness of the states may be influenced by a certain "case" and the "state." The scientist maintains that direct state intervention negatively influences competitiveness.

However, it is rather a debatable assertion, especially at the present time against the backdrop of financial crisis, when the governments drastically meddle with economic process and take measures to find the way out of the crisis. Argumentativeness of M. Porter viewpoint is corroborated by recent developments. For instance, there is a toughening of regulation and supervision of activities of financial companies in the USA from the late 1990s. In order to cope with this task there was created Financial Services Oversight Council, and the Federal Reserve System was given new powers to become an integrated control authority ("consolidated supervision") for all financial institutions. There was also created the National Bank Supervisor. On the whole President B. Obama administration implements a plan of restoration of social and economic stability. In 2009 there was passed "American Recovery and Reinvestment Act of 2009." The Primary goal of the programs financed under this law is demand promotion and new job creation.

The European Union's antirecessionary program is also basically connected with perfection of the state regulation system of financial sector and supervision of financial institutions. In order to stabilize the situation in the European Union, there was considerably (from 440 billion to at least 1 trillion Euros) increased the European Fund of Financial Stability (EFSF) within the framework of the antirecessionary program. Considerable part of the moneyed assistance is intended to help small-scale business. There is a large-scale crediting of partner banks. The said banks will perform functions of the intermediaries to provide funds to the business community within implementation of the "Small Business Act."

In Russia, announced economy modernization is carried out by means of active measures of public regulation:

- Perfection of institutional environments;
- Formation, as a whole, of a new model of regulation; mobilization of investments into the human capital assets;
- Perfection of the technical regulation system in order to offer a strong inducement for the enterprises to enhance technological level of their production;

- Modernization of the regulation system in the financial markets to provide higher reliability of the financial services sector.

M. Porter generalizes from facts that taking part in the competition are not only direct manufacturers but also consumers, suppliers, and other potential market participants, as well as manufacturers of alternative products—all of them make competitive forces to influence a certain field of activity in a varying degree.

M. Porter's research finding was the concept of the Five Competitive Forces. Porter five forces analysis is a framework to analyze the level of competition within an industry and business strategy development. It draws upon industrial organization economics to derive five forces that determine the competitive intensity and therefore attractiveness of a market; it specifies the determinants making the greatest impact on economic entities operating in a competitive market. According to the concept competitive situation in a certain market can be characterized as a collaborative effect of the Five Competitive Forces:

- Threat of new entrants;
- Threat of substitute products or services;
- Bargaining power of customers (buyers);
- Bargaining power of suppliers;
- Intensity of competitive rivalry.

However, modern researches in the field of competition, more specifically, works of Paul Krugman, deny the theory of "ideal" market competition. The criticism consists in the fact that the market cannot control itself; in other words, one can hardly speak about any standard rules for the economic entities in the market. Accordingly, a priority is placed on the problem each CEO is facing at every level of economic management (at the level of the country, industry, corporation)—how to win in the competition, i.e., how to be competitive in the market.

S. Frolov offers structuralization of approaches to considerations of competitiveness concept of the country by three basic groups:

- Competitiveness at the expense of domestic sources (manpower, natural resources, technological resources, etc.);
- Competitiveness at the expense of foreign trade activities and sweeping of the world markets (through foreign trade and direct foreign investments);
- Competitiveness on the basis of an institutional approach (competitive growth of the country due to strengthening of institutional entities—companies, regions, and industries).

According to S. Frolov, the first group deals with such an approach to competitiveness of the country, which is characteristic of the Consultative Group on Competitiveness of the European Commission. In accordance with this approach, competitiveness includes elements of productive efficiency (productivity), cost-effectiveness, and profitability; it is intended to increase living standards and social welfare. This case poses the question: should competitiveness reflect the ways of increasing living standards and the level of the jobs availability, or nonetheless it is just a consequence rather than the characteristic feature of the country competitiveness?

The second group as per S. Frolov is presented by the American scientists and the organizations:

Approach of the US Competitiveness Policy Council, whereby country competitiveness is an ability to make goods and services corresponding to the needs and interests of the world market pursuant to improvement of the living standards of the population in the long run;

Approach of the White House Council of Economic Advisers in the days of President Clinton whereby competitiveness is an ability to make goods and services capable of meeting requirements of the international competition pursuant to the simultaneous steady growth of the living standards of the population;

Approach of the European Union according to which competitiveness is understood as an ability to make goods and services which take examination in the international markets pursuant to the simultaneous maintenance of high and steady level of incomes;

Approach of B. Scott and D. Lodge defines competitiveness as an ability of the country to create, manufacture, distribute, and service products in international trade pursuant to the simultaneous growth of profitableness in using resources of the country. In this aspect, crude oil production and marketing is rather attractive and meets the market demand. However, how can a country be competitive if it depends on the raw materials marketing only?

The third group as per S. Frolov covers the approach formulated by R. Ferer and K. Chaharbaghi, whereby competitiveness is relative rather than absolute. Competitiveness depends on the level of shareholders and consumers and financial power which specify their ability to operate and respond to competitive environment and defines potential of the population and technologies in performing require strategic changes.

This done and following structuralization, S. Frolov challenges the said approaches by describing them as, to a considerable extent, unilateral and inconclusive in assessment of competitiveness of a country. It is possible to agree with this statement and underline that the approaches under review do not report in depth the innovative level of competitiveness and specifically take notice of trade relations only.

According to omnibus research of A. Lusse, the current approaches to competitiveness are distributed into six basic groups which the author has characterized as follows:

- Macroeconomic approach;
- "State" approach;
- Microeconomic approach;
- Resource approach;
- Social and cultural approach;

- Concept of competitive advantages.

According to the Macroeconomic approach, competitiveness of the country addresses the capacity of its economy operatively to adapt to varying conditions of the world market environment on-the-fly. This ability depends on economic development of the country and is expressed in such indicators as balance of payments position, general government deficit, size of the state indebtedness, foreign exchange rate fluctuation, etc. Pursuant to the approach accepted by the White House Council of Economic Advisers in the late 1980s and in the early 1990s, competitiveness of a country is reflected in the fact of its effective economic cooperation with other states, as far as it is successful and upside of the trade and payments balance indexes.

According to the State approach, competitiveness of the country is secured by the policy of the government, in particular, in the field of export and import regulation, and depends on degree of the government protection of national interests in the international political and economic institutions.

According to the Microeconomic approach, competitiveness is defined by the management efficiency at all levels of the enterprise.

According to the Resource, competitiveness of national economy is defined by availability of low-cost (in good supply) natural resources and labor power. The country achieves the most significant results in those areas, where production factors, firstly, are cheap; hence production cost price is rather low and, secondly, these factors are available in good supply; due to this fact supply can respond to any growth in demand for products on-the-fly.

Within the framework of the Social and cultural approach, competitiveness is treated as a wide phenomenon touching upon all the spheres of society life and domain. It is claimed that competitiveness of economy is defined by a series of characteristics with the social model of economic management as the basic value.

All the afore-cited approaches have one common trait: each of them makes it possible to specify a certain characteristic (or a number of characteristics) which in the judgment of their authors is a key parameter; the factor determines the level of economy competitiveness. Accordingly, the statements concerning enhancement of economy competitiveness within the framework of each approach taken separately have rather categorical nature. Besides, analysis of development of the countries with handsome economic results shows that the countries with almost the same initial level of development achieved the specified results by means of absolutely different ways; this prejudices the possibility of explanation of economy competitiveness on the basis of only one key factor or even a group of factors.

For example, some countries achieved considerable successes in increasing the living standard and advancement of the national goods in the world markets with the deficiency of their state budget (Japan, Korea, and the USA) and high interest rates (Italy and Korea). Other countries, poor in natural resources and with high cost of labor force (Germany, Japan, and Switzerland), have been developing more successfully than the countries with inexpensive resources. The same is related to the strong state support and attempts to form "national" models of management, etc.

As is obvious from the foregoing, there is a legitimate question whether it is possible to build a single-factor model of competitiveness as a matter of principle. We believe that competitiveness of economy should be considered as a complicated phenomenon which cannot be formally described within the framework of the current limited approaches.

G. Kulikov gives critical consideration to D. Hart's approach which also offers classification of competitiveness approaches similar to the abovementioned, emphasizing six tenors to be used by the advocates of this try theory in their attempt to explain one or another change in the world competitiveness:

- Macroeconomic approach;
- State approach;
- Neo-corporate approach;
- Coalition approach;
- Culture logical approach;
- Social and state approach.

G. Kulikov specifies the following basic aspects of competitiveness approaches according to D. Hart's classification.

For instance, as per D. Hart's interpretation the macroeconomic approach is based on such parameters as cost of manufacture factors, aggregate demand, savings and investment rates, and the rate exchange of world currencies; his approach is based on the basic economic conditions which are specified by the market forces and affected by the state policy in the least possible degree. An imperfection of this approach to the explanation of competitiveness according to D. Hart is obliteration of importance of technology and education. He insists that modern technologies compensate deficiency of resources and other productive factors, as well as high or increasing labor costs; education gives birth to knowledge and skills which facilitate creation and propagation of new technologies.

As per D. Hart, the followers of the state approach believe that the governments are rather independent in relation to the civil society and that the government's role in creation and maintenance of national advantage is considerable. However, G. Kulikov points out that there is no common opinion about the extent of the government's influence on formation and development of economy competitiveness.

The corporate approach as per D. Hart does not explain the change in competitiveness; quite the contrary, it is concentrated on such aspects as flexibility of response to the economic changes and maintenance of balance of economic and political stability, which would lead to success or failure in economic activities of the state or in its political legitimacy.

D. Hart specifies the works of D. Lodge and E. Vogel as apologists of the culture logical approach. By the said authors all ideologies are based on individualism or communitarism, in which connection communitarism societies of East Asia (Japan,

South Korea and Taiwan) are adapted to the changing economic conditions much faster than more developed industrial countries with their individual societies (USA, Great Britain, and France).

The coalition approach specified by D. Hart is based on the assumption that the state policy is defined by negotiations between social influential groups and irrespective of the state. In this case, the state becomes an agent of a coalition of specific social circles (representatives of industry, finance, commercial business, agriculture, etc.).

D. Hart also notes importance of the social and state approach dealing with social and state system and claims that relations between society and the state (the union of the government, business and labor) have an effect on the ability of the country to create and propagate new technologies as the basic factor of international competitiveness. According to D. Hart, the state consists of a system of institutes, which include "triple (government—business—labor) boards and commissions, state enterprises, and the organizations of other forms of ownership. The state and public society operate in close cooperation and supplement each other. D. Hart specifies that "in the modern industrially developed countries two groups of civilian population—business and the organized labor—represent the special importance, especially for solution of the issues connected with competitiveness of industrial sector."

The various approaches to interpretation of the country competitiveness concept, as stated above, specify a lack of the unified competitiveness theory. There is a multitude of factors, reasons, and characteristics of competitiveness of the countries and regions only. However there is no objective and complete theory of competitiveness. Consequently, there are no stable and integral concepts of international competitiveness for the time being, in spite of the fact that there are plenty of works by prominent scientists on the issues of competitiveness now.

A number of scientists try to develop their own interpretations of "competitiveness" concept and "international competitiveness" different from dominating "Porter's interpretation" (studies by M. I. Gelvanovsky, K. L. Ryzhkov, S. V. Emelianov, R. A. Fathutdinov, D. Hart, etc.).

One cannot but agree with S. Frolov that the studies related to the last group and possessing undoubted scientific value, nevertheless, do not solve the main task—developments of the unified approach to assessment and provision of international competitiveness and national economy, namely:

M. I. Gelvanovsky's works formulate the concepts of competitiveness at three levels of economic activities (macro-, micro-, and meso-level) and include useful studies concerning the influences of the rate of exchange on competitiveness;

K. L. Rozhkov's dissertation and monograph have laid the basis for the qualitative analysis of competitiveness and formulated typology of the countries depending on the character of competitive advantages;

S. V. Emelianov has performed the fact analysis of competitiveness of the American manufacturers in her monograph. The said analysis is a qualitative one to a greater extent; pursuant to methodology it is rather a monitoring of the manufacturers' activity of a separate country as opposed to its competitiveness analysis

R. A. Fathutdinov's works pose a critical analysis of M. Porter's concepts.

According to A. S. Bychkova, fundamental reasons responsible for plural interpretations of competitiveness concept are various positions of economists, as well as the fact that the manufacturer is considered to be a corporation or an industry or the entire economy as a whole.

I. P. Faminsky also notes multivariant approach of factors and conditions of competitiveness assessment in his characterizing the matter point of analysis and assessment of competitiveness,

The similar point of view is also expressed by P. S. Zavialov who states that "there is no unified universal standard competitiveness concept." In this connection, he notes that "there should be required research and application of a set of methods of the quantitative analysis and competitiveness assessment in the aggregate taking into account its sandwich-type properties, relativity and specificness. In addition to the above binding upon are domestic (intraindustry, regional) and foreign (international) comparisons of competitiveness parameters."

I. A. Spiridonov supports the ideas of the specified authors and underlines that "the methodological plan requires development of conceptual approach where the international experience in the sphere of increasing competitiveness of national economy should be accounted too."

In this context, R. A. Fathutdinov believes that in the educational and business literature the concept of competitiveness, competitiveness, competitive advantages, competitiveness forms and methods, principles competitiveness management, etc., are addressed in each specific case, separately from each other, individually, exclusively. Therefore, it is necessary to agree with M. I. Albakov who mentions R. Dekart's thoughts that if we give exact interpretation to the concepts it will be possible to relieve the world of the burden of one-half of errors. M. I. Albakov believes that competitiveness of national economy is rather a new category which is poorly developed by the world science. In his opinion, statements of some authoritative economists calling into question the very existence of the country competitiveness problem testify to the fact that the subject matter is not yet developed.

The classical economic theory itself contains a number of various concepts explaining success of specific country in the international competitiveness. So, the economic theory shows that international trade is a means for the country to develop specialization and enhance productivity of available resources and consequently increase the amount of goods and services and raise the standard of well-being.

In the early twentieth century, the Swedish economists E. Heksher and B. Olin established a doctrine whereby every participant of the international trade process strives to export the goods which in the course of their production require heavy use of certain productive factors which the management entity possesses in rather greater amount rather than its partners. However, when V. V. Leontief examined the structure of US export and import in 1947, it was expected that the said research would support US positions in the export of capital-intensive goods and import of the labor-consuming goods. However there was another situation, and this result was known as the "Leontief's paradox."

The concept of comparative advantages and its modern modifications have a number of essential lacks which may include inter alia negation of such factors as the movement of the qualified labor and the capital from one the country to another.

It is possible to agree with M. I. Albakov who believes that a number of the assumptions within the framework of the classical theory (for example, work is the only productive factor; there is full employment; there are only two countries to merchandise and make a market of two goods only; production costs remain constants; transport expenses are equal to zero; foreign trade is free from restrictions, etc.) in modern conditions are of little use for explanation of success of a certain country within the framework of the international competitiveness. It is possible to agree also with his statement that the fundamental defect of the classical theory is an ability to explain how the high-level diversification of the intra-industry foreign trade of the developed countries is stipulated in the modern conditions. An example is the US automobile business. The concept of comparative advantage as per M. I. Albakov can explain this model of trade through sterilizing and defeating the purpose of this concept only, for example, by means of asserting that Germany has comparative advantage in production of "BMW" and the USA—in production of "Ford."

In fact, basic part of world trade is accounted for by relations between the developed countries which have comparable resource potential. It is inconsistent with the Heckscher–Ohlin theory whereby the most favorable partnership should develop between the countries with the maximum economic distinctions. For example, the USA should have the most extensive barter with Mexico, the economic system of which considerably differs from the American one, instead of Canada, whose economic situation is close to the US economy. However, in practice Canada is the most active trading partner of the USA.

As can be seen from the above, it is arguable that an attempt to narrow down competitiveness of the national economy to comparative advantage has appeared to be unsuccessful regardless of how it is characterized: labor productivity (Ricardo concept) or availability of intensively used productive factors in increasing number (Heckscher–Ohlin theory). The problem of national economy competitiveness in similar interpretation of its economic substance is considered exclusively from the point of assumption, which makes the relative character of the said category unaccounted.

Modern economists try to prove that in order to achieve successful development of foreign trade, there should be similarity in economy of the countries—partnership, rather than distinctions. So, B. Balassa was one of the first scientists who paid attention to the visible tendency in international trade in the second half of the twentieth century: the developed countries are more and more engaged in trade of differentiated goods of one industry among themselves more and more. As a result, he developed the theory of the country competitiveness based on the intra-industry trade of differentiated goods which is specified by such standard reasons as the economy of scale effect, differentiation of demand, and overlapping demand theory.

Economy of Scale and Differentiation of Demand In the conditions of intra industry trade the production is highly specialized in each of the partner countries, that, finally, raises the general level of production in these countries, and a wide range of products within the framework of one commodity group become available to the buyers.

Overlapping Demand Theory This hypothesis was proposed by Swedish economist Staffan Burenstam Linder in 1961. The hypothesis addresses economic scheme of the international trade mainly from the point of view of demand. Proceeding from the assumption that consumers from different countries with comparable level of incomes have similar tastes (this yields the term "overlapping demand"), S. Linder claims that a country would be more competitive in selling the goods with wide experience in manufacture and home market. The overlapping demand theory will be more suitable under condition of more unified distribution of the population incomes in each of the partner—countries. However, the assumption of the "overlapping demand" is not universal—for example, the consumers of China and Russia even if they have comparable level of incomes can hardly have similarity of tastes.

Yu. Kurenkov and V. Popov hold the similar view and state that during industrial development in the market environment there are new competitive conditions emerging to change the general vector of competitiveness from using mainly comparative national advantages to the use of dynamically varying competitive advantages, based on scientific and technical achievements and innovations at all stages of the production cycle from creation of products by a manufacturer to their distribution to consumers. They note the following features of comparative and competitive advantages. Comparative advantages are inherited by a nation by nature; they are static and are not reproduced. Competitive advantages are dynamical and connected with innovations, development of the human capital assets, and intelligence and they are boundless inherently. Combination of specific comparative and competitive advantages of the country strengthens its competitiveness within global economic space.

Yu. Kurenkov and V. Popov subdivide the full suite of competitive advantages in the aggregate into casual competitive advantages which are caused by happy circumstances, but not directly by the activity of economic management of the country entities, and into competitive advantages which are deliberately and purposefully formed by the entities of economic management. Competitive advantages of the first kind are unstable and volatile, as they are casual by their nature; therefore they are named lowest order competitive advantages. Competitive advantages of the second kind, according to Yu. Kurenkov, and V. Popov, are stable and nonvolatile; they express characteristics of the real manufacture and promote its efficiency growth and consequently they are named high-order competitive advantages.

According to K. L. Rozhkov, an evidence of global competitiveness of a nation is ability to reproduce human resources. He addresses competitiveness of the countries as a special phenomenon which has been enhanced recently in connection with the special importance of reproduction of human resources for economic growth in the conditions of globalization of social sphere. S. Shavruk also believes that the level of education and qualifications of the manpower becomes a dominant factor defining competitiveness of a nation now.

Distinctions in approaches to evaluation of the country competitiveness are reflected, first of all, in the definitions of different scientists. There are as many definitions of international competitiveness as many authors writing on this issue.

M. I. Albakov treats competitiveness of national economy as an integrated property defined by interaction of economic and political factors under specific institutional conditions which provides positive economic effect from participation in the international competitiveness. Accordingly, the economic content of the said category consists in economic relations of the country following interaction of the above-specified factors which allow receiving the expected effect. The positive effect, unfortunately, can be stipulated by a temporary situation in the market. The definition offered by M. I. Albakov in no way connects innovation and competitiveness.

R. A. Fathutdinov analyzes competitiveness in biological, technical, social, and economic systems. It appears to him the concept of "competitiveness" concerning technical systems characterizes an ability to compete in the said market to meet the systems' requirements by means of providing optimum level of qualitative and resource indicators, and competitiveness concerning social and economic systems—ability to produce competitive goods (service) to be sold at the foreign or home markets.

R. A. Fathutdinov reasonably notes that HR competitiveness (scientists, experts, workers, etc.) specifies competitiveness of technologies, technical, social, and economic systems, and, finally, the better competitiveness of the goods and services, the better competitiveness of the nation, the efficient use of resources, and the population living standards. The index of the country competitiveness brings into focus (synthesizes) all results of quality and resource-intensiveness of work of all the management objects at all levels. R. A. Fathutdinov claims that the index of country competitiveness is an integrated indicator of its development level, an indicator of maturity of the market relations.

Agreeing with R. A. Fathutdinov's approach, it should be noted that the scientist brings the definition of competitiveness of the social and economic systems to the goods level, and this approach practically meets M. Porter's opinion. That fact that R. A. Fathutdinov believes that it is possible to bring competitiveness of the whole system to competitiveness of one element only is indicative of the absence of holistic and system approach.

The influential international organization The World Economic Forum in its annually published report "Global Competitiveness" defines national competitiveness from the point of view of intermediate-term (5 years) economic growth. Provided that the concept of national competitiveness is widely treated as an ability to support stable high rates of growth of real "per capita" income measured by rates of growth of the gross domestic product per capita in real terms. The project managers believe that the general approach, they accepted, unlike other approaches makes it possible to specify and analyze fundamental factors of economic growth. Whereas there is a chance to evaluate efficiency of various governmental and corporate programs, to forecast their real influence onto the level of competitiveness and long-term economic development. However in the long run brings the said approach to the countries competitiveness to the ability to sell goods. The definition accepted in the project of the World Economic Forum, as follows from its content, has considerable similarity to definition of competitiveness as efficiency of use of resources (as per M. Porter) where gross domestic product per capita is offered as an efficiency indicator.

However comparative approaches to competitiveness of national economies essentially differ. M. Porter holds that the category of competitiveness should be considered at the industry level. The similar opinion was stated by authors of the report of Expert Institute "Competitiveness of the Russian Economy" who claim that while analyzing the problems connected with competitiveness, it is necessary to pass from global categories "country," "industry" on to narrower categories—"economic sector," "sub-industry." The similar point of view is reflected in documents of the European Management Forum, where it is underlined that competitiveness of the companies to a certain extent is influenced by the general situation in the country which is defined by economy dynamism, flexibility of financial system, provision of manpower, country participation in the international division of labor, and social and political situation.

From our point of view, it is impossible to identify competitiveness of the companies and competitiveness of the national economies. The simple sum will not give us systemacity and integrity. The whole has other properties than the properties of its elements. The whole is always more than the sum of its components. One has to agree with G. Kulikov who supports P. Krugman's statement that identification of the companies' competitiveness with the countries' competitiveness is a "dangerous passion" and claims that the similar definition in the relation to the countries' competitiveness causes much more problems than in case of the analysis of the companies. Rigorous but reasonable opinion of M. I. Gelvanovsky specified that, in the theory of competitive advantages of the country, M. Porter having connected micro–meso–macro-level has circumvented a problem of macrocompetitiveness; as a matter of fact, he brought it to the meso-level. It enabled M. Porter to avoid the problems which are not concerning economy directly, and to focus attention on the pragmatic problems of the level of separate firms or their industry associations. According to M. I. Albakov's fair point of view the company as a system is an element of the higher order system—industries, corresponding to the national economy in the same way. A system is a real complex of the phenomena and processes and a communication between them. A. Lusse assumes that in explicit form the competitiveness concept is a property of exclusively goods. A. Lusse argues that exactly innovations provide rise in the efficiency of production and lead to the leadership change in the competitiveness. Therefore, in his opinion, it is possible to agree with the authors who connect competitiveness of the firms with the scientific and technical progress expressed either through investment activities or through Research and Development. In addition to the above, A. Lusse claims that competitiveness of a firm, financial and industrial group, or an industry can be more exactly defined as an ability to form and keep stable competitive advantages. A state is not a holder of competitive advantages; it creates environment, conditions for their formation only. Accordingly, a state cannot implement (to keep and develop) available competitive advantages. It is a prerogative of a company.

By competitiveness of a nation A. Lusse means an ability of its economic institutes to form favorable conditions to create and keep by the firms (financial and industrial groups, industries, and sub-industries) the stable competitive advantages leading to growth in the living standard in the country with optimum (as per Pareto) distribution of income received by the firms from competitiveness growth. A. Lusse mentions B. Hendrikson's researches, who, as the basic distinctive feature of competitive economy, defines well-being growth, but such a growth of well-being which is provided at the expense of investments into the physical and human capital.

L. Klein as the basic distinctive feature of competitive economy puts forward an availability of stable rates of economic growth (3–4 % per year), and that should provide stable growth in the standards of living.

J. Ross defines competitiveness of economy through the "added value, which is brought into the goods by Research and Development." D. Sax modernized competitiveness concept in light of the criticism by P. Krugman with regard to identification competitiveness of the companies with competitiveness of the country. In his opinion, there is a red line for each company below which the company cannot do its business further on. P. Krugman believes that the countries unlike the companies have no specific red line; they cannot go bankrupt and stop their existence in case of deterioration of their competitiveness in the foreign markets. He also notes that the positive balance of foreign trade does not always testify to competitiveness of economy.

According to D. Sax, the economy would be competitive in the world if economic institutes and a policy of the country provide stable and fast economic growth, i.e., competitive countries are the countries which choose institutes and a policy aimed at promoting long-term growth. One has to agree with this statement, the only question is what institutes and policy promote long-term growth? Is it possible to follow the point of view of the American business circles only?

G. Kulikov distinguishes concepts of real and nominal competitiveness in development of his approach to definition of competitiveness.

Real competitiveness of a nation in G. Kulikov's interpretation is an admissibility of national industries of economy in the conditions of free and fair market to make the goods and services which meet requirements of both domestic and foreign markets with the simultaneous growth of real incomes of the wage labor. Real competitiveness requires openness and justice of markets of the partners of the trading country, high quality and innovation of the goods and services from the country of manufacture, as well as the constant growth in the living standards of its citizens. Real competitiveness is possible only in the event the national companies are able to project, make, and effectively distribute the goods and services, when the prices and the quality meet requirements of both foreign and domestic consumers without direct grants, mass layoffs, or wages restraint.

Nominal competitiveness can be reached by implementation of a certain policy of the government creating the macroeconomic environment for domestic manufacturers by direct state grants and restraint of wages.

According to A. Seleznev, competitiveness is a position of the country or a commodity producer stipulated by economic, social, and political factors in the domestic and foreign markets, expressed through the indicators (indexes), including through the high level of incomes and wages under condition of openness for the international competitiveness. There are a number of questions concerning this definition. How does the country position in the home market reflect competitiveness in the foreign market? Why should one definition have aspects of macrocompetitiveness and microcompetitiveness? As it is obvious that high level of incomes can take place in case of export of raw materials to foreign countries, is the country favorably exporting raw materials competitive? In this case, it is possible to say that economies of the majority of the countries from the developing group are competitive. Being aware of inconsistency of such definition, A. Seleznev tries to connect some other aspects with competitiveness and specifies that competitiveness of economy is shown in aggregate abilities to make and sell competitive high-technology products, to form the niches in the world markets, to involve various resources from the world economy, and to possess economic stability against negative influence of the international competitiveness.

F. Klotsvog performed an important analytical research where he addressed the problems and tendencies of development of the Russian regions and provided a target forecast of their economic dynamics on the basis of macrostructural model of economy. F. Klotsvog's model includes six interconnected functional blocks:

- National economic performances (gross domestic product, final consumption, investments into fixed capital);
- Industry indicators (total output of the industry, average wholesale price of a product);
- Indicators of manufacture and use of production (expense factor per piece, quantity of imports of a product, quantity of export of a product, product expense factor per piece of volume of investments, etc.);
- Indicators of external economic relations (restriction on export and import of the major types of production); financial and cost indexes (amortization of the fixed capital, profit, compensation of employees, etc.);
- Indicators of manpower (quantity employed and a number of unemployed).

However, disputable are both allocation of blocks and equations for calculation of indicators for each block, namely, as per F. Klotsvog, it is the sum of products of corresponding indicators.

Various approaches to the essence of "competitiveness" concept have stipulated distinctions as a part of factors to influence competitiveness and approaches to their analysis.

So, I. Tochitskaya names six factors, the availability of which, in her opinion, is determinant for provision of competitiveness of the territory:

- Quality of labor;
- Availability of the research centers;
- Favorable business climate;
- Availability of industrial clusters with developed network of the vertical and horizontal communications to lower the costs of an industrial infrastructure and facilitate transmission of information;
- Developed infrastructure;
- Favorable conditions for life-sustaining activities.

A. Evtuhovich refers the following to the fundamental factors influencing the level of competitiveness:

- Modern structure of economic activities and advanced transport infrastructure;
- Level innovation and the human capital assets;
- Availability of a network of partner communications between competitor corporations, and a network of institutes and the public capital;
- Availability of the local leaders, capable of uniting local management entities round the strategy of development approved by the said management entities.

According to M. I. Yandiev, among important factors of increasing national competitiveness a special role belongs to the industrial and scientific and technical policy and concentration of financial resources on directions with priority importance for the country. Besides, M. I. Yandiev specifies national legislation to provide environment favorable for development of competitive manufactures, for independent foreign policy and security, for domestic political and social stability; he also underlines dependence of competitiveness of a nation on its economic and military power and political decisiveness in the world.

Abovementioned review of the Russian and foreign approaches to formalization of intuitively understood economic category "competitiveness," to specification and study of the factors influencing competitiveness of economic objects of the micro–meso–and macro-level, as well as the generalized analysis of merits and demerits of the approaches considered above, makes it possible to make findings of the availability of mature theoretical foundation and considerable practical experience in this area and the available preconditions to work out the general approaches to creation of the competitiveness management theory.

Dealing with the current condition of the economic theory of the firm management (management theory), it is possible to say that it was worked out in parallel to development of the theoretical foundation connected with concepts "competitiveness" and "competitiveness," and at the present stage there is an obvious interrelation between the general theory of management and the theory of competitiveness management. Within the frameworks of the modern theory of management of economic objects of various levels, one of the tasks of such management is the growth of competitiveness.

It is worth mentioning that preconditions to the statement of availability of communication between competitiveness management and firm management existed as far back as in the nineteenth century. In 1886, Henry Taun delivered a report "An Engineer in the capacity of Economist" at the meeting of the American Society of Mechanical Engineers, which said that an engineer should be interested in something more than just a technical efficiency, namely calculation of expenses, incomes, and profits. By this statement he, as a matter of fact, has suggested to combine managerial processes of development, creation, and marketing of the products with the processes of economic management of the factory and goods sale. This suggestion about association of two independent managerial processes in one to provide high economic efficiency of sale of the finished goods, as a matter of fact, became the beginning of development of the management science concerning the entire life cycle of production, and consequently, the beginning of development of competitiveness managerial process objects.

Henry Taun's idea has been further developed by F. U. Tailor, who has stated principles and directions of development of the American industry on the basis of scientific and technical progress, standardization, and unification. He has offered conceptual determination to the managerial process and characterized it as the "organization of production," based on experimental data according to calculations of physical work components and subsequent analysis of these components in order to achieve the maximum results.

In his most known work "*General and Industrial Management*" (1916), Henri Fayol specifies 14 fundamental principles of management; moreover separate principles are still important in the present days. For example, autocracy and unity of direction—common plan—one manager, division of labor, scalar chain of management.

One more management approach was offered by M. Weber (1864–1920). According to his theory, a firm was considered as a bureaucratic structure. As per M. Weber, management should be built on impersonal, especially rational basis, and this form of management has been defined by him as bureaucracy. Such concept envisaged clear definition of official duties and responsibility of the employees, conducting of formal reporting, division of property, and management. It was the bureaucracy that made it possible for many firms to achieve high efficiency; therefore the term "bureaucracy" had no negative connotation in M. Weber's approach.

In 1930 in the USA, there was formed an association "The International Society for the Advancement of Economic Theory in its Relation with Statistics and

Mathematics" which included such prominent economists as Ragnar Frisch, Charles F. Roos, Joseph A. Schumpeter, Harold Hotelling, Henry Schultz, Karl Menger, Edwin B. Wilson, Frederick C. Mills, William F. Ogburn, J. Harvey Rogers, Malcolm C. Rorty, Carl Snyder, Walter A. Shewhart, Oystein Ore, Ingvar Wedervang, and Norbert Wiener. Foundation of the Econometric Society was a starting point of creation of mathematical school of economists. Later, in the 50s of the twentieth century on this basis there was formed a school of quantitative methods in the management of economic processes. This scientific direction has its followers and continues to develop now and as a result we have profound understanding of complicated administrative problems thanks to development and application of economic and mathematical models with wide use of quantitative methods. The most known representatives of this school are R. Ackoff, S. Beer, A. Goldberger, R. Lewis, and L. Klein. Within the framework of quantitative school of the management science, there has been elaborated a considerable number of principles, rules have been developed, and approaches. There were generated two mainstreams:

First of all, production is addressed as a "social system";

Secondly, there is system and situational analysis with application of mathematical methods and computers.

Changing environment resulted in changing of management concepts and an object that has resulted in the change of theoretical approaches to solution of economic problems. In the late 1960s–1970s, besides the process approach, there was widely used a system approach to a firm management, and in the 1980s–1990s—situational approach.

The system approach to the firm management addresses processes and phenomena in the form of complete set of elements, structures, and the forces they drive. The systems have a hierarchical structure, horizontal and vertical communications, certain functions, centripetal and centrifugal tendencies, straight and feedback link, and exogenous and endopathic development factors. Within the system interpretation, a firm is considered as a system, i.e., as a unit including various interconnected elements. General nuances in the administrative activity make it possible to count much more variants of decisions and possible consequences of their acceptance. Supporters of the system approach believe that making specific decision should be connected with specific situation: both foreign and domestic factors and circumstances.

Situational or "case" approach is both a way of thinking and a set of specific activities. This approach developed in the Harvard Business School is aimed at development of situational thinking and direct use of the theoretical knowledge; it is based on analysis of the real situations and allows taking typological decisions. The situational approach, unlike the process and system approaches, is widely used in nonstandard cases and situations of uncertainty, unexpected, and nonstandard behavior of environment which, as per I. Ansoff, is called turbulence now.

At present the above specified approaches are widely used in practical terms in the process of management of economic entities, including for solution of problems concerning creation of competitive advantages. After we generalized the aforesaid

Table 2.1 Principal stages and directions of development of the competitiveness management theory

Development of doctrinal foundations concerning competitiveness management:
Development of industrial and economic relations;
Coming into existence of the concept "competition";
Development of the world economic science in the field of competition;
Coming into existence of the theory of management of economic entities;
Coming into existence of the concept "competitive advantage";
Coming into existence of the theory of "competitiveness";
Formation of doctrinal foundations concerning competitiveness management.
General-theoretical foundations of competitiveness management:
Economic laws;
Economic laws of the market relations;
Theoretical laws of organization and management, concerning the issues of competitiveness and creation of competitive advantages, in statics and dynamics;
Laws and approaches to competitiveness management;
The theory competitiveness management of entities.
Conceptual bases for creation of the theory of scientific field "Competitiveness Management":
Concept and definition of competitiveness management system;
Purposes and functions of competitiveness management;
Characteristic features of competitiveness management on micro—meso-and macro-levels; evaluation and ranging of factors of the foreign and domestic environment from the point of view of the object competitiveness management;
Parameters and indicators of competitiveness management system;
Methods, means, and technologies of management and decision-making.
Methodological bases of the management competitiveness theory:
Methodology of development and creation of competitiveness management systems for production, firm, and industry;
Methods of competitiveness evaluation for production, firm, industry;
Methods of creation of competitive advantages;
Methodology for management of the factors having effects on competitiveness and creation of competitive advantages;
Methods of planning, organization, receiving, and processing of information, protection of information, control and communications in management;
Mutual influence and interface of various management systems.
Theoretical and practical bases of competitiveness management mechanism:
Development of specific competitiveness management systems for economic entities (algorithms, mathematical models, building concepts);
Development of the building technology;
Development of technical means applied in competitiveness management systems;
Methodology and practice of using competitiveness management systems.
Theoretical bases for assessment of efficiency of competitiveness management systems:
Methodology of assessment of economic benefits from application of competitiveness management systems;
Criteria of assessment of efficiency of the functioning system;
Methods of analysis of functioning of competitiveness systems.

and studied historical development of the economic theory, we hereby offer our vision of sequence of theorization and development of competitiveness management theory, specified in Table 2.1. From a historical view and in consideration of development of the economic theory and the theory of competitiveness management, it is possible to formalize specific sequence of creation and development of the theory of competitiveness management of economic entities in the form of a table.

As things now stand, the theory of competitiveness management is at the stage of forming methodological basis on the principal economic laws and postulates, describing interaction of economic entities, as well as at the stage of development of the law of competitiveness management. This monograph analyzes the methods to create competitive advantages and shows the way to control them; it presents a general methodology of competitiveness management system at various levels of economic management, based on the evaluation of competitiveness of production, firm, and an industry.

Taking into consideration that many analysts specify deficiency of effective economic toolkit to exercise competitiveness management, this monograph presents the following solutions of this problem:

- Development of economic tools for quantitative assessment of competitiveness of production, firm and industry;
- Specification of effective methods of state regulation of the processes providing growth of competitiveness of national economy;
- Investigation of economic tools to evaluate efficiency of the projects and programs to a high degree of accuracy, aimed at enhancement of competitiveness of economic entities.

So, it is arguable that the theory competitiveness management is at the stage allowing consistent transformation to forming methodical basis on the fundamental economic laws and postulates, which describe interaction of economic entities, and to study experience concerning creation of competitive advantages and development of corresponding methods for their management, development of the general methodology of competitiveness management systems at various levels of economic managing, and, as a result, to start working out and substantiation of the law of competitiveness management.

2.2 Postulates, Hypotheses, and Model of Competitiveness Management

The economic theory lays emphasis on short-term, middle-term, and long-term business cycles. The most known among them are the following:

- Kitchin cycles;
- Inventory cycles (2–4 years);

- Juglar cycles (7–12 years), depending on volumes of investments into fixed capital which in turn initiate change of GNP, inflation, and employment;
- Kuznets swing (cycles) or long fluctuations possessing the biggest amplitude in the building industry (20 years);
- Kondratiev cycles (40–60 years).

Kondratiev constructed an economic theory of long waves, big cycles of conjuncture: he specified polycyclicality of economic dynamics and revealed interrelation of business cycles with cyclic processes in other spheres of society. These cycles define interrelation of development of scientific and technical progress with cyclicality of innovations.

Kondratiev cycles include two stages in the cycle: expansion stage (economic revival and growth) and recession (recession and depression). The beginning of expansion stage is necessarily preceded by the crisis and depression periods. Depression forces to search for possibilities of survival, and innovation process can provide them.

German researcher G. Mensch (1979) defined such phenomenon as the "trigger effect of depression," meaning that depression launches innovation process. G. Mensch has shown that innovation process is nonuniform and cyclic and every time this process comes to an end with formation of innovation clusters in the course of innovations diffusion. The time to start innovation process takes a long period covering a phase of depression and partially the beginning of revival phase.

American researcher M. Friedman (1987) claimed that the start of innovations takes place in the period of economy revival. Actually when the state finds itself near the trigger point, an industry or a firm starts activating the processes of creating competitive advantages to ensure economic development at the account of increasing efficiency of their activities, including for the account of the process management affecting enhancement of competitiveness of products, firm and industry, or the state as a whole. Such processes may include:

- Essentially new products with attractive end-user performance, unavailable earlier in the commodity markets,
- Innovation technologies to pass over to new generation of manufacture or to enter the following technological practice;
- Creation of materials with unique properties, various types of engines, and other technical equipment.

The processes of development of essentially new products, innovation technologies, and their commissioning take a long time interval. Therefore, the real start of innovations is not taking place at once, on the contrary—after some time required for creation and commissioning of innovations in manufacture, marketing in the commodity markets; and only then "economic" revival comes.

Innovations do not come into being spontaneously; this process connected with scientific and technical progress depends on economic and political conditions. The speed one can enter a market of products created on the basis of innovation solutions is defined by efficiency development management and manufacturing application of innovation activity results. Efficiency of the management depends on methods and tools applied (by business or state) subject to the current economic situation, available priorities, or the innovation policy.

Management of creating and commissioning of innovations securing competitive advantages is connected with involvement of significant amount of various resources. It should be evaluated in what conditions and for the sake of what purposes and with what efficiency these resources would be involved. In our opinion involvement of various resources to develop innovation solutions to create new and more competitive products, to ensure growth competitiveness of a firms (industry or a states as a whole), should be carried out with the first signals from competitiveness management systems concerning occurrence of any risks connected with the loss of commodity markets, or with financial and economic instability (regarding the firms, industry, state, and world economy as a whole). Such signals occur for example against background of new competitors in the commodity markets, in the event of evidence of a coming crisis or other negative phenomena in economy. If, by virtue of inefficiencies and inopportunity of the beginning of intensive management to create competitive advantages to enhance competitiveness, these processes are getting late, then comes the depression and stagnation period. A way out of stagnation requires intensive competitiveness management aimed at providing fast growth of economy.

The reasoning set forth above provides an opportunity to form the *first postulate of competitiveness management*:

> During the periods of depression and economic stagnation in order to ensure growth of production and products sales an intensive competitiveness management should be performed with involvement of considerable financial resources to create competitive advantages for the products товаров or firms.

Such management is carried out until expenses for creation of competitive advantages cease to provide earnings gain; then there will be required an alternation of generations of the output products.

The competitive advantages should maximize the firm profit thanks to growth in the sales volume and an establishment of a price which not only completely defray expenses but also provides an opportunity to receive desirable rate of return.

Profit maximization can be reached at the expense of output of hi-tech innovation products with the high added value. It is important to note the absence of direct dependence of innovations efficiency from the investments in their creation. Big volume of investments does not always generate highly effective innovations providing significant growth of competitiveness of production and a firm as a whole. Moreover, there may be situations when rather small investments ensure more attractive result in the plan increasing competitiveness.

In the modern context the information on innovation technologies is disseminated so quickly that in order to keep high-level competitive advantages, it is necessary to provide a continuity of process of creation and application of innovation solutions.

Competitiveness management should take place from the beginning of creating the goods and it should extend its life cycle until the moment the income from realization of the said goods still provides stable development of the firm. Availability of the products' competitive advantages finally brings growth in the demand for the products and hence the increase in revenues and reduction of the project payoff period.

The situation when the increase in revenues is equal to carried expenses is called a "break-even point." With the corresponding competitiveness management, the break-even point moves toward reduction of output. Every manufacturer wants to reduce the project payoff period; in other words, it means faster approach to the break-even point when the manufacturer starts receiving profit.

The break-even point or BEP is counted according to the formula:

$$\text{Break} - \text{even point} = \text{fixed costs}/(1 - \text{share of variable costs});$$

$$\text{Share of variable costs} = \text{variable costs}/\text{production output (volume of sales)}.$$

The break-even point here reflects production level to be provided for compensation of all expenses forming the cost of production. Calculation of the break-even point is extremely important for every production company. The lower production output in the break-even point the more investment-attractive and competitive production is.

Small production output can provide covering of expenses pursuant to the following conditions:

- Investments in manufacture and expenses from use of productive factors are low, i.e., they are used effectively enough; it can be done at the expense of the corresponding policy of a firm, more effective use of resources, in particular, as a result of application of innovation solutions, commissioning of new economic technologies, in other words—at the expense of thought over production competitiveness management;
- Demand for the products is rather high at the current and/or forecasted prices, and it is provided by availability of competitive advantages as compared to the goods of competitors; the prices level may be kept at the expense of continuous application of innovation solutions only.

As can be seen from the above, it is validly held that competitiveness management should be carried out most intensively in the beginning of development, during the preparation of production, and before achieving the break-even point of the manufacture, to be exact until the moment when the firm starts receiving profit from the sales.

With reference to the manufacture innovation process, a break-even point, in our opinion, should be counted with allowances made for expenses for creation of competitive advantages, i.e., expenses for scientific studies, research and development, and commissioning of innovation technologies, which in view of their specificity should be included in fixed costs.

At the initial R&D stage when new technologies are not yet commissioned and former goods are being produced (with former tendencies of production output growth and price), accounting cost for creation of competitive advantages within fixed costs leads to their growth and, accordingly, shifts to the right of the break-even points. This can explain unwillingness of many firms to invest in the manufacture requiring development of innovations.

If the firm creates highly competitive marketable products which are in greater demand than the products of the firms-competitors and competitors are unable to copy such technologies or to make more competitive products within a short time, then with the commissioning of this new competitive production and its sales growth, the sales revenue and, hence, the profit will start to grow at a fast pace.

If we compare a company successfully introducing innovations with a traditional company which is not using innovations as a mechanism competitiveness management, it is possible to say that profit of the innovation company, despite the higher costs, will be essentially bigger if compared with a traditional company, as demand for production, sales volumes, and consequently the sales revenue of the innovation company will be considerably higher than the similar indicators of the compared traditional company. Time interval of closing the break-even point of the innovation company will be essentially shorter than the one of traditional company—the competitor. This is rather attractive to the proprietors, shareholders, and investors both in case of required modernization and expansion of manufacture and in the event of other ways of development. The innovation-type company carrying out competitiveness management and increasing competitive advantages by means of working out and commissioning of innovation solutions and technologies in the processes of manufacture has much more chances to involve additional financial resources: to receive bank credit or to mobilize strategic investors. Capital investments of the innovation-type company working out and introducing innovation technologies under condition of carefully thought over marketing policy is a ticket to success of competitive advantages for intermediate- and long-term prospect.

In graphic form, the above process broadly speaking is illustrated in Fig. 2.1, where T is a traditional company, I—innovative company, and P_b—break-even point.

Figure 2.1 shows the revenues, expenses, and profit of two companies: traditional company and innovative company. It is obvious that the profit of the company dealing with innovative developments, despite higher costs, is considerably larger as compared with the traditional company, since demand for its production, its sales, and, consequently, company revenues considerably exceed similar indicators of the company brought into comparison. This being the case, the break-even point (output volume when the revenues = expenses) is reached more quickly by the innovative company, rather than its competitor; this is rather attractive, both for proprietors and the shareholders, as well as for investors if it becomes necessary to modernize, expand production, and have other options of development. The

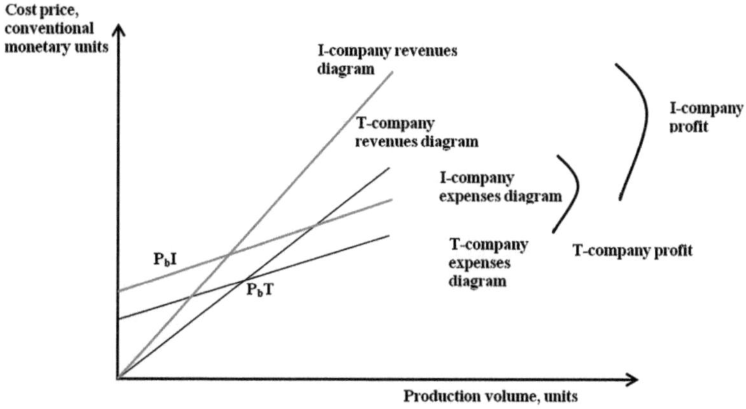

Fig. 2.1 The simplified schematic diagram of development of the companies exercising competitiveness management (I) and ignoring these processes (T)

company exercising competitiveness management and increasing its competitive advantages by means of development and commissioning innovative solutions and technologies has much more chances to involve additional funds: to receive bank credit or to mobilize strategic investors. Company capital investments in development and commissioning of innovative technologies taking into account carefully thought over policy in the field of marketing—formula for success—middle-term and long-term competitive advantages (depending on production and the industry). A common example is development of various types of high-technology and science-intensive products at the expense of big financial investments in creation of innovative technologies and their manufacturing application.

The reasoning set forth above provides an opportunity to form the *second postulate of competitiveness management*:

> Most intensive competitiveness management should be carried out from the moment of the beginning of production until the firm starts receiving profit on sales, sufficient for its stable development. As soon as the profit starts falling, it is necessary to pass over to the products with essentially new consumer properties, possessing high competitiveness in the commodity markets.

The implications of the second postulate of competitiveness management are as follows.

Intensive competitiveness management with involvement of considerable financial resources should be carried out until expenses for creation of competitive advantages of the products and the firm fail to provide growth of its income; then alternation of the products generations will be required. Some reduction in expenses for research and development and growth in sales will lead to faster profit improvement. In addition to the above, the closer innovations to the basic products are the better, the longer competitive advantages are the longer life term of production and the period of receiving high profit.

As can be seen from the above, it is possible to formulate *the third postulate of competitiveness management*:

> In order to keep the maximum value of profit in the long run there will be required creation of competitive advantages connected with both improvement of the basic characteristics of production and commissioning of new goods which were not available in the markets before at the expense of application of achievements of fundamental and applied science.

In order to create competitive advantages income-generating on a long-term horizon, it is necessary to apply radical innovations based on large scientific discoveries and inventions. Such innovations form the basis of new generations and directions of development of engineering equipment and technology.

Definition of competitiveness management time span is an important issue.

In order to answer a question on the time frame of competitiveness management at microeconomic level, that is, firm level, we consider dependence of marginal cost and marginal profit on additional unit of output, relying on the Law of increasing opportunity costs and the Law of diminishing marginal returns.

Let's have the following argument. After overcoming the break-even point, the firm starts receiving marginal (max) profit. The said process is due to decrease in max costs of the firm. As a result there is a moment, when maximization of marginal profit and minimization of marginal costs are achieved.

As a result there is a moment, when maximization of marginal profit and minimization of marginal costs are achieved as it is shown in Fig. 2.2

Relying on the Decreasing returns law and the Increasing costs, we can draw a conclusion that in the course of production, the critical, trigger point is the volume of output with the minimum of marginal costs and the maximum of marginal profit. From this time, at increase in production there is a growth of marginal costs and decrease in marginal profit.

Quite naturally, when there is no commissioning of innovation solutions and technologies, new ways of manufacture, or aggressive marketing policy, such

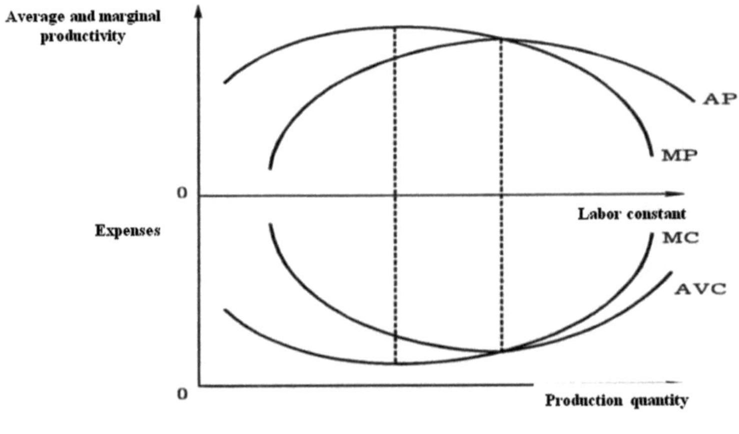

Fig. 2.2 Interrelation of dynamics of the company marginal expenses and marginal profit

tendency may turn into uncontrolled process and lead to falling of the firms' competitiveness in the market, its shakeout, and further—bankruptcy. In order to avoid it, there should be performed planning and forecasting of the situation development and in due time to activate the process of competitiveness management concerning commissioning of innovation technologies and solutions in the sphere of manufacture.

In view of the above said, important inference should be drawn that competitiveness management concerning production, firm, or an industry should be performed on an ongoing basis. If competitiveness management does not provide due effect or if the balance point of marginal costs and marginal profit is reached, the strategy competitiveness management should be changed. The substantiation of updated strategy management is performed on the basis of results of the next SWOT analysis of the strong and weak sides of production and the firm. By results of this work with a view to influence the factors which can enhance production competitiveness, the plan documents should be amended with regard to new purchasing, industrial, financial, and marketing policy.

Implementation of competitiveness management function increases expenses in the short-term period; however in the longer period of commissioning at the expense of more economic innovation technologies and growth of production competitiveness, short-term expenses will be paid off and will provide an opportunity to increase marginal and cumulative profit.

Timely measures on escalating competitive advantages of the goods or commissioning of the new goods with higher consumer properties do not exclude the possibility of occurrence of various risks, capable of affecting production competitiveness.

Let's consider how we can use mechanisms of competitiveness management to undercut negative influence of external effects (for example, occurrence of crisis or growth of risks) which cause growth of both cumulative and marginal costs and lead to decrease in marginal profit, for two scenarios:

- The scenario of increase in production and marginal profit improvement;
- The scenario of marginal cost escalation and increase in production.

Scenario 1

Increase in production and marginal profit improvement.

Let's consider a situation when the firm status is characterized by a part of a curve of the marginal costs, having a negative inclination (i.e., there is an increase in production and growth of marginal profit).

In this case, negative influences will give rise to increase in costs and, accordingly, decrease in marginal profit under increase in production. In the event there is no competitiveness management, such situation can proceed throughout a long period and the market won't be able to improve the firm position, whereupon it will be compelled to take advantage of borrowed funds, or to declare itself bankrupt, or to scale down production. In case of negative external effects, the curve of marginal costs will be positive and more abrupt than earlier—in view of aggravation of the situation at the expense of negative external effects. As can be seen from the above, the firm will face problems of increase in costs, deterioration of competitive advantages (it is by itself the biggest risk for a firm), reductions of output, profit, staff, and, as a consequence, falling of competitiveness in the market.

Such situation requires commissioning of more economic innovation technologies, use of more hi-tech equipment with greater productivity, or enhancement of production competitiveness by affecting the quality or carrying out of a corresponding marketing policy. In this case, even with the increase in production, the firm management can predict when there will come the moment of reduction of marginal costs and profit improvement.

Production competitiveness management will provide an opportunity to carry out timely management and reduce the crisis period for a firm. In turn, growth of production competitiveness will lead to enhancing growth of profit whereupon the firm will be able to overcome crisis consequences as soon as possible.

Scenario 2

Marginal Cost Escalation and Increase in Production

Let's consider a situation when the firm status is characterized by a curve of marginal costs having a positive inclination (i.e., there is growth of marginal costs under the increase in production).

In this case the firm is obviously lacking effective competitiveness management and efficient planning and forecasting. In addition to the above negative external effects can aggravate such situation. If there are no commissioning of innovation technologies, no enhancement of the products quality or no corresponding marketing policy, bankruptcy of the firm and its shakeout are inevitable.

In such a situation the majority of firms usually scale down production, however it is not the best way out, as the drop in production leads to insignificant cost reduction (whereas fixed costs remain at the former level, or may grow owing to negative external effects). Besides it is impossible to precisely predict economic indicators for a firm in the future: curtailment of production leads to shakeout, and new positions will be quickly filled by new players possessing bigger competitive advantages, using more innovative solutions to overcome the crisis.

Implementation of measures on competitiveness management in the short-term period will increase expenses, however within a short time, in view of commissioning of more economic innovation technologies, or owing to growth of production competitiveness in some other manner, short-term expenses will be paid off; there will be a possibility to increase marginal profit and to achieve its maximization.

The reasoning set forth above provides an opportunity to form the *fourth postulate of competitiveness management*:

> Competitiveness management should be activated in the event of risks capable to somehow cause cost-push and-or a falling-off in demand for the products and when it is impossible to receive scheduled profit.

The moment of termination of the active phase in competitiveness management depends on special aspects of development of specific industry and a firm.

There are enterprises and economy sectors where competitiveness management should be continuously performed in an active mode. This principle has special value for the markets' functioning in a mode of a perfect competition and oligopoly, when there are many emerging new players in the market.

In the markets of imperfect competition or in the market of monopolistic competition when the entrance to the market is complicated, a point of "damping" the process of active competitiveness management shall be the moment when there is a marginal cost reduction and profit improvement under the increase of the firm production output.

So, as follows from its content competitiveness management represents a complicated phenomenon uniting a set of relatively independent, but nevertheless, inextricably intertwined mechanisms to provide creation, application, and maintenance of competitive advantages on the basis of economic theories, laws, postulates, hypotheses, and processes.

The said four postulates (and their consequences) concerning competitiveness management made it possible for the authors of this monograph to put forward a number of hypotheses about competitiveness concept and behavior and to develop main principles of competitiveness management.

Distinctive feature of the offered approach to formalizing description of dynamics competitiveness and management impact on competitiveness indexes is the use of mathematical models based on the theory of the linear differential equations. It is important to emphasize the fact, notwithstanding that, in our model the dynamics of specific competitiveness indexes in time will be described by a system of linear differential equations; actually, competitiveness management itself can enter this model in a nonlinear manner.

The mathematical models presented in the monograph serve as a qualitative illustration of the offered hypotheses of competitiveness management and are intended to demonstrate the offered ideas. On the other hand, the use of mathematical models provides an opportunity to state more strictly the offered theoretical approach to competitiveness management.

So, let us present definition of competitiveness and formulate the basic hypotheses for competitiveness properties (hypotheses 1–3) and for competitiveness management (hypotheses 3*, 4–6).

Definition Competitiveness is an estimated category of a possibility to outperform a competitor under postulated condition, described by competitiveness index, presenting a numerical vector:

$$Q = \begin{pmatrix} q_1 \\ q_2 \\ \vdots \\ q_N \end{pmatrix},$$

where q_i, $i = 1, \ldots, N$—virtually specific competitiveness indexes, taking nonnegative values, that is:

$$q_i \geq 0, \quad i = 1, \ldots, N$$

As well as at any vector values, on a set of competitiveness indexes we put in a partial order. Usually utility functions are used for these purposes, but in our model we confine ourselves to the elementary partial order of the following type:

$$Q^1 \leq Q^2 \Leftrightarrow q_i^1 \leq q_i^2, \; i = 1, \ldots, N.$$

The put in partial order reflects an assumption that in our model the bigger value of the specific competitiveness index corresponds to more high competitiveness. As can be seen from the above, it is possible to form the first hypothesis for competitiveness.

Hypothesis 1 *Competitiveness can be presented a vector of specific competitiveness indexes. Specific competitiveness indexes are virtually nonnegative numbers.*

The problem competitiveness management means that the study is focused on the process competitiveness changing in time under the influence of various factors.

It is known that many economic processes are discrete in time; however in our model we shall assume that specific competitiveness indexes are time continuous and diminishing in the absence of management actions, that is, they meet the following conditions:

$$q_i = q_i(t), \quad t \geq 0$$

and

$$q_i(t') > q_i(t''), \quad t' < t''.$$

This assumption reflects the property of "diffusion" inherent in any quality indicators. As can be seen from the above, it is possible to formulate the second hypothesis for competitiveness—a hypothesis of continuous diffusion of competitiveness indexes.

Hypothesis 2 *Specific competitiveness indexes are functions of time, and in the absence of the factors positively influencing competitiveness, there is a diminishing of specific competitiveness indexes in time.*

Certainly, the state of affairs when competitiveness indexes are diminishing owing to natural diffusion cannot suit us; therefore we come to the next fundamental provision formulated as a consequence of hypothesis 2.

Consequence of Hypothesis 2 *In order to keep competitiveness at the desired level, there should be continuous competitiveness management with a view to increase specific competitiveness indexes.*

By reason of its general sense competitiveness is an indicator, which reflects superiority of the object under consideration (product, enterprise, industry, country) over competitors. Therefore, during competitiveness calculation, it is necessary to take into account not only state of the said object, but also status of competing objects. On the other hand, there is often a necessity to calculate competitiveness indexes regardless of competitors. As can be seen from the above, it is necessary to divide competitiveness into external and internal competitiveness (in other words, into subjective and objective competitiveness), prompting an opportunity to formulate the third hypothesis for competitiveness.

Hypothesis 3 *Competitiveness of the object is divided into external competitiveness which is calculated on the basis of interaction of the object with competitors, and internal competitiveness which is calculated on the basis of comparison of the object objective indicators.*

Let's consider an example to explain the said hypothesis. Let us assume that an unknown firm creates a new smart phone which outperforms modern iPhone of the well-known firm. If we consider a sales volume as criterion of competitiveness, the new smart phone (in the short-term period) will be inferior to the fashionable and well-known brand. In this case, external competitiveness will be worse as compared to the competitor. In order to evaluate competitiveness in the long run, it is necessary to take into account objective indicators; therefore internal competitiveness of the said product will be better.

This example reflects the fact that de facto there is both perfect and imperfect competition. In this case, we face an imperfect competition owing to the market entry threshold for smart phones.

So, it is possible to add hypothesis 3 with hypothesis 3*.

Hypothesis 3* *In the event of perfect competition, it is necessary to be guided by external competitiveness, and in case of imperfect competition, it is necessary to consider internal competitiveness.*

Whereas according to hypotheses 1 and 2 specific competitiveness indexes $\boldsymbol{q_i}\,\boldsymbol{(t)}$ are continuous functions of time, the basic mathematical model describing dynamics of competitiveness indexes may be written down in the form of a system of ordinary differential equations as follows.

Let us assume that $Q(t)$ is a vector competitiveness index at the moment of time $\boldsymbol{t}$. Then, in the absence of effects on competitiveness, we write down the model of dynamics of competitiveness indexes in the form of the following system of N linear homogeneous differential equations:

$$\frac{dQ(t)}{dt} = A(t)Q(t), \quad (1^*)$$

where $A(t)$—matrix of diffusion of the specific indicators, representing a square dimension matrix $N \times N$.

According to hypothesis 2 in the absence of management actions and positive external factors specific competitiveness indexes $\mathbf{q_i}$ **(t)** should diminish.

In order to reflect this property of specific competitiveness indexes in the model, we assume that the proper values of λ matrix $A(t)$ are satisfied as a matter of convention:

$$\mathrm{Re}\lambda_i(t) < 0, \quad i = 1, \ldots, N; \quad t \leq 0.$$

This condition means that if real components of the proper values Re (λ_i (t)) of the matrices of diffusion of specific indicators are negative, then condition of stability of the zero solution on the first approach for Eq. (1**) is satisfied and, accordingly, it is possible to write that under initial condition

$$Q(0) = \begin{pmatrix} q_1(0) \\ q_2(0) \\ \vdots \\ q_N(0) \end{pmatrix}, \quad q_i(0) \geq 0, \ i = 1, \ldots, N$$

There is

$$\lim_{t \to \infty} q_i(t) = 0, \ i = 1, \ldots, N.$$

Next, we show that according to consequence of hypothesis 2 to keep up with other companies at the set level, it is necessary to have continuous competitiveness management, aimed at an increase of specific competitiveness indexes. In our model of dynamics of competitiveness indexes, this requirement we shall be accounted as follows.

Let us have M measures $\boldsymbol{u_j(t)}$, providing an opportunity to influence $\boldsymbol{N}$ specific competitiveness indexes $\boldsymbol{q_i(t)}$, described by specified above system $\boldsymbol{N}$ of differential equations (1**). Then competitiveness management may be presented in the form of time-dependent M-dimensional vector $\boldsymbol{U(T)}$:

$$U(t) = \begin{pmatrix} \boldsymbol{u}_1(t) \\ \boldsymbol{u}_2(t) \\ \vdots \\ \boldsymbol{u}_M(t) \end{pmatrix}, \quad t \geq 0.$$

In order to account influence of management actions on competitiveness, we put in the equation competitiveness (1**) a vector of competitiveness management $\boldsymbol{U}$ $\boldsymbol{(T)}$ as the linear pattern:

$$\frac{dQ(t)}{dt} = A(t)Q(t) + B(t)U(t) \qquad (1^{**})$$

where $B(t)$ is a rectangular matrix of dimension $N \times M$ named a matrix of management possibilities.

Economic rationale of matrix $B(t)$ is in the fact that it provides an opportunity to consider influence of management actions on the speed of changing specific competitiveness indexes and the character of their change in time. Dependence of the matrix of management possibilities on time reflects the fact that influence of management actions on the character of changing specific competitiveness indexes can vary in due course.

According to hypothesis 3, the competitiveness indexes except for the natural diffusion and internal management actions are influenced by competitors' activities and other external factors. We shall consider this requirement in the trend data mathematical model of competitiveness as follows:

Let external factors are described K-dimensional vector $F\ (T)$:

$$F(t) = \begin{pmatrix} f_1(t) \\ f_2(t) \\ \vdots \\ f_K(t) \end{pmatrix}, \quad t \geq 0.$$

By analogy with the approach for accounting of management actions, for the influence vector of external factors we shall use transitive matrix $C(t)$ of dimension $N \times K$ which we name an external effects damping matrix.

The Economic rationale of external effects damping matrix lies in the fact that its elements show degree of influence of external factors on competitiveness dynamics of the modeled object.

Let's assume that influence of external factors on specific competitiveness indexes is additive. Therefore, in order to account influence of external factors on competitiveness, we shall put a vector of external effects $\boldsymbol{F(t)}$ in competitiveness Eq. (1**) as a linear pattern:

$$\frac{dQ(t)}{dt} = A(t)Q(t) + B(t)U(t) + C(t)F(t).$$

So, with the account of natural diffusion of specific competitiveness indexes, purposeful management actions, and external factors (negative or positive), the dynamics model of competitiveness management will assume the following final form of the ordinary differential equations:

$$\frac{dQ(t)}{dt} = A(t)Q(t) + B(t)U(t) + C(t)F(t). \qquad (2.1)$$

Where Q (t)—vector competitiveness index (dimension N),
A (t)—diffusion matrix of specific indicators (dimension $N \times N$),

U (t)—vector of competitiveness management of (dimension M),
B (t)—management possibility matrix (dimensions N × M),
F (t)—vector of external factors (dimension K),
C (t)—external effects damping matrix (dimension N × K).

In what follows, a task of management always means presence of the set target of management. Besides there may be put restrictions on management and, supposedly, presence of the so-called payment for distinguish management. In order to formalize the purpose of management, restrictions on management, and payment for competitiveness management, we shall use Stieltjes measure, that is, we shall consider as prescribed the functionals having rather common form of Stieltjes integrals, in which range of definition is presented by solution of Eq. (2.1). Use of Stieltjes integral will provide a joint stance to consider functionals, depending on function ***Q*(*t*)** within the entire time interval.

We shall define the purpose of competitiveness management within the limits of the dynamic model of management of the said system of the equations (2.1) by the following target functional ***J*(*Q*)**, calculated on the multitude of competitiveness indexes ***Q*(*t*)**:

$$J(Q) = \int_0^T G^Q(t, Q(t)) dH^Q(t). \tag{2.2}$$

where

G—is a function of current value of competitiveness index, which we assume to be, generally speaking, unstable, i.e., depending ОТ ***t***,
H—is a function to put Stieltjes measure at an intercept [0.T] and it is assumed to be nondecreasing.

The economic interpretation of the target functional ***J*(*Q*)**, for example, may be proceeds of the product sale, enterprise profit, etc.

From the economic point of view, special interest may take the values of competitiveness index ***Q*(*t*)** within the set points of time, for example, in the terminal point, that is, in the end of the analyzed period of time. So for example, in this particular case the target functional will be presented in the form of Mayer functional.

Important competitiveness properties to be considered in modeling shall be possible presence restrictions on management and, so-called, payments for selection of management.

We put restrictions on the management as follows:

$$U(t) \in W, \quad t \in [0, T]. \tag{2.3}$$

where W is a multitude of possible managements. Let us note that in certain situations a multitude of possible managements W may, in turn, depend on time, on the values of competitiveness indexes, and/or on the managements chosen before.

Let's put functional *I(U)* which has Economic rationale of a payment for the chosen management and is set on a vector of management functions *U(t)* in the form of Stieltjes integral as follows:

$$I(U) = \int_0^T G^U(t, U(t)) dH^U(t). \tag{2.4}$$

Taking into account restrictions on management (2.3) and payments for management (2.4), it is possible to formulate a problem of optimum competitiveness management as follows:

To find such admissible management *U(t)* which delivers maximum to the functional, being a difference between the values of target functional and corresponding payment for management:

$$(J(Q) - I(U)) \rightarrow \max_{U(t) \in W} \tag{2.5}$$

For solution of this problem, it is necessary to choose the following algorithm of competitiveness management:

$$U = K(Q), \tag{2.6}$$

which under conditions of observability and management provides the system "lock-in" and required number of managements practically without dependence on the proper values of diffusion matrix A, that is, practically compensates the natural diffusion of specific indications of competitiveness.

Economic rationale of observability and management conditions consists in the fact that it is necessary to have a possibility to measure competitiveness indexes and to influence them either expressly or by implication.

The algorithm of optimum management $\boldsymbol{K(Q)}$ is generally found by Bellman equation, and in that specific case (with the use of quadratic functional by Riccati equation.

It should be noted that, generally speaking, this model of dynamic competitiveness managements is not completely reduced to the task of optimum management. Equation (2.1) takes into account external factors, which are formed by competitors and operate, generally speaking, against competitiveness index. In this sense, the model is close to the theory of differential games.

Later in this section, we shall address a competitiveness management method based on the hysteretic-type management. Such approach has clear economic interpretation and leads to solution of the problem of competitiveness maintenance at the desired level.

Hysteretic approach provides an opportunity to effectively solve a problem of competitiveness management with the account of internal and external factors influencing competitiveness. An important characteristic of the said approach is the fact that this method leads to management which, on the one hand, corresponds to competitiveness management actions realized in practice, and on the other hand—provides an opportunity to avoid transition to the so-called sliding mode.

As mentioned above, the primary goal of competitiveness management is competitiveness index maintenance at the set level. Owing to effect of competitiveness index diffusion caused by matrix $A(t)$, we need continuous management to keep competitiveness at the desired level.

Optimum management as a solution of an extreme problem (2.5) is rather a complicated mathematical issue. However, many difficulties caused by purely mathematical reasons are not always essential in solution of economic problems. On the other hand, economic methods of competitiveness management are often restricted in their implementation.

Setting of the problem of competitiveness management within the frames of hysteresis approach can be formulated as follows.

Let's assume that during each fixed point of time t_0 on vector of specific competitiveness indexes $Q(t_0)$, it is possible to calculate specific integral scalar-valued function $\boldsymbol{IQ}(\boldsymbol{Q}(\boldsymbol{t}))$:

$$IQ : R^n \to R.$$

The Economic rationale of function $\boldsymbol{IQ}(\boldsymbol{Q}(\boldsymbol{t}))$ consists in defining competitiveness level at the time being.

Let's assume that competitiveness management goal is the maintenance of specific competitiveness indexes within the set range. Then it is possible to write down that the purpose of competitiveness management is maintenance of such specific competitiveness indexes (vector Q) which provide the following conditions:

$$IQ(Q(t)) \geq Q^*_{\min},$$

where $Q^*_{\min}$—the minimum desired level of competitiveness.

Let's designate through $Q^*_{\max}$ a certain set level of competitiveness which satisfies condition $Q^*_{\max} > Q^*_{\min}$.

Then the management on the hysteresis basis is built according to the following formula:

$$H(Q(t)) = \begin{cases} 0, & IQ(Q(t)) \geq Q^*_{\max} \\ U(t), & IQ(Q(t)) < Q^*_{\min} \end{cases}.$$

As the vector of management functions $U(t)$ is aimed at competitiveness growth, then hysteresis-type management makes active the activities for competitiveness enhancement while the integrated competitiveness index has less values $Q^*_{\min}$ and is kept until the integrated competitiveness index does not have value more than $Q^*_{\max}$. "Cross target" between values $Q^*_{\min}$ and $Q^*_{\max}$ creates so-called hysteresis "loop" required to avoid possibility of transition to the sliding mode in competitiveness management.

It is possible to show that if the matrix of possibilities of managing effects $B(t)$ provides an opportunity for competitiveness management $U(t)$ to raise competitiveness level to preset values, then the management on the basis of hysteresis brings to comprehensible management which solves the task by means of the most economical way.

As can be seen from the above, it is possible to formulate the fourth hypothesis concerning competitiveness, namely a hypothesis of competitiveness management.

Hypothesis 4 *Competitiveness management enhancement should be launched at the time when competitiveness integral index becomes less than the set minimum value, and should be continued until the moment when this index exceeds the set maximum value.*

It is noteworthy that competitiveness management on the basis of hysteresis principle has a clear economic rationale, namely: in order to achieve the necessary effect active competitiveness measures to enhance competitiveness should be taken within a prolonged period. The hysteresis principle provides an opportunity to formalize the said requirement to possible managements of competitiveness.

The above models are applicable in conditions of perfect competition; just such situations make sense to speak about competitiveness management by means of activities which are expressed by additive component $B(t)U(t)$ in Eq. (2.1).

In the situations of imperfect competition such management cannot solve the task of competitiveness management, or this management will not be justified from the economic point of view. In conditions of imperfect competition, it is necessary to use innovation management methods established by the following hypothesis.

Hypothesis 5 *Management by means of innovations should lead to change of production functions.*

High competitiveness in the long-term period can be reached due to development and commissioning of innovation technologies for creation of essentially new goods, i.e., as a matter of fact, at the expense of changing production functions.

On the basis of a hypothesis 5, let us put the third additive component in the model of competitiveness management, described by Eq. (2.1), to reflect the possibility of competitiveness management by means of changing production functions:

$$\frac{dQ(t)}{dt} = A^{U(t)}(t)Q(t) + B^{U(t)}(t)U(t) + C^{U(t)}(t)F(t) \tag{2.7}$$

Let's carry out qualitative analysis of the final equation (2.7).

According to the theory of the linear differential equations, positive additive components in the right part of the equation (2.7) render exponential influence on the values of corresponding components of vector Q.

The first additive component in the right part provides an opportunity to exercise competitiveness management by means of changing diffusion matrix of specific indexes of competitiveness $A(t)$. This component of the managerial competitiveness process consists in realizing such changes of diffusion matrix which lead to reduction of real components of proper values λ of matrix $A(t)$ as the exponential character of solutions of Eq. (2.7) will be defined by these real component of proper values λ. Performing this condition will provide reduction of diffusion of competitiveness indexes; moreover even small reduction of diffusion effect of competitiveness will essentially enhance the result of competitiveness management.

Similarly, the second additive component of equation (2.7) provides an opportunity to exercise competitiveness management due to such changes of matrix of possibilities managing effects $B(t)$ which will lead to essential increase of competitiveness as this matrix reflects technological possibilities of management of specific competitiveness indexes. And accordingly, even a small change of matrix factors $B(t)$ will render exponential influence on competitiveness indexes.

The third additive component in the right part of Eq. (2.7) provides an opportunity to exercise competitiveness management by means of changing the matrix of damping external effects $C(t)$ which is responsible for possibilities to resist negative external factors from the point of view of competitiveness. Often the basic decrease in competitiveness takes place because of external factors' influence; therefore possibilities on lowering this negative influence are rather important.

Management on the basis of innovations can provide substantial growth of competitiveness even with a small amount of investments. As can be seen from the above, it is possible to formulate the following hypothesis of competitiveness management on the basis of innovation approach.

Hypothesis 6 *Competitiveness management on the basis of innovation approach that is in conditions of changing production functions, it provides an opportunity to reduce influence of risks causing growth of production costs and reduction of profit.*

Let's consider the general issues of competitiveness management in the conditions of an imperfect competition. Competitiveness management in the conditions of an imperfect competition from the point of view of an individual object, for example, individual enterprise, was already examined above.

At the same time, there is a problem of managing imperfect competitiveness from the point of view of more general system. As per definition, enhancement of competitiveness is a response to competition. Hence, in competitive systems all the objects tend to continuous enhancement of competitiveness. However, often, perfect competition is replaced by a system with imperfect competition, which leads to the objects in this system reducing rates of competitiveness growth, and this negatively affects economic efficiency of the entire system.

In such situation, there is a problem of competitiveness management, not within the limits of separate competing objects, within the framework of certain state regulation competitive environment in order to form perfect competition that, finally, should lead to an increase of competitiveness of individual objects and, as a consequence, to increase economic efficiency of the entire system.

Mathematical description of competitiveness management process in the conditions of the perfect and imperfect competition, as well as logical reasoning on the markets of perfect competition, provides an opportunity to make a conclusion that there are no markets of perfect competitiveness in its pure form.

In practice, there is superposition of conditions of the various market structures proving depending on this or that situation in the market, which in turn is defined by cyclicity of economic development.

From our point of view, in spite of the availability of various sorts of cycles in economy, commissioning of competitiveness management can make a direct impact on development of national economy, industry, or an enterprise and to soften negative influence of the specified objective business cycles. Development of the country, industry, and an enterprise depends on consistency, periodicity, and intensity of the process of development and commissioning of innovation technologies.

In the event of insufficient and poor management competitiveness, a nation or a firm can reach a critical point very quickly and find itself on the verge of a crisis. Such situation, if possible, requires radical updating of the entire system of innovation development of the state or a cardinal change of innovation policy of a firm with involvement of intellectual and financial resources, sufficient for creation of essentially new types of production and radical modernization of manufacture. If the firm does not go bankrupt, and the country does not face a debt crisis, economic recovery will soon take place. In order to avoid a possible crisis situation, it is necessary to undertake preventive (or proactive) measures. This is the only way to supervise threat of achieving critical point to avoid crisis from the part of a state, industry, or a firm.

2.3 Competitiveness Management Law

In consideration of evolution of the market competitiveness concept, George Joseph Stigler noted that by the middle of the twentieth century, definition of competitiveness might have been narrowed to the term which would only mean nonavailability of monopoly power in the market. However such definition is not enough to study mechanisms of competitiveness management which is understood today as a certain evaluative category to outperform a competitor in the specified conditions. In this context, it would be safer to treat the concept of competitiveness as a "natural property of commodity, service and economic agent to act in the market on an equal basis with the similar like products, services or competing economic agents available in the market."

Evaluation of competitiveness most often is performed in order (qualitative) scale which usually specifies only high, average, and low competitiveness.

Low-level competitiveness in the fierce struggle for commodity markets can be accompanied by the so-called phase transitions of competitiveness management trajectory. It is presented by specific turning points (or trigger points) characterized by collapse of political and economic health of the states in competitive environment which may be accompanied by military hostilities sometimes. From the end of the twentieth and beginning of the twenty-first centuries, such turning points arise not only due to limited access to the natural resources but also because of increasing influence on competitiveness exercised by the innovations based on modern scientific and engineering solutions, because the countries with high innovative potential and without access to the basic vital resources try to do their best in order to get them to ensure their superiority in the world.

Among the instruments to increase competitive advantages used by commodity producers, both political and economic factors are applied almost on pari passu basis. For example, change of political regime in Iraq was aimed at obtaining access to cheap and qualitative oil followed by provision of competitive advantages for a number of companies concerning energy expenses. Change of political orientation and a course of business development of some states by means of "color," "velvet," and even bloody coup d'etat provided signing on economy of these states of large monopolies and companies on a preferential basis and, as consequence, have led to replacement of national manufacturers from domestic markets of the said states.

The fact of possessing a big set of competitive advantages makes big companies highly competitive in the world markets and may lead to their monopolistic takeover of a particular market. In order to resist such scenario of events, the developed countries have their antimonopoly organizations, called to control market processes and to prevent monopolization and collusive behavior in the market. However, a rule of thumb states that the antimonopoly organizations cannot solve this question in a big way, and "scarcely fair trading" for commodity markets is being aggravated in the modern economic context.

All this brings the necessity to look for theoretical and practical laws in the field of creating and buildup competitive advantages on the basis of new principles—principles of competitiveness management.

The problem of competitiveness and market evaluation first of all consists in definition of the market under investigation, structure of economic relations generated in the said market, and would-be directions of its transformation. It is exactly the level of variety of possible structures of the market to be one of the major characteristics to specify immunity of the market to possible changes of its borders and structure of economic relations of the market agents.

The analysis of the market structure begins with description of economic agents in the market. Each specific market is characterized, first of all, by the number of available sellers and buyers.

The buyers are ranged on the basis of such indicators as their share of the market, volumes of purchases, and territorial position within the market geographical borders.

The similar description is used for the sellers; the only difference is with the volumes of sales being analyzed instead of the volume of purchases.

Territorial distribution of the sellers in the market under consideration is also analyzed here.

Besides, the market is analyzed from the point of view of development of its infrastructure: transportation system, warehouse network, and availability of auxiliary production.

The descriptive analysis of the market is followed by calculation of the set of analytical indicators of the market structure. Use of the system of analytical indicators makes it possible to classify the markets under investigation in order of their centralization and to receive preliminary assessments of the markets structures.

Analytical indicators of the market structure may be divided on direct and indirect indexes as a matter of convention.

Direct indexes immediately mirror degree of the firm influence on the market concern, as exemplified by Bain Index, Tobin's Q Ratio, and Lerner Index.

Indirect indexes characterize the market situation as a whole, thanks to which it is possible to evaluate the level of independence of an individual firm in the cause of taking market decisions. Indirect indexes are Herfindahl–Hirschman Index, coefficient of relative concentration, entropy rate, dispersion of market units, and Gini coefficient.

Each of the listed analytical indicators of the market structure has specific calculation methodology. The specified indicators of the market structure are basically characterized by the fact that they offer static evaluation of the market situation.

Use of analytical indicators will be more productive and informative if we consider dynamics of indicators variation in time.

The major factor to define the structure and type of the market, level of concentration, and competitiveness of the market is availability and height of the market barriers. Analysis and evaluation of the market barrier height should be performed on the basis of collection and analysis of the problem-oriented information which meets the requirements of completeness and quality. This review in turn requires definition of major factors responsible for competitiveness in the said market.

According to M. Porter's model of competitive struggle, briefly reviewed in Sect. 2.1, the following groups of factors are used to analyze competitiveness at the market:

- Intensity of competitive rivalry in the said market—influence of sellers;
- Threat of substitute products or services and their influence;
- Threat of new entrants—influence of potential competitors;
- Bargaining power of suppliers—influence of suppliers;

- Bargaining power of customers—influence of buyers.

Each of Porter's five forces mentioned above may have a various activity-specific effect on the situation in the industry. Aggregate effect of these forces defines not only general characteristics of competitive rivalry in the industry but also a place of particular firms in the market and their success.

From the mentioned five groups which influence the level of market competitiveness, there is a group of factors ("Threat of new entrants") directly associated with market barriers which actually define the level of dependence of the market from the higher-ranking economic system. Prior to analyzing the market barriers' height it is worthwhile to evaluate the contribution of the "threat of new entrants" to the general characteristic of market relations.

During empirical formation of operating influences on competitiveness of market participants producing goods and services, as a rule, they define the barrier height for new entrants individual to the following factors influencing detrimental to competitiveness:

- Positive returns to scale;
- Vertical integration;
- Diversification of activity;
- Product differentiation;
- Elasticity and rates of growth in demand.

Let's characterize each of the listed empirical factors of competitiveness and evaluate their influence on the market entry barriers within the context of firms.

Positive Returns to Scale An indicator to characterize the entry barriers due to positive returns to scale is the so-called minimum effective output the economic substance of which consists in the following.

If the scale of production (output volume) increases, it leads to reduction in expenses and accordingly to reduction in price. When production volume achieves the minimum effective output, expenses stabilization leads to prices stabilization.

Henceforth, to define the minimum value of long-term average expenses, it is necessary to have, first, a guarantee that the process of production and consumption of the said product is stable. This fact may be established by analyzing price level during the "market significant interval of time," provided that the average indicators within this time frame may be considered reliable in some specified sense.

Secondly, it is necessary to estimate the Standard Deviation (root-mean-square deviation)—σ of the price values of specific product of the different enterprises from the average indicators. With this end in view, it is necessary to trace a situation within such time interval when this root-mean-square deviation can be evaluated with comprehensible reliability.

It is worthwhile to speak about positive returns to scale as an essential barrier to enter the market only in the event the market demand is limited. With the value of output volume exceeding the market demand value, expenses start to grow sharply. The firm starts working to no purpose, as if "selling at a sacrifice."

As can be seen from the above, first of all, it is necessary to specify the minimum value of the long-term average expenses concerning production of a product (goods). Proceeding from the assumption, that the market price would not exceed the minimum value of the average production expenses, it is possible to define would-be market demand in the product units (for example, on the basis of expert polling). Potential demand for the said product and dynamics of demand saturation are of great value here.

In order to specify these indicators we offer the following procedure.

There should be determined spread in values of the trading range and expenditures case by case and individual to every firm. This being the case, there may be four cases here:

1. If the value range (spread) (3σ) is not crossed—*very high barrier.*
2. If the value range (spread) is crossed, but does not cover the average prices and expenses—*moderately high barrier.*
3. If the spread of expenditures covers the average price or the value range covers average expenses—*moderate barrier.*
4. If the spread of expenditures forms low price or the value range is defined by low expenses—*low barrier.*

Actually, as can be seen from the above, this is the way to determine the level of the market power of the deeply rooted firms in the aggregate.

As a whole, the evaluation of the barrier height due to positive returns to scale is carried out through two positions:

- It is necessary to specify the barrier greatest possible level which is defined as a relation of the market significant interval of the sales volume to the averaged (through all firms-producers) difference of price and expenses;
- As it is empirically established that the positive returns to scale are suitable in case when the average value of the added value per one employee in big enterprises $C^{\partial}_{\kappa n}$ exceeds the average value of the added value per one employee in small enterprises of the same industry $C^{\partial}_{\text{мп}}$, it is necessary to have an advantage index of big enterprises on the expenditure side and calculated according to formula $K_{\kappa n} = C^{\partial}_{\kappa n}/C^{\partial}_{\text{мп}}$ not less than 1.25 within the market under review.

Vertical Integration Vertical integration strengthens the market power of some firms doing business in the market, through connection of the said firms with the higher-ranking economic system.

At determining the influence of vertical integration on the barrier height, it is necessary to establish, first of all, the fact of integration. For this purpose, we should define if there are firms in the said market for which we note an appreciable correlation of the variance processes of the market price with respect to their products. If there is a positive correlation of the market price between firms dealing with the end-product manufacturing at different stages, then the fact of vertical integration proves to be true. By means of such analysis, it is possible to reveal clusters of vertically integrated firms. Simultaneously with positive correlation in the same market, there may be negative correlation between price formation process of the firms in the vertically integrated clusters and firms outside of the said clusters.

There is provided to evaluate the impact of vertical integration on the barriers' height in the following way:

1. If the market is reasonably "clusterized" the factor of vertical integration essentially raises the height of the entry barriers. As can be seen from the above, in some cases this factor may be more important than the factor of positive returns to scale. Such situation can testify to an obvious monopolization of the market.
2. If there is a negative correlation in addition to positive correlation, it means that the vertical integration does not change type of the market and there is a place for free competitiveness.
3. If there is no positive correlation, it is possible to consider impact of vertical integration on the entry barriers as insignificant; otherwise, there is no vertical integration.
4. There may take place an intermediate option when correlation is available, but it not very high. Then the level of vertical integration impact on the barrier height can be estimated by a correlation value—coefficient from 0 to 1. It is worthwhile to say that if there is a complete clusterization of the market at low correlation, it means availability of strong institutional factors of raising the entry barrier.

Diversification of the Firm Activity Diversified firm as a rule is bigger in size and due to this fact it brings an essential contribution to the specific part of the market entry barrier which is defined by the positive returns to scale.

During evaluation of diversification contribution from the firm activity to the market entry barrier height, it is worthwhile to use point scale where 0 points correspond to the minimum barrier height and discretization interval of the barrier height is equal to 1 point.

Then the firms' diversification contribution to formation of the market entry barrier height can be evaluated in the following way.

In order to define the number of diversified firms in the market, it is necessary to fix the firms with the total volume of their products sale exceeding volume of sales in the said specific market. Then, for every diversified firms we should define indicator $\boldsymbol{V_{exmar}}$ being a part of the firm volume of sales beyond the said market which can be used for buildup of its activities in the market. Keeping in mind that diversified firms are already occupying a certain part of this market (V_{enmar}), their coefficient of impact on the barrier height of $\boldsymbol{K_{divim}}$ will be calculated according to the following formula:

$$K_{divim} = 1 + V_{exmar}/V_{enmar}.$$

In order to define contribution of diversified firms to the barrier height, for example, specific to positive returns to scale, this barrier height in points should be multiplied by coefficient $\boldsymbol{K_{divim}}$.

Product Differentiation Product differentiation means modification (sometimes only external modification) of the products which satisfy the same requirement and have the same basic characteristics. Output of the differentiated product does not mean at all that the firm leaves this particular market.

As an illustration of product there are different cigarette brands, cars, and home appliances. While being distinguished by packing, marking, and insignificant internal modifications, the products continue to be the same trade brand.

Calculation of the product differentiation contribution into the value of the market entry barrier height is as follows.

In order to identify cluster of the firms which pay special attention to product differentiation, there is a good reason to consider the number of the firms which incur essential expenses for advertising of their products and positive company image. Average expenses of such firms exceed average expenses throughout the market (for similar products), at the same time their product price is above the average price throughout the market. As this takes place, the increase in price in relative units exceeds the increase in expenses.

For firms which incur essential expenses for advertising of their products and positive company image, it is necessary to evaluate their sales volume in bulk sales of similar products in the said market.

As a result, in order to calculate the influence coefficient of product differentiation on the barrier height, as well as to the influence coefficient of the firm diversification activity, it is considered that base case calculation of the barrier height is performed according to the factor of positive returns to scale. The distinction consists in that, in a case of the firm diversification activity we evaluate potential expansion of operations, and in case of product differentiation expansion of operations is already under way, and we only take note what contribution to the barrier height has actually taken place due to product differentiation. Coefficient of influence $\boldsymbol{K_{dif}}$ of product differentiation may be evaluated by ratio of excess average price of production ($\boldsymbol{Q_c}$) to excess of average expenses ($\boldsymbol{Q_t}$) according to the following formula:

$$K_{dif} = 1 + Q_c/Q_t.$$

Elasticity and Rates of Growth in Demand Price elasticity in demand limits excess price over the marginal expenses in the markets with imperfect competition. If demand is not elastic, the firms may increase the price in comparison with expenses to a greater extent than in conditions of elastic demand. Besides, the lower the elasticity demand, the easier for a dominating firm to limit the market entry and simultaneously to have considerable economic profit.

Concentration level depends inversely on the rates of growth in demand: the bigger the rates of growth in demand, that is, the faster is the growth of consumer market, the easier for new firms to enter the industry, and the lower concentration level and, hence, the higher the level of market competitiveness.

It is recognized that demand conditions, though they can create industry entry barriers, are basically out of the firms' control. However, as far as the firms sticking to innovative policy of development are concerned, the fact of the barrier height dependence on the rates of growth in demand for new (innovative) products is of great importance from the point of view of purposeful regulation of influence on the market barrier height.

For the firms established in the said market, a possibility to control the entry barrier height is connected with additional expenses, similar to the event of product differentiation, but without any possibility to use these additional expenses for increase of prices. Moreover, there may be observed reduction of prices during the increase of expenses. This will not make it possible for weaker firms to upgrade their production facilities and be prepared for a boom in demand for innovative production. That is, in a sense, there is a preparation for a sharp buildup of the entry barrier. Therefore, it is important to launch institutional deflation factors for innovative-focused firms which are not so powerful.

We shall consider some characteristic features of competitiveness management mechanisms within the context of various countries.

While analyzing competitiveness management mechanisms we should take into account both external and internal competitive advantages. For further examination of this question, we shall group the principal competitive advantages on the basis of their occurrence and form three groups:

1. *Resource group*—competitive advantages due to availability of cheap natural resources and favorable climatic conditions,
2. *Structural group*—competitive advantages defined by the level of economic development of the state and internal economic environment, which the labor cost depends on,
3. *Technological group*—the competitive advantages defined by the level of scientific-and-technological advance.

Table 2.2 provides an example of groups of the countries depending on the availability of one or another competitive advantage.

Distribution of the countries by groups according to types of their competitive advantages can scarcely ever be executed unequivocally as a concrete country can possess particular competitive advantages characteristic for all three groups simultaneously or to one or two groups only.

There may be observed further division into particular groups of "preferences" within one group for different countries.

In the event we are interested in competitiveness management in the markets with high-tech products, this division is substantially distinguished by expenses for

Table 2.2 Distribution of countries by types of their competitive advantages

<table>
<tr><th></th><th>I
Resource group</th><th>II
Structural group</th><th>III
Technological group</th></tr>
<tr><td>Source of competitive advantage</td><td>Cheap natural resources and favorable climatic conditions</td><td>Level of the state development and the and internal economic environment to provide cheap labor</td><td>Level of scientific and technical progress and economic development</td></tr>
<tr><td>Examples of the countries possessing specific competitive advantages</td><td>Saudi Arabia—oil, Iran—gas, Chile—copper</td><td>Tajikistan, Uzbekistan—cheap and low-skilled labor</td><td>USA, EU countries (Germany, Finland, Sweden, etc.), Japan—high economic development and availability of powerful scientific-and-technological basis</td></tr>
<tr><td rowspan="4">Examples of the countries possessing competitive advantages of various types</td><td colspan="2">Russia—diversified and rich in natural and climatic resources, cheap labor
Chile—cheap labor and rich in natural resources (copper)</td><td></td></tr>
<tr><td></td><td colspan="2">India, Korea—cheap and both low-skilled and highly skilled labor with simultaneous high level of scientific and technological progress: development of hi-tech production, information and communication technologies, etc.</td></tr>
<tr><td colspan="3">China—rich in natural resources, cheap and both low-skilled and highly skilled labor with simultaneous high level of scientific and technological progress</td></tr>
<tr><td colspan="3">USA—included into groups I and III in view of availability of rich natural resources, high social and economic level, development of hi-tech production, information & communication technologies</td></tr>
</table>

manufacture of particular types of technologies and by market saturation by objects of intellectual property right.

It is possible to make the following examples of such division within a group of countries possessing competitive advantages of the same type, namely—technological.

Specialization according to criterion "patenting":

- USA—mainly in the sphere of medicine;
- Japan—systems of information processing in a broad sense, including photo, TV, manufacture of modern musical instruments;
- Germany—mainly mechanical systems, engines and car components, organic chemistry.

Each of these countries has other types of technologies and products patented too, including recurring ones (in comparison with the countries of the same group), but specialization by countries is clearly evidenced.

Specialization according to criterion "technological development":

- USA—production of military and industrial supercomputers and their software, production of air and space engineering equipment, lasers, biotechnology, and advanced environmental technologies;
- West European countries—building of nuclear power stations, production of pharmaceutical preparations, communication equipment, a number of transport mechanical engineering industries;
- Japan—production of industrial robots, medical electronics, information systems, integrated circuits, new metals and ceramics, optical fibers, biotechnologies.

There are characteristic features of these countries in respect of their influence on specific industry-specific markets. For example, Japan takes leading positions in export of microelectronic components and the electronic consumer equipment, and the West Europe lags behind in such areas, as production of integrated circuits and semiconductors, manufacturing of microprocessors and biomaterials.

Let us provide brief characteristics of the groups of countries according to classification of their competitive advantages specified in Table 2.2.

We shall consider *the first group of competitive advantages—resources*. Resource competitive advantages can be concentrated within the borders of particular countries or interstate associations. As a rule, availability of resource competitive advantages in the territory is rather stable. Therefore, this group is especially important for the countries with developing or transition economy. With appropriate investments in innovative extraction and production activity, processing and transportation of natural resources competitive advantages of this group can be augmented. Under condition of successful combination of natural resources processing technologies with new technological processes in the group of manufacturing activities, these competitive advantages can sharply increase due to manufacture of high-technology products with high added value. This is the way, for example, followed today by OPEC countries, regulating price for oil and mineral oil in the world market.

Within the context of competitiveness, it is possible to specify the following objective laws, characteristic of resource competitive advantages:

- With effective control over the processes of creating new products with application of resource competitive advantages, competitiveness of the countries of this group can consistently increase. The countries which do not sufficiently possess competitive advantages of the first group may want to take possession of the said resources in order to enhance their own competitiveness in the world market;
- Protecting their natural resources, the countries with resource competitive advantages can be dragged by the countries without resource competitive

advantages in economic, political, and other wars. It can be said with confidence that military conflicts in the struggle for this group of competitive advantages are a trigger point in competitive rivalry;

- Dependence of national economy on the use of only specific natural resources leads to high dependence of this country on conjuncture of the world prices for the said resources;
- Possession of particular resources can create conditions when the country has an opportunity of more tight control over the prices for the resources, up to dictation of its conditions to consumers;
- Specialization in resource competitive advantages in the long run can bring a deterioration in performance of national economy in view of demotivation in development of innovative technologies (including energy saving solutions and resource-recovery technologies) in order to enhance new competitive advantages and promote scientific and technological progress, which would end in a number of social and economic problems and growth of regional and structural disproportions in economy.

Structural competitive advantages (the second group) are basically formed in the developing countries and countries with transition economy. These countries have high percent of migration abroad, low employment, low cost of services, including municipal and household as well as leas of land and industrial premises, etc.

As economy development advances, the structural competitive advantages are gradually losing their economic importance and appeal. However, at the initial stages of economic growth, structural competitive advantages of the country promote active mobilization of investments and hi-tech involvement of foreign companies. It leads to enhancement of competitiveness of local products, provides replacement by national manufacturers of the foreign products, and promotes buildup of export of local high-tech products to the world markets. China, Brazil, and India can be held as an example of such economic policy.

Capturing of the world markets by products of the countries with structural competitive advantages can bring economic wars. So, for example, the USA exerts political pressure upon against China by trying to appreciate Chinese Renminbi yuan, as well as create specific economic barriers against the Chinese goods in the markets of the USA and other countries where they sell American products.

Countries with structural competitive advantages try to get competitive advantages of the first and the third group, more often at the cost of economic methods, more rarely—political. China is especially aggressive in its activities. It intensively promotes migration of its population and creation of small and middle business in the territories of other countries by Chinese migrants. China takes out shares of large banks and highly technological companies, etc.

For the time being, the countries with structural competitive advantages do not yet provoke transformation of competitive struggle into military conflicts, as there are powerful political and military-technical constraining factor in the world now. However the countries' desire to enter the world advanced markets, generally speaking, does not exclude military conflicts provoked by competitive rivalry.

Within the competitiveness context, it is possible to specify the following objective laws, specific to structural competitive advantages:

1. Structural competitive advantages due to development of economy of the countries, where they are formed, lose their economic importance.
2. Buildup of competitiveness of these countries at the expense of structural competitive advantages, mobilization of investments, and commissioning of innovations leads to replacement of the export goods from their domestic markets and provides development of export.
3. In the process of development of their economy, the states with structural competitive advantages may want to acquire competitive advantages of the first and the third group.
4. The struggle of the states with structural competitive advantages for the world markets and possession of competitive advantages of the first and the third group may escalate into economic and political wars in the foreseeable future and provoke military conflicts in the event constraining factors are low. Hence, in this case competitive struggle can also lead to a turning point, to a situation when the state is on the verge of a crisis.

The third group—*technological competitive advantages*—was generated in advanced countries and develops at a fast pace. Technological competitive advantages are provided by scientific and technical progress, as well as historical, political, and economic conditions. Economy of the countries possessing the third group of competitive advantages, such as the USA, European Union, Canada, and other industrially developed countries, continuously contributes into innovative development.

There is a continuous growth of financing innovative activities against the growth of similar investments in the countries with mainly structural and/or resource competitive advantages in industrially developed countries. Therefore, in the near future, there is a high probability in certain sectors of economy of the countries with technological competitive advantages that they may lose their competitive value due to technological development of the countries which previously possessed basically structural or resource competitive advantages.

Countries with technological competitive advantages are facing a big threat in terms of overproduction of commodities owing to saturation of the current markets and backlog in capturing new commodity markets that results in commodity crises. On the other hand, commodity money generates financial and economic crises. So, for example, one of the reasons of financial and economic crisis in the USA in 2007 may be overproduction of the basic world currency (US dollar) and a "soap bubble" of unsecure mortgage. Besides, one more version has the right to existence, though a disputable one this is objective cyclicity of development of any economy on the basis of the theory of the big waves by N. D. Kondratyev.

One of the possibilities to maintain technological competitive advantages for the countries is an acquisition of competitive advantages of the first and the second group—resource and structural groups. This is the case when economic and political wars are possible; moreover, such military conflicts between the countries or groups of countries are already coming into existence, though, more often under the veiled reasons.

So, influence of technological competitive advantages on economic development is defined by the following natural laws in the sphere of competitiveness:

1. Continuous growth of investments into science and innovative activity leads to essential enhancement of competitiveness of products and firms in the short-term and long-term periods, prolongs their life cycle, and may prevent commodity crises.
2. Diversion of financial resources from innovative sphere and real sector of economy into the area of financial speculative operations may bring financial crises.
3. Process of buildup technological competitive advantages besides continuous investment into scientific and technological progress and innovative activities requires creation of economic and political conditions for obtaining competitive advantages of the first and the second groups (resource and structural groups).
4. Buildup of technological competitive advantages allows creating high competitive products of the future generations and improves the image of the state in the world.
5. Creation of innovative technologies of the future generations allows developing such goods and services, when it will be difficult to simulate or copy them and henceforth to outperform them in the short term and mid term. In this context, technologically advanced countries (Japan, USA, and others) are interested in development of the most advanced products.

Integrated analysis of the above objective laws in the sphere of competitiveness makes it possible to expose the logic of competitiveness management laws and specifies a number of qualitative features of competitive relations in the modern markets.

First buildup of competitive advantages takes place on a continuous basis and is provided not only at the expense of application of innovative solutions requiring continuous development of intellectual potential for their creation, but also at the cost of methods of economic regulation and political pressure.

Secondly during buildup of competitive advantages which do not provide creation of commodities with essentially new consumer properties giving a chance to form additional markets, there may be preconditions to crisis and conflict situations in the world economy.

Thirdly the struggle for competitive advantages of any of the above types (resource, structural, and technological advantages) in the event of depletion of economic and political possibilities leads to military conflicts.

Fourthly in order to avoid formation of triggering event for trigger point, commodity producers, in case of slowing competitiveness of their commodities and reduction in income, should launch production of commodities with essentially new consumer properties to create conditions of forming additional markets. This point can be named a transition point to creation of new commodity markets.

This is the way, for example, commodity market of computer equipment was created in the late eighties and in the nineties of the last century; and in the beginning of 2000s there were created markets of mobile telecommunication, the Internet, etc.

However, not all the industries of economy of a particular country can be simultaneously ready to participate in essentially new markets. It leads to stagnation and outflow of investments into the sphere of financial speculative activities instead of the sphere of creating innovative solutions to provide production of commodities with essentially new consumer properties.

In consideration of the abovementioned objective laws in the sphere of competitiveness, it is possible to give the following findings on the fact that without consideration of competitiveness management and without indicating inefficiency and/or insufficiency of such management, it is possible to reach a turning point which would be followed by financial losses, bankruptcy, loss of goodwill, etc.

As can be seen from the above, it is possible to claim that there are objective economic and sociopolitical conditions when an economic agent at the state level either passes over this turning point or keeps away from this point. If we do not consider such conditions, the state may face an extremely negative situation with poorly predicted consequences.

All this causes exclusively high requirement in competitiveness management according to the above objective laws which can be formulated in the form of empirical economic competitiveness management law[1]:

> Competitiveness management law is an economic law, according to which purposeful and continuous management of product competitiveness and industrial engineering takes place on the basis of competitive advantages, and in case of their under-intensive generation demand for product is cut and the organization faces a risk of bankruptcy. Elimination of bankruptcy risk requires purposeful competitiveness management to create goods with essentially new consumer properties, providing formation of new commodity markets and stable economic development in order to lessen the risk of bankruptcy situations.

[1] As is known, a concept of law in economy and management of economic processes is of conditional character. Rigorous definition of the law even in the natural phenomena is limited by certain conditions. For example, the Ohm's law is not exercised in ultralow temperatures when superconductivity takes place. The laws in economy, as "internal, essential, stable, recurring cause-and-effect relations within the system of production relations" (New Economic Dictionary, - M, New Economy Institute, 2008), a fortiori, cannot have the absolute character beyond the control of economic agent. Using a concept of law within a context of competitiveness management, the author tries to underline the specified objective law which proves to be more strong when there is a more effective feedback (from effect to cause) in the economic structure—which already finds itself within the possibility space of the Manager, i.e., Organizer of economic activities. At the same time, failure to follow the specified objective laws will rather lead to the same effect as a result of deviation from indicative planning—growth in the loss of opportunities.

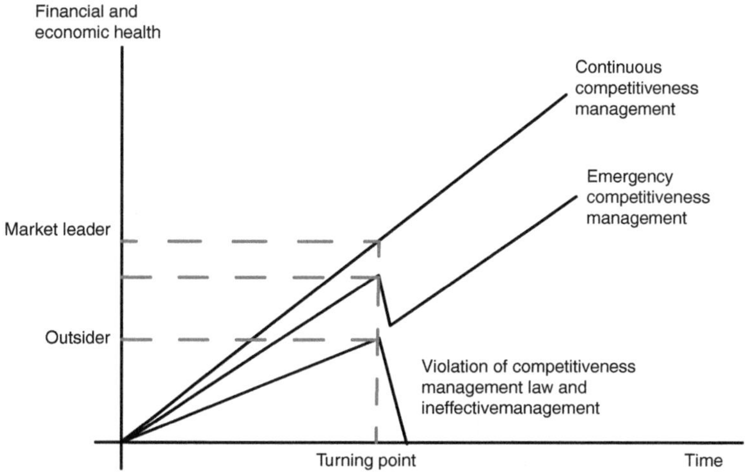

Fig. 2.3 Influence of competitiveness management on financial and economic health of a firm or a state

The way the organization of competitiveness management, according to the above specified empirical law, influences financial and economic health of a firm or a state is illustrated schematically in Fig. 2.3.

So, for example, continuous (permanent) compliance with the law leads to better financial and economic indicators at the expense of high sales, caused, in turn, by high demand for commodities with competitive advantages. In this case, a firm, a segment of industry, or a state has a possibility to prevent accumulation of specific internal factors forming a competitiveness trigger point; provided there are external crises it would be easy to overcome it. In this situation, such factors as diversification of activity and vertical integration have a leading positive role in competitiveness management.

If a firm, a segment of industry, or a state anyhow reached a trigger point and found themselves in a crisis phase, the situation will be different: there will be sharp deterioration of financial and economic conditions and, as a result, there will be required emergency increase in financial investments in the process of competitiveness management. Competitiveness management in this case will consist of the following: increased financing of Research and Advanced Development and innovative projects concerning commissioning of new types of commodities, replacement of fixed assets (purchase of expensive equipment), training of personnel with a view of new equipment, etc.

If done right after a little while the firm or the country will gather momentum and pace of growth and restore the financial and economic indicators. In this situation, such factors as positive returns to scale and product differentiation have a leading positive role in competitiveness management. While continuing to exercise permanent competitiveness management, this firm or the country, most likely, will not face a turning point any more in the foreseeable future.

In the event of violation of substantive provision of competitiveness management law, namely in case of ignoring competitiveness management processes, the economic agent will quickly reach the turning point and goes into bankruptcy.

There are four consequences of empirical law on management competitiveness given below.

Consequence 1 Demand for commodities depends on the current and new competitive advantages moreover stable buildup of competitive advantages allows extending the term of life cycle of the products. Prolongation of life cycle of the goods is expedient until expenses for creation of competitive advantages are paid off, and at the expense of these competitive advantages there will be ensured an income sufficient for stable economic development commodity producer.

Consequence 2 In the event the expenses for creation of competitive advantages are higher than the economic benefit of their introduction which should provide stable economic development of commodity producer, the latter should provide conditions to launch production of the commodities with essentially new consumer properties by this time. The products with new consumer characteristics shall be an important condition of organizing additional commodity markets the development of which would prevent commodity and financial crises and reduce risk of military conflicts because of competitive struggle.

So, the competitiveness management law governs the following:

- Prolongation of life cycle and provision of competitiveness of the goods in the market;
- Alternation of generations of commodities and creation of the products with new consumer properties;
- Competitiveness of the products in the commodity markets and innovative activities of commodity producers.

Consequence 3 Creation of competitive advantages is a cost-based process from the point of view of financial investments; therefore production of highly competitive commodities and their sale should provide buildup of the firm possibilities; otherwise there would be financial problems resulting in holdup in development of new competitive advantages.

Consequence 4 In order to stimulate innovative activity of a firm, there will be required financial resources and other instruments and mechanisms which should be forwarded to support Research & Developmental, commercialization of innovations, replacement of fixed assets (purchase of hi-tech equipment, etc.), personnel training, acquisition of innovative technologies, and so forth.

Above listed four consequences of competitiveness management law from the point of view of the market theory may be interpreted as provision of specific values of elasticity figures and rates of growth in demand.

Practical application of competitiveness management law makes it possible to implement the following functions:

- Integration function;
- Stimulation function;
- Distribution function.

Integration function means accounting of interaction and interdependence of the basic economic laws and theories—law of value, supply and demand, marginal costs increase, diminishing marginal utility, comparative advantage, factor productivity, labor theory of value, social use value, marginal product, and productivity.

As the economy development is based on competitive struggle, competitiveness management law unites results of various laws and theories in the area under consideration. Possibility implementation of this integration function depends on the current measures of state economic regulation and political and economic situation in the state and world economy.

Stimulation function within the framework of competitiveness management law promotes improvement of consumer properties of the commodities, modernization of production facilities, curtailment on demand for production resources and operation of products, and creation of new generations of commodities and production facilities.

Distribution function according to competitiveness management law means that, on the one hand, producers in commodity markets are distributed into groups according to their product competitiveness indexes, and on the other hand, there is a stimulation of commodity producers to redistribute resources for creation of competitive advantages of their goods.

So, that's where we are. The meaning of the functional value of competitiveness management law is in the following:

- Competitiveness of the goods;
- Growth in demand;
- Creations of products with essentially new consumer properties;
- Opening of new markets;
- Reduction in risks of economic crises and conflicts.

Competitiveness management law plays the leading role in the contemporary economic world. It is clearly manifested in crisis and post-crisis situations when the most significant value is attached to the mechanisms designed to effectively integrate the country into the world hi-tech economy and to lower (whenever possible—to prevent) negative influence of the crisis on innovative processes.

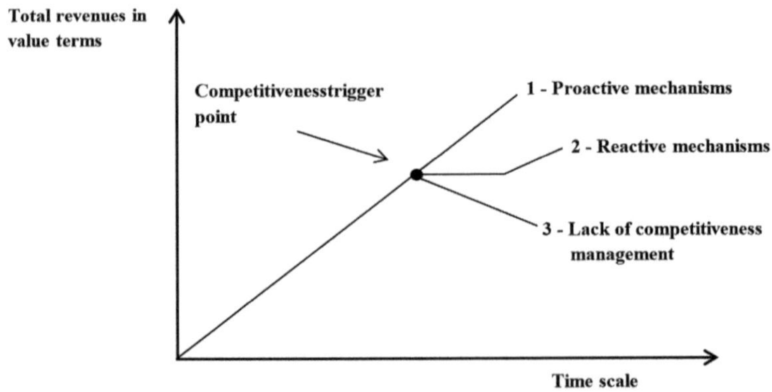

Fig. 2.4 Influence of competitiveness management processes on economic performance of a firm

The process of competitiveness management uses specific mechanisms to provide stable economic development and control one or another of negative phenomenon or to prevent it.

Economic stability arrangements include special mechanisms of preventive character and mechanisms to lower potentially negative role of growing instability of the world economic system, designated by L. S. Blyahman as proactive and compensation (response) mechanisms of accordingly.

Figure 2.4, with a view to illustrate the effect of competitiveness management processes on economic performance of a firm, shows a graph of revenue growth of a company which upon reaching a turning point has a possibility to develop in three directions:

1. With application of proactive mechanisms or, in other words, performing competitiveness management;
2. With application of compensation (or response) mechanisms;
3. Without performing competitiveness management.

The above graph shows that the most effective from the point of view of revenues and retention of financial stability is the first option providing application of proactive mechanisms of competitiveness management. Lack of competitiveness management, upon reaching a trigger point, can lead to the company bankruptcy in the long run.

Some of the above mechanisms of competitiveness management are already present in the state regulation practice in Russia and some are planned for introduction in the long run, but many mechanisms are new for domestic regulatory system. In this context, we shall consider in detail some of the most important and pressing mechanisms in the modern context, applicable for effective competitiveness management.

In order to provide strategic stability of national economy, both the state and the firms should comply with competitiveness management law. Economic stability in conditions of the global environment instability can be based on a wide spectrum of "growth points" of domestic market, hence, the basic mechanism aimed at retention of stability, buildup of competitive advantages in locomotive industries, and diversification of economy. In addition to the above, it is necessary to take into account long-term, strategic character of stability, that is, diversification should be based on either the industry sectors with good prospects of long-term development and capable to remain a growth area of national economy for a long time or the industry sectors creating preconditions for development of such production facilities in the future. At last, problem number one at present in the context of strategic stability is orientation to high rates of growth. The highest rates of growth are provided by the industry sectors generating the maximum added value; accordingly, support mechanisms should be focused on stimulation of development of such industries and economy spheres.

We are of the opinion that the most effective mechanisms of competitiveness management, including for the purposes of sustainable development of Russia, are proactive mechanisms, namely, the mechanisms of state regulation aimed at preventive, anticipatory influence on factors capable of making a negative impact on economic development. In the context of retention of strategic stability, the basic task of proactive mechanisms shall be development of economy sectors to enhance general stability of the economic system, as well as prevention of detrimental effect on economy from the part of various kinds of globalization manifestations.

The said problems can be solved through application of proactive mechanisms of two basic types—strategic and operational designation.

Mechanisms of strategic designation, first of all, are aimed at diversification and modernization of the Russian economy in order to reduce its dependence on base material sectors and, as a consequence, to increase stability of economic development.

Mechanisms of operational designation have mainly economic character, instead of organizational one.

At the present stage of development of global economy with its specificity caused by a high level of development of financial infrastructure, financial mechanisms are especially specified among such proactive mechanisms. Financial mechanisms can be considered as a priority, including because of the fact that the basic threat to stability in the conditions of globalization is constituted by financial markets with their unstable conjuncture and high volatility act. Specifically proactive mechanisms of operational designation should be focused on the prevention of these threats.

Besides, among mechanisms of proactive character, it is possible to specify hedging of adverse price adjustments (for example, by means of options), insurance and reinsurance of export deliveries, optimization of currency relations aimed at minimization of losses of the Russian exporters and borrowers from foreign-exchange fluctuations, and other financial engineering methods.

The practice of adoption of advanced financial technologies, aimed at reduction of risks, should also cover the activity of the state authorities—from the Ministry of Finance which is issuing bonds for the foreign markets (there is a risk of adverse foreign-exchange rates) to financial and investment structures, such as Investment fund (for which investment risk in foreign securities is characteristic) and industrial companies of national level.

Compensation mechanisms are focused on overcoming of globalization negative factors which can worsen the situation in national economy. Now, taking into account mainly raw-material orientation of economy and export of Russia, the basic threat to stability of development is constituted by unstable conditions of the world commodity markets and to a smaller extent—financial markets on which investment situation in the country essentially depends. In this context, compensation mechanisms should be built, first of all, in order to liquidate consequences of reduction of prices for production of the Russian export on which stability of the national economy depends.

It is possible to outline six applications of compensation mechanisms in competitiveness management:

1. Indemnification of the state budget losses;
2. Stabilization of home market conditions;
3. Enhancement of stability against the negative influence of globalization factors;
4. Import substitution;
5. Development of scientific and innovative industry sector;
6. Development of information and communication technologies.

The first area—indemnification of the state budget losses is presented by the Stabilization Fund of the Russian Federation; therefore the said area of compensation mechanisms can be considered as protected.

Stabilization Fund is a built in economy stabilizer; it provides additional stability to public finances and can be a source of financing investment programs to reduce budgetary expenses for the future periods. In 2008, the Ministry of Finance of Russia has divided Stabilization Fund into Reserve Fund and National Wealth Fund.

The reserve fund is formed at the expense of oil and gas incomes (tax on the extraction of commercial minerals; oil, gas, and mineral oil export duties). A certain part of oil and gas incomes in the form of oil and gas transfer is annually allocated for financing expenses of the federal budget.

The second area—stabilization of domestic market conditions during huge sales swings in foreign markets and formation of capacity reserves for the leading Russian companies closely connected with the global markets.

For a long period, the government of the Russian Federation has been pursuing a policy of strong ruble. On the one hand, it shows a relative stability of the Russian economy. On the other hand, it affects development of domestic industry in an extremely negative way. Strong ruble means cheap import and leads to toughening of the price competitiveness in domestic market. As a result, domestic manufacturers do not stand this competitiveness.

Besides, negative consequences for home market and, first of all, for commodity producers have low world prices threatening production profitability.

As can be seen from the above, one of the areas of use of compensation mechanisms is an evening-out of dependence of the Russian manufactures on the world markets, stabilization of supply and demand, and formation of stable internal prices and stable financial position of commodity producers.

The third area of employment of compensation mechanisms is improving stability against negative influence of globalization factors, which are most significant for the Russian economy and companies.

We are of the opinion that there should be an encouragement of creating stabilization funds by such intracorporate business structures (by analogy with Stabilization Fund at the macroeconomic level). Such stimulation can be carried out by both administrative methods—for the state national companies and economic methods—for private corporate sector by means of granting tax privileges. It is possible to use the mechanisms thereto similar to the ones already applied for retention of stability of the second-level banks—obligatory resource reservation in the Central bank of Russia.

A goal for formation of intracorporate stabilization funds is a stable functioning of enterprises even in conditions of an adverse price conjuncture in the world markets when production becomes unprofitable. Traditional management in such conditions is cost improvement, decline of production, etc. It may be achieved specifically at the expense of reduction of workplaces, optimization of production structure, liquidation of noncore business, and rolling back social programs.

Formation of intracorporate stabilization funds would make it possible to do without such social and economic restrictions at the expense of the said funds during adverse periods and to keep human recourses and industrial potential of the enterprise, as well as its social programs.

The fourth area of using compensation mechanisms is import substitution. Now, in the Russian Federation there are government programs in the field of creation and commissioning of innovations, mobilization of domestic and foreign investments and technologies, as well as adoption of corresponding laws in the field of custom barriers. In other words, the need of competitiveness management is acknowledged at the state level and in some industry sectors competitiveness management is implemented now. These are the state activities to increase competitiveness and investment appeal of the high-technology complex, development of home market and export support, development of domestic hi-tech complex as a basis for modernization of other industry sectors, perfection of this complex structure, and development of HR potential.

The modern state innovative policy consists in definition of purposes and mechanisms of stimulation of priority innovative programs and projects. This policy helps the Russian industrial output to move to a new qualitative level, capable of providing its competitiveness in the world markets and, as a consequence, its realization in various countries and world regions.

The fifth area of compensation mechanisms is development of scientifically innovative sector. In modern conditions, innovations are the major factor of economic development. They are realized both in the material form and by commissioning of more effective forms and ways of production and services management and labor management, etc. Innovations create competitive advantages to the individual countries and regions in the international market; they possess a key role in implementation of the basic imperative of the modern paradigm of sustainable development—harmonious combination of economic growth, social progress, and environment protection.

An innovative component, which is the basis for the GDP growth in the majority of the developed and new industrial countries, can be considered as an embodiment of newly established scientific knowledge in traditional economy sectors. There is a tendency to increase a share of resources of the society aimed at development of science, education, and information technologies which form a skeleton of economy of postindustrial stage of development of the modern society.

Distinctive feature of such economy is a transition from mass production based on stringent standards to the flexible systems capable of responding to the market conditions online. Such systems are large modern production facilities on the way of vertical decomposition and establishment of horizontal network communications between their divisions, which objectively promotes development of initiative and independence of small business teams and individual innovators on all production phases.

It is generally agreed that dynamism of innovative sphere (the upward tendency of fundamental science and applied studies, consecutive adoption of high technologies) creates the basis of stable growth of national economies. But the issue remains open why, in the presence of objective preconditions and obvious necessity to make a major technological leap, individual economic agents of the global economic cooperation (Russia among them) cannot always employ these factors in the proper way?

The sixth area of compensation mechanisms is connected with information contours of innovative development, i.e., with development of information and communication technologies.

There are no concurrent views on hierarchy of soft and hardware tools of information and communications technologies for the time being. Information and communications technologies are subdivided into three technological groups—base group, primary group, and secondary group.

The first group includes the products forming element base of all set of information facilities—integrated circuits of various complexity, magnetic and optical drives, etc. They can be compared with "foundation blocks" on which information and communication systems are erected. Basic technologies are the very sphere where fundamental science is aligned with applied science and where there is an approbation of new scientific effects and phenomena (Research and Advanced Development).

The second group (primary information and communications technologies) is made by facilities where information in one form or another is both initial and final product, namely, computers, telecommunication equipment, and communication means.

The third group, information and communications technologies, covers the entire information-computer field. As can be seen from the above, the prospects of the majority of nonmilitary nature products in the category of information and communications technologies are specified by amounts of industrial expenses and their commodity value, i.e.—by market mechanisms.

This classification underlines the fundamental role of the basic information and communications technologies in development of hi-tech industries and makes it possible to evaluate more specifically the degree of threats and risks connected with the global information and formation of competitive advantages.

Now the role of information and communication technologies in competitiveness management at various levels (national, industry-specific, and organizational) is rather great. During the last decade, there was formed a stable tendency of building systems with artificial intellect which provide transition of many functions concerning data collection, processing, and control over various processes from human being to the automated information and analytical systems. The basic efforts of the leading world powers have been aimed at formation of single information space and are aimed at creation of technical equipment, automated systems, and networks intended for transmission and processing of information at the most advanced level.

Development of information and communications technologies is in line with the world tendencies of globalization and internationalization, in particular shown in activation of innovative and technological convergence consisting in mutual influence and interpenetration of technologies. Borders between specific technologies are being erased, and end results appear to be within the framework of interdisciplinary research studies and cross-sectoral issues.

The processes of innovative and technological convergence connected with development of new scientific and technological areas promote achievement of positive synergetic effect which leads to buildup of competitive advantages to provide a state with scientific and economic preferences to ensure growth of international competitiveness on the basis of creation and application of intellectual management systems.

This movement in line with the world competitive leadership should pass three stages:

I stage Development and application of uniform organizational and information mechanisms at all the hierarchical levels of the companies' management systems aimed at optimization of preparation and managerial decision-making.

The specified mechanisms constitute the basis to form an integrated managerial space, and in aggregate they present a multilevel information management system with a possibility to increase the volumes of automation and enhance its quantitative and qualitative characteristics of collection, processing, storage, and distribution of information used for managerial decision-making.

At the present stage, there is an implementation of the following organizational and managerial transformations:

- Formation of a new managerial paradigm;
- Transition to the managerial paradigm based on convergent spaces;

- Formation of transboundary distributed innovative clusters;
- Formation of convergent management infrastructure.

II stage Development of managerial mechanisms to use hardware and software architecture of programming innovative behavior of the companies should reach the world level by means of unification split-level modules of network-centric management based on intellectual information technologies.

The specified module represents a basis of integrated transboundary target-oriented electronic content. At the said stage, it would be possible to perform control over the chains of managerial transactions both with synchronous work of the organizational structures and upon incurrence of mismatch between them in the international, industrial, territorial, and corporate aspects of management.

At this stage, there is an implementation of the following organizational and managerial transformations:

- Formation of transboundary electronic content;
- Modernization of enterprises on innovative basis;
- Concentration of global impact disruptive innovations;
- Joining technological platforms of the developed countries.

III stage Formation of distributed transboundary electronic managerial environments and using this basis for expansion of intercorporate financial and economic coordination and scientific and technical cooperation of the companies to provide their international competitiveness and harmonious integration into world economy.

At the final stage, there are the following global changes based on adoption of convergent infrastructure:

- Formation of investment asymmetry;
- Transition to export of hi-tech production and services;
- Concentration of excess profit from innovations in the country;
- Formation of new intercorporate agglomeration;
- Achieving world competitive excellence.

It is worth noting that achieving world competitive excellence is based on various levels of competitiveness management on the basis of development of information and communications technologies being an important part of the management system of firms, industry sectors, and a state. In modern conditions, it is exactly the effective competitiveness management and development of integration by means of information and communications technologies that can overcome inertia of old organizational forms gaining the upper hand in the business sector of the developing countries, as well as to provide competitiveness growth in domestic and world markets.

2.4 Substantiation of Competitiveness Management Law on the Basis of Mathematical Modeling

According to empirical law formulated in Sect. 2.3 concerning competitiveness management, successful development and holding of financial and economic indicators of enterprises require stable competitiveness management.

Ignoring of the market signals, that is, neglect of competitiveness management, leads to deterioration in demand for commodities and, as a consequence, to deterioration of financial and economic indicators of an enterprise.

Competitiveness management law has a natural mathematical interpretation in terms of theory of dynamic systems management.

When building a mathematical model of competitiveness management, we shall use the methods of evolutionary functional and differential equations in Banach spaces and stipulate correctness of the system of equations using substantive provisions of the empirical concerning competitiveness management that we put in.

Let's put the following designations of key parameters the dynamics of which will be described by our model:

Q(t)—function describing result of competitiveness management of a firm. We shall assume that this function describes all actions of enterprises competitiveness management in an integral way. We shall consider this function as positive; as this takes place larger values of this function correspond to BETTER competitiveness management. Zero values of this function mean full ignoring of competitiveness management;

D(t)—function describing level of demand for the goods, manufactured by the firm under review. This function is supposed to be positive too.

F(t)—function describing an integrated indicator of financial and economic health of the enterprise. It is an alternating function.

Let's assume that function Q(t) describing competitiveness management is defined.

Demand function D(T) and function F(t) possessing an economic sense of financial and economic indicator should be calculated on the basis of functional differential equations to describe demand behavior and financial and economic indicators according to the principal law of competitiveness management.

Taking into account defined designations, we shall present mathematical model of competitiveness management in the form of the following system of two functional differential equations:

$$D'(t) = a_1 \left(\int_{t-T_1}^{t} Q(s)ds - H_1 \right)_+^{\alpha} - a_2 D(t) + a_3 \int_{t-T_2}^{t} D'(s)ds$$
$$- a_4 (D(t) - H_2)_+^{\gamma} \tag{2.8}$$

$$F'(t) = a_5 D(t) + a_6 \int_{t-T_2}^{t} D'(s)ds \tag{2.9}$$

$$a_1, a_2, \ldots, a_6 > 0, \quad T_1 > 0, T_2 > 0, H_1 > 0, H_2 > 0$$
$$D(0) = D_0, \quad F(0) = F_0$$

Cutoff function is used here:

$$(x)_+ = \begin{cases} x, & x \geq 0 \\ 0, & x < 0 \end{cases}$$

Let's consider consistently members in equations (2.8) and (2.9) and we shall give them economic treatment.

According to the competitiveness management law, activities aimed at improving competitiveness lead to an increase in demand for the goods. Therefore, the first summand in Eq. (2.8):

$$I_1 = a_1 \left(\int_{t-T_1}^{t} Q(s)ds - H_1 \right)_+^{\alpha}, \quad 0 < \alpha < 1$$

leads to increase in value of the demand function with nonzero competitiveness management. We shall consider in detail this summand. Competitiveness management integral—functions Q(t) on the interval $[t - T_1, t]$—reflects the fact that demand function influenced by competitiveness management not only at the specified moment but during the previous moments too. On the other hand, influence of management on demand function takes place with a delay in time; therefore the integral in this summand is under cutoff sign.

The second addend in Eq. (2.8):

$$I_2 = -a_2 D(t)$$

is a dissipative summand and expresses the fact that without competitiveness management the demand for the goods will be reducing. The mathematical role of this summand consists in the fact that demand function values exponentially disappear with time.

The third addend in the first equation (2.8):

$$I_3 = a_3 \int_{t-T_2}^{t} D'(s)ds$$

reflects the market response to changes of demand function. In other words, total (integrated) change of demand function during the previous points of time is reflected in change of demand function in real time. This addend can be treated as inertia of demand function.

The fourth addend in the first equation (2.8):

$$I_4 = -a_4(D(t) - H_2)_+^{\gamma}, \quad \gamma > 1$$

is a nonlinear restriction of growth of demand function in the said mathematical model. Mathematical function of this addend consists in the fact that after achievement of a certain threshold H_2, demand function is sharply limited in growth. This limitation is natural in the economic model under review.

Let's pass to economic interpretation of the summands in the equation (2.9).

The first summand in Eq. (2.9):

$$I_5 = a_5 D(t)$$

reflects natural connection between growth in demand for the goods and financial and economic status of the enterprise. The second addend in the equation (2.9):

$$I_6 = a_6 \int_{t-T_2}^{t} D'(s)ds$$

expresses influence of change of demand function during the previous points of time on financial and economic health of the enterprise in real time. This summand plays a role of inertial component for the function describing financial and economic status of the enterprise.

As the above mathematical model of competitiveness management in the form of two functional differential equations has a certain mathematical specificity, the proof of soundness of this model that is the proof of solution of this system of equations is specified below.

Proof of the Soundness Theorem for Competitiveness Management Model

We shall use a method of approximation with the help of differential inclusions for solution of the system of equations (2.8 and 2.9). We shall describe this method for an abstract evolutionary functional differential equation.

Let's put in functional spaces in which it is possible to consider evolutionary inclusions. We shall consider a terminal time interval $[0, T]$ and a pair of Banach spaces E_0 and E_1, and we assume here that the space E_1 is dense and is continuously enclosed in space E_0.

Now we shall consider one-parametrical families of functional spaces:

$$\begin{array}{ll} H^T = L_\infty(0,T;E_0), & T\in(0,T], \\ V^T = L_\infty(0,T;E_1), & T\in(0,T] \end{array}$$

and

$$W^T = W^1_\infty(0,T;E_1), \quad T\in(0,T].$$

In connection with these spaces, we shall put in operators of restriction of the function from space H^T to piece $[0,T]$

$$P_T : H^T \to H^T.$$

We also put in the operator of extension of function from space H^T to piece $[0,T]$

$$I_T : V^T \to V^T,$$

defined according to the following formula:

$$w(t) = (I_T v)(t) = \begin{cases} v(t), & t\in[0,T] \\ v(T), & t\in[0,T]. \end{cases}$$

Through I_0, we shall designate the operator which according to element from E_1 compares constant function from space V^T, taking on the specified value.

Let's put in a designation for the closed sphere in space H^T for any $v_0\in H^T$:

$$B^T_\delta(v_0) = \{v\in H^T \|v - v_0\|_{H^T} \le \delta\},$$

for $\delta > 0$

Let's consider continuous operator

$$A : V^T \to H^T.$$

Let's put in one more operator

$$A_T = P_T A I_T : V^T \to H^T.$$

Let's study the evolutionary equation with parameter $T\in(0,T]$:

$$u'(t) = A_T u(t), \quad t\in[0,T]$$

With this equation, we shall consider the entry condition:

$$u(0) = \varphi \in E_1.$$

Definition of Equation Solution

Solution to the problem with fixed $T \in (0, T]$ is function u from the space V^T, which is in accord with this equation.

Under the general conditions for operator A, of course, it is impossible to hope for solution of the problem.

Let's approach the equation by differential inclusion.

For predetermined number $\delta > 0$, we shall consider inclusion

$$u'(t) \in B_\delta^T(A_T u(t)), \quad t \in [0, T].$$

We shall consider this inclusion together with initial condition

$$u(0) = \varphi \in E_0.$$

Definition of Solution of Differential Inclusion

For defined $T \in (0, T]$ and $\delta > 0$ function $u \in V^T$ is called solution of evolutionary inclusion, if u is in accord with this inclusion.

Let's prove the theorem of local resolvability of evolutionary problem.

Soundness theorem

Let us assume that the initial condition φ is in accord with the following conditions:

$$\varphi \in E_1$$

and

$$A_T I_0 \varphi \in V^T.$$

Then for every $\delta > 0$, there is $T > 0$ when at these δ and T there is a solution of differential inclusion.

Corroboration

We take number $\tau \in (0, T]$ and construct function of space V^τ under the following formula:

$$u^\tau(t) = P_\tau I_0 \varphi + t A_\tau I_0 \varphi.$$

Owing to conditions on φ, we have $u^\tau \in V^\tau$. Therefore we can construct the following function:

$$F^\tau(t) = \left(\frac{d}{dt} - A_\tau\right) u^\tau(t).$$

Function $F^\tau(t)$ belongs to space H^τ. Moreover, it has the following appearance:

$$F^{\tau}(t) = P_{\tau}AI_0\varphi - P_{\tau}AI_{\tau}[P_{\tau}I_0\varphi + P_{\tau}tAI_0\varphi].$$

Let's show that for any set positive number δ exists such τ, when the norm of function F^{τ} in space H^{τ} is less than δ.

Let's put in a designation

$$v^{\tau} = P_{\tau}I_0\varphi + P_{\tau}tAI_0\varphi.$$

Function $I_{\tau}v^{\tau}(t)$ looks like

$$I_{\tau}v^{\tau}(t) = \begin{cases} \varphi + t(A\varphi)(t), t \in [0, \tau] \\ \varphi + \tau(A\varphi)(t), i \in [0, \tau]. \end{cases}$$

Let's show that $I_{\tau}v^{\tau}$ has limit $I_0\varphi^{\tau}$ in space V^T at $\tau \to 0$

Actually we have

$$\|I_{\tau}v^{\tau} - I_0\varphi\|_{V^T} \leq \sup_{t \in [0,\tau]} \|t(A\varphi)(t)\|_{E_1} + \sup_{t \in [\tau,T]} \|\tau(A\varphi)(\tau)\|_{E_1} \leq$$
$$\tau\left(\sup_{t \in [0,\tau]} \|(A\varphi)(t)\|_{E_1} + \|(A\varphi)(\tau)\|_{E_1}\right) \leq 2\tau\|AI_0\varphi\|_{V^T}.$$

It follows

$$\|I_{\tau}v^{\tau} - I_0\varphi\|_{V^T} \to 0, \quad \tau \to 0.$$

Now we can evaluate norm $\|F^{\tau}\|_{H^T}$ as follows:

$$\|F^{\tau}\|_{H^T} = \|P_{\tau}AI_0\varphi - P_{\tau}AI_{\tau}[P_{\tau}I_0\varphi + P_{\tau}tAI_0\varphi]\|_{H^{\tau}} \leq$$
$$\|AI_0\varphi - AI_{\tau}[P_{\tau}I_0\varphi + P_{\tau}tAI_0\varphi]\|_{H^T} = \|AI_0\varphi - AI_{\tau}v^{\tau}\|_{H^T}.$$

There is a value

$$\alpha(\tau) \in V^T, \quad \alpha(\tau) \to 0, \quad \tau \to 0,$$

When the following takes place

$$\|AI_0\varphi - AI_{\tau}v^{\tau}\|_{H^T} = \|AI_0\varphi - A(I_0\varphi + \alpha(\tau))\|_{H^T}.$$

Whence owing to continuity of operator $A : V^T \to H^T$ it follows that there is value

$$\beta(\tau) \in H^T, \quad \beta(\tau) \to 0, \quad \tau \to 0,$$

And we have

$$\|AI_0\varphi - A(I_0\varphi + \alpha(\tau))\|_{H^T} = \|AI_0\varphi - AI_0\varphi + \beta(\tau)\|_{H^T} = \|\beta(\tau)\|_{H^T}.$$

As can be seen from the above, we established that

$$\|F^\tau\|_{H^\tau} \to 0, \quad \tau \to 0.$$

Now with $\tau^* > 0$ $\left\|F^{\tau^*}\right\|_{H^{\tau^*}} \leq \delta$ where $\delta > 0$—defined value. Then function

$$u^{\tau^*}(t) = P_{\tau^*}I_0\varphi + tA_{\tau^*}I_0\varphi$$

shall be solution of the differential inclusion at $T = \tau^*$

Now, the theorem is completely proved.

This proved theorem establishes soundness of our mathematical model, which in turn confirms provisions of competitiveness management law.

In particular, we can formulate the following conclusions.

1. Competitiveness management should be rather effective to support financial and economic indicators of the enterprises to provide progressive development.
2. Insufficient competitiveness management will inevitably lead to sharp decrease in financial and economic indicators of the enterprise and its bankruptcy.
3. Retention of financial and economic indicators of the enterprise will be more effective by performing continuous competitiveness management than by emergency (short-term) management, which may be required during partial or full loss of commodity markets, reduction in price competitiveness of the goods, and other factors.
4. In case of insufficient competitiveness management, there is a crisis point when financial and economic indicators of the enterprise take the plunge or emergency measures aimed at competitiveness management to restore financial and economic indicators are required.

2.5 Approaches to Competitiveness Management Under Various Types of Competitiveness

The first most complete theoretical abstract theorems concerning competitiveness and its driving forces were conceived in the middle of the eighteenth century. The credit is due to the representative of classical political economy A. Smith who believed that the principal method of competitive struggle is price adjustment. As this takes place, he noted that the market economy which is not governed by collective will and disobeys a single concept, nevertheless, conforms to the strict market rules of conduct. According to these rules, the free competitiveness serves as a force to provide interaction supply and demand and to counterbalance the market prices.

Ideas of the market price regulation owing to competitiveness were developed by D. Rikardo. Provisions concerning perfect competition, the theoretical model of which he developed, helped to understand how the "natural" prices in the long-term balance harmonize with principles of decentralized management and how the said principles promote economy development.

Neoclassical version of competitiveness interpretation, as was treated by one of its fathers—English economist A. Marshall, connects it with the struggle for rare economic benefit. The logic of this approach consists in the fact that the majority of benefits are rare in the sense that their number is less than potential public needs. Therefore, owners of the said benefits have a possibility to distribute wealth, being guided by self-interest. They present conditions or criteria (required level of prices, quality, etc.) and depending on execution of these conditions they decide who deserves the goods and who does not deserve.

From the end of the nineteenth century, the economic theory witnessed another concept of competitiveness gaining momentum, which came out on top later. Among its authors were F. Edgeworth, A. Kurno, J. Robinson, and E. Chamberlin. According to this concept, the market is called competitive when the number of firms selling a homogeneous product is so great and the share of a particular firm in the market is so small in such a way that no firm can independently affect the price of the product by means of changing the sales volume.

The classics, speaking about competitiveness, meant only perfect competition in which frameworks' interdependence of the sellers is so small that it may be neglected. In the competitive market, all the firms are independent from each other in the sense that activities of one firm do not render any market effect on behavior of other firms. Under such competitive behavior—competition—no firm can become a leader in the market, that is, monopoly shall be impossible.

Eventually as economic relations may be amended from time to time, the concept of competitiveness of neoclassical understanding has become obsolete. Discontent of the current model of perfect competition has been caused by excess attention rendered to its one type only (price competitiveness) and impossibility to specify with its help the main point of competitive activity. Friedrich August von Hayek more definitely expressed that one should take into account the fact that the state system already exists… and the process of competitiveness takes place in already existing system. If the model of perfect competition would ever exist in the real state, there would be no restrictions in all fields of activity. But actually it is impossible, as restrictions from the part of the state are vital.

Critics of the perfect competition model specified the elements of monopoly which are penetrating economy and are not embodied in the existing concept of competitiveness. Francis Ysidro Edgeworth (mathematical description), Abba Lerner (monopoly power and its evaluation), Johan Gustaf Knut Wicksell (competition and price discrimination), Joseph Alois Schumpeter, and above-named F. Hayek made significant contribution to theoretical models of oligopoly and monopoly later.

The last years faced criticism of both the model of perfect competition where all characters tend to the so-called Pareto-optimality (when a gain of one of economic agent does not worsen an economic situation of all other economic agents) and the entire orthodox (neoclassical) theory with an evolutionary economic theory coming up to take its place.

Evolutionists claim that the market is a system with the main driving power presented by the processes of the balance disturbance, that is, the processes opposite to the principle of Pareto-optimality. The basic position in the evolutionary theory consists in the fact that the progress is moved by nonequilibrium processes. Evolutionists present economy as a system in which development is focused on growth of variety and complexity of technologies, goods and services, and ways of organization of production and management. From the point of view of the evolutionary theory, transition to essentially new technologies (especially during its initial stages) depends not on the prices and effective demand but on the needs of economic agents interested in the new technologies. Researchers have shown that the leaders are those companies which create technologies in compliance with the future needs of their clients. At the same time, scientists believe economy has peculiar features concerning pari passu both the drive to balance and dislocation of balance. To this we can add that the specified property is characteristic for any live systems and is provided with homeostasis mechanisms. We observe that not only economic but also technical systems increasingly make use of the specified mechanisms and self-organizing mechanisms. Hence, synthesis of the classical and evolutionary theory is inevitable, but at a new level with the arising evolutionary theory being developed and neoclassical theory being simultaneously reconsidered within its frameworks.

It is important to keep in mind that groundbreaking technologies should be aimed at the future and meet both social and economic perspective requirements and ecclesiastic requirements. This basic provision is directly related to competitiveness management of a product, a firm, an industry, and a country as it will be said below.

By the middle of the twentieth century, there have been formed general representations about the subject matter of competitiveness and its basic driving forces taking the form of postulation of four classical models of market competitiveness: perfect competition, monopolistic competition, oligopoly, and pure monopoly. Positions of this group of scientists in contemporary western economic science are so strong that the term "competitiveness" ("competition") is more often used in the said understanding.

The focus of attention is not a competition of economic agents in price making and not determination of the fact who and why was the winner, but determination of a basic possibility (or impossibility) to influence an independent economic agent on the general price level in the market. If such influence is impossible, it is a question of the market of perfect competition, otherwise—one of the versions of imperfect competition.

At present the specified models (twentieth century) are supplemented with the model of evolutionary theory demanding a new type of competitiveness, connected with provision of new needs and beyond the control of the prices and effective demand.

The specified models explain in the context competitiveness management below.

Perfect competition is such a type of market structure which assumes performance of following conditions:

- Production output of a corporation is insignificant and does not influence the market prices;
- The goods sold by every manufacturer are homogeneous;
- Buyers are well informed about the prices;
- Sellers do not enter into a collision concerning the prices and take their own line;
- Producers can enter the industry and leave it free.

Perfect competition is a condition to create a market mechanism for formation of the prices and self-adjustment of the economic system through achievement of equilibrium state when egoistical intentions of specific individuals work to the benefit of the society. Perfect competition has the following basic positive features:

- Promotes more effective use of resources;
- Encourages manufacturers to respond to changes of manufacture or the buyers needs in a flexible way;
- Creates favorable conditions for commissioning of latest achievements of science and technology;
- Provides freedom in choosing and freedom of action;

Weak points of free competitiveness may include:

- Inability of conservation of nonreproducible resources;
- Does not ensure development and production of the shared use goods and services;
- Does not create conditions for development of general education, municipal economy;
- Does not contain mechanisms to prevent stratification of society and social injustice.

Theoretically the market of perfect competition consists of a number of independent small firms which due to their small sizes cannot influence the market price. They make homogenous products and the buyers possess the absolute information on the goods quality, prices, and gain from trade. Perfect competition is "pure," that is, it does not depend on interventions of the state and monopolies. Absolutely competitive markets in modern economics are very rare; it would be rather an ideal than a reality. Actually, many markets in modern economics are possessed by several big firms, sometimes by two or three only.

From the perspective of competitiveness management and creation of competitive advantages in the market, hypothetically it is possible to assume that we consider a market with perfect competition. On the one hand, in case of perfect competition there cannot be any management as such in the market environment, as it is understood that the market regulates itself, but on the other hand, any firm in the market and possessing stable position there a priori is engaged in competitiveness management and buildup of competitive advantages.

As can be seen from the above, it is possible to assume that even in case of "ideal" market with perfect competition, the firm should operate its competitiveness.

Research studies of many scientists testify to the fact that there is no perfect competition in its pure form in the modern world.

As it was specified above, imperfect competition is in contrast to perfect competition.

Imperfect competition has the following specific types of market situations:

- Oligopoly—monopoly when several big firms supervise manufacture and sale of goods in a particular territory;
- Pure monopoly is a full contrast to pure competitiveness when there is only one seller of the goods possessing full control over its quantity; access to the market is closed for would-be competitors;
- Monopsony is a type of the market structure when there is only one buyer of certain goods.

Table 2.3 presents basic types of imperfect competition.

Let's consider a question: whether it is possible with the help specific tools to control competitiveness of an object in conditions of the market with perfect and imperfect competition.

The work of economist E. Raihlin "The Foundations of Economic Theory. The Microeconomic Theory of the Resource Input Markets" presents the situations, when:

- Production market is a market of perfect competition, and resource input market is a market of imperfect competition.
- Production market is a market of imperfect competition and resource input market is a market of imperfect competition too.

Concerning a question how the equilibrium is achieved and how the incomes are defined in the resource input market of imperfect competition, E. Raihlin considers conditions of discriminating and nondiscriminating monopsony.

Let's consider a situation when production market is a market of perfect competition, and the resource input market is a market of imperfect competition.

Table 2.3 Types of an imperfect competition

	Sellers		
Buyers	Many	Many	Many
Many	Bilateral polypoly	Oligopoly	Monopoly
Several	Oligopsony	Bilateral oligopoly	Monopoly limited by oligopsony
One	Monopsony	Monopsony limited by oligopoly	Bilateral monopoly

Function of demand for production of the enterprise in conditions of this theoretical organizational market structure as per E. Raihlin in general shall be written as follows:

$$MRP_{VF} = MP_{VF} \cdot P_Q,$$

where

MRP—marginal revenues under the production factor
VF—introduced variable which is understood as a work, or a capital, or technology
Q—number of production units
MP—marginal output
P—production cost

Let us assume that $MP_{VF} = \frac{1}{\sqrt{VF}}$;
then $MRP_{VF} = \frac{P_Q}{\sqrt{VF}}$.

Equilibrium values in the resource input market of imperfect competition ($\boldsymbol{MRC_{VF} = MRP_{VF}}$) are different depending on whether monopsony discriminates against price or not (here *MRC*—marginal expenses for a variable factor).

In case when *price discrimination is absent*, market equilibrium is defined as

$$P_{VF} = MP_{VF} \cdot P_Q,$$

where

$$MRC_{VF} = P_{VF}, MRP_{VF} = MP_{VF} \cdot MR = MP_{VF} \cdot P_Q,$$

So

$$MRC_{VF} = MRP_{VF}.$$

where ***MR***—marginal revenues

Figure 2.5 graphically illustrates what is happening in the market when additional resource is input.

Figure 2.5 shows lines $\boldsymbol{MRP_{VF}}$ and $\boldsymbol{MRC_{VF}}$ for discrimination and not discrimination of monopsony.

The cross point of lines $\boldsymbol{MRP_{VF}}$ and $\boldsymbol{MRC_{VF}}$ is an equilibrium point (or a break-even point). It follows from analysis of Fig. 2.5 that it is possible to determine the incomes in case of discriminating and nondiscriminating monopsony. As can be seen from the above, we can make a conclusion on appropriateness of enhancing competitiveness by introduction of additional units of economic resource.

The value of "economic" types of revenues in the resource input market with nondiscriminating monopsony is equal to the area of rectangle ***QHAD*** plus the area of the figure under curve ***MRP*** and above straight line ***HA***. The value of "economic" types of revenues in the resource input market with nondiscriminating

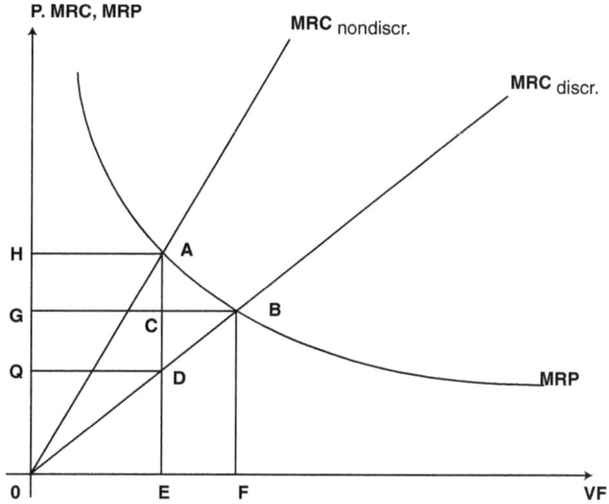

Fig. 2.5 Equilibrium for discriminating and nondiscriminating monopsony

monopsony is equal to the area of rectangle ***GHAC*** plus the area of figure ***ABC*** plus the area of the figure under line ***MRP*** and above straight line ***HA***.

Discriminating monopsony employs a greater number of resource input than nondiscriminating monopsony. Such price discrimination is beneficial to those who offer services of their own production factors in the markets of economic resources. Henceforth, discriminating monopsony is compelled to make more serious general expenses (***TC***) as it employs a greater number of resource input. Besides, "noneconomic" revenues per one unit of resource input $\left(\frac{TC}{VF}\right)$ appear to be lower in conditions of employment of discriminating monopsony as compared to nondiscriminating monopsony. As far as "economic" revenues are concerned, comparison shows that they are also bigger in case of nondiscriminating monopsony as compared to discriminating monopsony.

We believe that competitiveness management in perfect competition should be performed by both management of additional resources input and by management of the process of choosing priority points of the said resources application. The process of management will be effective when the firm sells more goods with higher qualitative characteristics. The goods price will be defined by minimization of resources input and their effective use.

Now we shall consider a situation when both commodity market and the resource input market are the markets of imperfect competition.

Transition of commodity market from the market of perfect competition to the market of imperfect competition leads to necessity of using smaller resources in the resource input market. Being aware of the marginal product function in monetary form, equilibrium values can be defined depending on whether monopsony is discriminating or nondiscriminating.

Demand function in this case looks like:

$$MRC_{VF} = MP_{VF} \cdot MR, \text{ where } MR \neq P_Q.$$

The major condition of equilibrium remains invariable:

$$MRC_{VF} = MRP_{VF}.$$

The analysis shows that transformation of commodity market from the perfect market to the market of imperfect competition actually negatively influences the number (VF) and the price (P_{VF}) of employed resource. The volume of services of resource input required by monopsony is reduced. As a result, there is also a reduction in payment for the services rendered by the economic resource. These factors ($VF\downarrow$ and $P_{VF}\downarrow$) affect production expenses too, that is, the amount of revenues of the owners of the said economic resource both in general and per unit of services of the input resource, accordingly.

In conditions of imperfect competition, there is a struggle for increase in income. Hence, it is necessary to reduce costs which should lead to reduction in the cost price of production. Here, there is a problem of cost improvement with preservation of qualitative characteristics of production which would provide superiority or at least equality with competitors.

We shall carry out analysis of the market outlook properties (precondition concerning quantifiability, additivity, and homogeneity); we shall formulate problems concerning search of such volumes of production consumption which lead to the minimum expenses on the part of consumer, as well as to quantitative evaluation of competitiveness of the manufacturer.

For the henceforth analysis, we shall make the following assumptions:

Let us assume that at the point of time $t \in T$ there is $n(t)$ of the enterprises, and each of these enterprises produces only one type of products under brand G_i in number $Q_i(L_i(t), K_i(t), A_i(t))$ $(i = 1, \ldots, n(t))$ and sells the products in the consumers market for the price $p_i(t)$

Let us assume that every one among these consumers buys at the point of time $t \in T$ a set of production available in the market $G_i(i = 1, \ldots, n(t))$

We assume that consumer makes a choice concerning both the amount of the products $Q_i(t)$ $(i = 1, \ldots, n(t))$ and their properties—technical characteristics.

Let us assume that $Z_i(t)$ $(i = 1, \ldots, m(t))$ is a set of technical characteristics (consumer properties) of production G_i which can change from time to time; then there will be a possibility to investigate dynamics of both the output volumes and production consumption G_i $(i = 1, \ldots, n(t))$ and dynamics of production property change

In order to analyze dynamics of the products property we should quantify the said properties, i.e., to provide a possibility to measure quality in quantitative values.

Let us use the following preconditions to be met by production properties: G_i $(i = 1, \ldots, n(t))$:

- Quantifiability which means that production properties can be identified and described both qualitatively and quantitatively, i.e., it is possible to write down that one production unit G_j $(j = 1, \ldots, n(t))$ contains $\alpha_{ij}(t) \geq 0$ units of property $Z_i(t)$ $(i = 1, \ldots, m(t))$;
- Homogeneity which means that if one unit of production G_i $(i = 1, \ldots, n(t))$ contains $\alpha_{ij}(t)$ of property units $Z_i(t)$ $(i = 1, \ldots, m(t))$, then $Q_j(t)$ of this production units contains $\alpha_{ij}(t)Q_j(t)$ property units $Z_i(t)$;
- Additivity which means that if $Q_j(t)$ units of production G_i $(i = 1, \ldots, n(t))$ contain $\alpha_{ij}(t)Q_j(t)$ property units $Z_i(t)$ $(i = 1, \ldots, m(t))$, and $Q_k(t)$ units of production $G_k (k = 1, \ldots, n(t))$ contain $\alpha_{ik}(t)Q_k(t)$ units of the same property $Z_i(t)$, then $Q_j(t)$ units of production G_j and $Q_k(t)$ units of production G_k contain $\alpha_{ij}(t)Q_j(t) + \alpha_{ik}(t)Q_k(t)$ property units $Z_i(t)$ $(i = 1, \ldots, m(t))$.

On the basis of the said preconditions, we receive the following system of equations:

$$\begin{cases} \alpha_{11}(t)Q_1(t) + \alpha_{12}(t)Q_2(t) + \ldots + \alpha_{1n}(t)Q_n(t) = a_1(t) \\ \ldots\ldots\ldots\ldots\ldots\ldots\ldots\ldots\ldots\ldots\ldots\ldots \\ \alpha_{m1}(t)Q_1(t) + \alpha_{m2}(t)Q_2(t) + \ldots + \alpha_{mn}(t)Q_n(t) = a_m(t), \end{cases} \tag{2.10}$$

where $a_i(t) \geq 0 (i = 1, \ldots, m(t))$—quantity of property $Z_i(t)$ in consumption bundle $Q_i(t)$ $(i = 1, \ldots, n(t))$ at the point of time t.

In the vector form, the system of equations (2.10) will look like:

$$A(t)\vec{Q}(t) = \vec{a}(t),$$

where $A(t)$ matrix:

$$A(t) = \begin{Bmatrix} \alpha_{11}(t) & \ldots & \alpha_{1n}(t) \\ \ldots & \ldots & \ldots \\ \alpha_{m1}(t) & \ldots & \alpha_{mn}(t) \end{Bmatrix},$$

$\vec{Q}^T(t) = (Q_1(t), Q_2(t), \ldots, Q_n(t))$ and $\vec{a}^T(t) = (a_1(t), a_2(t), \ldots, a_m(t))$ — vectors.

As can be seen from the above, there is a possibility to formulate a problem of looking for such volumes of consumption $Q_i(t)$ of production which would lead to the minimum expenses on the part of consumer for consumption bundle $G_i (i = 1, \ldots, n(t))$:

$$M(t) = p_1(t)Q_1(t) + p_2(t)Q_2(t) + \ldots + p_n(t)Q_n(t) \to (\min)$$

with

$$\begin{cases} \alpha_{11}(t)Q_1(t) + \alpha_{12}(t)Q_2(t) + \ldots + \alpha_{1n}(t)Q_n(t) \geq a_1(t) \\ \ldots\ldots\ldots\ldots\ldots\ldots\ldots\ldots\ldots\ldots\ldots\ldots\ldots\ldots \\ \alpha_{m1}(t)Q_m(t) + \alpha_{m2}(t)Q_m(t) + \ldots + \alpha_{mn}(t)Q_n(t) \geq a_m(t), \end{cases}$$

where $p_i(t)\,(i = 1, \ldots, n(t))$ is the price at the point of time t for one unit of production G_i

Let us use n-dimensional space of products (consumption bundles)

$$Q_n^+\{(Q_1(t), Q_2(t), \ldots, Q_n(t)) | Q_1(t) \geq 0, Q_2(t) \geq 0, \ldots, Q_n(t) \geq 0\}$$

and m-dimensional space of the said products properties

$$A_m^+\{(a_1(t), a_2(t), \ldots, a_m(t)) | a_1(t) \geq 0, a_2(t) \geq 0, \ldots, a_m(t) \geq 0\}.$$

Matrix $A(t)$ can be considered as a linear operator transforming vectors $\vec{Q}(t) \in Q_n^+$ in vectors $\vec{a}(t) \in A_m^+$.

Let's assume that the consumer in the commodity market solves a problem of rational behavior like:

$$u(Q_1(t), Q_2(t), \ldots, Q_n(t)) \rightarrow (max)$$

under constraints

$$\begin{aligned} &p_1(t)Q_1(t) + p_2(t)Q_2(t) + \ldots + p_n(t)Q_n(t) \leq M(t) \\ &Q_i(t) \geq 0 \quad (i = 1, \ldots, n(t)). \end{aligned}$$

together with the task of choosing an optimum combination of properties: $(a_1(t), a_2(t), \ldots, a_m(t))$:

$$\begin{cases} \alpha_{11}(t)Q_1(t) + \alpha_{12}(t)Q_2(t) + \ldots + \alpha_{1n}(t)Q_n(t) \geq a_1(t) \\ \ldots\ldots\ldots\ldots\ldots\ldots\ldots\ldots\ldots\ldots\ldots\ldots\ldots\ldots \\ \alpha_{m1}(t)Q_m(t) + \alpha_{m2}(t)Q_m(t) + \ldots + \alpha_{mn}(t)Q_n(t) \geq a_m(t). \end{cases}$$

When we solve this problem, we shall receive evaluation of new production market outlook and come to a quantitative evaluation of competitiveness of the enterprise which entered the market with this production.

As can be seen from the above, we can make a conclusion that competitiveness management can and should be performed regardless of the market competitiveness model (perfect competition, monopolistic competitiveness, oligopoly, pure monopoly) as every firm in the market tends to strengthen its positions and to raise competitive abilities. The relevance of conclusions made by the authors of this monograph regarding necessity for competitiveness management in conditions of imperfect competition is motivated among other factors by the fact that the Nobel Memorial Prize in Economic Sciences in 2014 is awarded to French economist Jean

Tirole claiming that "if such markets (authors' note: the markets dominated by big companies) are not regulated, this will lead to socially undesirable results."

Strengthening of competitive positions of a firm and obtaining of positive economic and social effects as a result of its activities shall be possible only at the expense of development of innovative production with essentially new consumer and physical properties and effective competitiveness management by means of application of corresponding management tools and mechanisms which will be considered henceforth in this monograph, namely: techniques for evaluation of competitiveness of production and an enterprise, evaluation of their innovative potential, monitoring of dynamics of the basic indicators of competitiveness, management using weak signals, risk assessment, etc.

Conclusions It follows from the foregoing that that the theory of competitiveness management is being dynamically developed under the influence of tendencies of prompt innovative transformations in Russian and world economies and the changes in approaches to the management of an enterprise and an industry, etc. As things now stand, the theory of competitiveness management is at the stage of formation of methodological bases which rest on the fundamental economic laws and postulates describing interaction of economic agents. The theory is being filled with new theoretical and practical solutions of economic problems concerning buildup of competitive advantages and formation of corresponding methodological tools to be described within the framework of this monograph.

Postulates and hypotheses concerning competitiveness management formulated and mathematically sounded in this chapter reveal main point, processes and interrelations between them, and economic agents in the course of competitiveness management providing a possibility to have a system view of the said processes and to extend idea of methods and approaches to effective management of a firm.

Elaborating the specified postulates and hypotheses, the authors formulate a new economic law—Competitiveness Management Law. The point is that if a firm development takes place on the basis of creation and buildup of its competitive advantages at the expense of production of goods and services with essentially new consumer properties, as well as additional sales markets for the said goods and services, it would lead to growth in demand for the goods and services it produces, followed by provision of stable economic development of the manufacturer and reduction of risks and trigger points in development of a firm and an industry as a whole, a region, and a nation.

Competitiveness management law is an economic law, according to which purposeful and continuous management of product competitiveness and industrial engineering take place on the basis of competitive advantages, and in case of their under-intensive generation, demand for product is cut and the organization faces a risk of bankruptcy. Elimination of bankruptcy risk requires purposeful competitiveness management to create goods with essentially new consumer properties, providing formation of new commodity markets and stable economic development in order to lessen the risk of bankruptcy situations.

Theoretical Bases of Competitiveness Management 3

3.1 General-Theoretical Fundamentals of Competitiveness Management

Competitiveness management law formulated in Sect. 2.3 as well as the postulates and hypotheses of competitiveness management put forth in Sect. 2.2 according to their manifestation in economy are equally evident and significant as many fundamental economic laws (law of supply and demand, law of increasing opportunity costs, law of diminishing factor productivity, etc.). So, for example, one of the major laws of economy—the law of demand—is the exponent of shift in demand, and therefore the enterprise revenues, owing to change of price competitiveness of the goods or services (implementation of price policy, optimization of production expenditures, and logistical, administrative, and other functions included in the price of the goods or services).

The main economic agent of establishing a theory of competitiveness management consists in studying of economic agentive laws within the system of managing competitiveness of processes and development of relevant methods and techniques.

The subject of the theory of competitiveness management is the activity of economic agents aimed at enhancing of competitiveness at the particular economic level.

Peculiar feature of the theory of competitiveness management is in analysis of competitiveness of economic agents of various levels of hierarchy. The number of such levels depends on the depth of analysis of the general economic structure.

The theory of competitiveness management has three levels: production and enterprises, productive industries, and national economy (micro-level, meso-level, and macro-level, accordingly). This division from our point of view is optimal as it allows tracing synergies between all levels of competitiveness of national economy.

From the point of view of productive industries, product competitiveness is at the heart of economic category of "competitiveness" and hence the enterprise, since competitiveness of enterprise depends on the available level of competitiveness of the products.

A. Chursin, Y. Makarov, *Management of Competitiveness*,
DOI 10.1007/978-3-319-16244-7_3

Accordingly, competitiveness of national economy consists in competitiveness of productive industries being part of it.

Competitiveness management is such organization of economic processes which provides achievement of advantages in competitive struggle. In other words, competitiveness management is a deliberate action on the economic process under control, leading to the defined change of its condition or retention in the desired condition. The purpose of competitiveness management is adjustment of competitiveness of economic agent as a result of strategic, tactical, or operational planning. In order to meet a goal objective, the economic agent should form a governing external influence. Set of the specified elements, connections, and relations there between within the management system forms a structure of competitiveness management system. By so doing, the task of managing competitiveness of a complicated system is limited to provision of such functional transformations of parameters which would be appropriate according to the specified criteria of efficiency of competitiveness management.

Competitiveness management should provide task-oriented economic processes through collection and processing of information on the health of economic agent and environment and making decisions concerning influence on economic agent and their execution.

Competitiveness management process means ability and skill to have a purposeful influence on the economic agent in order to reveal its competitive advantages on micro- , meso-, and macro-level and enhance them.

There is a close interdependence between all levels of competitiveness—production, enterprise, productive industry, and the state within the system of competitiveness management.

Competitiveness of a country and an industry, in the long run, depends on the possibility of a particular enterprise to manufacture competitive goods with consumer, price, and qualitative characteristics (in comparison with me-too products) defining its success in the domestic and foreign markets. Production of competitive goods and successful activity of the enterprise shall be impossible without balanced political, social, and economic system to determine initial conditions of its functioning.

Now we proceed to definitions of three-level competitiveness system.

At the micro-level (i.e., at the level of production, manufacturing facility, and enterprise), one should distinguish two categories of competitiveness:

- Competitiveness of the enterprise as an efficiency of its industrial-marketing activity in the market;
- Product competitiveness as a potential distinguishing feature compared to the similar production in consumer demand.

Many authors connect competitiveness of enterprise only with competitiveness of its production, believing this concept to be a basic one in the system of competitiveness of enterprise, and its other components to be derivatives. However, the concept of enterprise competitiveness is more complicated and is treated in scientific literature rather ambiguously.

Product competitiveness is understood as its ability to meet requirements of specific consumer within a particular market and a certain period of time according to indicators of quality and consumer expenses for acquisition and operation (or consumption) of the said products.

Product competitiveness is mainly characterized by the price, quality, and their correlation. It would appear reasonable that high-quality products in a combination with low price would have the highest competitiveness. However, there is a tendency in the modern world according to which production based on innovative technologies possesses unique competitive advantages, and the price component cannot be a determinate. In such a manner, it may be concluded that the basic component of the product competitiveness, a manufacturer places an emphasis, should be defined depending on a specific market situation and particular market.

The low-price policy as a basic component of product competitiveness can be applied in following cases:

- low price to enter the market;
- low price used by an enterprise as a barrier for new competitors to enter the market;
- decreasing price as a response to competitors' activities.

It should be pointed out that the buyer is interested in full expenses for acquisition and operation of the products; as this takes place, level of operation expenses may be a determinate feature in purchasing many types of the goods.

As previously mentioned, a product quality competitiveness component in modern conditions is a determinate one. According to the experts, product competitiveness on 70–80 % depends on quality, which is shown through a measure of utility value of the particular consumer cost.

Product quality is understood as set of its consumer properties to satisfy specific consumer requirements to production. A consumer is interested in both the quality of a product and provision of the qualified additional services connected with the said products.

Production quality for a consumer can be evaluated in the following formula:

$$Q_c = a^* Q_{goods} + b^* Q_{ass.goods} + c^* Q_{serv}$$

Where

***Q*c**—quality for the consumer;
Q_{goods}—Product quality;
$Q_{ass.goods}$—Quality of associated goods and services;
Q_{serv}—Quality of the service;
a*, *b*, and *c—parameters to express the weight ratio defining measure of significance for the consumer of one or another components of the product quality.

There is a strong interrelation at the micro-level between two categories—competitive capacity of an enterprise and product competitiveness. As it was mentioned above, product competitiveness is one of the major factors to provide competitiveness of an enterprise. Enterprise ability to compete in a certain commodity market directly depends on product competitiveness and a set of the economic methods applied in activity of the said enterprise and affecting results of competitive struggle. Product competitiveness is a necessary but not a sufficient condition of competitive capacity of an enterprise. This circumstance is resulted in particular from the following distinctions of the said categories:

- Firstly, product competitiveness is defined for a short period of time from the economic point of view, and evaluation of the enterprise competitiveness is performed for a long period.
- Secondly, the level of product competitiveness is defined with reference to its every type and evaluation of the enterprise competitiveness covers all the nomenclature of production (and not only the stock list).
- Thirdly, only the owner who defines expediency of industrial activity is interested in competitive capacity of an enterprise on the basis of specific conditions. The consumer here is not interested in expenses for manufacture and its efficiency in evaluation of product competitiveness.

Competitiveness management at the product level can be presented with the help of the model including the following variables:

- Initiating of industrial activities i.e., decision to launch manufacturing of new high-technology products
- Lag development i.e., the period of time required for implementation of preparation of production output
- Readiness for production output
- Manufacture
- Commodity manufacture
- Production deliveries
- Commodity funds
- Production consumption
- Planned commodity funds
- Efficiency of the products sales
- Production implementation lag i.e., period of time for its sale in the market
- Consumer (market) prices and their fluctuation (dynamics)
- Market policy of industrial groups of a particular sector (productive industry) of the high-technology manufacture
- Potential ability of consumption of the said type of production
- Level of real consumption of the said type of production
- Welfare measure (standard of living) of the end production user

Figure 3.1 illustrates general model structure of hi-tech products competitiveness management.

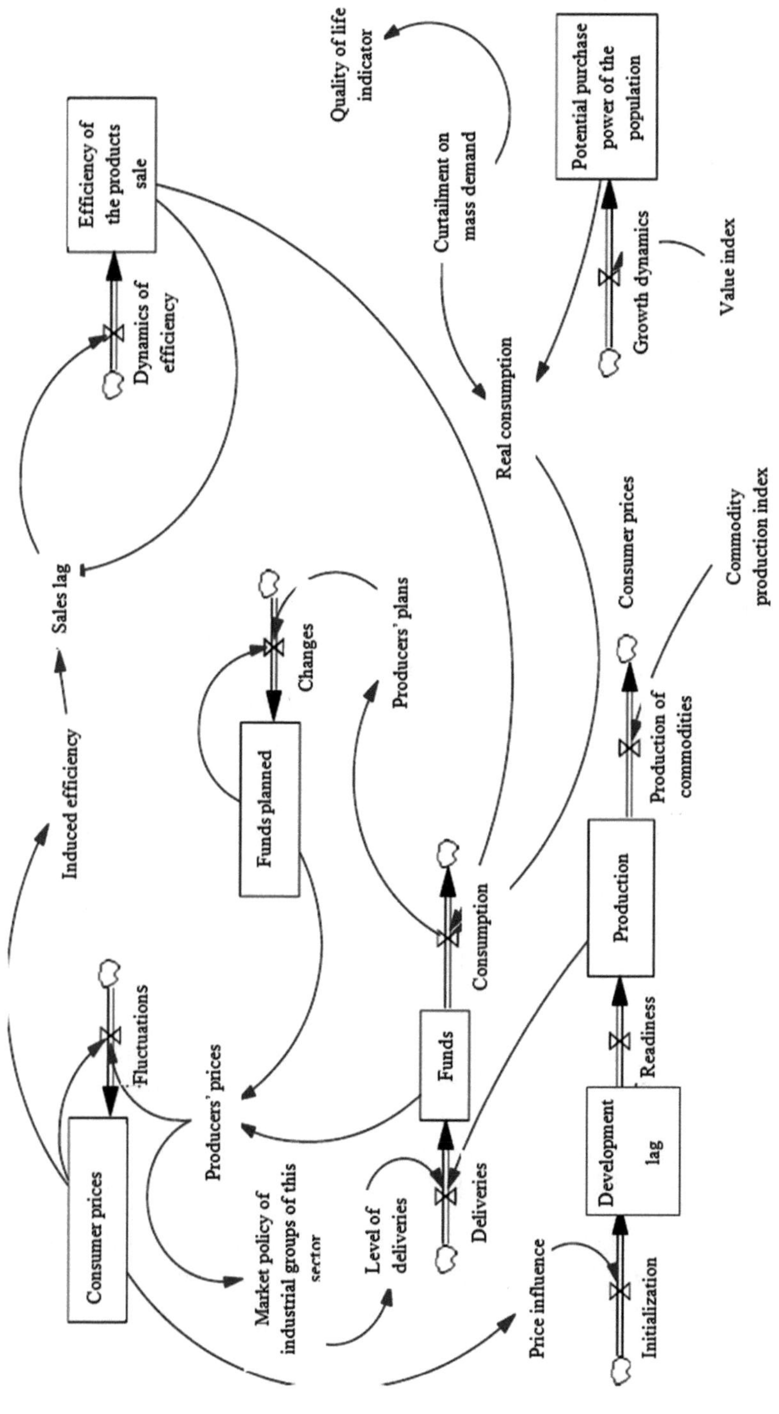

Fig. 3.1 Model structure of hi-tech products competitiveness management

This competitiveness model with specific type of production can be both applied in the form of independent analysis tools and integrated as a subsystem in models of higher meso- and macro-levels.

Competitive capacity of an enterprise, though considered within the framework of micro-level, is a higher level of management than the product competitiveness and is considered as a set of characteristics of enterprises specified by its innovative, scientific and technical, industrial, HR potential, and potential of its marketing services implemented in the course of production. On the other hand, competitive capacity of an enterprise depends on external social & economic and organizational factors allowing the enterprise to create production which is more attractive to consumers than production of competitors according to its price and nonmonetary factors. So, ability of an enterprise to successfully compete in the specific market depends on the product competitiveness and a set of social & economic and organizational factors as well as on the methods of the enterprise activities.

Competitiveness management at the level of an enterprise in scientific literature is treated as a set of activities performed in the course of development, production, sale, and after-sale services in order to provide the required level of the product competitiveness and the balanced influence on all the basic indicators of the enterprise activity on the basis of profit. If an enterprise is actively engaged in competitiveness management in its activities, quite naturally, it assumes aspiration of this enterprise to have high profit. In other words, the philosophy of competitiveness does not substitute the basis of appropriateness of the enterprise functioning and forms just another approach to their practical implementation.

Among the factors of competitive capacity of an enterprise defining its competitive advantages, we can specify the following:

- Novelty of employed equipment, technologies, tools, and computer aids (technical resources).
- Qualification of labor and its cost, demand for workers of specific specialties (man power resources).
- The cost depending on the earth quality, natural resources, minerals, forest resources, climatic conditions, and country geographical position (physical resources).
- The cost caused by availability and sufficiency of scientific and technical information, influencing competitiveness of the goods and services (resources of knowledge).
- Quantity and cost of capital which can be used for financing of the industry sector and an individual enterprise. Here, it is considered that the capital in its structure is nonhomogeneous and can have, for example, such forms as unsecured debt, secured debt, shares, etc.; and for each of these forms of the capital, there are specific conditions of functioning (monetary resources).

- Type, quality of available infrastructure, operating costs, and the user fee influencing the character of competition. These are the transport system, communication system, post services, etc. (infrastructural resources).

Enterprise competitiveness coefficients can be classified under external and internal factors.

External factors of competitive capacity of an enterprise shall be the factors making it possible to guide in the commodity market and to form strategy of development of the enterprise.

Competitive capacity of an enterprise is defined by the following basic external factors:

- Economic, administrative, and social regulation of economic activities on the part of regional and state control system.
- Basic characteristics of the current markets where products are being sold and forecasts the development of external and domestic markets (segmentation, capacity, possibilities of competitors, etc.).
- Social security level, political and economic situation in the state and beyond its boundaries, activities of political parties, human rights, and public and nongovernmental organizations.

The basic internal factors defining competitive capacity of an enterprise are as follows:

- Financial and economic condition of the enterprise.
- Industrial and operational management.
- Effectiveness of the management system;.
- Quality and condition of technical and technological systems.
- Scientific, technological, financial and economic, and HR potentials.
- Efficiency of advertising.
- Effectiveness of decisions concerning material support of an enterprise and product movement.
- Marketing.
- Level of the service organization.

Competitiveness management (namely, specific influences on the factors specified above in all the fields of the enterprise activity and in all the stages of production) will make it possible to enhance efficiency, productivity, and profitableness of the enterprise at the cost of synergistic effect from integration of managerial processes. Principal directions of competitiveness management at the level of an enterprise and possible synergistic effects are illustrated in Table 3.1.

Internal competitiveness management should be combined with the management of a wide arsenal of external resources, many of which may be quickly changed under the influence of poorly controlled processes about which development one can hardly have any idea. In order to control these, various and

Table 3.1 Basic directions of competitiveness management and enhancement of operating efficiency at the level of enterprise

Direction of the enterprise competitiveness management	Potential effect
Production	Synchronization of the general and local levels of production Efficiency of logistics and performance of deliveries Improvement of production management of configured products and spare parts servicing
Finance	Acceleration of financial settlements Optimization of the working assets; Integration and support functions for exchequer and regulation of monetary operations
Man power	Automation of processes, allocation of HR for performance of strategic functions; More efficient workforce management; Control of expenses for workforce management
New product promotion	Acceleration of innovative products deliveries into the market; Improvement of the products compliance with the market requirements; Cooperation with partners in the field of the goods deliveries.
Environment, health, and safety	Identification and reduction of risks connected with ecology, health, and safety; Processes management in ecology, health, and safety; Management and accounting in the corporate safety policy.
Marketing	Optimization of sales and investments into marketing; Coordination of marketing and sales; Customer retention.
Supply	Directional flows and centralization of purchases; All-round execution of contracts; Improvement of the control over suppliers.
Sales	Introduction of the sales strategies to promote sales growth; Sales commitment to the most profitable possibilities of the client; Increase in efficiency of commercial divisions.
Service	Superb service management; Optimization of using accessible means for service; Increase in volume of specialized types of sales.
Management of supply chains	Understanding of the global dynamics of demand; Supply and demand synchronization; Effective organization of deliveries system.
Management in the sphere of information technologies (IT)	IT employment to enhance competitiveness of the enterprise; Reduction in value of the general IT asset value; Efficiency of installed software.
Assets management	Assets control improvement; Increase of the period of the assets' performance efficiency; Safety precautions and application of assets.

complicated new management mechanisms are being developed for supervision of business processes, as well as planning and resource management systems and modern methods of strategic planning based on the systems thinking.

So, for example, the leading international research and consulting organization Gartner, specializing in the markets of information technologies, develops a theory and corresponding software applications, the use of which in the context of competitiveness management makes it possible to pass from functional-hierarchical methodology on to system-process methodology of competitiveness management. As research tools within the framework of system-process methodology for evaluation of the enterprise competitiveness potential in various industries, there may be used the following six easily duplicated software applications to model economic processes (developed by the experts of IT research and advisory firm Gartner):

- "Hype Cycles"—to analyze efficiency of investments into development of new technologies.
- "Magic Quadrants"—to analyze potential of competing suppliers in the market.
- "Market Scopes"—to define the rating of individual market participants.
- "Vendor Ratings"—to analyze suppliers' potential.
- "Market Forecasts"—to forecast markets dynamics.
- "Market Share Analysis"—to analyze market shares.

Competitiveness management on the basis of the specified applications is formed within the framework of the business processes' general architecture.

The possibilities for management of various and complicated processes integrating all the processes—from manufacture to sales and provision of services—are formed by new generations of the systems of planning and management of the enterprise resource (e.g., duplicated ERP (Enterprise Resources Planning) business applications, also put into the economic science and practice by Gartner experts) and modern methods of strategic planning based on the systems thinking.

ERP technology is an effective tool of the product competitiveness management of the companies in the world market as implementation of this technology is based on the principles of management rooted in the block of the international quality standards. Application of ERP technology provides essential benefits to consumers in respect of its operation and service. Competitive advantages ensured by application of the concept of planning and enterprise resource management are connected with a possibility in rather short terms to considerably lower expenses for creation, manufacture, and products operation simultaneously with the high quality. Therefore, technologies of planning and management of enterprise resource become an obligatory condition for provision of presence and competitiveness in the foreign markets.

Perfection of production processes during competitiveness management promotes growth of an overall performance of each division of the enterprise separately and interaction of all the links of value chain as a whole. On the basis of the theory of complex quality management and methodology of continuous perfection of all aspects of economic activities of an enterprise, it is possible to reach high degree of control over competitiveness management. Competitiveness management has a task to improve the work results by means of development of system decisions aimed at:

- Reduction of the cycle duration.
- Elimination of unproductive losses.
- Improvement of flexibility.
- Improvement of quality.

Thanks to development and introduction of innovative technologies and structures promoting interaction, joining together efforts and networking the value chain can become something big, than simply the sum of separate links. These processes, structures, and stimulus include target accounting of expenses, system of measurement with orientation to productivity, as well as the systems of compensation, the early warning, and control. The said measures are aimed at creation of a possibility of winning by all the parties by elimination of structural conflicts between internal divisions and referencing of efficiency indicators of each structural unit to its contribution into success of other parts of the system.

Enterprise competitiveness management through the affecting factors specified above, coupled with advanced achievements in the field of information technologies, will produce the greatest effect and will allow to carry out escalating of competitive advantages within the shortest terms. Specifically, for provision of competitiveness, the leading world manufacturers tend to considerably reduce production cycle, thereby reducing time interval from the first conception date to the idea embodiment in a batch production.

The model structure of competitiveness management at the enterprise level, specified in Fig. 3.2 which includes the basic subjects to management (factors) within the system of competitiveness management, allows understanding the way the economic agents are functioning. This computed appearance model can be used for scenario analysis following results of response of target parameters to changing of varied parameters of the model. With the help of such an analysis, it is possible to evaluate consequences of various possible decisions taken by the market competitors.

The general model of the product competitiveness management at the enterprise level (Fig. 3.2) includes the following variables:

- Level of waste-free production.
- Manufacture of renewable materials.
- Processed materials.
- Level of application of renewable materials.
- Material stocks.
- Level of application of new materials.
- Level of deliveries.
- Transport.

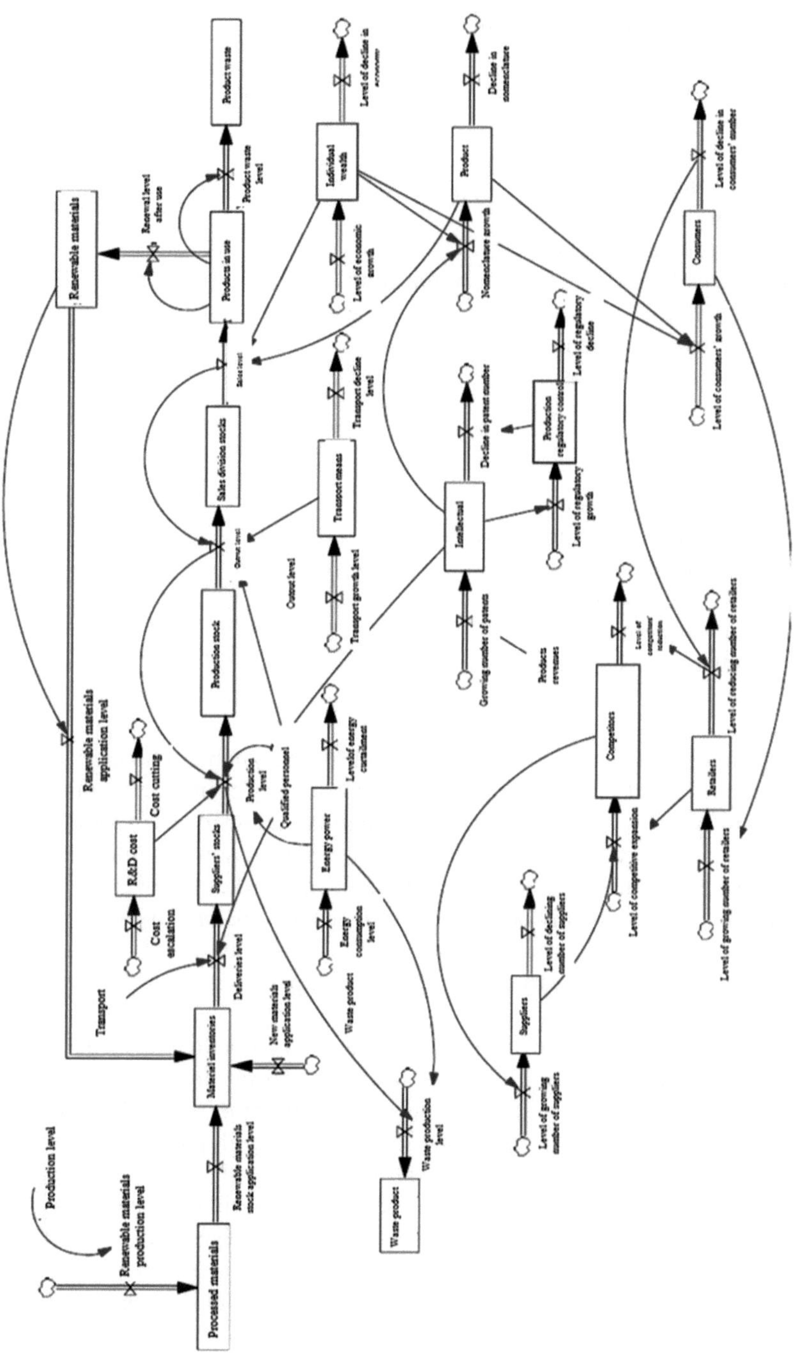

Fig. 3.2 Model structure of hi-tech products competitiveness management at the enterprise level

- Suppliers' stocks.
- Production level.
- Expenses for research and development (R&D).
- Level of deliveries.
- Transportation expenses.
- Industrial stocks.
- Level of production output.
- Stocks of the sales division.
- Sales level of the products.
- Level of the products application.
- Level of renewal after the products application.
- Renewable materials.
- Level of application of renewable materials.
- Level of production wastes.
- Qualified personnel.
- Energy consumption.
- Standard of well-being.
- Intellectual property (patents).
- Standard regulation of manufacture.
- Variety of production output.
- Manufacturers-competitors.
- Suppliers of competitors.
- Retailer (sellers) of competing products.
- Consumers.

In order to illustrate activity of this complicated system, we need several interconnected "networks." For example, to present activity of industrial enterprise, it is possible to specify several networks representing various types of variables—orders, materials, money funds, workforce and equipment, administrative personnel, etc. connected together by means of information network; moreover, every one of the said networks can be divided into several separate parts. Advantage of the similar dynamic models consists in the fact that it is possible to see how the value variability of one or another variable influences competitiveness in the modeling experiments.

Now let's go over to the following hierarchic step of competitiveness concept: to competitiveness management *at meso-level or at the industry level.*

Competitiveness management at the industry level is the most problem-plagued level of management due to its weak theoretical development. Theoretical approaches to competitiveness management at the level of productive industry have been studied for rather a short period of time. In particular, analysis of the state system of competitiveness management in productive industries of the Russian Federation makes it possible to draw a conclusion on conceptual weakness of the said approaches leading to permanent reorganization and is a consequence of nonavailability of the state strategy in the field of transition to modern technologies and to innovative way of development.

Competitiveness at the level of a separate industry is defined in the scientific literature as an ability to compete in the internal or external (international) market with satisfactory rates of return. It can be expressed as an average productivity in the said industry, i.e., the value of output per unit of labor and monetary unit of invested capital (or, in other words, mean value of costs per unit of the finished goods for the enterprises of the said productive industry).

Let's specify this definition as follows. Industry competitiveness is a category of national economy, which is:

- defined by indicators of efficiency of the industry functioning in the national and international markets;
- constituted by a set of internal and external characteristics of the industry and the enterprises being a part of it which, in turn, define ability of this productive industry to effectively function in the markets, in comparison with competitors, and to receive possibilities for further development of this productive industry in so doing.

The industry competitiveness management would make economic substance in the event; it is performed through the formation of competitive advantages of the enterprises within this productive industry.

In the context of competitiveness management, we shall put forward the following ideas:

- Competitive productive industry is a relative category because the most important thing would be how the indicators are measured up against the similar indicators of competitors, instead of the said indicators themselves.
- Competitiveness of productive industry is interconnected with competitiveness of a separate enterprise and the national economy.
- Competitive industry has a developed structure and includes a group of highly competitive enterprises; it has effective design and experimental and industrial technological bases; it applies flexible system of innovative, scientific and technical, industrial, material, and commercial cooperation both within the framework of this productive industry and with other industries in the country and abroad.

It is believed that competitiveness management of productive industries should be based on the forecast of competitiveness dynamics in terms of the cause-and-effect relations defining a key indicator—market share of productive industries in the total market sales. The core of industry competitiveness is productivity—all other measurements depend on this factor, directly or indirectly. In the context of analyzing the state influence, the data at this level has more informative value as opposed to analysis of the enterprises activities, as this influence can be complex valued and in comparative perspective projection with other productive industries both in the country and abroad.

Competitiveness management of the industries can be carried out on the basis of regulation of the following competitiveness coefficients (or their combinations):

- Labor productivity.
- Specific remuneration of labor.
- Capital intensity and research intensity.
- Products technological level.
- Body of knowledge and scientific achievements required for independent development of production and reproduction.
- Content of technical bases for implementation of design and engineering developments.
- Degree of export orientation and import dependence of productive industry.
- Quality of conformance of the level of productive industry development to the general level of development of the national economy.
- Degree of production utilization in various productive industries, etc.

Schematically, competitiveness management model at the level of productive industry is depicted in Fig. 3.3, illustrating a set of cause and effect relationship between the following system-related basic variables connected in the closed contour:

- Productive industry share in the world market.
- HR potential of R&D.
- Physical potential of R&D.
- Organizational potential of R&D.
- Industrial potential of productive industry.
- Level of productive industry budgeting.

Key indicator of competitiveness—productive industry's share in the world market—is representative of productive industry positioning in the world market.

Growth or decline in production sharing of the high-tech industry in the world market depends on corresponding integrated factors which are calculated on the basis of indicators of the processes dynamics in the model subsystems. Accordingly, the concept of competitiveness management of the high-tech industries should be developed with application of the data which can serve as sources of formalized indicators for analysis of dynamics of production sharing of the high-tech industry in the world market.

Competitiveness at the macro-level (i.e., at the state level) is formed at the expense of competitiveness at the level of industries in aggregate.

Model of national competitiveness is an integrated composite model which includes various parameters representative of product competitiveness and competitiveness of the national organizations manufacturing the said products, but not including competitiveness of productive industries. It is evident that competitiveness of the state, as a determining factor of economic growth, finally, depends on

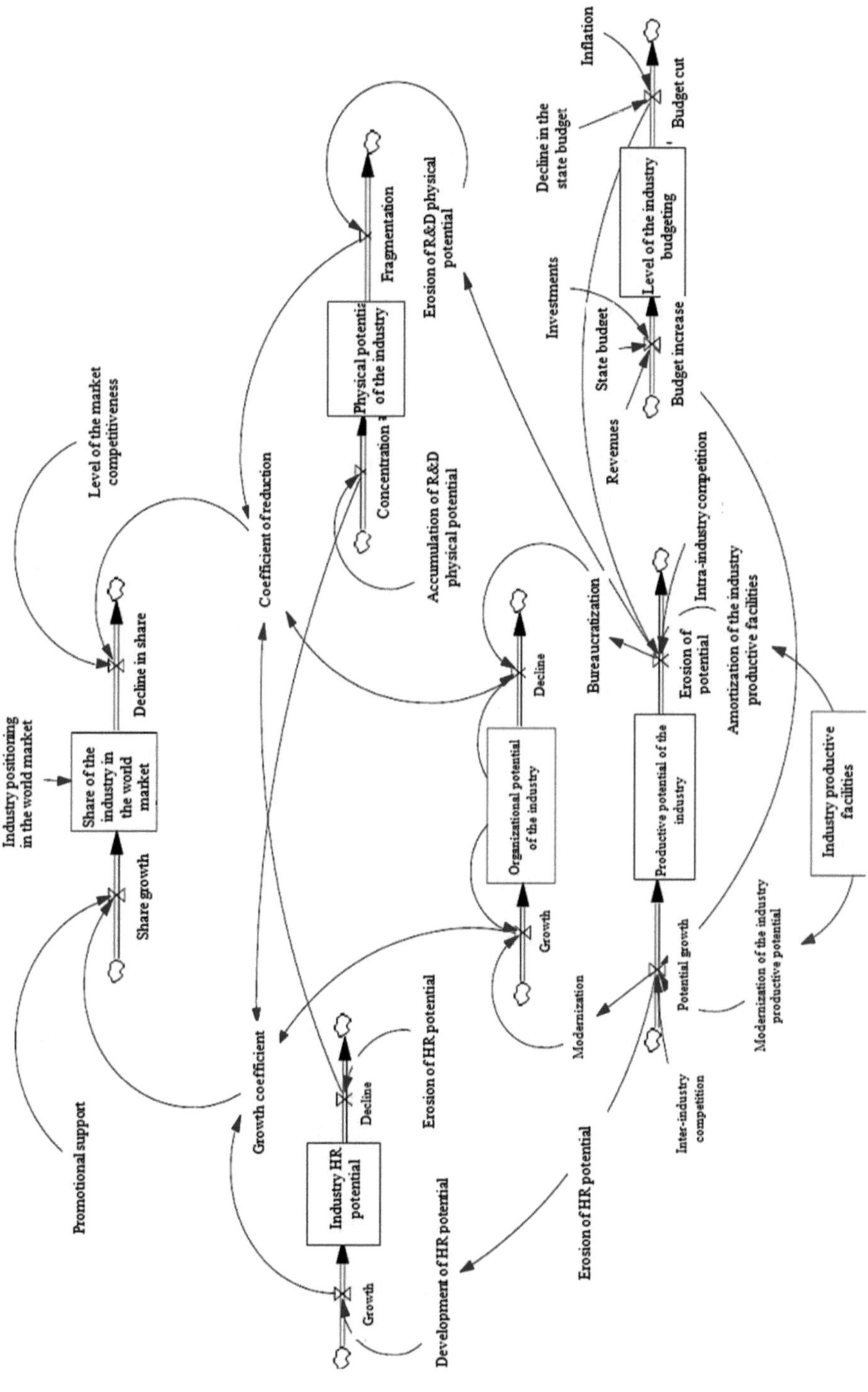

Fig. 3.3 Model structure of hi-tech products competitiveness management at the industry level

the possibility of a particular manufacture to produce competitive goods for which the characteristics determine its success in domestic and foreign markets.

Saturation of many market segments serves to the competition getting ever more and wider international character and new forms and methods of competitive struggle being conceived.

Taking part in competitiveness management at the macro-level are all leading countries of the world: USA, Japan, Germany, China, European developed countries, etc. However, only a few countries can build stable and competitive economy without developed markets, effective sources of innovations, and widespread application of high technologies. The result of efficient competitiveness management at the macro-level is embodied in top marks of the countries in the world ratings.

3.2 Dynamic Model Building for Production of Competitive High-tech Goods

Considering the fact that, as referred to in Sect. 3.1, the basis of economic category "competitiveness" is formed by product competitiveness. Sections 3.2–3.5 present theoretical approaches to mathematical modeling of production process for competitive science-intensive products, and dynamic study of corresponding performance indicators, including the modeling examples.

In order to build a model for production of competitive goods by various enterprises engaged in one-product production, we shall imagine competitive products' production process as the following chain:

- Investments as a possibility to create innovations.
- Innovations as a possibility to create competitive products.

In order to describe dynamics of the said innovative chains, we shall logically form a system of ordinary differential expressions.

Let's begin with the elementary model building.

Let us assume that unknown functions in this system are production indicators determining competitiveness coefficients.

Assume that there are two competing firms available.

Let $u_i = u_i(t)$ $(i = 1, 2)$ denote investments of n-th enterprise into development of innovations at the point of time $\boldsymbol{t}$, and $p_i = p_i(t)$ $(i = 1, 2)$ denote innovations of n-th enterprise.

It would appear reasonable that innovations contain new technical solutions and in doing so enhance products' competitiveness.

Let's consider the simplest case when there is a direct proportion between investments and innovations with a certain fixed factor $a_i > 0$ though it is not always correct.

So, for the sake of simplicity, at the first stage, we assume that

$$p_i(t) = a_i u_i(t) \quad (i = 1, 2). \tag{3.1}$$

Keep in mind that, as a practical matter, every enterprise does not know investments of the competitor enterprise as they make trade secret. However, in our elementary statement of a problem, there is no need for specific information about investments of competitor enterprises or other indicators being trade secrets.

Our purpose is qualitative study of below system of nonlinear ordinary differential equations and, in particular, study of influence of one or another parameter on dynamics of competitiveness coefficient.

Let $x_{i1j} = x_{i1j}(t) \quad (j = 1, \ldots, \mathrm{J}_1)$ denote index number of industrial production of n-th enterprise, the *growth* of which corresponds to competitiveness improvement. For example, it can be quality of products, labor productivity, etc.

Let $x_{i2j} = x_{i2j}(t) \quad (j = 1, \ldots, J_2)$ denote index number of industrial production of n-th enterprise for which the *decrease* corresponds to competitiveness improvement. For example, it can be production cost price.

Competitiveness coefficient of j-th index number of industrial production, the growth of which promotes competitiveness improvement, for the first and the second enterprise is determined from the formulas

$$K_{11j}(t) = \frac{x_{11j}(t)}{x_{21j}(t)}, K_{21j}(t) = \frac{x_{21j}(t)}{x_{11j}(t)}; (j = 1, \ldots, J_1). \tag{3.2}$$

Competitiveness coefficient of j-th index number of industrial production, the decrease of which promotes improvement of the enterprises competitiveness, for the first and the second enterprise is determined from the formulas

$$K_{12j}(t) = \frac{x_{22j}(t)}{x_{12j}(t)}, K_{22j}(t) = \frac{x_{12j}(t)}{x_{22j}(t)}; (j = 1, \ldots, J_2). \tag{3.3}$$

Competitiveness coefficient of n-th enterprise for the specific type of production is defined as follows:

$$K_i(t) = \sum_{i=1,2} \sum_{j=1}^{J_i} a_{lj} K_{ilj}(t). \tag{3.4}$$

where $a_{lj} > 0$—weighing coefficients $\sum_{l,j} a_{lj} = 1$.

For the sake of simplicity, we do not use multipliers corresponding to output index and a number of elements of the output products, considering that they are included in weighing coefficients.

Let's assume that for the first group of index numbers of industrial production $x_{i1j}(t)$, *the rates of their change* are directly proportional to innovations with some fixed positive coefficients $b_{i1j}(t) > 0$, i.e.,

$$\frac{dx_{i1j}(t)}{dt} = b_{i1j}p_i(t) \quad (i = 1, 2, j = 1, \ldots, J_1). \tag{3.5}$$

For the second group of index numbers of industrial production $x_{i2j}(t)$, it would appear reasonable that the rates of their change are proportional to innovations with some fixed negative coefficients $b_{i2j}(t) < 0$, i.e.,

$$\frac{dx_{i2j}(t)}{dt} = b_{i2j}p_i(t) \quad (i = 1, 2, j = 1, \ldots, J_2). \tag{3.6}$$

It is evident that investments $u_i(t)$ depend on product competitiveness coefficient $K_i(t)$.

It would appear reasonable that investments $u_i(t)$ go to development of innovations only in case when competitiveness coefficient $K_i(t)$ is more than a certain threshold value $c_i > 0$, and investment are proportional to value $K_i(t) - c_i$ with some fixed factor $d_i > 0$, i.e.,

$$u_i(t) = d_i(K_i(t) - c_i). \tag{3.7}$$

Number $c_i > 0$ will be named as threshold of the borrowed investments.

In a case when $K_i(t) < c_i$, negative investments are understood as the enterprise expenses from internal reserves for continuation of innovative activity.

From correlations (3.1)–(3.7), we receive the following system $2(J_1 + J_2)$ from nonlinear ordinary differential equations describing dynamic model of changing index numbers of industrial production $x_{i1j}(i, l = 1, 2, j = 1, \ldots, J_1)$:

$$\frac{dx_{ilj}(t)}{dt} = (-1)^{l+1} r_{ilj}\left(\sum_{k=1}^{J_1} \alpha_{1k}\frac{x_{i1k}(t)}{x_{s1k}(t)} + \sum_{k=1}^{J_2} \alpha_{2k}\frac{x_{s2k}(t)}{x_{i2k}(t)} - c_i\right) \tag{3.8}$$

$$(i, l = 1, 2, j = 1, \ldots, J_1, \ s = 2 \text{ if } i = 1; s = 1 \text{ if } i = 2),$$

Where

$$r_{ilj} = a_i b_{ilj} d_i,$$

c_i—constants.

Product competitiveness is influenced by a number of internal and external factors: equipment of the enterprise, energy cost, cost and quality of raw materials, quality of component parts and good timing of their delivery by suppliers, etc. Some of these factors can sharply strengthen their influence during crisis. These factors can be accounted in the form of parameters, equations' factors depend on, as follows:

$$r_{ilj} = r_{ilj}(g,h), \quad a_{lj} = a_{lj}(g,h), \quad c_i = c_i(g,h),$$

where

$g = (g_1, \ldots, g_{N_1})$—vector of indicators corresponding to internal factors;
$h = (h_1, \ldots, h_{N_2})$—vector of indicators corresponding to external factors.

Besides, factors r_{ilj}, a_{lj}, and c_i can depend on time, in this case, the system of Eq. (3.8) becomes nonstationary.

Figure 3.4 shows schematic representation of manufacturing flow chart for competitive high-tech goods by two competitor enterprises, for which the mathematical model is presented in the form of system of the ordinary nonstationary nonlinear differential equations (3.8) in the assumption of directly proportional (linear) dependence between investments and innovations.

Development (next level of the study) of the general model of competitiveness is represented by accounting of nonlinear character of dependence of innovations on investments. In this case, dynamics model of the index numbers of industrial production can be written down as follows:

$$\frac{dx_{ilj}(t)}{dt} = (-1)^{l+1} r_{ilj} f_i(K_i(x(t)) - c_i), \tag{3.9}$$

$$(i = 1, \ldots, N, l = 1, 2, j = 1, \ldots, J_1)$$

where

$f_i : \mathbb{R} \to \mathbb{R}$—Monotone increasing of uneven function describing dependence of innovations on investments,

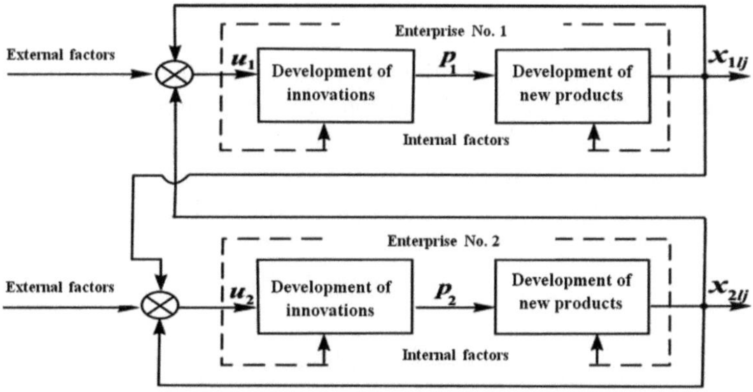

Fig. 3.4 Schematic representation of manufacturing flow chart for competitive high-tech goods of competitor enterprise

$$r_{ilj} = b_{ilj} d_i,$$

c_i—Positive constants;
b_{ilj}—Modules of dynamics proportionality factors of performance indicators from innovations,
d_i—Proportionality factors for investment of innovations depending on competitiveness of the enterprise,
c_i—threshold values determining level of competitiveness from which the investors can be interested in the enterprise.

Product competitiveness coefficient of n-th enterprise is determined under the formula

$$K_i(t) = \sum_{i=1,2} \sum_{j=1}^{J_i} a_{lj} K_{ilj}(t), \tag{3.10}$$

Where

$\alpha_{lj} > 0$—Weighing coefficients,

$$\sum_{l,j} \alpha_{lj} = 1$$

Contrary to the formula (3.4), competitiveness coefficient of j-th index number of industrial production for n-th enterprise, the growth of which promotes competitiveness increase, is determined under the formula

$$K_{i1j}(x(t)) = \frac{x_{i1j}(t)}{M_j(t)}, \quad (i = 1, \ldots, N, j = 1, \ldots, J_1) \tag{3.11}$$

where

$$M_j(t) = \max_i x_{i1j}, \;\; x(t) = \{x_{ilj}(t)\}, \;\; (l = 1, 2). \tag{3.12}$$

Competitiveness coefficient of j-th index number of industrial production for n-th enterprise, the decrease of which promotes enhancement of competitiveness of the enterprises, is determined under the formula

$$K_{i2j}(x(t)) = \frac{m_j(t)}{x_{i2j}(t)}, \quad (i = 1, \ldots, N, j = 1, \ldots, J_2), \tag{3.13}$$

where

$$m_j(t) = \min_i x_{i2j}. \tag{3.14}$$

Analogous to model (3.8), we assume that coefficients of equations depend on a number of internal and external factors; moreover, some of these factors can sharply strengthen their influence on competitiveness during crisis, and we will consider this dependence in coefficients of equations (3.9) as follows:

$$r_{ilj} = r_{ilj}(g, h), \quad a_{lj} = a_{lj}(g, h), \quad c_i = c_i(g, h),$$

where

$g = (g_1, \ldots, g_{N_1})$—vector of indicators corresponding to internal factors;
$h = (h_1, \ldots, h_{N_2})$—vector of indicators corresponding to external factors.

Besides, as in general, factors r_{ilj}, a_{lj}, and c_i can depend on time, and then if we take this dependence into account, the system of equations (3.9) becomes unstable.

The results received in this section make it possible to draw the following *conclusion*:

Dynamic models of high-tech competitive production can be formalized by means of nonlinear ordinary differential equations, the qualitative and numerical analysis of which is capable of determining performance indicators and competitiveness coefficient depending on time.

3.3 Dynamics Study of Performance Indicators of Competitive Production in Modeling

In order to study qualitative properties of solutions of nonlinear system of differential equations, we shall consider dynamics of high-tech competitive production of two enterprises in following four modeling cases:

I. There is a unique index number of industrial production , the growth of which promotes enhancement of competitiveness, and the threshold values of the borrowed investments are less than 1.
II. There is a unique index number of industrial production, the growth of which promotes enhancement of competitiveness, and the threshold values of the borrowed investments are more than 1.
III. There is a unique index number of industrial production, the decrease of which promotes enhancement of competitiveness, and the threshold values of the borrowed investments are less than 11.
IV. There is a unique index number of industrial production, the decrease of which promotes enhancement of competitiveness, and the threshold values of the borrowed investments are more than 11.

3.3.1 Case I

Let us assume that $J_1 = 1$ and $J_2 = 0$, i.e., there is a unique index number of industrial production, the growth of which promotes enhancement of competitiveness. Actually this assumption narrows down the class of considered real models very much. However, it is convenient for qualitative investigation of properties of the system of equations, which in this case will take on the appearance of

$$\begin{aligned}\frac{dx_1(t)}{dt} &= r_1\left(\frac{x_1(t)}{x_2(t)} - c_1\right),\\ \frac{dx_2(t)}{dt} &= r_2\left(\frac{x_2(t)}{x_1(t)} - c_2\right),\end{aligned} \tag{3.15}$$

Where

$$r_1, r_2, c_1, c_2 > 0,$$

$x_i(t)$—index number of industrial production of n-th enterprise.

Let's assume that threshold values of the borrowed investments $c_1, c_2 < 1$.

It corresponds to the stable development of economy based on investments, since even in case competitiveness coefficient is a little bit less than 1, the investor is ready to put up capital in production.

As both performance indicators $x_1(t)$ and $x_2(t)$ should be positive, we consider behavior of system (3.15) solutions in the first quadrant. In so doing, an important role will be played by straight lines $x_2 = x_1/c_1$ and $x_2 = c_2x_1$, since there is a change of derivative sign on these straight lines $x_1'(t)$, $x_2'(t)$.

From the assumption $c_1, c_2 < 1$, it follows that lines $x_2 = x_1/c_1$ and $x_2 = c_2x_1$ divide the first quadrant into three angles

$$\begin{aligned}A &= \{x = (x_1, x_2) : x_2 > x_1/c_2, x_1, x_2 > 0\},\\ B &= \{x = (x_1, x_2) : c_2x_1 > x_1/c_2, x_1, x_2 > 0\},\\ C &= \{x = (x_1, x_2) : x_2 > c_2x_1, x_1, x_2 > 0\}.\end{aligned}$$

In area A, the index number of industrial production of the first enterprise decreases, and the index number of the second is growing. In area B, both index numbers of industrial production are growing. In area C, the index number of industrial production of the first enterprise is growing, and the index number of the second enterprise is decreasing.

For behavior analysis of performance indicators and competitiveness coefficients, Fig. 3.5 graphically shows behavior of phase curves on the plane x_1, x_2.

From the system of equations (3.15), we have

$$\frac{dx_2}{dx_1} = r\frac{x_2/x_1 - c_2}{x_1/x_2 - c_1}, \quad r = r_2/r_1. \tag{3.16}$$

Isoclinic lines of the fields of directions for Eq. (3.16) are straight lines $x_2 = kx_1$, where $k > 0$.

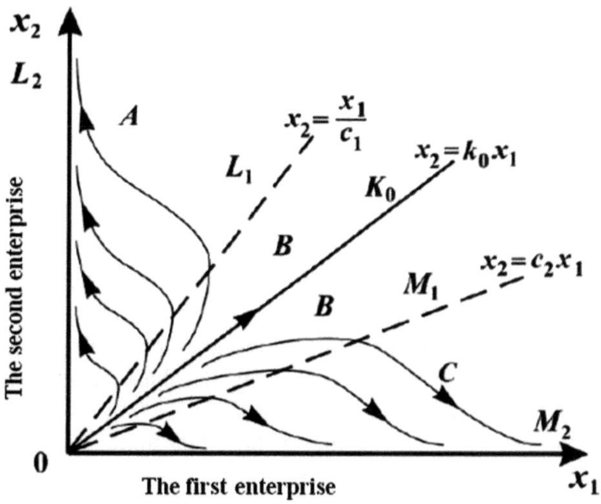

Fig. 3.5 The graphic of index numbers of industrial production of two enterprises under stable development of economy

On these straight lines, derivative $\frac{dx_2}{dx_1}$ is equal to a constant calculated under the formula

$$\frac{dx_2}{dx_1} = r\frac{k - c_2}{1/k - c_1}. \tag{3.17}$$

The isoclinic lines passing through point 0, the slope ratio of which is equal to slope ratio of the field of directions, meet the condition

$$r\frac{k_0 - c_2}{1/k_0 - c_1} = k_0,$$

Hence

$$k_0 = (1 + rc_2)/(r + c_1).$$

From assumption $c_1, c_2 < 1$, it follows that $c_2 < k_0 < 1/c_1$.

As can be seen from the above, half-line $K_0 = \{x = (x_1, x_2) : x_2 > k_0 x_1, x_1 > 0\}$ belongs to angle B (Fig. 3.5).

For the points in angle m, the following inequalities are performed:

$$x_2/x_1 - c_2 > 0 \quad \text{and} \quad x_1/x_2 - c_1 > 0\,.$$

it follows that

$$\frac{dx_2}{dx_1} < 0 \quad (x \in A). \tag{3.18}$$

Let's consider behavior of the field of directions on sides of angle A

$$L_1 = \{x : x_2 = x_1/c_1, x_1 > 0\} \quad \text{and} \quad L_2 = \{x : x_1 = 0, x_1 > 0\}.$$

It is evident that

$$\lim_{\substack{x \to x^0, \\ x \in A}} \frac{dx_2}{dx_1} = -\infty \left(x^0 = \left(x_1^0, x_2^0\right) \in L_1\right), \quad \lim_{\substack{x \to L_2, \\ x \in A}} \left|\frac{dx_2}{dx_1}\right| = \infty. \tag{3.19}$$

Formulas (3.18)–(3.19) imply that in angle $\vec{a}(t) \in A_m^+$, the phase curves beginning on half-line $u(Q_1(t), Q_2(t), \ldots, Q_n(t)) \to (\max)$ have a vertical inclination. Then the slope ratio of the field of directions, remaining negative, decreases in modulus. The slope ratio goes to$-\infty$ when the phase curve approaches half-line $Q_i(t) \geq 0$ $(i = 1, \ldots, n(t))$ (Fig. 3.5).

Moreover, it is possible to show that under some T_1, $0 < T_1 < \infty$, the solution possesses the following property: $x_1(t) \to 0, x_2(t) \to +\infty$ where $t \to T_1$.

In each point of angle $p_i = p_i(t)$, the inclination of the field of directions is negative, i.e.,

$$\frac{dx_2}{dx_1} < 0 \ (x \in C). \tag{3.20}$$

Let's consider behavior of the field of directions on the sides of angle C:

$$M_1 = \{x : x_2 = c_2 x_1, x_1 > 0\},$$
$$M_2 = \{x : x_2 = 0, x_1 > 0\}.$$

It is evident that

$$\lim_{\substack{x \to x^0, \\ x \in C}} \frac{dx_2}{dx_1} = 0 \ \left(x^0 \in M_1\right) \quad \lim_{\substack{x \to M_2, \\ x \in C}} \frac{dx_2}{dx_1} = 0. \tag{3.21}$$

Formulas (3.20)–(3.21) imply that in angle C, the phase curves beginning on half-line M_1 have a horizontal inclination (slope ratio is equal to 0). Then the slope ratio of the field of directions becomes negative. When the phase curve approaches half-line M_2, the slope ratio goes to zero (Fig. 3.5).

It is possible to show that under certain T_2, $0 < T_2 < \infty$ the solution possesses the following property: $x_1(t) \to +\infty$ and $x_2(t) \to 0$ under $t \to T_2$.

Further we consider behavior in angle B of the phase curves beginning above straight line K_0.

Owing to relation (3.17), slope ratio $\frac{dx_2}{dx_1}$ of the field of directions on isoclinic line $\{x : x_2 = kx_1, x_1 > 0\}$ $(k_0 < k < 1/c_1)$ monotonously increases as k is increasing, in such a case,

$$\lim_{\substack{x \to x^0, \\ x \in B}} \frac{dx_2}{dx_1} = +\infty \ \left(x^0 \in L_1\right).$$

As can be seen from the above phase curves in angle B, beginning above half-line K_0, while monotonously increasing coefficient of the inclination angle up to $+\infty$, reach half-line L_1 and then pass into angle A (Fig. 3.5).

In a similar fashion, it is possible to describe behavior of phase curves in angle B, beginning in the lower half-line K_0. Phase curves with time growth t monotonously reducing coefficient of inclination angle up to 0, reach half-line M_1, and then pass into angle C (Fig. 3.5).

Conclusions The economic substance of the above results concerning behavior of phase curves on the two-dimensional subspace of performance indicators x_1, x_2 consists in the following.

In case of market model of the chain "investments–innovations–competitiveness," during the stable development of economy, area C is the "area of guaranteed gain in the competition" for the first enterprise. If performance indicators (x_1, x_2) during the initial point of time are within area C, then competitiveness of the first enterprise goes to $+\infty$, and competitiveness of the second enterprise goes to 0. To reduce the size of area C, the second enterprise should reduce the threshold of the borrowed investments c_2.

Area A is the "area of guaranteed gain in the competition" of the second enterprise. If performance indicators (x_1, x_2) during the initial point of time are in area A, competitiveness of the second enterprise goes to $+\infty$, and competitiveness of the first enterprise goes to 0. To reduce the size of area A, the first enterprise should reduce the threshold of the borrowed investments c_1.

The most substantial case is competitive struggle in area B. If in the initial point of time performance indicators (x_1, x_2) are in area B, both the performance indicators increase (until point (x_1, x_2) is in area). However, the behavior of performance indicators and, hence, competitiveness coefficients varies, as soon as the phase curve reaches area B boundaries.

If in the initial point of time, performance indicators are in area B above half-line K_0, then after a while, they reach half-line L_1 After that, as it has been shown earlier, performance indicator x_1 starts decreasing, while performance indicator x_2 continues to increase.

If in the initial point of time, performance indicators are in area B below half-line K_0, after a while they reach half-line M_1. Then the performance indicator x_2 will start decreasing, and the performance indicator x_1 continues to increase.

If in the initial point of time, performance indicators (x_1, x_2) are on half-line K_0, then they will move along this half-line, monotonically increasing. In such a case, competitiveness coefficients will be constants,

$$K_1 = 1/k_0 \text{ where } k_0 = (1 + rc_2)/(r + c_1).$$

It is important to emphasize that straight line K_0, which is a multitude of dynamic equilibrium in competitive struggle, corresponds to unstable balance. For any performance indicators, which are during the initial point of time in a close vicinity of half-line K_0 but not belonging to K_0, after a while one of the parties wins in competitive struggle. To have certain balance in competitive struggle, it is necessary to control the system parameters.

3.3.2 Case II

We shall consider a situation studied in case I, believing now that $c_1, c_2 > 1$. It corresponds to a crisis condition of economy when the investor wishes to receive a guaranteed profit and invests capital only if the competitiveness coefficient is more than 1.

Then straight lines $x_2 = c_2 x_1$ and $x_2 = x_1/c_1$ also divide the first quadrant into three angles:

$$A = \{x : x_2 > c_2 x_1, x_1, x_2 > 0\},$$
$$D = \{x : x_1/c_1 < x_2 < c_2 x_1, x_1, x_2 > 0\},$$
$$C = \{x : x_2 < x_1/c_1, x_1, x_2 > 0\}.$$

In area A, the index number of industrial production of the first enterprise decreases and the index number of the second one is growing. In area D, both index numbers of industrial production are falling. In area C, the index number of industrial production of the first enterprise is growing, and the index number of the second one is falling (Fig. 3.6).

As well as in case of I, phase curve of the system of equations (3.15) are graphics of solutions of Eq. (3.16) with a corresponding selection of the movement direction.

Isoclinic lines of the field of directions for the Eq. (3.16) are straight lines $x_2 = kx_1$, where $k > 0$. On these straight lines, derivative $\frac{dx_2}{dx_1}$ is equal to the constant which is calculated under the formula (3.17).

Isoclinic line $x_2 = k_0 x_1$ has slope ratio k_0 equal to slope ratio of the field of directions.

From assumption $c_1, c_2 > 1$, it follows that $(1/c_1 < k_0 < c_2)$.

In such a case, $K_0 = \{x : x_2 = k_0 x_1, x_1 > 0\} \subset D$ (Fig. 3.6).

In each point of angle A, there are inequalities in $x_2/x_1 - c_2 > 0$ and $x_1/x_2 - c_1 < 0$.

Hence $\frac{dx_2}{dt} > 0$, $\frac{dx_1}{dt} < 0$. In such a case, movement on phase curves in angle A is carried out towards the increase of performance indicator $x_2(t)$ and decrease of performance indicator $x_1(t)$.

Let's consider behavior of the field of directions on the sides of angle A:

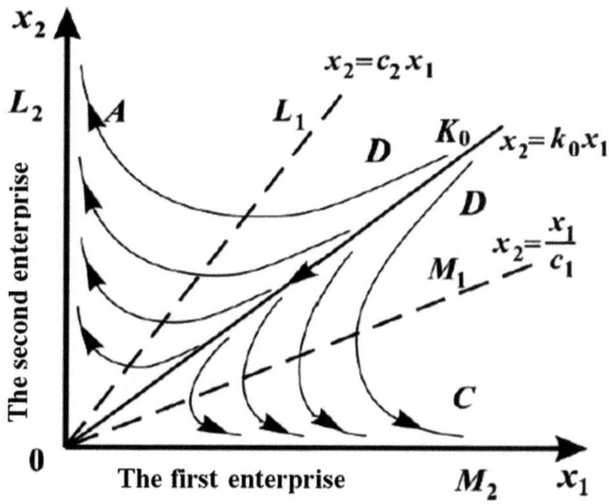

Fig. 3.6 The graphic of index numbers of industrial production of two enterprises under crisis development of economy

$$L_1 = \{x : x_2 = c_2x_1, x_1 > 0\} \text{ and } L_2 = \{x : x_2 = 0, x_2 > 0\}.$$

It is evident that

$$\lim_{\substack{x \to x^0, \\ x \in A}} \frac{dx_2}{dx_1} = 0 \ \left(x^0 \in L_1\right) \quad \lim_{\substack{x \to L_2, \\ x \in A}} \frac{dx_2}{dx_1} = -\infty. \tag{3.22}$$

The formulas (3.18 and 3.22) imply that in angle A, the phase curves beginning on half-line L_1 have a horizontal inclination (the slope ratio is equal to 0). Then the slope ratio becomes negative and goes to $-\infty$ during the approach of the phase curve to half-line L_2 (Fig. 3.6). Moreover, it is possible to show that under certain T_1, $0 < T_1 < \infty$, the solution possesses the following property: $x_1(t) \to 0$ and $x_2(t) \to +\infty$ when $t \to T_1$.

For the points in angle C, there are the following inequalities performed: $x_2/x_1 - c_2 > 0$ and $x_1/x_2 - c_1 < 0$. Hence, in each point of angle C, the inclination angle of the field of directions is negative, in such a case, $\frac{dx_2}{dt} > 0$, $\frac{dx_1}{dt} < 0$. As can be seen from the above, movement on phase curves in angle C is carried out towards increasing performance indicator $x_1(t)$ and decreasing performance indicator $x_2(t)$.

Let's consider behavior of the field of directions on the sides of angle C

$$M_1 = \{x : x_2 = x_1/c_1, x_1 > 0\} \text{ and } M_2 = \{x : x_2 = 0, x_1 > 0\}.$$

it is evident that

$$\lim_{\substack{x \to x^0, \\ x \in C}} \frac{dx_2}{dx_1} = -\infty \ \left(x^0 \in M_1\right) \quad \lim_{\substack{x \to M_2, \\ x \in C}} \frac{dx_2}{dx_1} = 0. \tag{3.23}$$

Formulas (3.20 and 3.23) imply that the phase curves beginning on half-line M_1 have a vertical inclination in angle C (the slope ratio is equal to $-\infty$). Then the slope ratio, remaining negative, goes to 0 on half-line M_2 (Fig. 3.6). It is possible to show, that under certain T_2, $0 < T_2 < \infty$, the solution possesses the following property: $x_1(t) \to +\infty$ and $x_2(t) \to 0$ under $t \to T_2$.

Let's consider now behavior of phase curves in angle C, beginning above straight line K_0.

Owing to correlations (3.17), the slope ratio of the field of directions on isoclinic line $\{x : x_2 = kx_1, x_1 > 0\}$ $(k_0 < k < c_2)$ monotonously decreases when k is increasing, in such a case,

$$\lim_{\substack{x \to x^0, \\ x \in B}} \frac{dx_2}{dx_1} = 0 \ \left(x^0 \in L_1\right) \tag{3.24}$$

In such a case, phase curves in angle D, beginning above half-line K_0, while monotonously reducing coefficient of inclination angle up to 0, reach half-line L_1 and then pass into angle A (Fig. 3.6).

In a similar fashion, it is possible to describe behavior of the phase curves in angle D, beginning below half-line K_0. Phase curves with the growth of time t, while monotonously increasing coefficient of inclination angle up to $+\infty$ reach half-line M_1 and then pass into angle C (Fig. 3.6).

Conclusions The economic substance of the above results concerning behavior of the phase curves on the two-dimensional subspace of performance indicators x_1, x_2 under crisis condition of economy consists in the following.

Under the crisis condition of economy, area C (as was in case I) is the "area of guaranteed gain in the competition" for the first enterprise.

If in the initial point of time, performance indicators (x_1, x_2) are in area C, then competitiveness of the first enterprise goes to $+\infty$, and competitiveness of the second enterprise goes to 0. Contrary to case I corresponding to stable development of economy, in this example, it is impossible to reduce the size of area C at the expense of change of threshold of the borrowed investments. On the other hand, the first enterprise, interested to increase area C can make it by reducing the threshold of the borrowed investments.

In a similar fashion, area A (as in case I) is the "area of guaranteed gain in the competition" for the second enterprise. Contrary to case I, in this example, it is impossible to reduce the size of area A at the expense of changing threshold of investments c_1. However, the second enterprise, interested in increasing area A, can make it by reducing the threshold of the borrowed investments c_2.

If in the initial point of time, performance indicators are in area D, then both performance indicators will be decreasing (until point (x_1, x_2) is in area D).

If in the initial point of time, performance indicators are in area B above half-line K_0, then after a while, they reach half-line L_1. After that, as it has been shown earlier, the performance indicator x_1 continues to decrease, and the performance indicator x_2 starts increasing.

If in the initial point of time, performance indicators are in area D below half-line K_0, then after a while, they reach half-line M_1. Then the performance indicator x_1 will start increasing, and performance indicator x_2 will continue to decrease.

If in the initial point of time, performance indicators (x_1, x_2) are on half-line K_0, then they will move along this half-line, monotonously decreasing. In such a case, competitiveness coefficients will be constants $K_2 = k_0$ and $K_1 = 1/k_0$.

Keep in mind that straight line K_0, which is a multitude of dynamic equilibrium in competitive struggle, corresponds to unstable balance. For any performance indicators during the initial point of time in the vicinity of half-line K_0, but not belonging to K_0, after a while one of the parties wins in competitive struggle.

The quoted above qualitative analysis of nonlinear differential equations shows that the above mathematical models describing dynamics of competitiveness indicators and being based on nonlinear differential equations accept a qualitative analyses of properties of these equations' solutions. Qualitative analysis of the basic equations modeling behavior of competitiveness indicators of two enterprises makes it possible to identify conditions to support competitiveness of both enterprises which is the principal task of competitiveness management in the high-tech productive industries.

3.3.3 Case III

Let us assume that $J_1 = 0$, and $J_2 = 1$ i.e., there is a unique index number of industrial production, the decrease of which promotes competitiveness increase, for example, production cost price.

Then the system of equations (3.22) will become the form

$$\begin{aligned} \frac{dx_1(t)}{dt} &= r_1\left(\frac{x_2(t)}{x_1(t)} - c_1\right), \\ \frac{dx_2(t)}{dt} &= r_2\left(\frac{x_1(t)}{x_2(t)} - c_2\right), \end{aligned} \tag{3.25}$$

where

$$r_1, r_2, c_1, c_2 > 0,$$

$x_i(t)$—index number of industrial production of n-th enterprise.

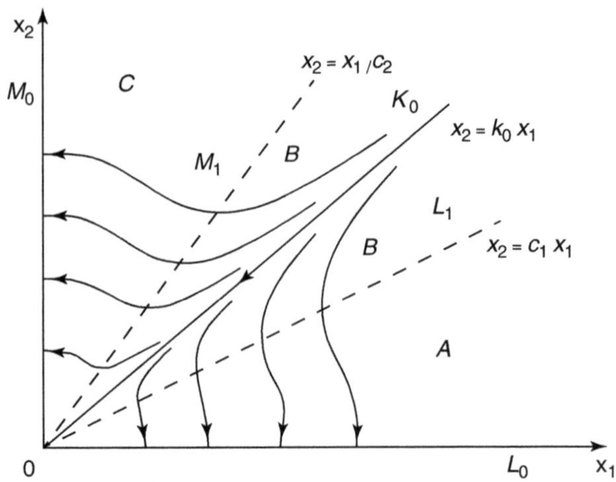

Fig. 3.7 The graphic of index numbers of industrial production of two enterprises under stable development of economy

Let's assume that threshold values of the borrowed investments $c_1, c_2 < 1$.It corresponds to the stable development of economy based on investments because even if the competitiveness coefficient is less than a unit, the investor is ready to invest in production.

As both performance indicators $x_1(t)$ and $x_2(t)$ should be positive, we consider behavior of solutions of system (3.25) in the first quadrant. In such a case, the important role will be played by straight lines $x_2 = x_1/c_2$ and $x_2 = c_1x_1$ as the derivative sign $x_1'(t)$, $x_2'(t)$ can vary on these straight lines.

Assumption $c_1, c_2 < 1$ implies that straight lines $x_2 = x_1/c_2$ and $x_2 = c_1x_1$ divide the first quadrant into three angles (see Fig. 3.7):

$$\begin{aligned} A &= \{x = (x_1, x_2) : x_2 < c_1x_1, x_1, x_2 > 0\}, \\ B &= \{x = (x_1, x_2) : c_1x_1 < x_2 < x_1/c_2, x_1, x_2 > 0\}, \\ C &= \{x = (x_1, x_2) : x_1/x_2 < x_2, x_1, x_2 > 0\}. \end{aligned}$$

In area ***A***, the index number of industrial production of the first enterprise is growing, and the index number of the second enterprise is decreasing. In area ***B***, both index numbers are decreasing. In area ***C***, the index number of the first enterprise is decreasing, and the index number of the second enterprise is growing.

In order to analyze behavior of performance indicators $x_1(t)$ and $x_2(t)$ and competitiveness coefficient $K_1(t) = \dfrac{x_2(t)}{x_1(t)}$ and $K_2(t) = \dfrac{x_1(t)}{x_2(t)}$, we map behavior of phase curves on the two-dimensional subspace x_1 and x_2.

From the system of equations (3.25), we receive

$$\frac{dx_2}{dx_1} = r\frac{x_1/x_2 - c_2}{x_2/x_1 - c_1} \tag{3.26}$$

where $r = r_2/r_1$.

Isoclinic lines of the field of directions for the Eq. (3.26) are straight lines $x_2 = kx_1$, where $k > 0$.

On these straight lines, derivative $\frac{dx_2}{dx_1}$ is equal to the constant which is calculated under formula

$$\frac{dx_2}{dx_1} = r\frac{1/k - c_2}{k - c_1}. \tag{3.27}$$

Isoclinic line passing through point **0**, slope ratio k_0, which is equal to the inclination angle of the field of directions, meets condition

$$r\frac{1/k_0 - c_2}{k_0 - c_1} = k_0. \tag{3.28}$$

This implies that

$$r/k_0 - rc_2 = k_0^2 - c_1k_0.$$

In this manner, $k_0 > 0$ is a root of equation

$$k_0^3 - c_1k_0^2 + rc_2k_0 - r = 0, \tag{3.29}$$

if the isoclinic line with the specified property exists.

Let's imply $P(k) = k^3 - c_1k^2 + rc_2k - r$. We prove that the multinomial has a unique positive root k_0, in such a case, $c_1 < k_0 < 1/c_2$.

Actually, if $k \geq 1/c_2$, then owing to condition $c_1, c_2 < 1$, we have

$$P(k) = k^2(k - c_1) + r(c_2k - 1) \geq k^2(k - c_1) > 0. \tag{3.30}$$

If $0 < k < c_1$, owing to condition $c_1, c_2 < 1$, we have

$$P(k) = k^2(k - c_1) + r(c_2k - 1) \leq r(c_2c_1 - 1) < 0. \tag{3.31}$$

On the other hand, when $c_1 < k < 1/c_2$ we have valid inequality

$$P'(k) = 3k^2 - 2c_1k + rc_2 > 2k(k - c_1) > 0. \tag{3.32}$$

It follows from (3.20)–(3.22) that the multinomial has a unique positive root k_0, in such a case, $c_1 < k_0 < 1/c_2$.

In such a case, it is proved that the half-line $K_0 = \{x : x_2 = k_0x_1, x_1 > 0\}$ belongs to angle **B** (Fig. 3.7).

For the points in angle ***C***, the following inequalities are performed: $x_1/x_2 - c_2 < 0$ and $x_2/x_1 - c_1 > 0$.

Hence

$$\frac{dx_2}{dx_1} < 0 \ (x \in C). \tag{3.33}$$

Let's consider behavior of the field of directions on the sides of angle ***C***:

$$M_1 = \{ :_2 = x_1/c_{2},_1 > 0\} \text{ and } M_0 = \{ :_1 = 0,_2 > 0\}.$$

It is evident that

$$\lim_{\substack{x \to x^0, \\ x \in C}} \frac{dx_2}{dx_1} = 0 \ \left(x^0 = \left(x_1^0, x_2^0\right) \in M_i; i = 0, 1\right). \tag{3.34}$$

Formulas (3.33 and 3.34) imply that in angle ***C***, phase curves have horizontal tangent lines in the points belonging to M_1. Then the slope ratio of the field of directions becomes negative, and on half-line M_0, phase curves have again horizontal tangent lines.

In each point of angle ***A***, the inclination angle of the field of directions is negative, i.e.,

$$\frac{dx_2}{dx_1} < 0 \ (x \in A). \tag{3.35}$$

Let's consider behavior of the field of directions on the sides of angle ***A*** $L_1 = \{ :_2 = c_1 x_1,_1 > 0\}$ and $L_0 = \{ : x_2 = 0, x_2 > 0\}$.

It is evident that

$$\lim_{\substack{x \to x^0, \\ x \in A}} \frac{dx_2}{dx_1} = -\infty \ \left(x^0 \in L_i, i = 0, 1\right) \tag{3.36}$$

The formulas (3.35 and 3.36) imply that in angle ***A***, phase curves in points belonging to L_1 have vertical tangent lines. Then the slope ratio of the field of directions becomes final negative, and on half-line L_0, phase curves again have vertical tangent lines.

Let's consider behavior of the phase curves in angle ***B***, beginning above half-line K_0.

Owing to relation (3.27), slope ratio of the field of directions $\frac{dx_2}{dx_1} > 0$ on isoclinic line $\{x : x_2 = kx_1, x_1 > 0\}$ $(k_0 < k < 1/c_2)$ is monotonously decreasing when k is increasing, in such a case,

$$\lim_{\substack{x \to x^0, \\ x \in B}} \frac{dx_2}{dx_1} = 0 \ \left(x^0 \in M_1\right)$$

As can be seen from above, the phase curves in angle ***B***, beginning above half-line K_0 by monotonously reducing the slope coefficient to ***0,*** reach half-line M_1 and then pass into angle ***C*** (Fig. 3.7).

In a similar fashion, it is possible to describe behavior of the phase curves in angle ***B,*** beginning below half-line. The phase curves with time growth ***t*** by monotonously increasing slope coefficient to $+\infty$, reach half-line L_1, and then pass into angle ***A*** (Fig. 3.7).

Conclusions The economic substance of the results concerning behavior of the phase curves on the two-dimensional subspace of performance indicators x_1, x_2 consists in the following.

In case of market model of the chain "investments–innovations–competitiveness" under stable development of economy, area ***A*** is the "area of guaranteed gain in the competition" of the second enterprise. If performance indicators (x_1, x_2) during the initial point of time are in area ***A,*** then competitiveness of the second enterprise goes to $+\infty$, and competitiveness of the first enterprise goes to ***0***. In order to reduce the size of area ***A***, the first enterprise should reduce the threshold of the borrowed investments, as well as in case I.

Area ***C*** is the "area of guaranteed gain in the competition" of the first enterprise. If performance indicators (x_1, x_2) during the initial point of time are in area ***C,*** then competitiveness of the first enterprise goes to $+\infty$, and competitiveness of the second enterprise goes to ***0***. To reduce the size of area ***C***, the second enterprise should reduce the threshold of the borrowed investments c_2, as well as in case I.

The most substantial is the model of competitive struggle in the field of ***B***.

If in the initial point of time, performance indicators (x_1, x_2) are in area ***B,*** then both performance indicators decrease (until point (x_1, x_2) is in area ***B***). However, the behavior of performance indicators and, hence, competitiveness coefficients vary, as soon as the phase curve reaches the boundaries of area ***B***.

If in the initial point of time, performance indicators are in area ***B,*** above half-line K_0, then after a while, they reach half-line M_1. After that, performance indicator x_2 starts to increase, and performance indicator x_1 continues to decrease.

If in the initial point of time, performance indicators are in area ***B*** below half-line K_0 after a while, they reach half-line L_1. Then performance indicator x_1 starts to increase, and performance indicator x_2 continues to decrease.

If in the initial point of time, performance indicators lie in half-line K_0, then they will move along this half-line, monotonously decreasing. In such a case, competitiveness coefficients will be constant $K_1 = k_0$, $K_2 = 1/k_0$ where k_0 is a material positive root of polynominal *P*(*k*). Note that in this case, half-line K_0 which is a multitude of dynamic equilibrium in competitive struggle corresponds to unstable balance. For any performance indicators in the initial point of time in the vicinity of half-line L_0 but not belonging to L_0, after a while one of the parties wins in competitive struggle. In order to keep a certain balance in competitive struggle, there should be a system parameters management.

3.3.4 Case IV

Let us consider a situation specified in case III, assuming that $c_1, c_2 > 1$. This case corresponds to the crisis condition of economy when an investor wants to receive guaranteed profit and invests only if the competitiveness coefficient is more than 1.

Then straight lines $x_2 = c_1 x_1$ and $x_2 = x_1/c_2$ divide the first quadrant into three angles:

$$\begin{aligned} A &= \{x : x_2 < x_1/c_2, x_1, x_2 > 0\}, \\ D &= \{x : x_1/c_2 < x_2 < c_1 x_1, x_1, x_2 > 0\}, \\ C &= \{x : x_2 > c_1 x_1, x_1, x_2 > 0\}. \end{aligned}$$

In field ***A***, the index number of industrial production of the first enterprise is growing, and the index number of the second enterprise is decreasing. In field ***D***, both index numbers are growing. In field ***C***, the index number of the first enterprise is decreasing, and the index number of the second enterprise is growing.

As well as in case III, the phase curves of the system of equations (3.25) are graphics of solutions of Eq. (3.26) with a corresponding selection of direction of movement.

Isoclinic lines of the field of directions for Eq. (3.26) are straight lines $x_2 = kx_1$, $k > 0$. On these straight lines, derivative $\frac{dx_2}{dx_1}$ is equal to the constant which is calculated under formula (3.28).

Isoclinic line $x_2 = k_0 x_1$, where k_0 is determined under formula (3.28), has the slope ratio equal to a tangent of inclination angle of the field of directions.

Formula (3.28) implies that $k_0 > 0$ is an equation root

$$P(k) = 0, \tag{3.37}$$

if the isoclinic line with the specified properties exists. Here, $P(k) = k^3 - c_1 k^2 + rc_2 k - r$.

Let's assume in addition that $c_1, c_2 \leq 3$. We prove that in this case, Eq. (3.37) has a unique positive root k_0, in such a case, $1/c_2 < k_0 < c_1$.

Actually, if $k \geq c_1$, owing to a condition $c_1, c_2 > 1$, we have

$$P(k) = k^2(k - c_1) + r(c_2 k - 1) \geq r(c_2 k - 1) > 0. \tag{3.38}$$

If $0 < k < 1/c_2$, owing to a condition $c_1, c_2 > 1$, we receive

$$P(k) = k^2(k - c_1) + r(c_2k - 1) \leq k^2\left(\frac{1}{c_2} - c_1\right) < 0. \quad (3.39)$$

On the other hand, $P''(k) = 6k - 2c_1 = 2(3k - c_1) \leq 2\left(\frac{3}{c_2} - c_1\right) \geq 0$ for $k > 1/c_2$. Therefore owing to (3.38, 3.39) multinomial $P(k)$ has a unique valid root k_0 within interval $(1/c_2, c_1)$.

By construction, isoclinic line $x_2 = k_0x_1(x_1 > 0)$ is a solution of differential equation (3.26) and

$$K_0 = \{x : x_2 = k_0x_1, x_1 > 0\} \subset B.$$

For the points in angle ***C***, the following inequalities are performed:

$$x_1/x_2 - c_2 < 0 \text{ and } x_2/x_1 - c_1 > 0.$$

Hence,

$$\frac{dx_2}{dx_1} < 0 \ (x \in C). \quad (3.40)$$

Let's consider behavior of the field of directions on the sides of angle ***C***: $L_1 = \{x : x_2 = c_1x_1, x_1 > 0\}$ and $L_0 = \{x : x_1 = 0, x_2 > 0\}$.

It is evident that

$$\lim_{\substack{x \to x^0, \\ x \in C}} \frac{dx_2}{dx_1} = -\infty \ \left(x^0 = \left(x_1^0, x_2^0\right) \in L_1\right). \quad (3.41)$$

$$\lim_{\substack{x \to x^0, \\ x \in C}} \frac{dx_2}{dx_1} = 0 \ \left(x^0 \in L_0\right). \quad (3.42)$$

Formula (3.40–3.42) imply that in angle ***C***, the phase curves have vertical tangent lines in the points belonging to L_1. Then the slope ratio of the field of directions becomes negative, and on half-line L_2, the phase curves have horizontal tangent lines.

In each point of angle ***A***, the inclination angle of the field of directions is negative, i.e.,

$$\frac{dx_2}{dx_1} < 0 \ (x \in A). \quad (3.43)$$

Let's consider behavior of the field of direction on the sides of angle ***A***:

$$M_1 = \{x : x_2 = x_1/c_2, x_1 > 0\} \text{ and } M_0 = \{x : x_1 = 0, x_1 > 0\}.$$

It is evident that

$$\lim_{\substack{x \to x^0, \\ x \in A}} \frac{dx_2}{dx_1} = 0 \ \left(x^0 \in M_1\right) \tag{3.44}$$

$$\lim_{\substack{x \to x^0, \\ x \in A}} \frac{dx_2}{dx_1} = -\infty \ \left(x^0 \in M_0\right) \tag{3.45}$$

Formulas (3.43–3.45) imply that in angle ***A***, the phase curves have horizontal tangent lines in the points belonging to M_1. Then the slope ratio of the field of directions becomes final negative, and on half-line M_0, the phase curves have vertical tangent lines.

Now let us consider behavior of the phase curves in angle ***D***, beginning above half-line K_0.

Owing to Eq. (3.26), the slope ratio of the field of directions $\frac{dx_2}{dx_1} > 0$ on isoclinic line $\{x : x_2 = kx_1, x_1 > 0\}$ $(k_0 < k < c_1)$ is monotonously increasing at growing $\boldsymbol{k}$, in such a case,

$$\lim_{\substack{x \to x^0, \\ x \in B}} \frac{dx_2}{dx_1} = +\infty \ \left(x^0 \in L_1\right)$$

In such a case, the phase curves in angle ***D***, beginning above half-line K_0 by monotonously increasing the slope coefficient up to $+\infty$ reach half-line L_1, and then pass into angle ***C*** (Fig. 3.8).

In a similar fashion, it is possible to describe behavior of the phase curves in angle ***D***, beginning below half-line K_0. The phase curves with time growth $\boldsymbol{t}$ by monotonously reducing slope coefficient up to 0 reach half-line M_1 and then pass into angle ***A*** (Fig. 3.8).

Conclusions The economic substance of the above results concerning behavior of the phase curves in the two-dimensional subspace of performance indicators x_1, x_2 under crisis condition of economy consists in the following.

Under the crisis condition of economy, area ***A***, as in case III, is the "area of guaranteed gain in the competition" of the second enterprise.

If in the initial point of time, performance indicators (x_1, x_2) lie in area ***A***, competitiveness of the second enterprise goes to $+\infty$, and competitiveness of the first enterprise goes to ***0***. Contrary to case III, in this example, it is impossible to change the size of area ***A*** at the expense of changing the threshold of the borrowed investments c_1. However, the second enterprise interested in increasing area ***A***, can make it by means of reducing the threshold of the borrowed investments c_2.

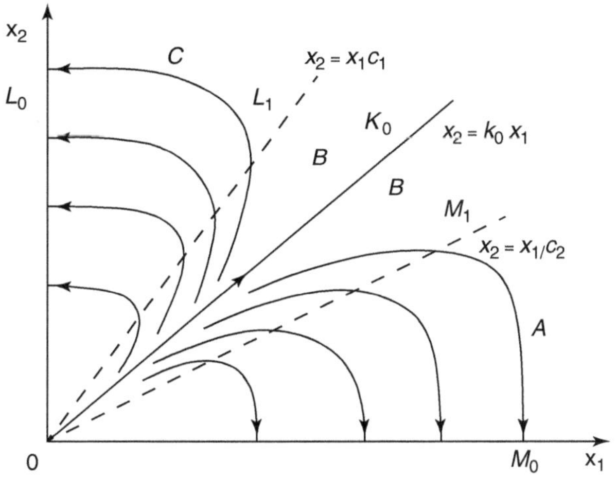

Fig. 3.8 The graphic of index numbers of industrial production of two enterprises under crisis development of economy

In a similar fashion, the area $\boldsymbol{C}$ (as in case III) is the "area of guaranteed gain in the competition" of the first enterprise. Contrary to case III, in this example it is impossible to change area $\boldsymbol{C}$ at the expense of changing the threshold of investments c_2. However, the first enterprise, interested in increase area $\boldsymbol{C}$, can make it by means of reducing the threshold of investments c_1.

If in the initial point of time, performance indicators are in field $\boldsymbol{D}$ further both performance indicators will be increasing until point (x_1, x_2) is in field $\boldsymbol{D}$.

If in the initial point of time, the performance indicators are in field $\boldsymbol{D}$ above half-line K_0, after a while, they reach half-line L_1. After that, as was shown earlier, the performance indicator x_1 will start to decrease, and performance indicator x_2 will continue to increase.

If in the initial point of time, the performance indicators are in field $\boldsymbol{D}$ below half-line K_0, after a while, they reach half-line M_1. Then the performance indicator x_1 will continue to increase, and the performance indicator x_2 will start to decrease.

If in the initial point of time, performance indicators (x_1, x_2) lie in half-line K_0, then they will move along this half-line, monotonically increasing. In such a case, competitiveness coefficients will be constant $K_1 = k_0$, $K_2 = 1/k_0$.

Keep in mind that straight line K_0, being a multitude of dynamic equilibrium in competitive struggle, corresponds to unstable balance. For any performance indicators, in the initial point of time in the vicinity of half-line K_0 but not belonging to K_0, after a while one of the parties wins in competitive struggle.

3.4 Dynamics Analysis of Performance Indicators of Competitive Products in General

In order to analyze the quality of mathematical modeling of competitiveness management, we shall consider dynamic model of changing performance indicators from Sect. 3.3 by writing down the system of nonlinear ordinary differential equations (3.15) in the following way

$$\begin{aligned}
\frac{dx_{11j}(t)}{dt} &= r_{11j}\left(\sum_{k=1}^{J_1} a_{1k}\frac{x_{11k}(t)}{x_{21k}(t)} + \sum_{k=1}^{J_2} a_{2k}\frac{x_{22k}(t)}{x_{12k}(t)} - c_1\right) \quad (j = 1, \ldots, J_1),\\
\frac{dx_{12j}(t)}{dt} &= -r_{12j}\left(\sum_{k=1}^{J_1} a_{1k}\frac{x_{11k}(t)}{x_{21k}(t)} + \sum_{k=1}^{J_2} a_{2k}\frac{x_{22k}(t)}{x_{12k}(t)} - c_1\right) \quad (j = 1, \ldots, J_2),\\
\frac{dx_{21j}(t)}{dt} &= r_{21j}\left(\sum_{k=1}^{J_1} a_{1k}\frac{x_{21k}(t)}{x_{11k}(t)} + \sum_{k=1}^{J_2} a_{2k}\frac{x_{12k}(t)}{x_{22k}(t)} - c_2\right) \quad (j = 1, \ldots, J_1),\\
\frac{dx_{21j}(t)}{dt} &= -r_{22j}\left(\sum_{k=1}^{J_1} a_{1k}\frac{x_{21k}(t)}{x_{11k}(t)} + \sum_{k=1}^{J_2} a_{2k}\frac{x_{12k}(t)}{x_{22k}(t)} - c_2\right) \quad (j = 1, \ldots, J_2).
\end{aligned} \tag{3.46}$$

Here
$r_{ilj},\ a_{lk},\ c_i > 0$ are constants,

$$\sum_{l,k} a_{lk} = 1,$$

$x_{i1j}(t)$—j-th index number of industrial production of the n-th enterprise, $(i = 1, 2,\ j = 1, \ldots, J_1)$ the growth of which promotes improvement of competitiveness,

$x_{i2j}(t)$—j-th index number of industrial production of the n-th enterprise, $(i = 1, 2,\ j = 1, \ldots, J_2)$ the growth of which contributes to competitiveness deterioration.

Let us denote the vector with positive coordinates x_{ilj} by $x \in \mathbb{R}^{2(J_1+J_2)}$, which are performance indicators.

According to formula (3.4), competitiveness coefficients $K_i(x)$ are calculated under formulas

$$K_i(x) = \sum_{k=1}^{J_1} a_{1k}\frac{x_{i1k}}{x_{s1k}} + \sum_{k=1}^{J_2} a_{2k}\frac{x_{s2k}}{x_{i2k}} \quad (i = 1, 2), \tag{3.47}$$

where $s = 2$, if $i = 1$ and $s = 1$, if $i = 2$.

Then the system of ordinary differential equations (3.46) will become

$$\begin{aligned}
\frac{dx_{11j}}{dt} &= r_{11j}(K_1(x) - c_1),\\
\frac{dx_{12j}}{dt} &= -r_{12j}(K_1(x) - c_1),\\
\frac{dx_{21j}}{dt} &= r_{21j}(K_2(x) - c_2),\\
\frac{dx_{22j}}{dt} &= -r_{22j}(K_2(x) - c_2).
\end{aligned} \tag{3.48}$$

Let's put in the following designations:

$$\begin{aligned}
A &= \left\{x \in \mathbb{R}^{2(J_1+J_2)}: \ K_1(x) - c_1 < 0, \ K_2(x) - c_2 > 0, \ x_{ilj} > 0\right\},\\
B &= \left\{x \in \mathbb{R}^{2(J_1+J_2)}: \ K_1(x) - c_1 > 0, \ K_2(x) - c_2 > 0, \ x_{ilj} > 0\right\},\\
C &= \left\{x \in \mathbb{R}^{2(J_1+J_2)}: \ K_1(x) - c_1 > 0, \ K_2(x) - c_2 < 0, \ x_{ilj} > 0\right\},\\
D &= \left\{x \in \mathbb{R}^{2(J_1+J_2)}: \ K_1(x) - c_1 < 0, \ K_2(x) - c_2 < 0, \ x_{ilj} > 0\right\}.
\end{aligned}$$

Note that some of these multitudes can be empty.

For example, if $J_1 = 1$, $J_2 = 0$, and $c_1, c_2 < 1$, then $D = \varnothing$, see case I in Sect. 3.3. This case corresponds to one index number of industrial production, when competitiveness improves at its increase. In this case, stable development of economy is considered.

If $J_1 = 1$, $J_2 = 0$, $c_1, c_2 < 1$ then $B = \varnothing$, see case II in Sect. 3.3. This case corresponds to one index number of industrial production, when competitiveness improves. In this case, crisis condition of economy is considered.

If $J_1 = 0, J_2 = 1$, and $c_1, c_2 < 1$, then $D = \varnothing$, see case III in Sect. 3.3. This case corresponds to one index number of industrial production, when competitiveness improves at its decrease. In this case, stable development of economy is considered.

If $J_1 = 0, J_2 = 1$, and $c_1, c_2 > 1$, then $B = \varnothing$, see case IV in Sect. 3.3. This case corresponds to one index number of industrial production, when competitiveness improves at its decrease. In this case, the crisis condition of economy is considered.

Let's prove now, that $A \neq \varnothing$.

Let us assume that $x_\varepsilon \in \mathbb{R}^{2(J_1+J_2)}$ is a point with coordinates $x_{iij} = \varepsilon(i = 1, 2, \ j = 1, \ldots, J_i)$, $x_{21j} = 1$, $(j = 1, \ldots, J_1)$; $x_{12j} = 1$, $(j = 1, \ldots, J_2)$.

Then $K_1(x_\varepsilon) = \varepsilon$ and $K_2(x_\varepsilon) = \frac{1}{\varepsilon}$. We choose $\varepsilon > 0$ so that $\varepsilon < \min\{c_1, 1/c_2\}$.

Then $K_1(x_\varepsilon) - c_1 < 0$ and $K_2(x_\varepsilon) - c_2 > 0$, i.e., $x_\varepsilon \in A$.

In such a case, it is proved that $A \neq \varnothing$.

In the same way, it is possible to illustrate that $C \neq \varnothing$.

Let's put in $(2(J_1 + J_2) - 1)$—dimensional smooth manifolds.

$$\begin{aligned}
L_1 &= \left\{x \in \mathbb{R}^{2(J_1+J_2)}: \ K_1(x) - c_1 = 0, \ x_{ilj} > 0\right\},\\
M_1 &= \left\{x \in \mathbb{R}^{2(J_1+J_2)}: \ K_2(x) - c_2 = 0, \ x_{ilj} > 0\right\}.
\end{aligned}$$

Let's imply $x(0) = x^0$ and $x(T) = x^T$, where $T > 0$.

Now we prove that if the vector of performance indicators during the initial point of time is in area ***A*,** then during the final time, the phase curve reaches one of coordinate planes $x_{11j} = 0$, $(j = 1, \ldots, J_1)$ or $x_{22j} = 0$, $(j = 1, \ldots, J_2)$. In such a case, the phase curve at increased $\boldsymbol{t}$ cannot reach manifolds L_1 or M_1.

Let us assume that $x^0 \in A$.We prove that the phase curve which is passing through point x^0, cannot reach manifold $L_1 \cup M_1$ for the final time. We assume the opposite: $x^T \in L_1 \cup M_1$, moreover, $T > 0$—the shortest time required for the trajectory to reach manifold $L_1 \cup M_1$. Without limiting generalities, we assume that $K_1(x^T) - c_1 = 0$ and $K_2(x^T) - c_2 \geq 0$. As $K_1(x^0) - c_1 < 0$, there should be interval $[t_1, t_2] \subset (0, T)$ so that on this interval, the competitiveness coefficient strictly increases, or it means that one of the performance indicators $x_{11j}(t)$ or $x_{22j}(t)$ strictly increases at $t \in [t_1, t_2]$, or one of the indicators $x_{21j}(t)$, $x_{12j}(t)$ strictly decreases. Hence, either the left parts of the first or the last equation of system (3.46) are positive, or the left parts of the second or the third equation of system (3.46) are negative. But it is contrary to the fact that the right parts of the first and the fourth equation of system (3.46) are not positive, and the right parts of the second and the third equations of system (3.46) are not negative. This conflict of results proves that the phase curve which is passing through point $x^0 \in A$ cannot reach manifold $L_1 \cup M_1$ for the final time.

Now we prove that the phase curve which is passing during the initial point of time $t = 0$ through point x^0 for final time reaches one of coordinate planes $x_{11j} = 0$ or $x_{22j} = 0$. It corresponds to the gain of the second enterprise in competitive struggle.

As it is proved above, along this phase curve,

$$K_1(x(t)) - c_1 < 0 \text{ and } K_2(x(t)) - c_2 > 0,$$

then owing to the system of equations (3.46)

$$\begin{aligned} &\frac{dx_{11j}(t)}{dt} < 0, \quad \frac{dx_{21j}(t)}{dt} > 0, \\ &(t \in (0, T), \quad j = 1, \ldots, J_1). \end{aligned} \tag{3.49}$$

$$\begin{aligned} &\frac{dx_{12j}(t)}{dt} > 0, \quad \frac{dx_{22j}(t)}{dt} < 0, \\ &(t \in (0, T), \quad j = 1, \ldots, J_2). \end{aligned} \tag{3.50}$$

Therefore, owing to formula (3.47) $K_1(t)$ is monotonously decreasing, and $K_2(t)$ is monotonously increasing. Hence, owing to the first and the fourth equations of system (3.49), we have

$$r_{11j}(c_1 - K_1(x^0)) \leq \left|\frac{dx_{11j}(t)}{dt}\right| \quad (t \in (0,T), \quad j = 1, \ldots, J_1). \tag{3.51}$$

$$r_{22j}(K_2(x^0) - c_2) \leq \left|\frac{dx_{22j}(t)}{dt}\right| \quad (t \in (0,T), \quad j = 1, \ldots, J_2). \tag{3.52}$$

Integrating the left and the right parts of inequalities (3.51) and (3.52) from ***0*** to T, we receive

$$r_{11j}(c_1 - K_1(x^0))T \leq x_{11j}^0 - x_{11j}^T \quad (j = 1, \ldots, J_1), \tag{3.53}$$

$$r_{22j}(K_2(x^0) - c_2)T \leq x_{22j}^0 - x_{22j}^T \quad (j = 1, \ldots, J_2). \tag{3.54}$$

Assuming that $x_{iij}^T = 0 \quad (i = 1, 2)$, we derive the following inequalities from (3.53) and (3.54):

$$T \leq \frac{x_{11j}^0}{r_{11j}(c_1 - K_1(x^0))} (j = 1, \ldots, J_1),$$

$$T \leq \frac{x_{22j}^0}{r_{22j}(K_2(x^0) - c_2)} (j = 1, \ldots, J_2).$$

In such a case, if in the initial point of time the vector of performance indicators x^0 belongs to manifold ***A***, then the second enterprise wins in competitive struggle for final time T; in such a case, time T is calculated from the above formula

$$T \leq \min_{i,j} \frac{x_{iij}^0}{r_{iij}(c_i - K_i(x^0))} \quad (i = 1, 2 \quad j = 1, \ldots, J_1). \tag{3.55}$$

In a similar fashion, it is possible to prove that $C \neq \varnothing$.

Besides, if the phase curve during the initial point of time $t = 0$ passes through point x^0 in area ***C***, then for final time T, the phase curve reaches one of coordinate planes $x_{12j} = 0, \ (j = 1, \ldots, J_1)$ or $x_{21j} = 0, \ (j = 1, \ldots, J_2)$, and there is calculation

$$T \leq \min_{i,j} \frac{x_{isj}^0}{r_{isj}(c_i - K_i(x^0))} \tag{3.56}$$

$$(i = 1, 2, \quad j = 1, \ldots, J_s, \quad s = 2 \text{ if } i = 1, s = 1 \text{ if } i = 2).$$

Same as previous, it is possible to show that the phase curve which is passing through point $x^0 \in C$, at increased $\boldsymbol{t}$ cannot reach manifolds L_1 and M_1.

Owing to the above stated, it is natural to name areas ***C*** and ***A*** the "areas of guaranteed gain in the competition" of the first and the second enterprises accordingly.

We investigate now a question whether there can be a nonempty manifold at the crossing of manifolds L_1 and M_1.

If $L_1 \cap M_1 \neq \varnothing$, we name point $x^0 \in L_1 \cap M_1$ as a special point of independent system of ordinary differential equations (3.15). By definition, in the special point, the right parts of the system of equations (3.15) become zero, i.e., both the growth and the decrease of performance indicators are not available.

In case $J_1 + J_2 = 1$, the system of equations (3.46) has no special points, see cases I–IV in Sect. 3.3.

Let's prove that in case $J_1 = 2$ and $J_2 = 0$, the system of equations (3.46) has no special points if $c_1, c_2 < 1$ and has an infinite set of special points if $c_1, c_2 < 1$.

Example 3.46. Let us assume that $J_1 = 2$ and $J_2 = 0$. Then the system of equations (3.46) will become

$$\begin{aligned} \frac{dx_{1j}}{dt} &= r_{1j}\left(\sum_{k=1,2} a_k \frac{x_{1k}}{x_{2k}} - c_1\right) \quad (j = 1, 2), \\ \frac{dx_{2j}}{dt} &= r_{2j}\left(\sum_{k=1,2} a_k \frac{x_{2k}}{x_{1k}} - c_2\right) \quad (j = 1, 2). \end{aligned} \tag{3.57}$$

Here $r_{ij}, c_i, \alpha_k > 0$ are constants, $\alpha_1 + \alpha_2 = 1$, x_{ij}—index numbers of industrial production of n-th enterprise, the growth of which promotes competitiveness improvement.

Point x^0 with coordinates x_{ij}^0 is a special one, in only case when equalities are satisfied

$$\begin{aligned} \sum_{k=1,2} a_k \frac{x_{1k}^0}{x_{2k}^0} - c_1 &= 0, \\ \sum_{k=1,2} a_k \frac{x_{2k}^0}{x_{1k}^0} - c_2 &= 0. \end{aligned} \tag{3.58}$$

Let's imply $z_1 = x_{11}^0 / x_{21}^0$, $z_2 = x_{12}^0 / x_{22}^0$, and $\alpha = \alpha_1$.
Owing to condition $\alpha_1 + \alpha_2 = 1$, we have $\alpha_2 = 1 - \alpha$.
Then the system of equations (3.28) will become

$$\left.\begin{aligned} &\alpha z_1 + (1-\alpha) z_2 - c_1 = 0 \\ &\frac{\alpha}{z_1} + \frac{1-\alpha}{z_2} - c_2 \end{aligned}\right\}. \tag{3.59}$$

From the first equation of system (3.59), it follows that

$$z_2 = \frac{c_1 - \alpha z_1}{1 - \alpha}. \tag{3.60}$$

Inserting this expression into the second equation of system (3.59), we have

$$\frac{\alpha}{z_1} + \frac{(1-\alpha)^2}{c_1 - \alpha z_1} - c_2 = 0.$$

Hence

$$\alpha c_1 - \alpha^2 z_1 + (1-\alpha)^2 z_1 - c_1 c_2 z_1 + c_2 \alpha z_1^2 = 0.$$

Let's imply $y = z_1$. Then

$$c_2 \alpha y^2 + (1 - 2\alpha - c_1 c_2) y + \alpha c_1 = 0. \tag{3.61}$$

If $1 - 2\alpha - c_1 c_2 > 0$, then Eq. (3.61) has no material positive roots.
Let's assume that

$$1 - 2\alpha - c_1 c_2 < 0. \tag{3.62}$$

In performing this condition, Eq. (3.61) has at least one material positive root in only case when

$$D = (c_1 c_2 - (1 - 2\alpha))^2 - 4\alpha^2 c_1 c_2 \geq 0$$

i.e.,

$$(c_1 c_2 - (1-2\alpha) - 2\alpha\sqrt{c_1 c_2})(c_1 c_2 - (1-2\alpha) + 2\alpha\sqrt{c_1 c_2}) \geq 0. \tag{3.63}$$

If $1 - 2\alpha - c_1 c_2 = 0$, then $D < 0$ and then Eq. (3.61) has no material roots. Owing to condition (3.62), the second factor in the left part of inequality (3.63) is positive. In such a case, condition (3.63) is equivalent to the following

$$(c_1 c_2 - (1-2\alpha) - 2\alpha\sqrt{c_1 c_2}) \geq 0. \tag{3.64}$$

Let's imply $\sqrt{c_1 c_2} = u$. Then inequality (3.64) becomes

$$\left(u^2 - 2\alpha u - (1-2\alpha)\right) \geq 0. \tag{3.65}$$

The roots of auxiliary equation

$$u^2 - 2\alpha u - (1 - 2\alpha) = 0$$

are calculated under formula

$$u_{1,2} = \alpha \pm \sqrt{\alpha^2 + (1-2\alpha)} = \alpha \pm (1-\alpha),$$

i.e., $u_1 = 1$, $u_2 = -1 + 2\alpha$.

Inequality (3.65) is satisfied in cases when $\sqrt{c_1 c_2} \leq -1 + 2\alpha$ or $\sqrt{c_1 c_2} \geq 1$ inequalities are satisfied.

Let us assume that $c_1, c_2 < 1$. Then inequality (3.65) is equivalent to the following inequality

$$\sqrt{c_1 c_2} \leq -1 + 2\alpha. \tag{3.66}$$

From inequality (3.66), it follows that

$$\alpha > \frac{1}{2}. \tag{3.67}$$

It is evident that (3.52) follows from (3.66).

So, performance of inequality (3.67) follows from condition of positivity of number $z_1 = x_{11}^0/x_{21}^0$. Owing to symmetry of the system of equations (3.59) relative to z_1 and z_2 with replacement of α for $1 - \alpha$, we have $1 - \alpha > 1/2$, i.e., $\alpha < 1/2$. The last inequality is contrary to inequality (3.67).

In such a case, it is proved that in a case where $c_1, c_2 < 1, J_1 = 2$, and $J_2 = 0$, the system of equations (3.46) has no special points.

Let us assume that now $c_1, c_2 > 1$. Then $c_1, c_2 > 1 > 1 - 2\alpha$, i.e., inequalities (3.52 and 3.54) are satisfied. Hence, both roots of Eq. (3.51)

$$y_{1,2} = \frac{c_1 c_2 - (1 - 2\alpha) \pm \sqrt{D}}{2\alpha c_2}$$

are real and positive.

Let's assume $z_1^1 = y_1 = \frac{c_1 c_2 - (1-2\alpha) + \sqrt{D}}{2\alpha c_2}$. Then using simple calculations, we receive

$$z_1^2 = \frac{c_1 - \frac{c_1 c_2 - (1-2\alpha) + \sqrt{D}}{2\alpha c_2}}{1 - \alpha} = \frac{c_1 c_2 + (1 - 2\alpha) - \sqrt{D}}{2c_2(1 - \alpha)} > 0. \tag{3.68}$$

Now $z_1^2 = y_2 = c_1 - \frac{c_1 c_2 - (1-2\alpha) - \sqrt{D}}{2\alpha c_2}$. Then from equality (3.50) and inequality (3.68), we receive

$$z_2^2 = \frac{c_1 - \frac{c_1 c_2 - (1-2\alpha) - \sqrt{D}}{2c_2}}{1 - \alpha} = \frac{c_1 c_2 + (1 - 2\alpha) + \sqrt{D}}{2c_2(1 - \alpha)} > 0. \tag{3.69}$$

So, we have proved that the system of equations (3.59) has two solutions (z_1^1, z_2^1) and (z_1^2, z_2^2) with positive coordinates. In such a case, the set of special points of the system of equations (3.57) looks like

$$L \cap M = \{x \in \mathbb{R}^4 : x_{11}/x_{21} = z_1^1, \ x_{12}/x_{22} = z_2^1, \ x_{ij} > 0\} \cup$$
$$\cup \{x \in \mathbb{R}^4 : x_{11}/x_{21} = z_1^2, \ x_{12}/x_{22} = z_2^2, \ x_{ij} > 0\}$$

From the reasons of continuity, it follows that in a case $c_1, c_2 > 1$, in case of any $J_1 \geq 2$ and $J_2 \geq 1$, the set of special points $L_1 \cap M_1$ is infinite.

It means that under a crisis condition of economy, there is an infinite set of points of $2(J_1 + J_2)$—dimensional phase space, where performance indicators of both enterprises do not vary, i.e., two enterprises face a simultaneous stagnation due to nonavailability of investments.

In case of stable condition of economy under any certain $J_1 > 2$ and $J_2 > 0$, the question on existence of nonempty set of special points remains open.

3.5 Dynamics Modeling of the Index Numbers of Competitive Products Output by Means of Functional Differential Equations with Regard to Lagged Effect

In the general case, it is necessary to take account of lagging in receiving information and managerial decision-making. Then, instead of the system of ordinary differential equations (3.46) specified in Sect. 3.4, one must study corresponding system of functional differential equations or the equations with lag variables.

In the construction of adequate dynamics model of competitive products, it is necessary to take account of the lagged effect in time. During modeling, the lagging can be included in various correlations:

In functional dependence of innovations on investments,
In functional dependence of performance indicators on innovations,
In functional dependence of investments on competitiveness coefficient, etc.

Availability of lagging is connected with the after-action effect. For example, creation of the innovations received as a result of investments requires some time τ. In such a case, the innovations received at the point of time τ should depend on investments at point of time $t - \tau$. In other words, there is a new lag variable $t - \tau$.

Taking into account these arguments, we derive functional differential equations describing dynamics model of competitive products output with regard to lagged effect.

Let's assume that there are two competitor enterprises.

Let $u_i = u_i(t) \quad (i = 1, 2)$ denote investments of the n-th enterprise into creation of innovations at the point of time τ, and $p_i = p_i(t) \quad (i = 1, 2)$ denote innovations of the n-th enterprise.

It would appear reasonable that with regard to lagging, innovations at the point of time τ are proportional to investments at the point of time $t = \tau_{i1}$ with particular fixed factor a_i, i.e.,

$$p_i(t) = a_i u_i(t - \tau_{i1}) \quad (i = 1, 2). \tag{3.70}$$

Where

$a_i, \tau_{i1} > 0$—constants,
τ_{i1}—lagging in the course of innovations.

Let $x_{i1j} = x_{i1j}(t) \quad (j = 1, \ldots, J_1)$ denote index number of industrial production of the n-th enterprise, the growth of which corresponds to competitiveness improvement. Quality of products can be use as such indicator, for example.

Let $x_{i2j} = x_{i2j}(t) \quad (j = 1, \ldots, J_2)$ denote index number of industrial production of the n-th enterprise, the decrease of which corresponds to competitiveness improvement. Production cost price can be used as such indicator, for example.

Competitiveness coefficient of the j-th index number of industrial production, the growth of which promotes competitiveness improvement, for the first and the second enterprises are determined from the formulas

$$K_{11j}(t) = \frac{x_{11j}(t)}{x_{21j}(t)} \quad (j = 1, \ldots, J_1), \tag{3.71}$$

$$K_{21j}(t) = \frac{x_{21j}(t)}{x_{11j}(t)} \quad (j = 1, \ldots, J_1), \tag{3.72}$$

accordingly.

Competitiveness coefficient of the j-th index number of industrial production, the decrease of which promotes competitiveness improvement, for the first and the second enterprises are determined from the formulas

$$K_{12j}(t) = \frac{x_{22j}(t)}{x_{12j}(t)} \quad (j = 1, \ldots, J_2), \tag{3.73}$$

$$K_{22j}(t) = \frac{x_{12j}(t)}{x_{22j}(t)} \quad (j = 1, \ldots, J_2), \tag{3.74}$$

accordingly.

Competitiveness coefficient of the n-th enterprise for a particular type of production is determined as follows:

$$K_i(t) = \sum_{l=1,2} \sum_{j=1}^{J_l} \alpha_{lj} K_{ilj}(t), \tag{3.75}$$

where $\alpha_{lj} > 0$—weighing coefficients.

Let's assume that for the first group of the index numbers of industrial production $x_{i1j}(t)$ the rates of their change at the point of time τ are proportional to innovations at the point of time $t - \tau_{i2}$ with some constant positive coefficients b_{i1j}, i.e.,

$$\frac{dx_{i1j}(t)}{dt} = b_{i1j}p_i(t - \tau_{i2}) \quad (i = 1, 2, \ j = 1, \ldots, J_1). \tag{3.76}$$

where $b_{i1j}, \tau_{i2} > 0$,

τ_{i2}—lagging in the course of innovations.

For the second group of the index numbers of industrial production $x_{i1j}(t)$, it would appear reasonable that with regard to lagging, the rates of their change at the point of time are t proportional to innovations at the point of time $t - \tau_{i2}$ with some constant negative factors $-b_{i2j}$, i.e.,

$$\frac{dx_{i2j}(t)}{dt} = b_{i2j}p_i(t - \tau_{i2}) \quad (i = 1, 2, \ j = 1, \ldots, J_2). \tag{3.77}$$

where $b_{i2j}, \tau_{i2} > 0$,

τ_{i2}—lagging in the course of innovations.

It is evident that investments $u_i(t)$ depend on product competitiveness coefficient $K_i(t)$.

It would appear reasonable that investments $u_i(t)$ are used in development of innovations only in case when competitiveness coefficient $K_i(t)$ is more than some threshold value $c_i > 0$, and investments at the point of time τ are proportional to value $K_i(t - \tau_{i3}) - c_i$ with some fixed factor $d_i > 0$, i.e.,

$$u_i(t) = d_i(K_i(t - \tau_{i3}) - c_i), \tag{3.78}$$

where $\tau_{i3} > 0$—lagging in the course of investment.

Similar to Sect. 3.2, in case when $K_i(t) < c_i$, negative investments are understood as expenses of the enterprise from internal reserves for continuation of innovative activities.

From correlations (3.70)–(3.78), we receive system $2(J_1 + J_2)$ of nonlinear functional differential equations describing dynamics model of change of the index numbers of industrial production $x_{ilj} \quad (i, l = 1, 2, \ j = 1, \ldots, J_l)$ with regard for lagging,

$$\frac{dx_{11j}(t)}{dt} = r_{11j}\left(\sum_{k=1}^{J_1} a_{1k}\frac{x_{11k}(t-\tau_1)}{x_{21k}(t-\tau_1)} + \sum_{k=1}^{J_2} a_{2k}\frac{x_{22k}(t-\tau_1)}{x_{12k}(t-\tau_1)} - c_1\right) \quad (j = 1, \ldots, J_1),$$
$$\frac{dx_{12j}(t)}{dt} = -r_{12j}\left(\sum_{k=1}^{J_1} a_{1k}\frac{x_{11k}(t-\tau_1)}{x_{21k}(t-\tau_1)} + \sum_{k=1}^{J_2} a_{2k}\frac{x_{22k}(t-\tau_1)}{x_{12k}(t-\tau_1)} - c_1\right) \quad (j = 1, \ldots, J_2),$$
$$\frac{dx_{21j}(t)}{dt} = r_{21j}\left(\sum_{k=1}^{J_1} a_{1k}\frac{x_{21k}(t-\tau_2)}{x_{11k}(t-\tau_2)} + \sum_{k=1}^{J_2} a_{2k}\frac{x_{12k}(t-\tau_2)}{x_{22k}(t-\tau_2)} - c_2\right) \quad (j = 1, \ldots, J_1),$$
$$\frac{dx_{21j}(t)}{dt} = -r_{22j}\left(\sum_{k=1}^{J_1} a_{1k}\frac{x_{21k}(t-\tau_2)}{x_{11k}(t-\tau_2)} + \sum_{k=1}^{J_2} a_{2k}\frac{x_{12k}(t-\tau_2)}{x_{22k}(t-\tau_2)} - c_2\right) \quad (j = 1, \ldots, J_2). \tag{3.79}$$

Here $\tau_i = \tau_{i1} + \tau_{i2} + \tau_{i3} > 0$—constant laggings,
$r_{ilj} = \ a_i b_{ilj} d_i > 0$ and $c_i > 0$—constants $(i, l = 1, 2, \ \ j = 1, \ldots, J_l)$.

In such a case, we have received the required system of functional differential equations.

As is known, for correct statement of initial problem for the system of ordinary differential equations (3.46), it is necessary to set values of unknown functions $x_{ilj}(t)$ corresponding to performance indicators at the point of time $t = 0$. In other words, we should consider the system of equations (3.46) with initial conditions

$$x_{ilj}(0) = x^0_{ilj} \quad (i, l = 1, 2, \ \ j = 1, \ldots, J_l)\,, \tag{3.80}$$

Contrary to the ordinary differential equations, in case of functional differential equations, initial conditions are set not in the point but at some interval. In such a case, for the system of functional differential equations (3.81), initial conditions look like

$$x_{ilj}(t) = \varphi_{ilj}(t) \quad (t \in [-\tau, 0] \quad i, l = 1, 2, \ \ j = 1, \ldots, J_l)\,, \tag{3.81}$$

Where $\tau = \max\{\tau_1, \tau_2\}$, $\varphi_{ilj}(t)$—the set functions, continuous in interval $[-\tau, 0]$.

As analogue of $2(J_1 + J_2)$—measured phase space used in Sect. 3.4. for qualitative analyses of the system of ordinary differential equations (3.46), in case of the system of functional differential equations (3.79), one must use infinite-dimensional phase space the points of which are the functions $\left(x_{ilj}\right)_t : [-\tau, 0] \to \mathbb{R}$ determined under formula $\left(x_{ilj}\right)_t = x_{ilj}(t + s)$.

For qualitative analyses of system (3.79) with initial conditions (3.82) or with boundary conditions, it is possible to use numerical methods. In application of numerical methods for solution of initial problem (3.79) and (3.81) for the system of functional differential, one must take into account the loss of solution smoothness in points $k\tau_i$ $(k = 1, 2, \ldots)$.

Conclusions In the construction of mathematical models describing dynamics of competitiveness coefficient of enterprises for the purpose of competitiveness management of the said enterprises, one must take account of lagging in managerial decision-making and economic processes. According to the qualitative analysis of nonlinear functional differential equations describing dynamics of the rates of competitiveness of the enterprises, management of the lagging factors can essentially influence changing of competitiveness followed by development of new approaches to competitiveness management of the enterprises which produce high-tech goods.

Quantitative Evaluation of the Product Competitiveness

4

4.1 Methodology of Quantitative Evaluation of the Product Competitiveness

Product competitiveness as a competitiveness of the goods, first of all, is a possibility of their distribution in the domestic or foreign markets in the presence of competitors.

The consumer often prefers such goods (products) which, per unit of consumption price (price + consumption cost), serve more needs than the goods of a competitor.

In general terms, competitiveness = useful effect/consumption price. Consumption prices for the capital goods (producer goods) are usually higher than the sale price. Consumption price is formed on the basis of the general expenses connected with the product's life cycle. Therefore, the goods with the lowest consumption price for all the product life cycle are the most competitive. It is useful to highlight in this regard that within the framework of the enterprise (firm), being actually sold are not only commodity items but a broad range of services important for the consumer and connected with the goods' life cycle and after-sales service of cars, equipment, and materials involved in consumption of the said goods at all the stages of the after-sales life cycle. It should be noted that the buyer may carry some financial expenses throughout a long period of time, subject to the goods life cycle.

Subject competition is competitiveness between the similar items and services of various firms which vary in price, degree of quality, and other figures. The concept of the products differentiation which has become a frequent practice in the markets of the developed countries is at the heart of the subject competition. This differentiation covers both consumer items and means of production, which is reflected in deepening of specialization and growing share of small-scale industries.

The relation between the subject form of competition and the product competitiveness is obvious. Entering a particular market with the goods, the manufacturer (seller), as a rule, in the majority of cases assumes there are similar items in the

A. Chursin, Y. Makarov, *Management of Competitiveness*,
DOI 10.1007/978-3-319-16244-7_4

market and, accordingly, takes this circumstance into account to ensure products' competitiveness.

The competition between the goods which meet one requirement is called a functional competition. The functional competition may take place even in case of the products with unique characteristics.

The interrelation between the functional form of competition and the product competitiveness has a latent character to a certain extent. With the functional form of competition, there is a "rivalry" of the products of various industries that meet the similar specific requirements.

Hence, entering the market, a seller should assume that its production will face a competition not only from the me-too products but also from the part of both functionally homogeneous and functionally heterogeneous groups of items in case they are substitution goods intended to meet the same requirements of the buyer. It bears reminding that manufacturers of the substitute products represent one of competitive forces, as per M. Porter.

Efficiency of managerial decision-making depends on timeliness, objectivity, and relevance of information. Besides, the information should not be fragmented when offered to the head; it should be provided in a compact and human-friendly way, displaying complete picture of the firm functioning and with account of external and internal factors it is influenced by.

External factors are created and regulated by the current market mechanisms, rather than by a separate firm (competitors, suppliers of raw materials, materials, components, and various types of service), indirectly influencing price policy, scientific & technical, and industrial policy of a firm, as well as by the state in the form of economic, political, and administrative mechanisms of the state control, specific and mixed capital firms, and industries in general (state laws, normative act, governmental decrees, standards, norms and rules, and political and economic conditions). These factors, depending on the state economic policy, act as the limitations of specific frameworks when a firm cannot do business beyond the scope (taxes, tariffs, and customs barriers), and as an incentive to create more competitive products, increase the industry export and gross output (grants, benefits, and investments).

Internal factors influencing competitiveness of the firm and its products are the technological level of production, qualification of personnel, development strategy, and its financial and economic policy. Under effective accounting, analysis, and management, the internal factors make it possible to create competitive advantages for the output products and the firm as a whole.

When new products appear in the market and give rise to increase of uncertainty level of consumer preferences, traditional methods of management of the specified factors can jeopardize their efficiency. In this case, mismatch of the products parameters to consumer requirements becomes an immediate cause of reduction in sales and growth of residual stock of the finished goods and, hence, deterioration of financial status of the firm. In order to avoid deterioration of financial situation and, as a consequence, loss of possibility of stable development, the firm in the sphere of management, creation, and introduction of competitive advantages should:

- Provide competitive advantage of the goods in the commodity markets;
- Provide new consumer properties to the goods in order to enter various markets with the help of advertising to form demand and sales promotion;
- Develop and master industrial production of essentially new goods with the high consumer properties to ensure sale on external and home markets;
- Develop flexible price policy.

Doing this requires performing evaluation of the products competitiveness within the sales framework in the following sequence:

- To perform analysis of the market and selection of the most competitive goods as opposed to the competitors in the said market;
- To determine the most essential characteristics of the various items determining their competitiveness in the commodity market;
- To calculate an integrated index of the product competitiveness.

The data for accounting and analysis of the firm activities should be taken on the basis of the principal objective of its activity—mission. The amount of such data with their priority ranking should be optimal to make it possible for the head to make a managerial decision concerning both the separate special case and the overall objective of the firm activities. However, in as much as even the optimum quantity of such data is a very considerable body, their analysis is a labor-intensive task; in practice, in many cases they resort to the methods of mathematical modeling which help to determine a basic composite index on the basis of calculation and accounting of the separate indices weighting. We shall illustrate how the product competitiveness is determined with the help of mathematical modeling.

Figure 4.1 offers a scheme of stage-by-stage evaluation of influence of various factors of external and internal environment on the product competitiveness.

A number of methods concerning product competitiveness evaluation are applied now: differential, complex, and mixed. The mixed method is chosen as the most comprehensible for evaluation of the product competitiveness level. The point is in the joint application of single and integrated indices (differential and integrated methods).

There is a following response protocol in the mixed method:

- The most important indices of the product competitiveness are used as individual (specific) figures compared with the similar competitiveness indices of the product sample.
- Other individual indices are integrated in groups with specified group (generalized) indices of the product competitiveness.
- On the basis of a set of generalized and specific indices, competitiveness level is evaluated by a differential method.

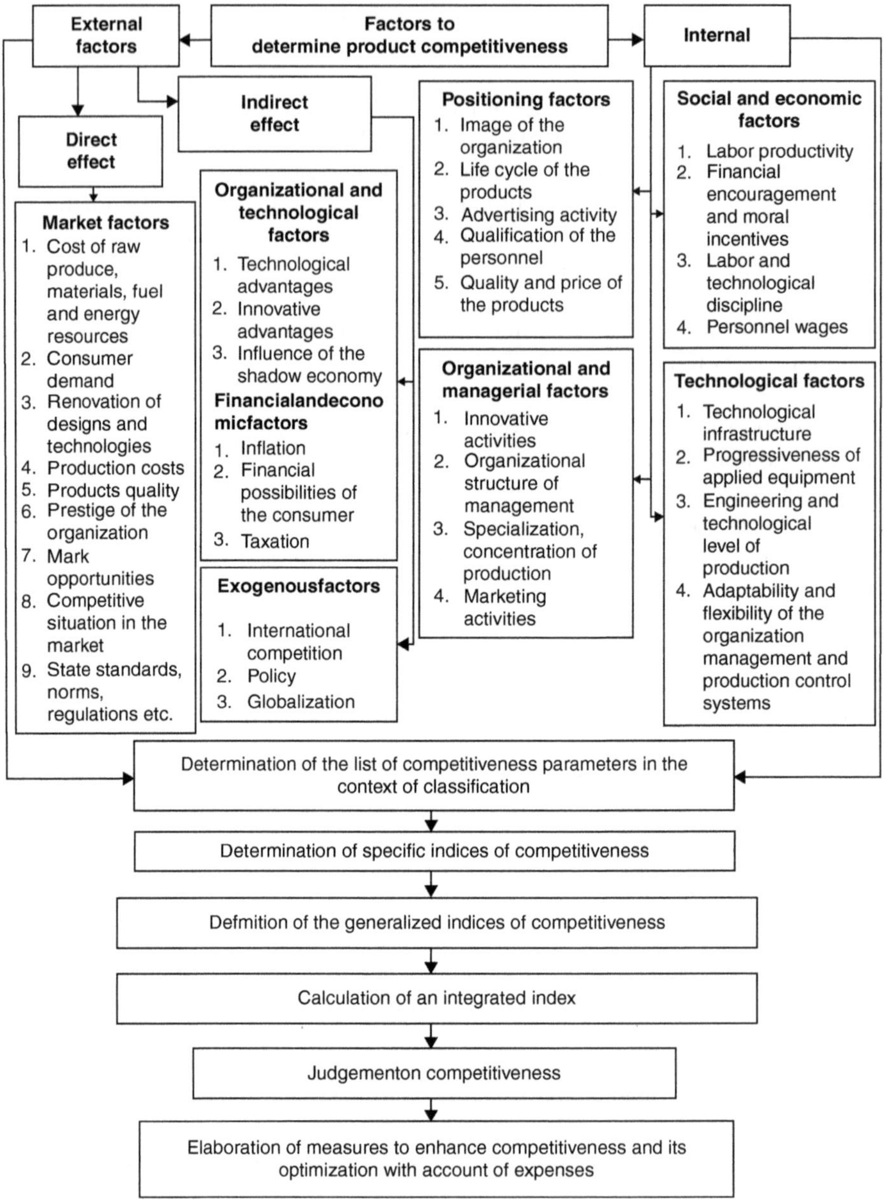

Fig. 4.1 Evaluation of influence of various external and internal factors on the product competitiveness

On the basis of Fig. 4.1, it is safe to say that in the course of evaluation of the product competitiveness, it is necessary to make correct choice and determine quantitative specific and composite indices.

Specific indices make it possible to estimate possible influence of external and internal factors on creation and marketing of the products. Specific index is a statistical basis for formation of the summary figures and composite indices and an initial basis for making managerial decisions on creation of a certain type of the products, their updating, or phasing out. Specific indices—coefficients of evaluation of the product competitiveness level—reflect its condition according to one or another characteristic: technical characteristics, cost of a particular type of materials, inflation, or custom duties. Specific indices characterize competitive properties of the products.

It is important to emphasize that it would be too low just to find out what factor influences competitiveness in a greater or lesser degree.

For objective evaluation of the product competitiveness, provisions should be made to determine the most significant factors influencing competitive manufacturing, to analyze them, and to forecast their change in the future in order to determine product competitiveness both in real time and in the long run with a reasonable degree of accuracy.

The composite indices are chosen so that their contents would have certain rational value to study the position of the products and tendencies of their life cycle. The composite index reflects interaction of a set (total or found in another way) of specific indices with an allowance for their weighting in this generalized interaction. During formation of composite indices, it is important to determine correctly the significance of specific indices as their components.

The composite indices determined on the basis of specific indices make it possible to form an integrated index of the product competitiveness within the framework of the mixed approach. It will give the chance to the head of a firm to make a judgment on competitiveness of the output products, and in case of need on the basis of available information, to make managerial decisions on regulation of the firm's competitive policy concerning the output products: to update the products, to take them out of production, and to increase output volume.

It is possible to offer the following methodology of determining specified indices.

Each product can be characterized by a certain set of specific indices S estimating competitiveness of the said products in the market. During analysis of specific indices, a key problem is the selection of a product sample to compare indices of production sample and the products under evaluation and define numerical value of competitiveness coefficient in such a manner.

In order to evaluate production competitive advantages, characterizing its scientific & technical potential, it is necessary to choose a set of corresponding parameters of product sample $S_0^{\prime}$ reflecting achievements of Scientific-Technological Progress (STP) in the field of creation of this type of production: technical characteristics, ergonomic, ecological and resource indices.

As other indices which do not reflect achievements of STP, there may be used a set of corresponding specific indices of goods sample S_0: economic, consumer, indices of required useful effect, and competitiveness.

Hence, among specific indices of production, provisions should be made to determine the indicators to be compared with the indices reflecting achievements of STP in the field of creation of this type of production:

$$S' \subset S \tag{4.1}$$

Specific indices of the product sample to be compared with the indices of output production are formed of two sets: sets of the indices provided by traditional mixed method S_0—indices of the buyers' requirements, parameters of competing goods, and a set of specific indices of the STP achievements in creation of this type of production S_0'.

The product competitiveness coefficient under the partial detail described by the corresponding specific index can be calculated by formula

$$K_i = \frac{s_i}{s_{i0}}. \tag{4.2}$$

where K_i—competitiveness coefficient according to the i-th specific index;
s_i—value of the i-th analyzed specific index out of the set of specific indices $(s_i \in S_0)$.
s_{i0}—value of the i-th basic specific index of the sample out of the set of its specific indices $(s_{i0} \in S_0)$.

Let us remark here that in the calculation of, for example, competitiveness coefficient at the rate of cost and prices, there is an inverse dependence:

$$K_i = \frac{s_{i0}}{s_i}. \tag{4.3}$$

In other words, from among formulas (4.2) and (4.3), we select the one according to which changing of index K_i corresponds to competitiveness increase. For example, if expenses for material purchasing are lower than the competitor's expenses for purchasing of the same material, then the products under consideration are more competitive according to this index which was to be proved in the formula in the form of inverse dependence of parameters (4.3).

In case of comparison of technical indices of production with the indices reflecting achievements of STP under this type of production, the competitiveness coefficient is calculated by formula

$$K_i' = \frac{s_i'}{s_{i0}'}. \tag{4.4}$$

where s_{i0}'—value of the i-th basic specific index (index of the sample) out of the set of specific indices reflecting achievements of STP $(s_{i0}' \in S')$.

It is obvious that in the context of the product competitiveness coefficients K_i and $K_i^{'}$, it is possible to draw the following conclusions:

- if $0 \leq K_i < 1 \quad \left(0 \leq K_i^{'} < 1\right)$, then product competitiveness according to index $s_i(s_i^{'})$ is lower than the competitiveness of the competitor's goods with which the products under consideration are compared;
- if $K_i > 1 \quad \left(K_i^{'} < 1\right)$, then product competitiveness according to index $s_i(s_i^{'})$ is higher than the competitiveness of the competitor's goods;
- if $K_i = 1 \quad \left(K_i^{'} = 1\right)$, then product competitiveness according to index $s_i(s_i^{'})$ is equal to the competitiveness of the competitor's goods under the similar parameter;
- if $K_i \approx 1 \quad \left(K_i^{'} \approx 1\right)$, then according to index $s_i(s_i^{'})$, the products are noncompetitive. This case is inadmissible in forming product competitiveness. For each and every index $s_i(s_i^{'})$, the competitiveness coefficient should be strictly larger than zero: $K_i > 1 \quad \left(K_i^{'} > 1\right)$. Otherwise the output products, being noncompetitive at least in terms of one of competitiveness indices, do not possess one of the necessary competitive advantages for their successful marketing, which becomes a "bottleneck" in formation of the product competitiveness , a risk to lose a part of commodity market and to lose in competitive struggle.

It should be noted that by comparison of specific scientific & technical indices of production with the corresponding indices reflecting achievements of STP, competitiveness coefficient will be always calculated by formula (4.4) and $0 < K_i^{'} \leq 1$, as the achievements of STP for all production companies are always new developments and innovations intended to enhance their competitiveness.

The composite indices can be calculated by the following formulas:

The composite index of the product competitiveness by cost

$$Q_c = \sum_{i=1}^{n_1} K_{c,i}\alpha_i. \tag{4.5}$$

where n_1—number of specific indices to characterize cost;

$K_{c,i}$—product competitiveness coefficient according to the i-th specific index to characterize cost of production (expenditure for materials and components, inflation, and wages);

α_i—coefficient reflecting weighting of this specific index in evaluation of the product competitiveness by means of the composite index.

The significance of specific indices, as a rule, is found through economic laws and is described by mathematical dependences as well as by expertise and assumes values $0 \leq \alpha_i \leq 1$. Moreover, during calculation of each composite index for weighting coefficients of the specific indices which constitute a part of the composite index, the condition should be met

$$\sum_{i} \alpha_i = 1. \tag{4.6}$$

As a mechanism to determine weighting of specific and composite indices of competitiveness of a product or a firm, etc., a modified method of analysis hierarchical structures is provided to use.

Provisions should be made to pay special attention to specific indices of the product competitiveness with the greatest weighting coefficients.

Within the framework of every composite index, there may be accounted the indicators reflecting achievements of STP in the field of creation of this type of production and other chosen samples. For example, in order to calculate a composite index of the product competitiveness by cost, it is necessary to consider both the index of the workers' wages, compared with the similar index of competitor's production (sample) and the cost parameter of the modern resources and components for this type of production under conditions of the current scientific & technical developments. Then expression (4.5) may be presented as follows:

$$Q_c = \sum_{i=1}^{j} K_{c,i}\alpha_i + \sum_{i=j+1}^{n_1} K'_{c,i}\alpha_i,$$

where $K'_{c,i}$—product competitiveness coefficient, characterizing its cost according to the i-th specific index compared with the corresponding specific index, reflecting achievements of STP by this type of production.

It should be noted that for the weighting coefficients of all specific indices (s_i and s'_i) in forming a single composite index, this condition is met (4.6). Hence, for weighting coefficients of specific indices of the product competitiveness by cost, determining $\boldsymbol{Q_c}$, this condition is met $\sum_{i=1}^{n_1} \alpha_i = 1$.

The composite index of the product technological level is determined in the same way:

$$Q_t = \sum_{i=1}^{j} K_{t,i}\alpha_i + \sum_{i=j+1}^{n_2} K'_{t,i}\alpha_i,$$

where $K_{t,i}$—product competitiveness coefficient according to the i-th specific index characterizing technological level of production (technical and technological characteristics);

$K'_{t,i}$—product competitiveness coefficient according to the i-th specific index characterizing technological level of production, compared with a corresponding index of achievements of STP by this type of production;

n_2—number of specific indices characterizing technological level of production.

Here this condition is met too $\sum_{i=1}^{n_2} \alpha_i = 1.$

The number of the composite indices required for accounting is found depending on complexity of the firm structure, type of the output products, and condition of the market where the products should be sold.

Besides the abovementioned composite indices of the product competitiveness by cost and technological level, there may determined:

- Information composite index of competitiveness with specific indices of competitiveness providing information about production in the market (about its advertising, firm brand) considered within its framework;
- Composite environmental coefficient of influence on product competitiveness (political and economic situation, administrative orders, behavior of competitors).

In general terms, the composite index of the product competitiveness can be presented by formula

$$Q = \sum_{i=1}^{j} K_i \alpha_i + \sum_{i=j+1}^{n} K_i' \alpha_i,$$

where K_i—product competitiveness coefficient according to the i-th specific index compared with the similar specific index of production sample;

K_i'—product competitiveness coefficient according to the i-th specific index compared with the corresponding index, reflecting achievements of STP by this type of production;

n_2—number of considered specific indices.

Here, the condition for all weighting coefficients is met too: $\sum_{i=1}^{n} \alpha_i = 1.$

The integrated index of competitiveness of the output products will be determined by formula

$$K_I = \sum_{i=1}^{N} Q_i \alpha_i / \sum_{i=1}^{N} \alpha_i,$$

where Q_i—composite index of the product competitiveness;

α_i—weighting coefficient of the composite index of the product competitiveness ;

N—number of composite indices of the product competitiveness taken into consideration.

It should be noted that condition $\sum_{i=1}^{N} \alpha_i = 1$ is met here too.

It is obvious that the purpose of any firm is achievement of such values of the composite indices of the product competitiveness when condition $K_I \to \max$ is met.

Hence, within the framework of determining product competitiveness and its management, there should be system-defined value of all specific and composite indices in achieving the set goal—enhancement of the product competitiveness:

$$\left.\begin{array}{ll} K_{i_1} > 0, & i_1 = 1, \ldots, N_1; \\ K'_{i_2} > 0, & i_2 = 1, \ldots, N_2; \\ Q_{i_3} = \sum\limits_{i=1}^{j(i_3)} K_{i_3}\alpha_{i_3} + \sum\limits_{i=j(i_3)+1}^{n(i_3)} K'_{i_3}\alpha_{i_3}, & i_3 = 1, \ldots, N_3; \end{array}\right\}. \tag{4.7}$$

$$K_I = \sum_{m=1}^{M} Q_m\alpha_m / \sum_{m=1}^{M} \alpha_m \to \max,$$

where K_{i_1}—product competitiveness coefficient according to the i_I-th specific index.

N_1—number of specific indices of the product competitiveness.

K'_{i_2}—product competitiveness coefficient according to the i_2-th specific scientific & technical index.

N_2—number of specific scientific-technical indices of the product competitiveness.

Q_{i_3}—i_3-th composite index of the product competitiveness.

$j(i_3)$—number of specific indices of the product competitiveness in the i_3-th composite index.

α_i—weighting index of the product competitiveness coefficient K_i (or K'_i).

$(n(i_3) - j(i_3))$—number of specific scientific-technical indices of the product competitiveness in the i_3-th composite index.

N_3—number of the composite indices of the product competitiveness.

$\sum\limits_{i_3=1}^{n(i_3)} \alpha_{i_3} = 1$ for any composite index Q_{i_3}.

K_I—integrated index of the product competitiveness.

M—number of the composite indices of the product competitiveness in the integral coefficient.

$\sum\limits_{m=1}^{M} \alpha_m = 1$ for integrated index K_I.

The integrated indices of competitiveness of all types of the firm production and analysis of specific and composite indices with account of their weight in the integrated index of competitiveness will make it possible for the firm management to determine so-called "bottleneck" in production of goods, namely, the least competitive products, and on the basis of the analytical data—to determine the reasons of low competitiveness of the said products. Whereas it will give a chance to make a managerial decision on the products competitiveness regulation, which includes the development of a number of measures concerning enhancement of competitiveness coefficients with too small value (by use of modern materials, processing means and methods, change of supplier or a commodity market), and to producing of updated items with new competitive advantages or to take this type of items out of production.

In so doing, the firm will get rid of the weak point in the activity in due time, anticipate would-be losses from selling noncompetitive goods, strengthen its positions in the market with no risk of losing competitiveness by the indices of the said production, and will raise the general competitiveness.

As noted above, in order to enhance objectivity and timeliness of making managerial decision and providing a possibility to avoid negative consequences as a result of constant influence of changing external and internal environment on the firm activity, the product competitiveness should be forecasted for a long term. With this aim in view, provisions should be made to provide forecasting of specific indices, for which the weighting is not lower than the set value (for example, $\alpha \geq 0,1$) with the help of modeling approach with account of the weighting coefficients. For such specific indices, it is necessary to provide their time-dependent behavior that will make it possible forecasting competitiveness coefficient in future, i.e., it is necessary to provide the task of a set of specific indices of the product competitiveness S and achievements of STP S' in time. Then formulas (4.1, 4.2, and 4.3) will become accordingly:

$$S'(t) \subset S(t);$$
$$K_i(t) = \frac{s_i(t)}{s_{i0}(t)};$$
$$K_i(t) = \frac{s_{i0}(t)}{s_i(t)}.$$

Forecasting of the indices reflecting achievements of STP in creation of this type of production is possible on the basis of scientific forecast of development of the industry, areas of science and technology, and perspectives of materials' developments and components. The formula (4.4) takes on the appearance of:

$$K'_i(t) = \frac{s'_i(t)}{s'_{i0}(t)}.$$

There should also be carried out forecasting for essential values of weighting coefficients making it possible to establish significance of the index in the long run:

$$\alpha = \alpha(t).$$

In consideration of the foregoing, there should be forecasted composite indices of the product competitiveness and an integrated of its competitiveness:

$$
\begin{aligned}
&Q_1 = Q_1(t);\\
&\dots\dots\dots\dots\dots\\
&Q_N = Q_N(t);\\
&K_I = K_I(t).
\end{aligned}
$$

Mathematical model (4.7) with due account for the time parameter takes on the appearance of:

$$
\begin{cases}
K_{i_1}(t) > 0, & i_1 = 1, \dots, N_1;\\
K'_{i_2}(t) > 0, & i_2 = 1, \dots, N_2;\\
Q_{i_3}(t) = \sum\limits_{i_3=1}^{j(i_3)} K_{i_3}(t)\alpha_{i_3}(t) + \sum\limits_{i_3=j(i_3)+1}^{n(i_3)} K'_{i_3}(t)\alpha_{i_3}(t), & i_3 = 1, \dots, N_3;
\end{cases}
$$

$$
K_I(t) = \frac{\sum\limits_{m=1}^{M} Q_m(t)\alpha_m(t)}{\sum\limits_{m=1}^{M} \alpha_m(t)} \to \max.
$$

Such mathematical model will make it possible to estimate product competitiveness depending on factors influencing it in time. On the basis of available data, the firm management can make managerial decisions for timely, purposeful regulation of the firm activity and forestall negative influences of changing external and internal environment on the product competitiveness, and use favorable conditions, as much as possible, for its enhancement at present and in future with forecasted in advance values of the product competitiveness , profit from its sale, and indices of external and internal environment reflecting these changes.

4.2 Assessment of the Impact of Change in the Products' Price on Its Competitiveness in the Middle-Term and Long-Term Forecast

Product competitiveness is influenced by a number of factors; however, for many goods and services, the major factor is the price of production. Significance of the price factor in management of the product competitiveness is that, as a rule, the enterprise has a possibility to change production price within bounds. In so doing, unlike control of other production characteristics, management in production price may be carried out in the most effective and productive way.

For the majority of goods and services, there is an inverse dependence of competitiveness on the price. Reduction in price increases competitiveness, and its increase, on the contrary, reduces competitiveness. At the same time, quantitative evaluation of production price influence on competitiveness is a big problem. In this connection, there is a necessity for construction of mathematical models establishing impact of change in the products' price on the indices of competitiveness of this production.

Another major problem to be investigated is impact of change in price on competitiveness depending on the time factor. In particular, provisions should be made to study a question on the price influence on competitiveness in the middle-term and long-term forecast.

Our approach to investigation of the impact of production price on its competitiveness is based on approaches of the theory of evolution functional differential equations. As is known, the functional differential equations can describe dynamic systems with time lagging and after-action. Use of these effects will make it possible for us to receive mathematical model which will give us a quantitative description of influence of the change in price on competitiveness in the middle-term and long-term forecast.

As the basic index of competitiveness, we choose relation "quality/price." "Quality" shall be understood to mean the composite index of production qualitative characteristics. Naturally, we assume that the higher the index value is, the more preferable this product is for consumers.

Let us put in the following designations:

K—index of production quality.
S—production price.
Q—index of the product competitiveness,

As we study dynamics of the index of competitiveness depending on change in price, we should consider change in time of competitiveness, qualities, and the prices instead of their static indices:

$Q(t)$—change of the index of competitiveness.
$K(t)$—change of the quality index.
$S(t)$—change in price.

As noted above, there is the following natural formula for these functions:

$$Q(t) = \frac{K(t)}{S(t)}. \qquad (4.8)$$

In order to find out the influence of change of quality indices and change in price on dynamics of the index of competitiveness, provisions should be made to have this correlation differentiated in time and to write down the differential equation

$$Q'(t) = \frac{K'(t)S(t) - K(t)S'(t)}{S^2(t)}. \qquad (4.9)$$

In differentiation, there should be required smoothness of the functions within this correlation though this assumption is a situation idealization, of course.

Let us consider a problem of constructing differential equations in the right part which includes derivative of production price.

The basic problem is that in actual economic processes, production price is changed jump-like and, hence, function of prices is not differentiated. As is known, derivative of discontinuous function may be treated as the generalized function. In case of derivative of jump function, such generalized function is Dirac delta. The basic problem with Dirac deltas is that these functions are not point functions. On the other hand, in a case when the Dirac delta meets in the right part of the differential equation, it can be interpreted as impulse force.

From the mathematical point of view, for consideration of impulse forces in the right part, it is necessary to understand the differential equations according to Caratheodory.

As is obvious, use of discontinuous functions as a function of prices leads to a number of serious computing difficulties; therefore, our understanding is that function of prices is continuously differentiable function.

For simplification, let us consider a case when the quality index value is constant. In this case, we have differential equation:

$$Q'(t) = \frac{K_0}{S^2(t)} S'(t), \tag{4.10}$$

$$K(t) = K_0. \tag{4.11}$$

This equation expresses influence of instant change in price on the index of competitiveness. However, in order to investigate a question of influence of change in price on competitiveness in the middle-term and long-term forecast, it is necessary to modify these differential equations to take into account the effects of time lagging and aftereffect. As already noted above, to take these effects into account, it is necessary to use modification of differential equations with the help of difference-differential equations and functional differential equations.

Let us consider influence of change in the products' price on its competitiveness *in the middle-term period*. With this aim in view, we modify our differential equation by adding the right part with the summands containing time lagging. This equation will be difference-differential equation:

$$Q'(t) = \frac{K'(t)S(t) - K(t)S'(t)}{S^2(t)} + \sum_{k=1}^{N} f_k\Big(Q(t-h_k), S'(t-h_k)\Big). \tag{4.12}$$

In this equation, values $h_k > 0$ are time lagging. We name this equation as difference-differential equation describing dynamics of the index of competitiveness in the middle-term period.

The meaning of this equation consists in the fact that dynamics of competitiveness index is influenced by not only instant change in the products' price but the value of competitiveness index in the previous values of time too. In the middle-term period, it is justified by the fact that competitiveness index depends on not only objective characteristics of production but on subjective opinion of the consumer concerning production too. As is known, the consumers' opinion possesses certain inertia. Therefore, in case of instant change in price of the products, the consumer's opinion will change with account of this opinion during the previous times of the middle-term period. Our model presents discrete time lagging which means that in the middle-term period, the consumer opinion on production undergoes rather a big change depending on change in product value. Summands in difference-differential equation describing dynamics of the index of competitiveness in the middle-term period, containing lag variables, depend on not only values of the index of competitiveness in the previous time readings but the price values in the said time readings. It expresses known psychological response of consumers to change in the products' price.

Let us consider the properties to be met by functions $f_k(Q, S')$.

First, functions f_k are nonnegative when S' has nonpositive value, and on the other hand, functions f_k are nonpositive when S' has nonnegative value for all Q.

Secondly, functions f_k do not decrease on the first argument with the second argument fixed.

Thirdly, we need continuity of these functions with respect to the first argument.

Fourthly, we need fulfillment of the condition:

$$\lim_{Q \to 0} f_k\left(Q, S'\right) = 0. \tag{4.13}$$

From these conditions, in particular, it follows that solution of the difference-differential equations remains nonnegative, which meets economic rationale of function $Q(t)$ as the index of competitiveness.

Let us consider the elementary example of difference-differential equation describing dynamics of changing competitiveness index in case the products' price is changing in the middle-term period:

$$Q'(t) = \frac{K'(t)S(t) - K(t)S'(t)}{S^2(t)} + \sum_{k=1}^{N} a_k Q(t - h_k), S'(t - h_k). \tag{4.14}$$

where a_k factors are negative and are decreasing by module with the growth of index k:

$$|a_1| \geq |a_2| \geq \ldots \geq |a_N|. \tag{4.15}$$

It is obvious that all assumptions are hence executed concerning properties of functions f_k.

In what follows, we consider the problem of influence of the change in products' price on its competitiveness *in the long-term period*.

In this case, we consider generalization of the differential equation describing dynamics of the index of competitiveness depending on change in price and modification of the differential equations by means of functional differential equations, with due account for the functions value during previous time. However, unlike consideration of the middle-term period, influence of the history of values of competitiveness indices cannot have any dependence during the discrete moments of time any more. Therefore, we should consider the distributed time lagging. This equation looks like:

$$Q'(t) = \frac{K'(t)S(t) - K(t)S'(t)}{S^2(t)} + \int_0^t F\Big(t-\tau, Q(t-\tau), S'(t-\tau)\Big)d\tau. \tag{4.16}$$

We will name this equation as functional differential equation describing dynamics of the index of competitiveness in the long-term period.

The economic rationale of this equation consists in the fact that the speed of the index of competitiveness depends on the previous history of values of the index of competitiveness and change in the product's price. Unlike the equation describing dynamics of the index of competitiveness in the middle-term period, time lagging in this equation is distributed through the entire time interval. Certainly, influence of change in price should decrease in due course.

Let us consider conditions function $F(t, Q, S')$ should meet.

First, function $F(t, Q, S')$ should be quickly decreasing by module according to first argument, i.e., there should be executed correlation for all Q and S':

$$\left|F\left(t, Q, S'\right)\right| \le \frac{C}{t^n}. \tag{4.17}$$

$$n \ge 1. \tag{4.18}$$

This condition expresses the fact that the influence of change in the products' price on its competitiveness in long-term perspective should be decreasing with the passage of time.

Secondly, function $F(t, Q, S')$ should be continuous on variable Q.

Thirdly, function $F(t, Q, S')$ should satisfy condition:

$$\lim_{Q \to 0} F\left(t, Q, S'\right) = 0. \tag{4.19}$$

Let us note here that in this case, we suppose that the sign of function $F(t, Q, S')$ can coincide with the sign of the third argument. Such situation is possible when the earlier overestimated price makes a positive impact on dynamics of the index of competitiveness at sharp reduction of price.

While investigating dynamics of the index of competitiveness in case of change in the products' price in the long-term perspective, it is necessary to consider random risk factors. The following circumstances can be the said risk factors:

- Serial spoilt production.
- Change of consumer demand.

- Activities of competitors.
- Change of the market conditions.

These circumstances are uncontrollable for the particular enterprise; therefore, in the mathematical model, it is necessary to consider them as stochastic processes. As it has already been noted, risk factors are composed of many circumstances of different nature. However, in our model, we take into account only integrated (generalized) risk factor by means of stochastic function.

Let us consider stochastic process $\xi(t)$. We assume that this stochastic process meets the following properties.

First, in any time interval $[0, T]$, the trajectory of stochastic process $\xi(t)$ is ten to one a function with final variation.

Secondly, there is such constant $C > 0$, which is ten to one

$$|\xi(t)| \leq C, t \in [0, T]. \tag{4.20}$$

The functional differential equation describing dynamics of the index of competitiveness depending on change in price has the following appearance in long-term perspective with account of risk random factors:

$$Q'(t) = \frac{K'(t)S(t) - K(t)S'(t)}{S^2(t)} + \int_0^t \left[F\left(t-\tau, Q(t-\tau), S'(t-\tau)\right) + e^{-(t-\tau)}\xi(t-\tau)\right]d\tau. \tag{4.21}$$

Let us consider now a question about management of the index of competitiveness by means of change in the products' price.

Competitiveness management is related to the most important problems of the enterprise. In an effort to increase indices of competitiveness, the enterprises have rather limited possibilities of competitiveness management. Competitiveness is influenced by the following major factors:

- Objective characteristics of the products.
- Products' price.
- Objective characteristics of competing products.
- Price of competing products.
- Opinion of consumers.

In addition to the above, the enterprise, as a rule, has a possibility to change objective characteristics of the products, their price, and opinion of consumers.

Change of objective characteristics of the products, as a rule, is associated with serious technological difficulties and huge span time. Moreover, implementation of innovations, as a rule, requires enormous financial expenses.

Influence on consumers' opinion about its own production is a necessary procedure for the big enterprises which is performed by means of advertising. However, influence on consumers' opinion is a challenging and unforecastable problem.

It would be much easier to exercise competitiveness management by means of change in price. Price change can be effectively carried out, which is important in competitive struggle. Change in price also is rather simple in a technical sense. On the other hand, the price factor of influence on competitiveness is one of the most important.

Representation of dynamic systems in the form of difference-differential equations and functional differential equations makes it possible to build effective schemes of optimum control of the index of competitiveness by means of price change.

Let us make some general remarks concerning management of competitiveness by means of the price.

First, provisions should be made in advance to establish limits of a possible change in price. The upper bound of the price in management has no basic value as the price increase leads to natural decrease in competitiveness. On the other hand, the lower bound of the would-be price cannot be less than a particular value. For example, as a rule, the price cannot be less than the cost price of production. Though, there are examples when some enterprises sell their products under cost in the hope of raising the sales and decreasing the cost price.

Secondly, control of the index of competitiveness by means of price change on the basis of difference-differential equations and functional differential equations faces a number of technical difficulties. Effects of time lagging and aftereffect which take place in the difference-differential equations and functional differential equations make serious impact on dynamics of the index of competitiveness.

Thirdly, control of the index of competitiveness by means of price change on the long-term period faces an inevitable problem of random factors of risk which can make serious impact. The risk factors considered above, with due account for their unforecastability, present serious difficulties in building optimum control of the index of competitiveness by means of price change on the long-term period.

Nevertheless, mathematical models developed above make it possible to implement algorithms in order to select specific price control to enhance competitiveness.

4.3 Cost-in-process as the Product Competitive Differentiator

Tendencies specific to the present stage of development of the world market and activities of the leading suppliers of commodity items and products should be taken into account by domestic manufacturers, for which the problems of the products competitiveness in the foreign market are no less important.

The solution of the product competitiveness management problem, which is one of the major problems at present, has a great impact on efficiency and survival of many production industries of the Russian economy directly influencing well-being and standards of living.

To control competitiveness of a firm or production means to carry out competitive activities in particular fields providing competitive advantages. The most important action, in our opinion, is application of innovative technologies providing high product competitiveness as a result of achieving specific characteristics of this production corresponding to requirements of the world market or surpassing the level of analogues, simultaneously maintaining competitive price.

Competitive price, first of all, can be reached at the expense of decrease in the cost-in-process of the output goods. This decrease is achieved at the expense of application of innovative technologies providing growth of labor productivity, decrease in energy and material consumption, continuity and duration of use of production equipment, etc.

Identification of expenses for designing and production and the factors determining or influencing cost value is essential for analysis of the cost-in-process and identification of the ways of its decrease. The general algorithm of investigating the influence of various factors can be presented in the form of sequence of steps of analysis, synthesis, selection and substantiations, and evaluation of results during every step of the study and as a whole upon completion.

In our case, for the specified task, we need to do the following:

- Describe the process of creating the sample in terms of the system approach i.e., to construct a "tree" of procedures to implement this process at all the stages of designing and developing, production engineering, and manufacturing.
- Determine the basic cost drivers at every stage of the life cycle; to determine specific system of factors to affect the cost-in-process(criterion of optimization) for every stage of life cycle i.e., to construct hierarchical information model of factors.
- Develop one-factor mathematical model to provide comparability of results on every step of impact estimate on the cost-in-process.
- Evaluate the impact of every factor on the cost elements and cost value as a whole.
- Develop multifactor mathematical model of optimization of the cost-in-process for the entire set of determining factors.
- Select a mathematical model of evaluation of reliability of results and determine decision-making rules for available results.

On the basis of application of the complex of the system analysis tools and construction of mathematical apparatus, recommendations concerning cost optimization for engineering and production by cost-in-process criterion will be provided.

Separate aspects of this problem are well studied and described in various sources. However, the methods specified in the literature and concerning solution of this problem do not possess integrity and generality of their application. These methods, as a rule, cover only one specific field of activity (Production or products sale), influence of one or a sets of specific homogeneous factors (parameters of reliability, operational readiness and operational margins, type of technology operation, etc.). The available mathematical methods considerably differ and, hence, do not provide comparability and required reliability of results.

So, statistical methods used for analysis and cost price calculations yield quite good results with available big statistical samples i.e., in case of large-scale manufacture, and the said methods are ineffective at the stages of developing of a new product and its small-scale manufacture.

The system analysis tools and mathematical models offered in this work are free from the abovementioned drawbacks.

Investigation of cost drivers for production and sale, as well as their contents and nature and degree of impact of the factors determining cost-in-process, is of great significance for analysis of the cost price and identification of ways of its decrease (Fig. 4.2).

Let us construct a mathematical interpretation of the cost price with the help of regression analysis.

For mathematical presentation of the cost price in the form of function, it is necessary to create a mathematical model to set specific mathematics between dependent variables y_i, $i = 1, \ldots, n$ being outcome variable (responses) and independent variables x_j, $j = 1, \ldots, m$ being input variables or factors.

Every mathematical model, though reflecting some characteristic features of the object of interest, never happens to be its exact copy. It is possible to create a set of models for the same object, when each of which describes only one index of interest. Selection of a suitable mathematical model is rather a hard job. Hence it appears that the mathematical model we select cannot always completely

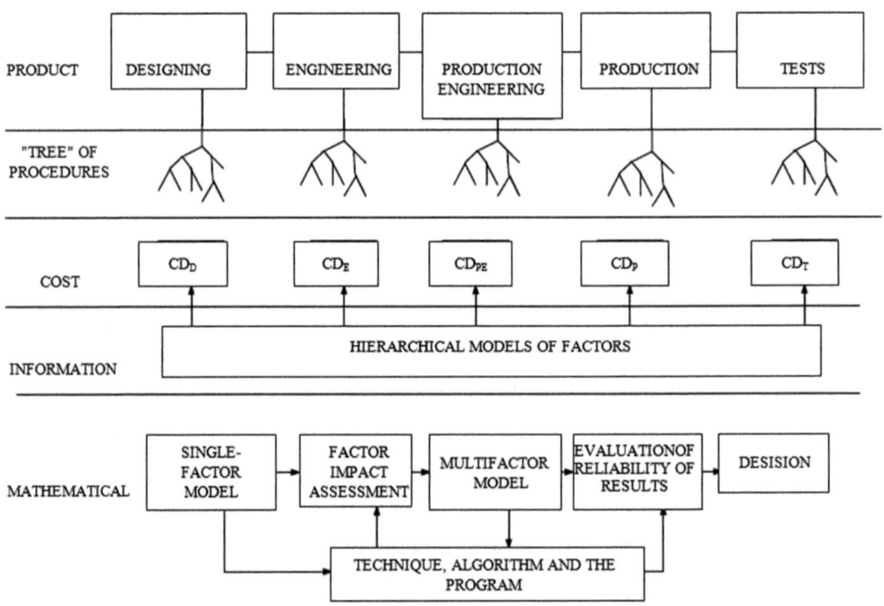

Fig. 4.2 General algorithm analysis of the change in cost price during the product's life cycle

correspond to the object of interest or to the process. Therefore, the model we receive requires its scrutiny.

In our case, we determine mathematical model as a conditional mathematical expectation of dependent variable under the preset values of the coefficients:

$$\eta(x_1, x_2, \ldots, x_m) = M\{y|x_1, x_2, \ldots, x_n\}.$$

This equation establishes dependence of change of the mean value of the object response (cost value) on change of factors and is called as an equation of regression.

The response (output characteristic) can be found as follows:

$$y(x_1, x_2, \ldots, x_n) = \eta(x_1, x_2, \ldots, x_n) - \varepsilon,$$

where ε—random disturbance influencing the object.

Action of a set of random disturbances on the object is equivalent to the single disturbance. If process under consideration is static, random disturbance $\varepsilon = 0$. Then for a random variable y_i, it is possible to write down

$$y_i(x_1, x_2, \ldots, x_n) = \eta = \sum_{i=1}^{n} \beta_i \cdot f_i(x_1, x_2, \ldots, x_n)$$

Moreover, functions $f_i(x_1, x_2, \ldots, x_m)$ are called regressors, and β_i—weighting coefficients of these regressors.

Let us introduce the concept "observation" connected with identification of function y_i in a particular tree node of factors x_i (Fig. 4.3).

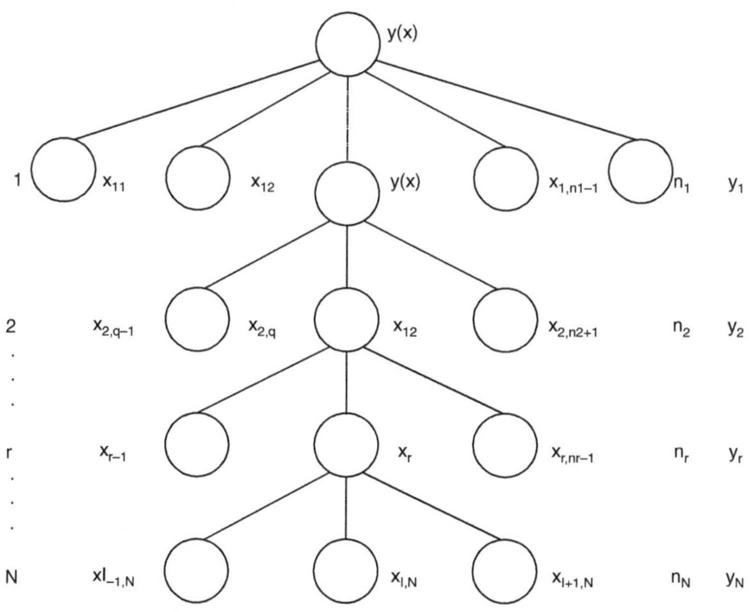

Fig. 4.3 Generalized tree of regressors

Hence, in observation $u = 1, 2, \ldots, N$, we have

$$y_u = \sum_{i=1}^{k} \beta_i \cdot f_{iu}$$

Let us make a table of observation (Table 4.1)
Here functions f_{iu} correspond to values x_{ju}.
Let us make a matrix of regressors:

$$F = \begin{Vmatrix} f_{11} & f_{12} & \cdots & f_{k1} & \\ f_{12} & f_{22} & \cdots & f_{k2} & \\ \cdots & \cdots & \cdots & & \cdots \\ f_{1N} & f_{2N} & \cdots & f_{kN} & \end{Vmatrix},$$

where each line has functions f_{iu} from model (2.1) in this observation, $u = 1, \ldots, N$.

Regressors can be calculated from initial structure of the model which is supposed to be known.

As the model $y_u = \sum_{i=1}^{k} \beta_i \cdot f_{iu}$ with $u = 1, \ldots, N$, observation provides an inexact copy of true character of function y_u; it can be specified by function

$$\widehat{y_u} = \sum_{i=1}^{N} b_i \cdot f_{iu}. \tag{4.22}$$

named as hypothesis y_u and used for evaluation of true value of a random variable η.

In order to receive estimated coefficients of the model or regression coefficients, there may be used least square method

$$Q = \sum_{u=1}^{N} \left(y_u - \widehat{y_k} \right)^2. \tag{4.23}$$

This method makes it possible to minimize value $\boldsymbol{Q}$. Value $\boldsymbol{Q}$ named regret function (risk function) can be received as small as we please.

Table 4.1 Table of observation

N_u	X_1	$X_2 \ldots X_n$	y
1	X_{11}	$X_{21} \ldots X_{n1}$	y_1
2	X_{12}	$X_{22} \ldots X_{n2}$	y_2
3	X_{13}	$X_{23} \ldots X_{n3}$	y_3
XXX...	...	....	...
N	X_{1N}	$X_{2N} \ldots X_{nN}$	Y_N

After transposing regressionor matrix $F = \begin{Vmatrix} f_{11} & \ldots & f_{k1} \\ f_{1N} & \ldots & f_{kN} \end{Vmatrix}$, i.e., changing places of the line and the columns, we receive transposed matrix. By multiplying the initial and transposed matrices, we find information matrix $G = F^T F$ which makes it possible to receive a system of standard equations. Doing this requires to multiply the transposed matrix by the column of responses of the table of observation. The result is that we have the right parts of the standard equations and, using the information matrix, we receive: $F^T F b = F^T y$, i.e., system of the standard equations.

Solving this system by the known methods, we receive values of coefficients $\boldsymbol{b_i}$, and we find function $\widehat{y}_u = \sum_{i=1}^{N} b_i \cdot f_{iu}$, i.e., we come to model $\widehat{y}_u$.

Hence, mathematical modeling tools give us a general technique for construction of various dependences on the basis of experimental data.

Let us consider a method which would help to solve a problem of the cost value optimization. By definition, cost value is expressed as the sum of cost of goods manufactured:

$$C = {}_1 + {}_2 + \ldots + {}_n = \sum_{i=1}^{n} {}_i$$

where

C—cost-in-process,
3_i—cost of goods manufactured.

It is possible to consider cost value ***C*** as a function from ***n*** independent variables. This function can be expressed by both linear and nonlinear dependence.

In general, this dependence can be written down as:

$$y = \sum_{i=1}^{n} y_i f_{im}, \quad m = 1, \ldots, k,$$

Variables f_{im} are function from ***t*** independent variables too. Function $f_i(x_1, \ldots, x_m)$ determines a category of expenses and depends on its variables x_i by both linear and nonlinear dependence. Cost function is also an amount of expenses according to the factors (parameters) that determine it:

$$f_i = \sum_{i=1}^{m} b_{ik} x_i, \quad k = 1, \ldots, t.$$

Let us assume that function f_i defines expenses for the technological level increase, the standard value for which is set, i.e., expenses on improvement of quality of the products are defined. In other words, it is a value which is related to and dependent on parameters, being its part.

Similar procedures should be performed for other expenses. Hence, we receive system of linear equations:

$$\left.\begin{array}{l} C_1 = b_{11}x_1 + \ldots + b_{1n}x_n \\ C_i = b_{i1}x_1 + \ldots + b_{in}x_n \\ C_n = b_{n1}x_1 + \ldots + b_{nn}x_n \end{array}\right\}. \tag{4.24}$$

Solving the system of linear equations by one or another method, we receive values of the coefficients $\boldsymbol{b_{ij}}$ as correction factors. By substituting these values in the model describing expenses, we receive an equation reflecting dependence of variable function f_i on independent parameters and its components. This equation can be both linear and nonlinear relating to its parameters.

Imposing conditions and restrictions on function f_i, it is possible to determine it as an objective function by one of optimization methods, i.e., to find its optimum.

Similar operations should be performed with all other functions f_i in order to find their optimum values.

By applying similar reasoning to model

$$y_u = \sum_{i=1}^{n} \beta_{im} \cdot f_i, \quad m = 1, \ldots, k \quad ,$$

We find values β_{im}.

By substituting the resulting values in the mathematical model determining function $\boldsymbol{y}$, we find the optimum of this function, i.e., optimum found cost value of the products. The multifactor mathematical model by its nature is invariant to any system of determining factors and is independent on the number of levels of observation and the number of factors at every level.

The specified model, being a basic model and possessing properties of adequacy for any stage of the product life cycle, does not guarantee high accuracy of results for each of them. Information specificity, volume of observation (statistical sample), and degree of uncertainty of the procedures carried out at every stage of life cycle require its specific modifications.

As an example, we describe the modified model of the product cost calculation at the production phase.

Product cost is a function of cost for its manufacturing. Expenses for the product creation depend on many factors. In doing so, the considerable role is played by quality indices. The basic quality indices of a product include reliability, durability, accuracy, and interchangeability of the product elements. These indices mainly depend on correct selection of the form tolerance and an arrangement of the product components and on their correct integration, i.e., character of parts mating. The entire product has a complicated set of interconnected details; therefore, all possible discrepancies from the form, sizes, arrangements of surfaces, or axes of details in one link cause discrepancies in other chain of the entire product, which in turn influences product quality indices as a whole, and consequently, the monetary evaluation of the product, i.e., its cost.

Let us carry out an analysis of the product cost calculation in case of change of the above qualities.

It is practically impossible to hold to the dimensions set by the design documentation in-process. Hence, there is one or another discrepancy from the absolute values and forms, i.e., there is a problem of the maximum permissible discrepancies of the details. The estimated substantiation of these acceptable deviations can be executed on the basis of the theory of dimension chains. The dimension chain is found by parameters independent of each other and united in closed contour and participating in the form of values related to this contour. Dimension chains are connections of smooth shaft and apertures. Then the problem of receiving the minimum discrepancies is reduced to reception within the specified limits of interspace Δ, the minimum size depending on the size of diameter of aperture $\boldsymbol{d_A}$ and a shaft $\boldsymbol{d}_{\mathrm{B}}$. In creation of a link of dimensional chain "aperture-shaft," the interspace is resulted from this connection. Hence, it is a master link, and diameters $\boldsymbol{d_A}$ and $\boldsymbol{d}_{\mathrm{B}}$ are making links which are subdivided into increasing and reducing links depending on the fact whether the master link increases or decreases

All the listed factors differently influence the product cost. Hence, it happens so that the product cost is function $C = f(x_1, x_2, \ldots, x_n)$ from independent parameters $\boldsymbol{x_i}$, describing considered factors. Function $C = f(x_i)$ expresses influence of indices on expenses.

The number of influencing factors is rather big, many of them have a qualitative character and sometimes are unequivocally expressed in quantitative indices, and some can possess considerable uncertainty.

To receive a type of function $C = f(x_1, x_2, \ldots, x_n)$ from purely theoretical preconditions is rather difficult. An important role is played in this case by analysis of the development background which provides the fact sheet concerning expenses and indices $\boldsymbol{x_i}$ in processing of the similar operations or manufacturing the similar product. Availability of operations analogues or products analogues creates conditions for application of statistical methods in forecasting of expenses for a perspective product.

Cost is a cost function; therefore, cost C_{3B} of a closing dimensional chain is composed of costs for every separate operation, i.e., $C_{3B} = C_I + C_2 + \ldots + C_N$, where each of the composed expenses is a function from independent parameters describing factors which define some quality indices of every separate link of the chain; for example, the value of the shaft diameter or an aperture.

It is practically impossible to receive an exact type of function from the theoretical preconditions. In order to solve the task, it is possible to use methods of regression analysis allowing to choose a function model which, whenever possible, reflects behavior of function of parameters and simple enough.

Two types of models have practical distribution:

Linear $y = b_0 + \sum_{j=1}^{n} b_j \cdot x_j$ and nonlinear, for example, like $y = b_0 \prod_{j=1}^{n} b_j x_j$.

Basically linear models are used as this type of models is simpler and makes it possible to receive more substantial and evident results, as well as it sufficiently estimates parameters of the selected model.

Model $y = b_0 + \sum_{j=1}^{n} b_j x_j$ will be linear relative to its coefficients and is the analogue of the function true value. True value of the function is understood to be a mathematical expectation of dependent variable at the specified values of the coefficients:

$$\eta(x_1, x_2, \ldots, x_n) = E(y|x_1, x_2, \ldots, x_n).$$

Actually measured output characteristic is

$$y(x_1, x_2, \ldots, x_n) = \eta(x_1, x_2, \ldots, x_n) + \varepsilon$$

where ε—random disturbance.

Action on the object of a set of random disturbances is supposed to be equal to one random disturbance with normal distribution, zero mathematical expectation, and dispersion equal to σ^2. Using concepts and methods of the statistic analysis, we express cost function in the form of linear model relative to coefficients of the model equation:

$$y = \eta + \varepsilon = \sum_{i=1}^{n} \beta_i f(x_1, x_2, \ldots, x_m) + \varepsilon$$

i.e.,

$$y = \sum_{i=1}^{k} \beta_i \cdot f_{ik} + \varepsilon$$

where $u = 1, \ldots, N$—numbers of observation.
k—number of parameters.

In case of dimensional chain, these observation will be in accord with changes of values of function f_{ik} depending on discrepancy of the shaft diameter sizes or the aperture, and probably, on other qualitative parameters determining the link.

Hence, the value y_n is a random value; therefore, it is impossible to determine exact values of coefficient β_i. With this aim in view, they use their evaluations, i.e., coefficients $b_1, \ldots, b_k$, being coefficients of the forecasted model:

$$\widehat{y}_n = \sum_{i=1}^{n} b_i \cdot f_{ik}.$$

In order to receive estimated coefficients of the initial mathematical model in the regression analysis, the least square method is used.

For evaluation of regression, coefficients' provisions should be made to find the least possible remainders. But, as there is a lot of measurements, there is a lot of remainders too; hence, it is necessary to use a combined characteristic depending on distinctions between observations and forecasts. To compensate distinctions in signs, the remainders are squared; as a result, we have a functional:

$$Q = \left(y - \widehat{y}\right)^T \left(y - \widehat{y}\right).$$

This functional is called a regret function. The method, allowing estimating regression model coefficient so as to minimize value Q, is called as the least square method.

For an evaluation of coefficients of the model equation, it is necessary to find ***min*** of functional Q; doing this requires differentiating Q by all coefficients b_i and equating every received equation to zero. As a result, we receive system of the standard equations which is solved in the context of parameters b_i. Hence, we found the minimum assessed estimates. These estimates are substituted in the forecasting model and as a result we have the best model.

The estimates received by the least square method possess the following basic properties:

- The estimates are not biased, i.e., their mathematical expectations converge on probability to their true values: $E(b) = \beta$.
- dispersions and covariances of the regression coefficient values are found according to formulas:

$$\sigma^2(b_i) = c_{ii}\sigma^2;$$

$$\operatorname{cov}\left(b_i b_j\right) = c_{ij}\sigma^2,$$

where c_{ii}—diagonal element of the matrix of dispersions—covariances, named matrix of errors.

This matrix originates from regression or matrix by multiplication of its left by transposed matrix and then applying a matrix contrary to the product, i.e.,

$C = F^T F^{-1}$ where c_{ij}—any other insignificant element;

The estimates received by this method are effective and have the least dispersions among all possible unbiased estimates; i.e.,

$$\sigma^2(b_i) = \sigma^2(\theta_i),$$

where θ_i—any linear subjective unbiased estimate β_i.

The evaluations are well founded, i.e., with N number of observation when they were received, they go to infinity ∞, $b_{iN} \to \beta_i$ in probability, i.e.,

$$\lim_{N\to\infty} P[|b_{iN} - \beta_i| < j] = 1$$

where j—any small positive number. The dispersion of the forecasted value $\widehat{y}$ is found as

$$\sigma^2\left[\widehat{y}(x)\right] = E\left\{\left[\widehat{y}(x) - \eta(x)\right]^2\right\}.$$

If regression model is selected correctly, then unbiased estimate of dispersion is set by equation

$$S^2_{oct} = \left[\sum_{n=1}^{N}\left(y_n - \widehat{y}_n\right)^2\right]/(N-k),$$

$\sum_{n=1}^{N}\left(y_n - \widehat{y}_n\right)^2 = Q_{ocm}$—residual sum of squares.
$(N-k) = v_{oct}$—degrees of freedom of the residual sum.

$$Q_{ocm} = Q_{res}$$

$$v_{ocm} = v_{res}$$

K—number of the model variables.
N—number of observations.

If random disturbances $\varepsilon_1, \ldots, \varepsilon_N$ are independent normally distributed random variables with the mathematical expectation equal to zero and identical dispersions σ^2, then evaluation vector has multidimensional normal distribution with the mathematical expectation β and matrix of dispersions—covariants $\left(F^T F^{-1}\right)\sigma^2$

ratio

$$\chi^2 = Q_{ocm}/\sigma^2 = \left(1/\sigma^2\right)\sum_{n=1}^{N}\left(y_n - \widehat{y}_n\right)^2$$

has distribution χ^2 with the number of freedom degrees $v_{ocm} = N - n$ (χ^2—normal normalized distribution).

Correct selection of the model plays a big role for definition of true value of the function which is rather a difficult process. For definition of the polynom (model) degree, at first, they begin evaluation of coefficients of the simplest model (relative to coefficients of the model equation) and verify whether the well-forecasted value according to the model complies with the actual value. In order to check the development, they use special statistical procedure named model verification. The model verification is one of the most important statistical procedures of regression analysis, testifying to the fact that the received model yields positive result and, hence, is selected correctly.

The selected model should be as simple as possible, it should include as few coefficients as possible, i.e., it should be the most cost-effective. In analysis of estimated coefficients of regression model, there may be a case when because of influence of random disturbances, they turn out to be different from zero when their true values are equal to zero. In this case, such coefficients can be neglected and the model may be simplified.

Hypothesis checking for regression coefficients equal to zero is called a test of significance. Test of significance is also one of the major characteristics of the selected model. Accuracy of estimated coefficients, i.e., a measure of their difference from true values, is found by means of confidential interval and the area.

The confidential interval is a piece with assessed value $\boldsymbol{b_i}$ being its center and which has specified in advance probability that it may include assessed value $\boldsymbol{\beta_i}$. Confidential intervals for some other random variables can turn out asymmetrical relating to their evaluations. Confidential areas are constructed in space of all regression coefficients. They have meaning similar to the interval.

Hence, before model verification, we introduce the following concepts.

Quality evaluations of regression coefficients and the model structure can be found from the residual sum of squares

$$Q_{ocm} = \sum_{n=1}^{T} \left(y_n - \widehat{y}_n\right)^2 = \sum_{n=1}^{T} \varepsilon_n{}^2$$

where $n = 1, 2, \ldots, N$—numbers of observation.

y_n—responses of observation.

$\widehat{y}_n$—forecasted value of the response.

By introducing an arithmetic mean from results of observation

$$\overline{y} = \frac{1}{N}\sum_{n=1}^{N} y_n$$

and by substituting expression y_n through $\overline{y}$ into the formula of the residual sum of squares, we receive expression

$$Q = Q_{ocm} + Q_R$$

where $\boldsymbol{Q}$—total (full) sum of squares,

$$Q_{ocm} = Q_{res}, \quad \text{i.e.},$$

$$Q = \frac{1}{N}\sum_{n=1}^{N}(y_n - \overline{y})^2,$$

Q_R—sum of squares caused by regression,

$$Q_R = \frac{1}{N}\sum_{n=1}^{N}\left(\widehat{y}_n - \overline{y}\right)^2.$$

Expression for Q is the basic equation for the dispersive analysis of result. The total sum of squares from the equation for Q is resolved into two components: Q_R—specified sum of squares and $Q_{ocm}(= Q_{res})$—residual sum of squares.

The specified sum of squares Q_R shows that the value $\widehat{y}_n$ within it determines k of linear connections between observations y_n as it includes k of estimated coefficients b_i, found under the same observations. Value $\overline{y}$ defines only one linear connection between them. Then the number of degrees of freedom for Q_R is equal to $v_R = k - 1$. The residual sum of squares $Q_{ocm}(Q_{res})$ reflects the influence of all reasons of dispersion of results $\overline{y}$ which are inexplicable regression. Number of degrees of freedom of this sum is equal to $v_{ocm}/v_{res} = N - k$. For the total sum of squares, the number of degrees of freedom is equal to $v = N - 1$ as it includes N observations with one linear connection $\overline{y}$.

However, by virtue of the fact that

$$Q = Q_{ocm} + Q_R,$$

Subsequently,

$$v = v_{ocm} + v_R.$$

For the residual sum of squares, it is possible to introduce a scalar (nonvector) record which is the most used, practically because it has no forecast therein i.e.,

$$Q_{ocm} = \sum_{n=1}^{T} y_n^2 - \sum_{i=1}^{k} b_i \sum_{n=1}^{N} f_{in} y_n.$$

Scalar expression of the residual sum of squares with due account for the forecast looks like

$$Q_{ocm} = \sum_{n-1}^{N} y_n^2 - \sum_{n-1}^{N} \widehat{y}_n^2.$$

The said mathematical tools are used in practical calculations of cost for various coefficients in the course of designing and product manufacturing.

There is a cost accounting program developed with evaluation of residual requirement depending on the volume of statistical sample (number of observations).

The calculations were performed for number of observation ***N*** **=*5, 8, 9, 10, and 15*** under the following conditions:

1. As the law of errors of the tests results χ^2 distribution is made.
2. For assessed value of regression coefficients and confidential intervals, Fisher and Student arrays and t_α -distributions were used.

Calculations have proved an adequacy of the selected model, as well as techniques and high convergence in probability of derived estimates.

Figure 4.4 shows the character of dependence of residual measures of inaccuracy of responses deviations $\mathbf{\Delta_y}$ (cost price variance) from its arithmetic mean value in the average sample number function ***N***.

The calculations also show that the offered techniques make it possible to receive the required decision which is proved by the resulting value of the adequacy coefficient for the selected model.

In cases when this coefficient is more than the tabulated point (i.e., the selected model does not fit the real model), provisions should be made to carry out repeated calculation in order to exclude possible errors in the process of calculation. In case of coincidence of the repeated calculation results, it is necessary to specify the initial formula of regression.

Hence, determination of the adequacy coefficient is one of the required conditions for scrutiny of selecting initial regression models.

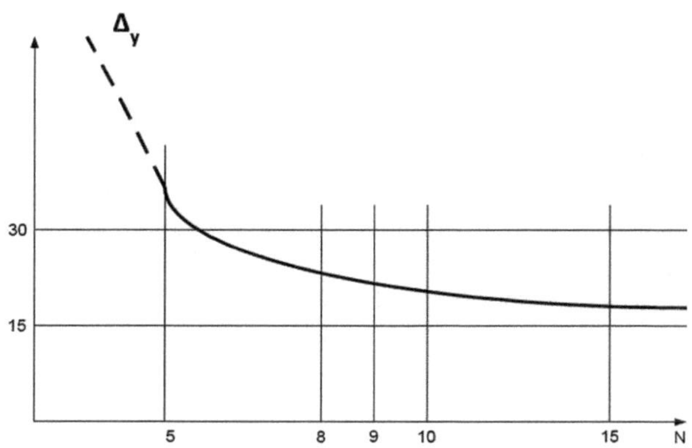

Fig. 4.4 Dependence of the cost price variance Δ_y on the number of observations N

The second constraint of validity of the postulated regression models is definition of significance of the multiple correlation coefficient which is an assessed estimate of dispersion of the forecasted value or a measure of determination, pointing to degree of nonlinearity of statistical dependence between observable values of response y_n and their forecasts according to model $\widehat{y}_n$. In the event computed, coefficient of multiple correlation appears to be more than the tabular one (from Fisher array), it is significant, and its value cannot be explained random disturbances only.

When the estimated coefficient of multiple correlations appears to be less or equal to the tabular value, it is insignificant, and the model does not explain dispersion of observations concerning their mean value. Insignificance of coefficient leads to the fact that dependence on included regressions is weak or completely absent, which may be stipulated by the following:

- Lack of strongly influencing coefficients in the model (the model is insufficient).
- Wrong structure of the models.

The third constraint of validity of regression models will be the values of confidential intervals for coefficients of forecasted (estimated) model. If the estimated confidential intervals appear to be more than the tabular ones, then the coefficients of the estimated model are significant; otherwise, they are insignificant.

The offered simulated mathematical model to determine and forecast the cost price of production makes it possible to determine and forecast the cost value of the products on a real time basis in modern rapidly developing market situation and especially in the conditions of current financial and economic crisis and unpredictability of changes in prices for raw materials, power resources, component parts, and tariffs of natural monopolies, and depending on the forecast results concerning change of one or another type of expenses determining cost value of production to make corresponding decisions relating to the level of cost price in order to provide the required profit on production.

Creation of high-quality and, at the same time, economic products is a pressing problem which can be solved with implementation of innovative technologies only aimed at both cutting of absolute value of production costs and relative reduction of expenses per unit of their effectiveness.

One of the primary goals of production is provision of required products quality, including obtaining of reliable operational characteristics. Qualitative manufacturing of the products consists in strict implementation of technical requirements to construction and manufacturing techniques. Quality of the products depends on perfection of design execution and technological level. However, quality criteria is not the only index to determine technological level of production, as at the present stage of development of technology as a science, the question of the economic feasibility is a branch of this science, equivalent to reliability and quality. Only comprehensive study of engineering and technological problems when the issues of accuracy, quality, reliability, and profitability are considered as a whole, can lead to correct, scientifically proven decisions.

Hence, the major problem of implementation of innovative technologies is cutting of production costs with provision of the necessary quality and competitiveness. Analysis of separate productive process makes it possible to be convinced that, first of all, they require automation of the operations which influence accuracy and quality characteristics of component parts and products most of all. Improvement of quality of output products and effective management and control of expenditure substantially influence the cost value of output products.

Another reserve of cost saving in mechanical engineering is optimization of tolerance for structural components to provide the necessary quality at minimum cost.

Commercialization of provisions is possible with mathematical modeling of tolerance and development of technological processes based on identification of objective laws between the indices of the products quality, accuracy of the sizes of designs elements, cost of production, and the "know-how." Optimization calculations of operational margins are rather labor consuming and are impossible without computer techniques. As the problems of increasing product profitability are connected with both design and technological problems and with economic problems of a firm, they should be considered as a part of the entire complex of problems of the integrated automated systems of designing and manufacturing. Productivity enhancement is a key task of economy. The major quality index of the firm activity is the cost of production.

In mechanical engineering, this index depends on a set of the coefficient objectively caused by design features of the product and organizational and technological process of manufacturing. Such design factors as number of original details, complexity and accuracy of their manufacturing, consumption and the prices of applied materials, and a number of other factors directly influence costs of production. The mode of influence of these coefficients mainly depends on adaptability to the level of manufacturability, i.e., allowance for optimum conditions of details manufacturing and their matched parts assembly. Products with identical design data and operational indices can have several variants of constructive decisions considerably differing from each other according to the cost price and, as a consequence, by the sale price because of different level of their adaptability to manufacture. There are organizational-technology factors influencing level of industrial expenses too. It is series, production specialization, volumes of application of unified details and assembly units, technological level of industrial equipment, organizational-technological level of all auxiliary services of a firm, qualitative level of production management, etc.

Hence, mathematical interpretation of the cost price will make it possible to control competitiveness of a firm or production and to implement measures for application of innovative technologies providing high product competitiveness as a result of enhancing characteristics of this production so that they would meet the world market requirements or be above the level of their analogues with competitive price. In turn, the competitive price in the market can be reached at the expense of application of innovative technologies providing growth of labor productivity, decrease in energy and material consumption, persistence of production equipment use, etc. All these measures will make it possible to lower cost value of the output products and, as a result, to increase product competitiveness in the world and domestic markets.

4.4 Updating of the Products as a Major Factor of Enhancing Competitiveness

Competitive advantages of the products, as a rule, are created at the stage of their designing and then at the stage of manufacturing preparation, sale, and advertising.

Updating of the products is an inescapable link in a chain of enhancing economic efficiency of the enterprise (for example, in the developed countries, automobile, aerospace, machine-building, and other companies update their production every year or 2 years). Therefore, provisions should be made to reveal the basic technical and economic conditions providing practical necessity of the output goods.

Efficiency of any product including a new one is measured by ratio of economic benefit (profit) to the total expenses connected with its development, manufacturing, and operation. In the market conditions, development of industrial enterprise depends on the profit received as a result of economic activities. Therefore, it should estimate necessity of updating of the output products to determine expenses and to establish optimum and economically expedient terms of updating.

Technical and economic conditions of updating output products, in practice, are found by a set of factors.

First, it is technical and operational factors of updating the products which specify:

- Irrelevance of consumer needs at a definite time period or expected level of technical and operational characteristics of the products being prepared for manufacturing by the competitor, ($TTX_з = \text{Engineering Specification}_{needs} - ES_n$) to similar parameters of the products to be withdrawn from production, ($TTX_c = \text{Engineering Specification}_{withdraw} - ES_w$). This condition in a formalized manner can be written down as follows: $TTX_з > TTX_c$;
- Conformity of the level of market requirement and consumer needs at a definite time period $TTX_з$ with parameters of new production ($TTX_н = \text{Engineering Specification}_{new} - ES_n$), i.e., $TTX_н \geq TTX_з$.

Secondly, economic factors of updating within the framework of economic interests and possibilities of both consumer of new production and its manufacturer, namely:

- Launch price for new product $Ц_н(\text{Price}_{new} - P_n)$ should not exceed the price of the product manufactured by competitors, financial possibilities of consumer $Ц_{зн}$, i.e., $Ц_н \leq Ц_{зн}$.

- Price for the products to be withdrawn from production $Ц_c$(Price$_{withdraw}$ – P_w) according to accepted practice of discounts from the wholesale prices should be in excess of the possible price of consumer for this product $Ц_{зс}$, i.e., $Ц_c > Ц_{зс}$ provided that $Ц_{зс}$ tends to zero.
- Profit per unit of cost for a new product $П_н$(P_n)should be in excess or equal to the profit per unit of cost for the period of updating upon the average within the enterprise (association) $П_{ср}$ (Profit $_{average}$ – P_a), i.e., $П_н \geq П_{ср}$.
- Profit per unit of cost for a product to be withdrawn from production, $П_c$ should be less than the profit upon the average within the enterprise $П_{ср}$, i.e., $П_{ср} > П_c$ provided that $П_c$ tends to zero.

According to the formulated baseline, production of a new product and its commercialization will be economically effective for an industrial enterprise (association), and the product will be competitive in the market if the following economic and technological conditions are met:

$$\begin{aligned} &TTX_н \geq TTX_з;\\ &Ц_н \leq Ц_{зн};\\ &П_н \geq П_{ср}. \end{aligned}$$

Phasing out of a product in this case is determined by the following conditions:

$$\left.\begin{aligned} &TTX_з \geq TTX_c;\\ &Ц_c \leq Ц_{зс};\;\; Ц_{зс} \to 0\\ &П_{ср} \geq П_c;\;\; П_c \to 0 \end{aligned}\right\}. \tag{4.25}$$

Technical and engineering conditions for the output of new production would be just the initial stage of substantiation of its updating and require further detailed elaboration and specification depending on specific significance of production, its demand at a definite time period, and conditions of its consumption and operation. Providing that each finished product is effective within the established standard term of operation when it provides specific and measured in rubles standard effect $Э_{Hi}$ (i—product serial number), and expenses connected with its development, manufacturing, and operation are determined, i.e., standard cost S_{Hi}, normative cost effectiveness connected with development, manufacturing, and operation of a particular *i*-th product shall be the normative effect of this product per 1 ruble of normative cost:

$W_{Hi} = Э_{Hi}/S_{Hi}$.

By plotting on the abscissa of serial numbers of the made items, and their normative efficiency—on the ordinates, it is possible to receive a graph providing insight into change of normative cost effectiveness in the course of enhancing technical and economic level of production of the mastered products, creation of new modifications of the earlier mastered products, and alternation of generations of production of a particular type (Fig. 4.5).

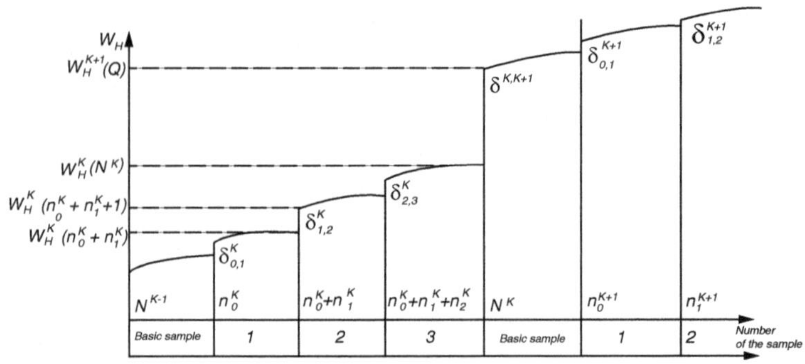

Fig. 4.5 Graphic model of development of a type of production

This graph represents an elementary model which displays objective laws of development of a type of production at the qualitative level. Figure 4.5 has the following designations:

n_0^k—total of the made items of the basic sample of the k-th generation;
n_j^k—total of the made items of the j-th modification of the basic sample of the k-th generation;
N^k—total of the made items of the k-th generation:

$$N^k = \sum_{j \to 0} n^k_{Hi};$$

W^k_{Hi}—normative efficiency of the i-th sample of the k-th generation; $1 \leq i \leq N^k$;
$\delta^k_{j,\, j+1}$—difference between initial normative efficiency of the products of $(j+1)$-th modification of the basic sample and available normative efficiency of the products of the previous j-th modification (the basic sample is considered as zero modification $j \geq 0$:

$$\delta^k_{j,\, j+1} = W^k_H\left(n^k_0 + n^k_1 + \ldots + n^k_{j+1}\right) - W^k_H\left(n^k_0 + n^k_1 + \ldots + n^k_j\right);$$

$\Delta^{k,k+1}$—Difference between initial normative efficiency of the products of the basic sample of the new $(k+1)$-th generations and available normative efficiency of the products of the last modification of the basic sample of the k-th (previous) generation:

$$\Delta^{k,k+1} = W^{k+1}_H(0) - W^k_H\left(N^k\right).$$

In the market conditions, the enterprise should master a new product when there is confidence in its economic feasibility, i.e., the incremental value of economic benefit at the expense of increasing normative efficiency of the products of a newly mastered sample in comparison with earlier produced should pay back expenses for reequipment (creation of capacities) and preparation of new manufacture in the established (normative) term.

Formally, it is possible to present it in the following type:

$$\sum_{i=i_0}^{i_0+\Pi'_{\Pi}(t_{ok})} W'_{Hi}S'_{Hi} + \sum_{i=i_0}^{i_0+\Pi_{\Pi}(t_{ok})} W_{Hi}S_{Hi} \geq S_{\Pi\Pi}, \tag{4.26}$$

where i_0—product number to launch the output of new sample.

t_{ok}—standard time of recoupment of expenses for reequipment (creation of capacities) and PLC preoperating phase.

$\Pi_{\Pi}(t_{ok})$ and $\Pi'_{\Pi}(t_{ok})$—number of old and new items to be made in time t_{OK} to meet requirements of the national economy in this type of production (hereinafter—Π_{Π} and Π'_{Π}).

$S_{\Pi\Pi}$—expenses for reequipment (creation of capacities) and PLC preoperating phase.

Normative efficiency and standard expenses vary inconspicuously from product to product in comparison with values $\delta^{k}_{j,\,j+1}$ and $\Delta^{k,k+1}$ and, as a consequence, they can be replaced by their arithmetic mean values which do not depend on value i:

$$\left.\begin{aligned} W_{Hi} &= \overline{W}_{H} \approx const;\\ W'_{Hi} &= \overline{W}'_{H} \approx const;\\ S_{Hi} &= \overline{S}_{H} \approx const;\\ S'_{Hi} &= \overline{S}'_{H} \approx const. \end{aligned}\right\}. \tag{4.27}$$

With an allowance for assumptions (4.27), inequality (4.26) is as follows:

$$\Pi'_{\Pi}\overline{W}'_{H}\overline{S}'_{H} - \Pi_{\Pi}\overline{W}_{H}\overline{S}_{H} \geq S_{\Pi\Pi}. \tag{4.28}$$

If we associate the values of $\overline{S}'_{H}$, Π'_{Π}, $\overline{S}_{H}$ and Π_{Π} representing the expenses on the production of old and new types of products which are in demand, so the following correlation is economically reasonable.

$$\overline{S}'_{H}\Pi'_{\Pi} \leq \overline{S}_{H}\Pi_{\Pi}. \tag{4.29}$$

Inequality (4.29) shows that in case of replacement of old products for new items of similar designation, there should be no increase in cost. Condition of lack of growth(reduction) of capital coefficient in introduction of progressive equipment instead of outdated equipment is one of application examples of this requirement.

The inequality (4.29) can be presented in the form of equation

$$\frac{\overline{S}_{\textit{н}}\Pi_{\Pi}}{\overline{S}'_{\textit{н}}\Pi'_{\Pi}} = 1 + \alpha, \quad 0 \le \alpha < 1, \tag{4.30}$$

where

$$\alpha = \frac{\overline{S}_{\textit{н}}\Pi_{\Pi} - \overline{S}'_{\textit{н}}\Pi'_{\Pi}}{\overline{S}'_{\textit{н}}\Pi'_{\Pi}}. \tag{4.31}$$

If we substitute values (4.30) and (4.31) in expression (4.28) we have:

$$\overline{W}'_{\textit{н}} - \overline{W}_{\textit{н}} \ge \frac{S_{\Pi\Pi}}{\overline{S}'_{\textit{н}}\Pi'_{\Pi}} + \frac{\overline{S}_{\textit{н}}\Pi_{\Pi} - \overline{S}'_{\textit{н}}\Pi'_{\Pi}}{\overline{S}'_{\textit{н}}\Pi'_{\Pi}}\overline{W}_{\textit{н}}. \tag{4.32}$$

The right part of inequality (4.32)—minimum economically expedient incremental value of efficiency normative.

Let us set $\overline{W}'_{\textit{н}} - \overline{W}_{\textit{н}} = \Delta W_{\textit{н}}$ and a great number of possible economically expedient values $\Delta W_{\textit{н}}$ and we set $\{\Delta W_{\textit{н}}\}_{\textit{э}}$,the right part of inequality (4.32) is the greatest lower bound of a great number $\{\Delta W_{\textit{н}}\}_{\textit{э}}$:

$$\frac{S_{\Pi\Pi}}{\overline{S}'_{\textit{н}}\Pi'_{\Pi}} + \frac{\overline{S}_{\textit{н}}\Pi_{\Pi} - \overline{S}'_{\textit{н}}\Pi'_{\Pi}}{\overline{S}'_{\textit{н}}\Pi'_{\Pi}}\overline{W}_{\textit{н}} = \inf\{\Delta W_{\textit{н}}\} = \Delta W_{\textit{н}}.$$

Taking into consideration that $\overline{S}_{\textit{н}}$, Π_{Π}, and $\overline{W}_{\textit{н}}$—constants and the more unconventional and more perfect the design of new sample is, the more the cost $S_{\text{пп}}$ is and less $\overline{S}'_{\textit{н}}\Pi'_{\Pi}$, it is possible to conclude that the incremental value of normative efficiency in alternation of production generations should be much more than in case of changing modifications, i.e.,

$$\Delta^{k,k+1} > \delta^{k}_{j,\, j+1}. \tag{4.33}$$

Correctness of inequality (4.33) brings assertion to the front that in new market conditions, fast alternation of generations is a key factor of the enterprise survival providing acceleration of innovation of every type of production.

Let us consider in detail the graphic model of development of the type of production presented in Fig. 4.5, with an allowance for specific character of the curves describing change of normative efficiency according to the increase of technical and economic level of production and quality of the mastered product samples and dynamics of the incremental value of normative efficiency during development of production of various modifications of the same basic sample.

Processes of increasing production efficiency of a particular product as a result of its technological processing and organizational-technical measures in order to increase the technical and economic level of production are precisely described by the logistical curves. It is obvious that process of changing normative efficiency, caused by the same factors and having as an independent variable the number of the made items of the j-th modification of the basic sample of the k-th generation, should have the same character. Figure 4.6 shows the graph of process $W_{H}^{k}(i)$, $i \in \left[n_{j}^{k+1}, n_{j+1}^{k}\right]$. Asymptote $W_{H}^{k\,j}$ shows a limit of potential possibilities of design technology of the j-th to modification of the basic sample of the k-th generation of production in increasing its normative efficiency.

In analysis of dynamics of incremental value of efficiency in mastering production of various modification of the same basic sample, it is convenient to take advantage of integrated function of the total incremental value of normative efficiency at the expense of consecutive development of modification of the basic sample. This function looks like

$$\delta^{k}(j) = \sum_{i=1}^{j} \delta_{i-1,i}^{k} \leq M_{k},$$

where M_k—total of modifications of the basic sample mastered until the alternation of generations;
i—modifications index, $i = 1, 2, \ldots, M_k$.

Practice shows that $\delta_{i-1,i}^{k}$ is decreasing with the growth of i, as the development potential in design of the basic sample is limited. Their identification and use in the process of creation and development of production of new modifications require increasing resources and time. It is easy to notice that $\delta^{k}(j)$ with the increase of j should grow more slowly and like a logistical curve should have a zone of saturation and an asymptote to characterize potential saturation point of the basic sample design (Fig. 4.7).

Discontinuation of the mastered sample and the beginning of new production take place in the zone of saturation $W_{H}^{k}(i)$ of dependence at the time of slowing rates of its growth to such a level when development of new sample becomes more effective than continuation of work regarding perfection of the old item.

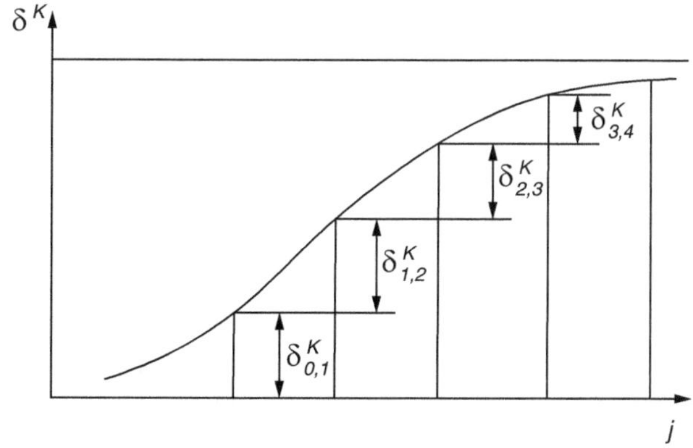

Fig. 4.6 Dependence of normative efficiency of design technology of the j-th modifications of the basic sample of the k-th generation $W_{H}^{k\,j}$ on the number of made items i

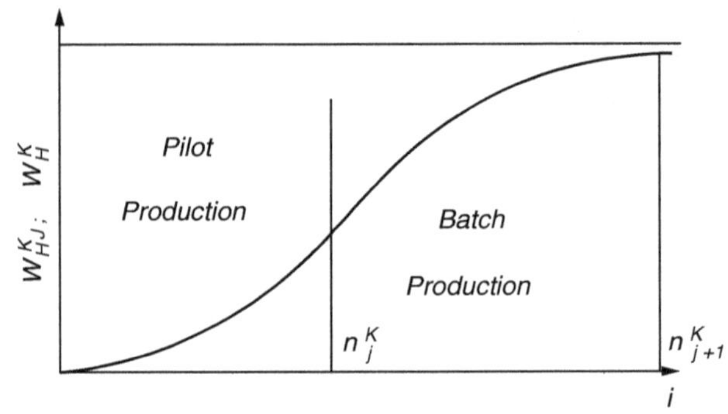

Fig. 4.7 Dependence of integrated function of the total incremental value of normative efficiency δ^k on the number of modifications of the basic sample j

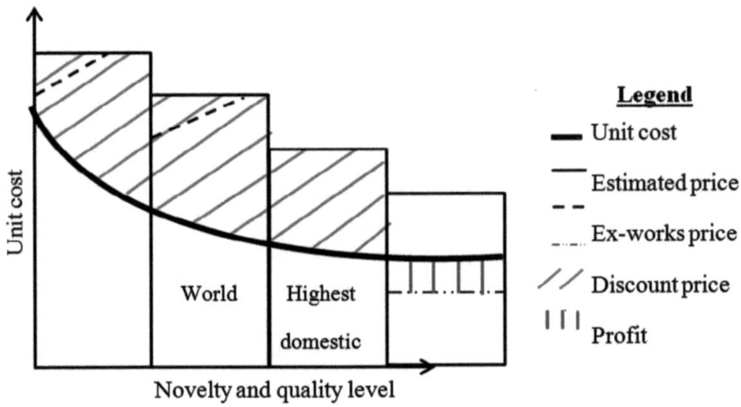

Fig. 4.8 Dependence of the unit price on the level of its novelty and quality

Alternation of generations of the output products takes place in the zone of saturation of function $\delta^k(j)$ at the time of reduction of increments $\delta^k_{i-1,1}$ when development of the new sample becomes more expedient on the economic aircraft rather than new modification of the old one.

Appropriateness of development of production of new samples and production generations in various conditions can be caused by the policy of prices only. The newly mastered products should be more profitable for a manufacturer than the previous one. Profitability level should be as high as the level of normative efficiency of a new product relative to the old one. In this case too, there should be time when development of a new product becomes more expedient on the economic aircraft, as the incremental value of profit from commercialization of new products will make it possible to pay back nonrecurrent expenditures for its development within a short period of time. The relation between the price and cost value of production changing according to the degree of novelty and quality of products is presented in Fig. 4.8.

At the early stages of development of the new sample, ex-works price can be essentially lower than the factory price the manufacturer would like to have. It is done in order to attract the buyers of new goods; then with the increase in demand, the price rises and becomes optimum for the manufacturer.

Actual processes of updating depend on:

- Prices for a new product (in comparison with the price for the previous item);
- Consumer cost of a new product (in comparison with consumer cost of the previous item).

Let us consider the process of production updating in terms of enhancement of economic efficiency of the enterprise (Fig. 4.9). Even in case of equality of profit from production and commercialization of old and new products, we should carefully analyze dynamics of production costs and the price of a new product. When the old product is replaced by a new item at the moment t_1 and production cost of a new product C_1 is equal to $Ц_0$, during time t_1–t_4, the company receives additional profit equal to two areas of Fig. A1'1. If the products replacement takes place later at the moments t_3 or t_4, except the specified loss of profit, the enterprise will not have any free production capacities, as production costs for a new product by the time point t_4 are lower than production costs of the old item by almost twofold.

$Ц_0$, $Ц_1$—old and new products' prices with the similar rate-of-return from commercialization;

C_0, C_1—production costs of old and new products

Timely updating of the output products provides additional profit to the manufacturer if updating is preceded by the careful economic analysis.

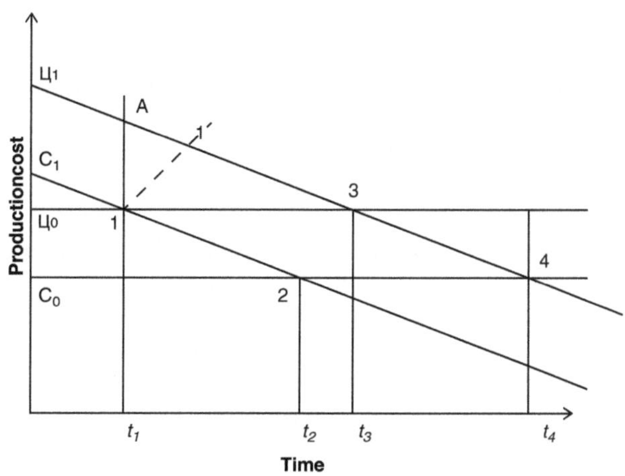

Fig. 4.9 Dynamics of production cost of the old and new products

Economic methods to determine time of new products output can be classified as follows:

- Analysis of time series;
- Structural analysis;
- Invariant analysis;
- Analysis of cross-sectoral linkages;
- Analysis of value limits;
- Analysis of threshold values;
- Substitution analysis;
- Strategic analysis.

Time series analysis makes it possible to display visually the most essential tendencies of changing capital–labor ratio, operation and maintenance cost of equipment, number of personnel and payroll budget, a technological level and volume of output products, and production capacities.

The problem of threshold values should be considered from the point of view of:

- possibilities to identify the limits of partial saturation and their occurrence time;
- possibilities to investigate new ways of setting new prices;
- uses of available economic provisions;
- establishments of the optimum correlation between full and partial updating.

The volumes of economic processes of replacement (updating) depend on the price for a new product (in comparison with the price for the previous item) and consumer cost of this new product (in comparison with the previous one). The new product price certainly depends on the market demand and is defined by the market; however, cost value of the output new production in many respects depends on quality and efficiency of Production Engineering Process (PEP).

While determining basic directions of PEP and scope of works by the directions, it is expedient to start with following positions.

PEP stage begins with the time of decision-making on production supply for the manufacture, and it includes creation of conditions to launch a batch production and proceeds until production achieves the necessary technical, technological, and economic characteristics providing its high competitiveness in the commodity market. Proceeding from the scheme in Fig. 4.10, we specify the scope of works in the following basic directions of PEP.

Scope of Works in the Basic Directions of Production Engineering Process

If we consider each of PEP stages in detail, it is possible to see that they, to one extent or another, create competitive advantages for the products at the expense of achieving goals of PEP performing and PEP indices (Table 4.2).

First, it is reduction of production costs which is one of the factors to determine the price of the goods. Other factors on which the goods' price depends are technical characteristics, demand for the goods in the market, and the sale volumes.

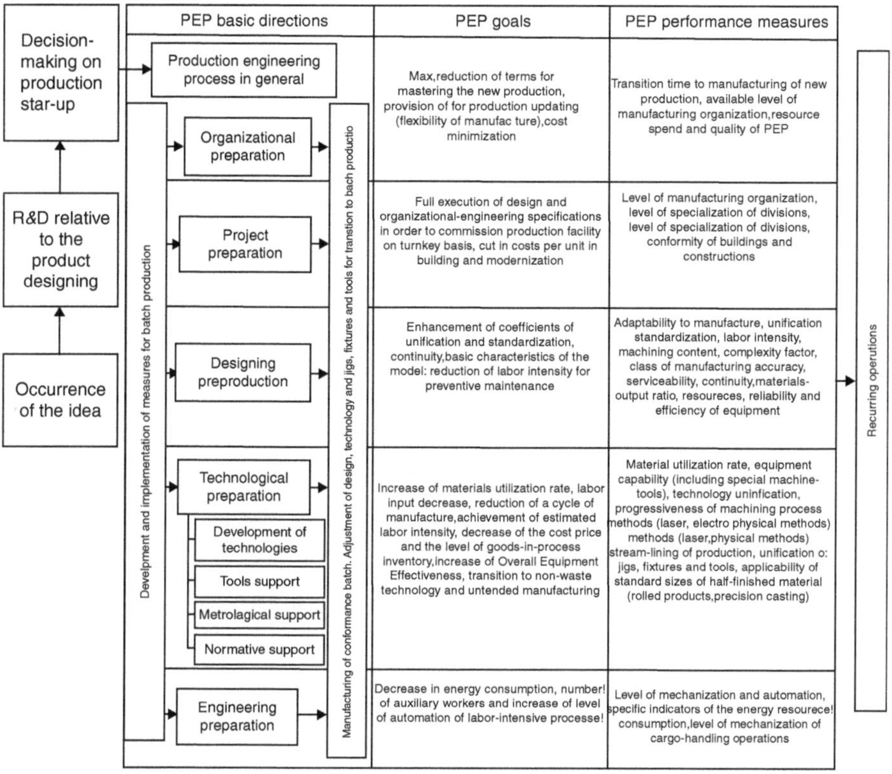

Fig. 4.10 Production Engineering Process

They are closely associated with industrial, marketing, and administrative costs. The price can and must include past sunk costs connected with designing and production engineering process, as well as deferred cost connected with after-sales services which the firm can defray to lower expenses in order to attract the buyers.

It is worth mentioning the costs connected with information processes during the period before the goods sale. Change of costs compels a firm to change the good's price not because it would like to receive big dividends, though such factor takes place too, but also for the objective reasons arising in the course of production and sale. The price increase for production of the firm does not bring it additional competitive advantages. On the contrary, this increase in price reduces competitive advantages. This fact forces the firm to reduce production costs at the expense of various activities. Doing this requires periodic costs analysis and with the help of control system (such system should work practically within every firm) to stop their growth by means of organizational-technical measures intended to decrease the production costs of the goods. It should be mentioned that internal costs of the firm can be stabilized and reduced by means of application of known methods of decrease in work labor input, increase of productivity, organization of cost-effective use of

Table 4.2 Scope of works in the basic directions of production engineering process

Types of works	Scope of works
Organizational preparation:	–Design development, organization of omnidirectional R&D required by PEP –Development of specifications for PEP, regulations, standards –Training of personnel to provide output of new production
Project preparation:	–Development of design assignments –Development of construction design documents –Drawing up of preliminary schemes of configuration of producing shops –Complex reconstruction of the buildings, shops, sites –Organization design –Regulation of production process
Designing preproduction:	–Development of design documents –Design fabricability testing –Preparation of documentation for batch production –Preparation of the documents on equipment operation, servicing, and restoration –Increase of indices of unification, processability, etc. –Perfection of operational qualities by results of analysis of consumer operation
Technological preparation:	–Development of technologies: designing of new technological processes, perfection of the current ones, development of typical and group processes –Development of programs for NC equipment, instructions, standards –Tool preparation: identification of required jigs, fixtures and tools (JF&T), multifunctional machine-tool attachments –Designing of the original machine-tool attachment, the special cutting tool, containers; development of JF&T manufacturing processes –Metrological support: identification on nomenclature of testing instruments; designing of original test facilities; development of inspection processes, adjustment of equipment –Normative support: development of norms for consumption of material, power resources, labor costs
Engineering preparation:	–Development of non-standard equipment –Development of mechanical equipment and automation aids –Installation, adjusting of equipment, and power supply systems –Provision of scheduled preventive maintenance –Development of safety precaution measures

resources, and other known measures. As a rule, production internal costs amount to 25–60 % of the general costs depending on complexity of the output products and availability of the minimum or maximum number of technological process stages required for production of particular production.

As to external costs, i.e., cost of materials, components, power resources, influence of intermediaries and the state economic policy, reduction of prices, increase in tariffs, taxes, provision of grants, etc., these costs amounting to 75–40 % are not directly influenced by the firm-manufacturer; therefore, advanced firms in an effort to win the market forecast change in prices of suppliers, tariffs, taxes, and other external factors influencing production costs. On the basis of this forecast, the firm prepares to avoid essential economic losses as a result of adverse influence of external factors. It provides stabilization of prices and a victory in the price competitive struggle.

Secondly, highly effective PEP should provide a possibility to alter production generations as a way to receive competitive advantages and perfect technological bases of manufacture, i.e., diversification of production.

Diversification of industrial production is assortment expansion, change of a type of production made by the firm, development of new types of manufacturing in order to increase production efficiency, receive economic incremental value, and prevention of bankruptcy.

Before starting diversification of production, the manufacturer should carefully study consumer demand in order to find out consumer's opinion concerning necessity and significance of one or another characteristic of updated products. Afterward, a manufacturer defines a number of the most important characteristics to be met by the products to increase the demand. Depending on type of the characteristics and how they can be provided at the expense of technical or processing methods, the manufacturer makes a decision on partial change of one or another element of the goods design or creates structurally new goods. For example, perfection of design and, in most cases, change of design take place in the motor industry, and only then there is a new type of car. Successful carrying out of diversification of production allows the manufacturer to establish a margin on the goods for additional constructive elements or new characteristics, and more often to raise the price or to increase the sales volume, to enter new markets, and to make the manufacturer's trade mark more attractive.

Diversification of industrial production will be successful if the technical and technological superiority of the products and the process is created at the expense of innovative solutions and technologies providing high quality of production and easy servicing. Results of diversification can be positive (high profit) if the manufacturer can considerably improve consumer properties of the goods, offer a wider set of accompanying services, and, as a whole, provide the consumer with the more values at the same price.

Thirdly, well-organized PEP with due account for perspective of its development can promote creation of essentially new goods which, in the beginning of production, will be claimed by only a certain small segment of the market, say, intended for a consumer with the big consumer ability. Creation of essentially new goods with use of advanced innovative technologies requires concentration of all resources of the firm and availability of highly effective, automated production.

It should be noted that though PEP is one of the known elements of creation of competitive advantages of the goods, however, even being highly effective it does not provide permanent competitive advantage in the market as there is a set of other factors influencing creation of competitive advantages of the goods.

Enhancement of efficiency of the specified processes requires specific organizational-technical measures. As a rule, they consist of the technical and technological offers connected, first of all, with improvement of quality and decrease of the cost price, i.e., the sale price and the output in the volumes claimed by the buyer. Measures to enhance quality of output products and to provide decrease of their cost price and increase in volume include increase of automation level of industrial and control and measure processes, application of low-waste technology, or ecologically pure "know-how." In other words, production of competitive goods for commodity markets should have all the newest innovative technologies which are economically justified and are supported with various types of resources of the firm-manufacturer.

4.5 Calculation Example for Product Competitiveness

In order to determine product competitiveness depending on its economic and technological parameters, we offer construction of the following mathematical model to provide objective evaluation of the product competitiveness in the form of system of functional dependences of the specific indices, presented in a general view:

$$F(u) = \begin{cases} f_1 = f_1(u_{1,1}, \ldots, u_{1,N_1}) \\ \cdots \\ f_w = f_w(u_{w,1}, \ldots, u_{w,N_w}) \end{cases}, \tag{4.34}$$

where f_i—i-th function reflecting interdependence N_i of specific indices of the product competitiveness $(u_{1,1}, \ldots, u_{1,N_1})$ where $i = 1, \ldots, w$, moreover, $u_{i,1} \in U, \ldots, u_{i,N_i} \in U$;

U—a set of all specific indices of the product competitiveness (including specific scientific and technical indices of the product competitiveness $u' i \in U' \subset U$ and risk factors $u_{iR} \in U \subset U$);

w—number of functional dependences of f_i in system $F(U)$.

It should be noted that the number of generalized indices should be optimum to identify product competitiveness; moreover, this system of generalized indices of competitiveness will have a complicated hierarchy considering various interrelations and interactions of one index with another.

Owing to noted above, in order to identify integrated coefficient of the product competitiveness, we should consider hierarchical system of the generalized indices located at various levels.

Within the framework of this hierarchical approach, specific indices of the product competitiveness are located at the first level:

$H_{1,i}$—quantitative value of the specific competitiveness index of the i-th product which is not the scientific and technical characteristic of the said product;

$H'_{1,i}$—competitiveness index of the i-th specific scientific and technical index of the product.

With due account for their weighting, the generalized index at the second level is found by formula

$$R_{2,j} = \sum_{i=1}^{m_{1,j}} H_{1,i}\beta_{1,i} + \sum_{i=1}^{M_{1,j}-m_{1,j}} H'_{1,i}\beta_{1,i}, \tag{4.35}$$

where $R_{2,j}$—j-th generalized index of competitiveness of the second level of generalization;
$m_{1,j}$—number of specific indices of the firm competitiveness;
$(M_{1,j} - m_{1,j})$ —number of specific indices of the product competitiveness, characterizing its scientific and technical condition, in which change can occur under the influence of scientific and technical achievements;
$\beta_{0,i}$—weighting coefficient of the i-th a specific index at the first level of generalization

$(i = 1, \ldots, M_{1,j})$, condition $\sum_{i=1}^{M_{1,j}} \beta_{0,i} = 1$ is met.

For any p-th level of generalization, the generalized indices will consist of the composite indices of the product competitiveness of the previous (p-1)-th level of generalization with due account for their weighting in this generalized index:

$$R_{p,j} = \sum_{i=1}^{M_{p,j}} R_{p-1,i} \cdot \beta_{p-1,i}, \tag{4.36}$$

Where $R_{p,j}$—j-th generalized index of the product competitiveness of the p-th level of generalization;
$M_{p,j}$—number of generalized indices of the previous level $R_{p-1,i}$ making index $R_{p,j}$;
$\beta_{p-1,i}$—weighting coefficient of generalized index $R_{p-1,i}$; moreover condition $\sum_{i=1}^{M_{1j}} \beta_{p-1,i} = 1$ is met.

The hierarchy top level (P) of the generalized indices of the product competitiveness will have generalized indices characterizing product competitiveness.

The number of such indices will depend on functional structure of production and its designation.

Hence, the use of formula (4.36) may generalize the integrated coefficient of the product competitiveness, which would quantitatively reflect the influence of specific and generalized indices, with due account for their weighting, influencing product competitiveness. Please note that at the final stage, i.e., at P-level, there should also be considered priority of the basic characteristics of production in forming its general competitiveness while identifying an integrated index of the product competitiveness, which are summarized with due account for weighting of the generalized indices of the hierarchy top level

$$H_{I,npo\partial} = \frac{\sum_{i=1}^{M_P} R_{P,i} \cdot \beta_{P,i}}{\sum_{i=1}^{M_P} \beta_{P,i}}, \tag{4.37}$$

where $R_{P,i}$—generalized index of the product competitiveness in the i-th direction of its activity.

$\beta_{P,i}$—weighting coefficient of index $R_{P,i}$ reflecting a share of competitiveness formed in this direction of the firm activity.

M_P—number of competitiveness generalized indices of the highest level of the hierarchy (basic characteristics of the product).

During the management of price and quality of production and effective variation, previously generalized and specific indices of competitiveness with their weighting, the integrated index of the product competitiveness within the framework of its activity should increase:

$$H_{I,npo\partial} \to \max. \tag{4.38}$$

On the basis of the above stated, there may be made the following mathematical model determining product competitiveness taking into account an optimality of the generalized indices of the firm competitiveness and existing interrelation of specific indices of the product competitiveness:

$$\begin{cases} f_{i_1} = f_{i_1}\left(u_{i_1,1}, \ldots, u_{i_1,N_{i_1}}\right), \quad (i_1 = 1, \ldots, I_f) \\ H_{i_2} > 0, \quad (i_2 = 1, \ldots, I_2) \\ H'_{i_3} > 0, \quad (i_3 = 1, \ldots, I_3) \\ R_{1,j_1} = \sum_{i=1}^{M_{1,j_1}} H_i \beta_{0,i} + \sum_{i=m_{11\,j_1}+1}^{M_{1,j_1}} H'_i \beta_{0,i}, \quad (j_1 = 1, \ldots, J_1) \\ R_{p,j_p} = \sum_{i=1}^{M_{p,j_p}} R_{p-1,i} \beta_{p-1,i}, \quad (p = 2, \ldots, P; \;\; j_p = 1, \ldots, J_p) \end{cases}, \tag{4.39}$$

$$H_{I,npo\partial} = \frac{\sum_{i=1}^{M_P} R_{P,i} \cdot \beta_{P,i}}{\sum_{i=1}^{M_P} \beta_{P,i}} \to \max$$

where f_{i_1}—i_I-th function reflecting interdependence N_{i_1} of specific indices of the product competitiveness $\left(u_{i_1,1}, \ldots, u_{i_1,N_{i_1}}\right)$; moreover, $u_{i,1} \in U, \ldots, u_{i,N_i} \in U$.

U—a set of all specific indices of the product competitiveness (including specific scientific and technical indices of the product competitiveness $u'i \in U' \subset U$ as well as risk $u_{iR} \in U \subset U$).

I_f—number of such functional interdependence.

$H_{1,i}$—specific index of competitiveness of the i_2-th production, without being a scientific and technical characteristic of production.

I_2—number of coefficients.

$H'_{1,i}$—competitiveness coefficient of the i_3-th specific scientific and technical index of production.

I_3—number of coefficients.

j_1-th generalized index of competitiveness of the first level of generalization.

$m_{1,j}$—number of specific indices of the product competitiveness, without being scientific and technical characteristic of production.

$(M_{1,j_1} - m_{1,j_1})$—number of specific scientific and technical indices of the product competitiveness R_{p,j_p}.

J_1—number of indices R_{1,j_1} at the first level of generalization.

$\beta_{0,i}$—weighting coefficient of the i-th specific index at the first level of generalization $(i = 1, \ldots, M_{1,j_1})$; the following condition is met:

$$\sum_{i=1}^{M_{1,j_1}} \beta_{0,i} = 1;$$

R_{p,j_p}—j_p-th generalized index of the product competitiveness of the p-th level of generalization.

M_{p,j_p}—number of the generalized indices of the previous level $R_{p-1,j}$ making index R_{p,j_p}.

J_p—number of indices R_{p,j_p} at the p-th level of generalization.

P—number of levels of generalization.

$\beta_{p-1,i}$—weighting coefficient of generalized index $R_{p-1,i}$ condition $\sum_{i=1}^{Mp,j_p} \beta_{p-1,i} = 1$ is met.

Indices $R_{1,i}$, $R_{p,i}$ $(p = 2, \ldots, P)$ and $H_{I,n\,po\grave{O}}$ can be repeatedly estimated after some time, for example, in a year. Change of these indices in time will show dynamics of the change of level of the product competitiveness in the directions of its activity that will help managers or directors in their decision-making concerning optimization of the products' properties.

With this aim in view, provisions should be made to provide a task within the framework of a set of specific indices of the products competitiveness U and achievements of $HT\Pi U'$ in time.

Then the formula takes on the appearance of

$$U^{'}(t) \subset U(t). \tag{4.40}$$

For mathematical model (4.39), all specific indices of the products competitiveness, weighting coefficients of all (specific and generalized) product competitiveness indices in formation of competitiveness will become

$$\begin{array}{l} \beta_{i,\,j} = \beta_{i,\,j}(t), \quad (i = 0, \ldots, P); \\ H_{i_2} = H_{i_2}(t); \\ H^{'}_{i_3} = H^{'}_{i_3}(t), \end{array} . \tag{4.41}$$

where t—time.

The generalized indices of the product competitiveness from the first to the P-th level will become

$$\begin{array}{l} R_{1,\,j_1} = R_{1,\,j_1}(t), \\ R_{p,\,j_p} = R_{p,\,j_p}(t). \end{array} \tag{4.42}$$

The integrated index of the product competitiveness will look like

$$H_{I,n\,po\grave{O}} = H_{I,n\,po\grave{O}}(t). \tag{4.43}$$

Mathematical model (4.39) takes on the appearance of

$$\begin{cases} f_{i_1}(t) = f_{i_1}\left(u_{i_1,1}(t), \ldots, u_{i_1,N_{i_1}}(t)\right), \quad (i_1 = 1, \ldots, I_f) \\ H_{i_2}(t) > 0, \quad (i_2 = 1, \ldots, I_2) \\ H^{'}_{i_3}(t) > 0, \quad (i_3 = 1, \ldots, I_3) \\ R_{1,\,j_1}(t) = \sum\limits_{i=1}^{M_{1,\,j_1}} H_i(t) \cdot \beta_{0,i}(t) + \sum\limits_{i=m_{11\,j_1}+1}^{M_{1,\,j_1}} H^{'}_i(t) \cdot \beta_{0,i}(t), \quad (j_1 = 1, \ldots, J_1) \\ R_{p,\,j_p} = \sum\limits_{i=1}^{M_{p,\,j_p}} R_{p-1,i}(t) \cdot \beta_{p-1,i}(t), \quad (p = 2, \ldots, P; \quad j_p = 1, \ldots, J_p) \end{cases}, \tag{4.44}$$

$$H_{I,npo\grave{o}}(t) = \frac{\sum_{i=1}^{M_P} R_{P,i}(t) \cdot \beta_{P,i}(t)}{\sum_{i=1}^{M_P} \beta_{P,i}(t)} \rightarrow \max$$

With the help of such mathematical model within the framework of the product competitiveness system, there will be calculated an integrated product competitiveness coefficient, and there will be forecasting of changes of the product competitiveness with due account for all the factors it is influenced by. It will make it possible to provide the firm management with the timely information on change of the product competitiveness at any stage.

Such information will give a chance to purposefully, in due time and objectively, make a decision on competitiveness regulation and perfection of competitive advantages of the output products and the firm in general: for example, concerning replacement of a particular type of equipment for a new one with established technical possibilities required by the firm; concerning change of materials in production and components possessing required competitive advantages; and concerning search and implementation of "know-how" to provide previously identified terms and quality.

Using mathematical model (4.44), we calculated integral coefficients of competitiveness of one purpose products.

The basis of calculation is presented by block diagram on Fig. 4.11.

Stage 1-2 Collection and analysis of statistical data on the medium-range aircraft of Russia, and identification of the basic indices to characterize this class aircraft.

Stage 3 Plotting of hierarchical structure of (aircraft) manufacturing based on splitting a number of indices into levels in the order of their importance (Table 4.3).

Stage 4 Calculation of integrated coefficients of the product competitiveness according to the scheme in Fig. 4.8 with due account for the above-offered calculation model of integrated indices of the product competitiveness.

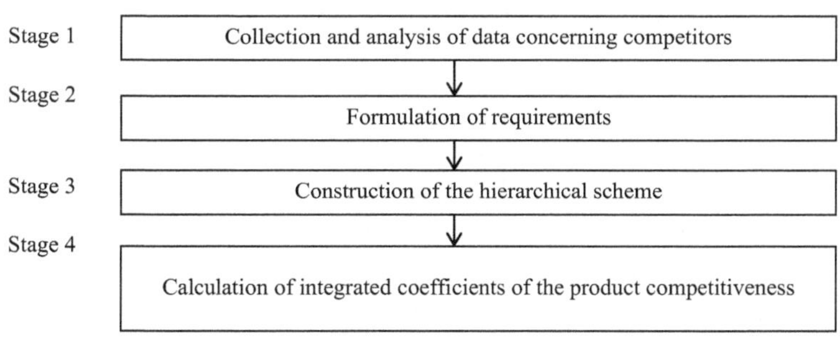

Fig. 4.11 Computation scheme for integrated coefficient of the product competitiveness

Table 4.3 Collection and analysis of statistical data concerning specific indices of competitiveness of the medium-range aircraft of the Russian federation

Levels	Specific indices	Types of aircraft					
		Tu-334-100	RRJ 75 LR	RRJ 95 LR	AN-148-100E	AN-148-100A	AN-148-200E
1	Price 1. Aircraft price, million rubles	10	24	27	14	16	18
	Operating performance: 1. Passenger seat configuration (pax)	102	75	98	98	100	102
2	Operating performance: 2. Maximum takeoff weight (t).	47,90	42,28	45,88	39,90	43,05	46,33
3	Operating performance: 3. Maximum payload (kg)	12,000	9,130	12,245	9,000	9,000	12,000
4	Operating performance: 4. Fuel consumption per 500 n miles under full load (kg)	2,890	2,264	2,408	2,094	2,094	2,574
5	Operating performance 5. Flying range (km)	2,800	4,550	4,420	3,350	4,800	3,200

Step 1 We will proceed from the known fact that product (service) competitiveness can enhance with the increase of only specific indices of the product competitiveness which we designate as $X_{k,i}$ (for example, passenger seat configuration) and with decrease of other indices which we designate as $X_{j,k}$ (for example, production price (service)).

Let us introduce the following basic designations:

P—current number of level.
P—number of levels.
i—indicator of the product competitiveness index; when it increases, product competitiveness increases too.
j—indicator of the product competitiveness index; when it decreases, product competitiveness increases.
k—number of competing goods.
$x_{i,k} = X_{i,k}/X_{i\ \max}$—standardized parameters of the product competitiveness, where $X_{i\ \max}$—the maximum value of the i-th index among T products.
$x_{j,k} = X_{j\ \min}/X_{j,k}$—"standardized" parameters of the product competitiveness.
$X_{j\ \min}$—minimum value of the j-th control index among K goods.

By means of this scheme, we receive standardized table of specific indices of the aircraft competitiveness presented in Table 4.3.

Step 2 The integrated index of the product competitiveness is calculated according to the scheme in Fig. 4.8. Calculation should be performed from the first level, in steps to the next level, for which the generalized indices were computed by formula (4.39). It should be noted that in identifying weighting coefficients β, an analysis method of the hierarchical structures was used. It should be noted that this analysis method of the hierarchical structures, developed by American mathematician T. Saati, is an original approach in the decision-making theory. The method was approved in a number of studies in the field of sociology, economy, and ecology and is a plausible model of a natural course of human reasoning while solving challenges of a hierarchical choice (Figs. 4.12, 4.13, and 4.14, Table 4.4).

Determination of Specific Indices of Quality at the First Level and Generalized Indices at the Second Level

With allowances made for the data in Table 4.3, we have standardized specific indices of the product competitiveness of the first level $H_{1,r}$—presented in Table 4.5.

Then, with the help of hierarchy analysis method, we find the priorities vector of the firms quality indices at the first level, presented in Table 4.6.

With allowances made for the formula (4.39), by multiplication of the transposed matrix presented in Table 4.6 and vectorβ_I, we receive generalized indices of the aircraft quality competitiveness at the second level, presented in Table 4.7.

As you can see in Table 4.6, AN-148-Ehas the highest quality indices.

Determination of Price Indices at the First and the Second Levels

With allowances made for the data presented in Table 4.3, we have standardized specific indices of the product competitiveness of the first level $H_{1,r}$—presented in Table 4.9.

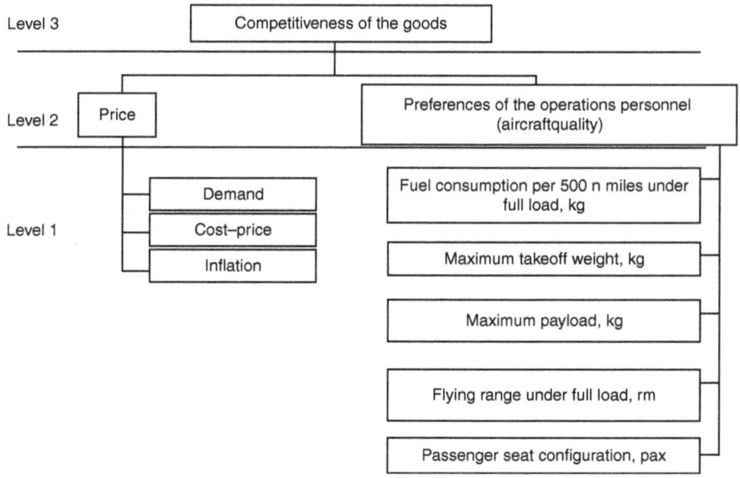

Fig. 4.12 Hierarchical structure product (aircraft) competitiveness

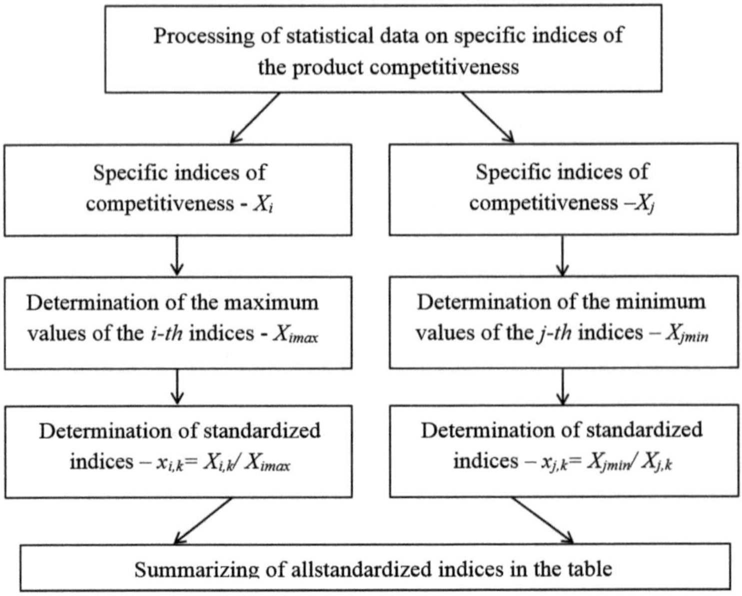

Fig. 4.13 Computation scheme for standardized indices of the product competitiveness

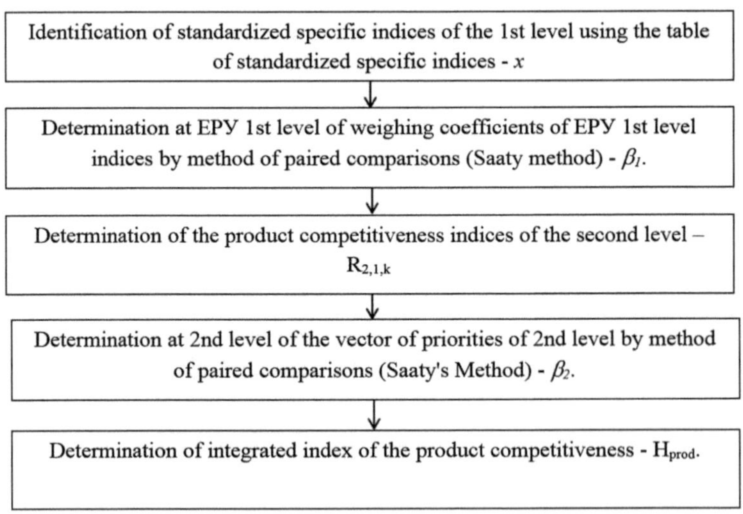

Fig. 4.14 Computation scheme for integrated indices of the product competitiveness

Table 4.4 Summary of all standardized indices of competitiveness of medium-range aircraft of the Russian federation

Levels	Specific indices	Types of aircraft					
		Tu-334-100	RRJ 75 LR	RRJ 95 LR	AN-148-100E	AN-148-100A	AN-148-200E
1	Price 1. Aircraft price, million rubles	0.8	1	1	0.8	0.8	0.8
	Operating performance: 1. Passenger seat configuration (pax)	1	0.926	0.893	1	0.962	0.893
2	Operating performance: 2. Maximum takeoff weight (t).	1	0.7353	0.9608	0.9608	0.9804	1
3	Operating performance: 3. Maximum payload (kg)	1	0.8827	0.9578	0.8330	0.8987	0.9672
4	Operating performance: 4. Fuel consumption per 500 n miles under full load (kg)	0.980	0.746	1	0.7350	0.7350	0.9800
5	Operating performance 5. Flying range (km)	0.5833	0.9479	0.9208	0.6979	1	0.6667

Table 4.5 Standardized specific indices of the aircraft competitiveness of the first level

Aircraft quality	Types of aircraft					
	Tu-334-100	RRJ 75 LR	RRJ 95 LR	AN-148-100E	AN-148-100A	AN-148-200E
1. Fuel consumption per 500 n miles under full load (kg)	0.7246	0.9249	0.8696	1.0000	1.0000	0.8135
2. Maximum takeoff weight (t)	0.8330	0.9437	0.8697	1.0000	0.9268	0.8612
3. Maximum payload (kg)	0.9800	0.7456	1.0000	0.7350	0.7350	0.9800
4. Flying range (km)	0.5833	0.9479	0.9208	0.6979	1.0000	0.6667
5. seat configuration (pax)	1.0000	0.7353	0.9608	0.9608	0.9804	1.0000

With the help of hierarchy analysis method, we determine the vector of priorities for specific price indices of the firm competitiveness of the first level, presented in Table 4.9.

With allowances made for the formula (4.39), by multiplication of the transposed matrix presented in Table 4.8 and vector β_2, we receive specific indices of the product competitiveness of the second level, presented in Table 4.10.

Table 4.6 Matrix of binary comparisons by means of hierarchy analysis method and priorities vector of the aircraft quality indices at the first level of hierarchy

Ranging of objects	1	2	3	4	5	6
1. Fuel consumption per 500 n miles under full load (kg)	1	2	4	6	8	0.4653
2. Maximum takeoff weight, (t)	0.5	1	2	4	8	0.28301
3. Maximum payload (kg)	0.25	0.5	1	2	3	0.1336
4. Flying range (km)	0.1667	0.25	0.5	1	2	0.0750
5. seat configuration (pax)	0.125	0.125	0.3333	0.5	1	0.0431

Table 4.7 The composite indices of competitiveness of aircraft the second level on quality

Types of aircraft	Quality indices of the second stage
Tu-334-100	0.7907
RRJ 75 LR	0.8998
RRJ 95 LR	0.8948
AN-148-100E	0.9403
AN-148-100A	0.9430
AN-148-200E	0.8462

Table 4.8 Standardized specific indices of competitiveness of the first level according to the price

	Types of aircraft					
Price indices	Tu-334-100	RRJ 75 LR	RRJ 95 LR	AN-148-100E	AN-148-100A	AN-148-200E
1. Advertized price	1	0.9777	08872	1	0.9615	0.8929
2. Demand	0.2	1	1	0.2	0.26667	0.3333
3. Inflation	0.6667	1	1	0.5	0.5	0.5

Table 4.9 Matrix of binary comparisons by means of hierarchy analysis method and the vector of priorities for specific scientific & technical indices of the product competitiveness of the first level

Alternatives	1	2	3	β_2
Cost value	1	3	7	0.6694
Demand	1/3	1	3	0.2426
Inflation	1/7	1/3	1	0.0879

Table 4.10 Specific indices aircraft competitiveness of the second level

Types of aircraft	Price indices
Tu-334-100	0.7766
RRJ 75 LR	0.9851
RRJ 95 LR	0.9245
AN-148-100E	0.76191
AN-148-100A	0.75235
AN-148-200E	0.7225

As you can see in Table 4.9, RRJ 75 LR has the highest Price indices.

AN type aircraft are not as good due to smaller number of orders and higher probability of financial risks.

Determination of Integrated Index of the Firm Competitiveness

Let us summarize the results of calculation of specific indices of the aircraft competitiveness of the second level, presented in Tables 4.7 and 4.10, and the data on specific indices of the second level in single Table 4.11.

Let us consider a case when the consumer is interested in the aircraft quality indices. Then, with the help of the hierarchy analysis method, it is possible to determine a vector of weighting for specific financial indices of the firm competitiveness of the second level, presented in Table 4.12.

With due account for the formula (4.39), by multiplication of the transposed matrix of Table 4.9 and the vector of priorities from Table 4.12, we receive integral coefficients of the aircraft competitiveness presented in Table 4.13.

As you can see in Table 4.12, if the price is less important as compared to the aircraft quality, RRJ 75 LR and RRJ 95 LR aircraft have the higher competitiveness, and Tu-334-100 has the least competitiveness.

In case when the price and quality of the aircraft are of equal worth, it is not difficult to receive the following evaluation presented in Table 4.14.

Table 4.11 Generalized indices of the aircraft competitiveness of the second level

Types of aircraft	Quality indices	Price indices
Tu-334-100	0.79066	0.7766
RRJ 75 LR	0.8998	0.9851
RRJ 95 LR	0.8948	0.9245
AN-148-100E	0.9403	0.7619
AN-148-100A	0.9430	0.7523
AN-148-200E	0.8463	0.7225

Table 4.12 Matrix of binary comparisons by means of hierarchy analysis method and the vector of priorities for specific indices of the firm competitiveness at the second level of hierarchy

Alternatives	1	2	β_l
Cost value	1	2	0.6667
Demand	0.5	1	0.333

Table 4.13 Integral coefficients of the aircraft competitiveness depending on the price priority

Types of aircraft	Integrated competitiveness coefficient of the aircraft
Tu-334-100	0.786
RRJ 75 LR	0.928
RRJ 95 LR	0.905
AN-148-100E	0.881
AN-148-100A	0.880
AN-148-200E	0.805

Table 4.14 Integrated coefficient of the aircraft competitiveness depending on priority of the quality

Types of aircraft	Integrated competitiveness coefficient of the aircraft
Tu-334-100	0.784
RRJ 75 LR	0.943
RRJ 95 LR	0.910
AN-148-100E	0.851
AN-148-100A	0.848
AN-148-200E	0.7844

As is obvious in this case, RRJ 75 LR and RRJ 95 LR aircraft have the higher competitiveness, and Tu-334-100 has the least competitiveness.

Conclusions Evaluation of the product competitiveness takes a key place in the competitiveness management system of a firm. Results of this evaluation form a basis for managerial decision-making, for identification of the vector and elaboration of the firm development strategy, as well as for commercialization of particular measures in various fields of activity (Research & Development, products quality improvement, reduction of production cost, products modification, diversification of production, suppliers of raw materials and trade channels, perfection of the marketing policy, etc.), as well as to forecast and plan financial and economic activities in the near-term period and in the long run. In order to receive objective, quantitative evaluations of the product competitiveness, we should use specific methodology, the development approaches of which are hereby offered by the authors of this monograph in this chapter.

The methodology of quantitative evaluation of the product competitiveness developed by the authors is based on the mathematical model, making it possible to compute competitiveness depending on the factors it is influenced in time. The mathematical model includes both specific and generalized indices of competitiveness.

The first group of indices makes it possible to estimate possible influence of external and internal environmental factors on creation and commercialization of production. They constitute a statistical basis for formation of integrated indices, initial basis for managerial decision-making on creation of a certain type of products, and their modification or phasing out. They reflect production status according to one or another characteristic: technical characteristics and cost of a certain type of materials, inflation, or custom duties. These indices reflect competitive properties of production.

The second group of indices is formed so that their subject matter had a particular rational value in order to study production status and tendencies of its life cycle. The generalized index reflects interaction of a set of specific indices with due account for their weighting in this coordinate action. The generalized indices, found on the basis of specific indices, make it possible to generate an integrated index of the product competitiveness within the framework of the system approach.

It will give a chance to the firm CEO to make a conclusion concerning output products competitiveness and, if necessary, according to the available information, to make managerial decisions concerning regulation of the firm competitive policy relating to the output products: to update production, to take it out of production, or to boost sales.

In order to have an objective evaluation of the product competitiveness, there should be specified an order of priorities and significance of the factors influencing competitive manufacturing, as well as their analysis and forecasting of their dynamics in the future. All this would make it possible to determine product competitiveness to a high degree of accuracy, both in the real time and in the long-term perspective.

One of the major coefficients of the product competitiveness is the products' price. Significance of the price factor is caused by the fact that the firm has a possibility to change production price within the known limits. Hence, unlike control of other products characteristics, production cost management can be carried out most operatively and effectively.

Another key problem to be investigated is the influence of change in price on competitiveness depending on the time factor. In particular, it is necessary to study a question of the price influence on competitiveness in the middle-term and the long-term forecasts.

The authors developed an approach to the study of the products' price's influence on their competitiveness based on application of the theory of evolutionary functional differential equations. As is known, functional differential equations can describe dynamic systems with due allowance for time lagging and aftereffect. Use of these effects makes it possible to receive mathematical model which would provide quantitative description of influence of the change in price on competitiveness in the middle-term and the long-term forecasts.

Mathematical models of evaluation of change impact assessment of the products' price, constructed by the authors, are relying on the system of difference-differential equations and functional differential equations. As a result, it is possible to build effective schemes of the optimum management of the index of competitiveness by means of change in price and to implement the algorithms for selection of a particular direction of the price management in order to enhance the product competitiveness.

Competitive price, in turn, can be reached at the expense of decrease in the cost price of the output goods. This decrease is reached at the expense of innovative technologies providing growth of labor productivity, decrease of energy and materials consumption, continuity and duration of the use of production equipment, etc.

Study of expenses for designing and manufacturing, as well as the factors determining cost value or influencing it, is of great importance for analysis of the cost price and identification of ways of its decreasing. The authors present general algorithm of the study of influence of various factors in the form of analysis sequence of steps, synthesis, selection and substantiations, and evaluation of results step by step and on the whole whenever done.

Mathematical interpretation of the cost price offered by the authors is based on regression analysis tools. This interpretation makes it possible to control product competitiveness, hence to take up specific measures to introduce innovative technologies providing high product competitiveness as a result of adjusting corresponding characteristics of this production according to requirements of the world market or above the level of analogues with the same competitive price.

The authors also arrived at the conclusion that it is necessary to identify basic technical and economic conditions to provide practical necessity of the goods output, which are specified by a set of factors, such as technical, operational and business factors, as well as to identify basic directions of manufacturing preparation being the basis for the products updating. It is obvious that the products' updating is a major link in a chain of enhancement of competitiveness and economic efficiency of the enterprise.

Relying on the computational methodology of the product competitiveness with application of mathematical approaches to assessment of the impact of change in price and production cost price on its competitiveness in the middle-term and long-term forecasts, as well as evaluation of influence of production updating on dynamics of competitiveness, the authors made a relevant calculation and verified techniques; they developed in the light of the data characterizing production medium-range aircraft of the Russian Federation. On the ground of the aircraft competitiveness integrated indices of six types, there was performed a benchmarking assessment, and a possibility of these assessments in the course of managerial decision-making depending on the firm priorities, "price and quality criteria," was illustrated.

Quantitative Evaluation of the Firm Competitiveness

5

5.1 Determination of Interrelated Competitiveness Indices of the Product and Firm

One of main objectives of any enterprise within the framework of market economy is enhancement of competitiveness and quality of the output products. As noted above, one of the main conditions of the enterprise competitiveness management is to develop a new technique of its analysis and "measurement" followed by a possibility to control the level of competitiveness of market entities and to make its comparative assessment. In the market conditions, the enterprise has an opportunity of further development only if it carries out effective economic activities. This principle brings all aspects of the enterprise activities under control of adjusted market conjuncture accounting, giving rise to necessity of working out a strategy of the enterprise competitiveness, provision of its continuous analysis, and evaluation.

At the micro-level one should distinguish two concepts of competitiveness: competitiveness of the enterprise as effectiveness of its industrial-marketing activity in the particular market and comparative product competitiveness (marketability) as a potential difference in consumer demand between it and similar production. Many authors associate competitiveness of the enterprise only with competitiveness of its products, believing this concept is a basic one in the system of enterprise competitiveness, assuming, as this takes place, that its other components are derivatives. The similar approach to competitiveness evaluation is presented in a number of publications. However, the concept of the enterprise competitiveness is much more complicated (more multidimensional) and is treated in the scientific literature rather ambiguously.

The concept of competitiveness of the product and the enterprise are measured up against each other as the whole and its parts. Competitive power (marketability) is one of the major coefficients to provide competitiveness of the enterprise. There is a strong correlation between these categories. Enterprise Capacity for compete in the particular commodity market directly depends on competitiveness of the goods

A. Chursin, Y. Makarov, *Management of Competitiveness*,
DOI 10.1007/978-3-319-16244-7_5

and a set of economic methods of the enterprise activities, affecting results of its competitive struggle.

Hence, competitive power is a necessary, but not a sufficient, condition of the enterprise competitiveness. This circumstance follows, in particular, from distinctions of the said categories:

- First, competitive power is determined for a short period of time from the economic point of view, and evaluating of the enterprise competitiveness is carried out for a long time.
- Second, level of the product competitiveness is determined in relation to its every type, and the evaluation of the enterprise competitiveness covers all product nomenclature (and not only the product portfolio).
- Third, competitiveness of the enterprise is of interest to its owner only, who determines appropriateness of industrial activity proceeding from concrete conditions. The consumer while evaluating the products competitiveness is not interested in production costs and its effectiveness.

The majority of on-line methods of the enterprise competitiveness evaluation are based on portfolio analysis and SWOT analysis or application of various industrial and financial indices characterizing industrial activity of the enterprise, its financial status, effectiveness of investments, etc. In so doing, the enterprise competitiveness is characterized by such basic indices as economic potential and effectiveness of the enterprise activities, level of its management, industrial, marketing, and research potential, financial status of the enterprise, goodwill of business, market strategy, innovative activity, condition, and qualification of manpower.

Some authors in their works describe competitiveness as a multidimensional category within the framework of the market complex, and for its "measurement" they use variables determining advantages, adaptability, and results of economic activities of the enterprise. Such approach offers to use following characteristics for evaluation of competitive advantages:

- Competitive pricing
- Advantages in costs
- Quality, design, packing, product operational characteristics
- After-sale service
- Speed of reaction to consumers demand
- Image; production assortment
- Contacts with suppliers
- Width of distributive network
- Advertising
- Personal sales technique
- System of marketing information
- Marketing studies

Adaptability of the enterprise is recommended to be quantitatively estimated by means of variables describing measures of adaptation to the market of consumer, price, and product policy of the enterprise, as well as the policy of production incentive and distribution of resources and products.

The results of economic activities of the enterprise can be measured by means of financial indices (return on investment and profit); market indices (sales volume and market Share of the enterprise); survival indices (cash receipts).

For an evaluation of the enterprise competitiveness, there may be used a system of indices of effectiveness of its industrial activity, financial status, effectiveness of the sales organization and promotion of goods, their competitiveness, and effectiveness of innovative projects.

Some authors consider time as one of the coefficients of achieving enterprise competitiveness. The separate directions of optimization of the time parameters of enterprise activities are as follows: speed of its adaptation, terms of payments, duration of production cycle, speed of decision making, etc.

As a whole, according to one of the Russian experts in the field of marketing and competitiveness R. A. Fathutdinov the enterprise competitiveness problem in the Russian economy is not discussed sufficiently both on theoretical and practical points of view now.

On the basis of analysis of the international experience, it is possible to provide classification of the basic approaches and methods of the enterprise competitiveness evaluation.

The most widespread method is investigation of the enterprise competitiveness on the basis of the theory of international division of labor. Prerequisite for achievement of strong competitive positions by the enterprise is availability of advantages which give a chance to provide rather low manufacturing expenses in comparison with the competitor.

There are widespread methods of the enterprise competitiveness evaluation based on the theory of effective competition. Their advocate believe that during the competitiveness analysis at the industry-sector level, it is necessary to pay attention, first of all, to the rivalry of the enterprises, as it is exactly the result of their activity to form the industry status. There are two basic approaches to determination of competitiveness criterion within the framework of this theory: structural and functional.

According to the structural approach, enterprise status can be evaluated in the light of knowledge of the industry monopolization level, i.e., concentration of production and the capital, and the barriers to new enterprises entering the market. The basic obstacles on the way of new competitors are: profitability of large-scale manufacturing; degree of production differentiation; absolute advantages in cost of existing enterprises; amount of capital required for organization of effective manufacturing.

Functional approach consists in determination of price-cost ratio, level of use of production capacities, production output, rate of return, etc. According to this approach, the enterprises with more efficient production and sales, effective financial management is more competitive. An example of the functional approach is the technique of American consulting company "Dun & Bradstreet" which is based on three groups of the market activity indices:

- Indices of effectiveness of industrial and marketing activity of the enterprise
- Indices of use intensity of the capital assets
- Indices of financial activity

Besides the said criteria, there are indices characterizing competitive power. Methods of the enterprise competitiveness measurement based on the functional approach of the theory of effective competition have received a wide circulation in the USA and Western Europe and can be recommended for use by domestic enterprises-exporters.

Advantage of the functional approach consists in use of indices which give a chance to draw conclusions on some directions of economic activities of the enterprise. However, it should be noted that this approach has also particular drawbacks as it does not take into account such important criteria of the enterprise competitiveness determination as availability of competitive potential, indices of ecological compatibility of production, social effectiveness, and image of the enterprise.

There are worth noticing methods of the enterprise competitiveness evaluation which are based on the firm and industry equilibrium theory and the theory of production coefficients. Criterion of competitiveness within the framework of such approach consists in possessing by the manufacturers of production coefficients which can be used with greater productivity as compared to the competitors. According to the equilibrium theory analyzed are the following:

- Credit interest rates
- Relative cost of purchased tooling
- Relative rates of wages
- Relative cost of material resources.

However, use of this method in the conditions of the Russian market economy is essentially limited for the following reasons:

- First, the equilibrium theory of production meets conditions of perfect competition, and the actual business environment is far from such form of the market.
- Second, the method is based on the theory supposing that the industry, as a result of its development, should reach an equilibrium position, and such position is not observed even in the countries with developed market economy.

Competitiveness of the enterprise is also evaluated according to quality of production with the help of polygonal profiles method. This method is one of few techniques to provide visualization of evaluation. Unlike other approaches, this method provides investigation of the market segments, evaluation of a possibility of changing production profitability, and the sale with allowances made for market requirements, as well as analysis of the marketing network. The method is based on identification of criteria of meeting requirements in relation to concrete product, on establishment of hierarchy of demand, their comparative significance within the spectrum which an ordinary consumer can evaluate. The scientific literature, as a rule, presents polygons of comparative characteristics of the enterprise competitiveness according to eight vectors of competence: concept, quality, price, finance, trade, after-sale service, foreign policy, presale preparation. The basic drawback of the specified method consists in the fact that it does not take into account effectiveness of industrial activity of the enterprise and is acceptable for the enterprises with only one type of production.

Being of interest are the so-called matrix methods of the enterprise competitiveness evaluation based on consideration of competition processes in dynamics and, in case of trustworthy information, permitting to make qualitative analysis of the enterprise competitive status. The said methods are evident and simple in terms of calculations. The advantages of these methods darken their drawbacks too: visualization is provided at the expense of simplified solution with the loss of its accuracy. Such methods make it possible to successfully identify goods status in the market and prospects for development of these goods according to their life cycle, showing position of several competitors and giving representation of their opportunities. The reality is that application of such methods is effective in combination with other more accurate methods, they illustrate.

A separate group includes the methods which connect the enterprise competitiveness level with the indices of quality of the output products or their quality and price. The quality is usually evaluated by means of composite index, which, in turn, is determined by an integrated method. Price index of a product is an aggregate cost including sales cost and costs of inputs in case of use of the goods. Finally, competitiveness index of the goods is expressed through "consumption efficiency." Hence, the higher the quality of the goods is and the lower their price, the better competitiveness of the goods. Such methods have a number of advantages, basic of which simplicity and presentation of an evaluation are. Besides, similar methods make it possible to consider an important aspect of competitiveness—competitive power is evaluated through price and quality criteria. At the same time they give a limited indication of about advantages and drawbacks of the enterprise activities as its competitiveness becomes competitiveness of the goods and is not related to the other aspects of activity.

The complex approach to evaluating competitiveness of the enterprise is implemented with the help of integral assessment method by means of two criteria characterizing degree of compliance with the consumer requirements and production effectiveness. Advantage of this approach is simplicity of calculations and a possibility of unequivocal interpretation of their results, and the basic drawback consists in incomplete characteristic of the enterprise activities.

Hence, this analysis of specified approaches and methods shows that the problems of evaluating competitiveness of the enterprises yield a relatively complete picture in the modern literature. As a whole, competitiveness of the enterprise is determined given the influence of market coefficients. However, as a rule, these coefficients do not provide complex quantitative evaluation of their competitiveness. Besides, common drawback of the specified methods is that they are not adapted to being used in conditions of formation of market relations and give incomplete characteristic of the enterprises being estimated.

Objective assessment of the enterprise competitiveness can be received on the basis of the system of competitiveness indices characterizing activity of this enterprise. The generalized competitiveness index can be calculated as follows:

$$K_T = J_T J_Э,$$

where J_T—index of competitiveness of commodity weight;
$J_Э$—index of relative effectiveness of the enterprise.

The index of competitiveness of commodity weight of diversified enterprise manufacturing various items can be calculated as the weighted mean value of competitiveness indexes of every product from the formula:

$$J_T = \sum_{i=1}^{p} \beta_i \frac{n_i}{n_{ib}} \cdot \frac{K_i}{K_{ib}} \cdot \frac{З_{ib}}{З_i},$$

As the indices of enterprise effectiveness may be taken labor productivity, capital assets rate of return, output profitability, etc. In theoretical terms it is possible to calculate the complex index of effectiveness $J_э$ including a number of specific indices of effectiveness E_J just as in qualimetry

$$J_э = \sum_{i=1}^{p} \gamma_j E_j / E_{jb},$$

where k—number of production indices effectiveness;
γ_j—coefficient of significance of the index of effectiveness;
E_j, E_{jb}—specific indices of effectiveness of this enterprise and competitor-enterprise, accordingly.

Taking into account the fact that indexes of competitiveness of commodity weight and relative effectiveness of the enterprise closely correlate among themselves, there is provided:

- To estimate level of competitiveness in the weighted mean value determined according to the indices of competitiveness of concrete goods in the concrete markets;
- To separately analyze effectiveness of the enterprise activities proceeding from competitiveness and effectiveness of every product in each market;
- To separately evaluate sustainability performance of the enterprise;

- To predict the listed complex indices for at least 5 years.

Competitiveness of the enterprise in statics is suggested to be evaluated according to the following formula:

$$K_{np} = \sum_{i=1}^{n} a_i b_j K_{ij},$$

where a_i—share of the i-th products in the sales volume for the period under analyses, unit shares;
b_j—index of significance of the j-th market where the goods are presented;
K_{ij}—competitiveness of the i-th products in the j-th market.

Share of the i-th products in the sales volume should to be determined from the formula:

$$a_i = V_i / V$$

where V_i—sales volume of the i-th products for the period under analyses;
V—total amount of sales of the enterprise output for the same period.

The advantage of two indices of the enterprise competitiveness noted above consists in accounting of its major component—competitive power.

Let us show the correlation between competitiveness indices of the product and the firm.

The index of product competitiveness is its integral property taking into account geometric middling, structural and substance properties of production and its structural components, as well as design, technological, consumer, economic, and other requirements according to consumption level.

The firm competitiveness index is an integrated index reflecting, on the one hand, ability of firm to produce competitive goods, and on the other hand, generalizing economic, technical, and other indices characterizing the firm.

Let us determine the general algorithm of building these indices:

1. We form vector $Z = (Z_1, \ldots, Z_n)$ of initial characteristics, each of which is required and sufficient for evaluation of the matter under inquiry.
2. We form vector $P = (P_1, \ldots, P_m)$ of the separate indices representing functions f_i of the vector of initial characteristics, characterizing the matter under inquiry.
3. We choose a type of systematizing function $K(P)$ to put in correspondence vector of separate indices $P = (P_1, \ldots, P_m)$ and integrated assessment K characterizing the matter under inquiry.

The matter under inquiry in this case is understood to be either the output or a firm.

According to the suggested structurally hierarchical model of the matter under inquiry, we put in additional determinations. We name the structural production element as Parts Assembly Unit (PAU) which can be an assembly unit or a detail and the set of technological operations of the firm characterized by specific similarity of applied means and ways of manufacture as Technological Conversion (TC).

The model of the matter under inquiry at an evaluation of competitiveness be as follows (Fig. 5.1):

In the general case, we consider *m*—technological conversion TC_j applied in the industry.

Hence,

$$TC = \left\{`TC_j | j = 1, 2, \ldots, m\right\} \tag{5.1}$$

In the general case, the integrated competitiveness index of the matter under inquiry is function:

$$K_{un} = f(У, Д, P, TC, TO, Q), \tag{5.2}$$

where У—a set of production assembly units;
Д—a set of production details;
P—a set of output characteristics;
Q—a set of the firm characteristics.

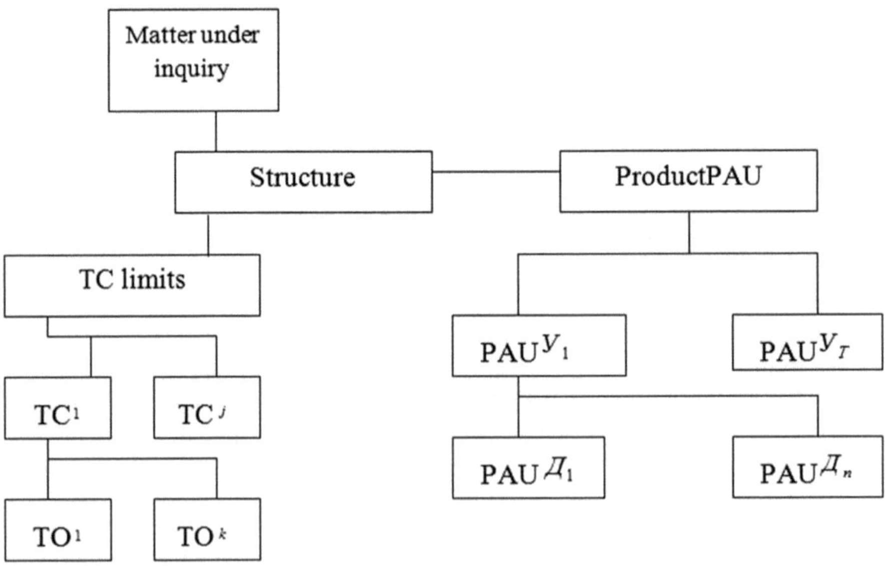

Fig. 5.1 Model of the matter under inquiry in evaluation of competitiveness: У—assembly unit; Д—detail

The integrated competitiveness index generalizes a set of specific indices of competitiveness K_i, in turn specific competitiveness index of the firm under inquiry is determined as an additive function relative to competitiveness PAU and applied TC:

$$K_i = \sum_{i=1}^{m} K_{PAU_i} + \sum_{i=1}^{n} K_{TC_i} \tag{5.3}$$

where m—number of PAU within production;

K_{PAU_i}—specific indices of competitiveness i-th PAU within production;

n—number of technological conversion used in manufacturing of PAU;

K_{TC_i}—specific competitiveness index corresponding to the i-th TC participating in manufacturing.

Characteristic feature of this model is that it has parameters characterizing output and parameters characterizing directly productive process.

Calculation of specific competitiveness index corresponding to specific technological conversion should be carried out with the use of mathematical model to be developed for every conversion.

A set of technological conversions used in the industry (5.1) has a big variety of specific features, from the big variety of applied equipment to specific conditions of its application.

In general terms in order to determine specific competitiveness index of technological conversion, we use entity decomposition (in this case conversion) on separate entities of the lower conversion (elements).

For every conversion, there should be determined a set of admissible elements $Э_i$ belonging to the said conversion:

$$Э_i^{TC_j} = \{Э_i | i = 1, 2, \ldots, n\}$$

Every element belongs to a particular class of elements technological conversion B_j too, making some set $B = \{B_j | j = 1, 2, \ldots, L\}$ where every element $Э_i$ can belong to one of considered classes B_j. For every class of elements, there is a set of elements to be determined

$$Д^{B_j} = \{d_h | h = 1, 2, \ldots, r\}$$

providing generation of all admissible elements of this class.

$$Э^{B_j} = \{Э_l | l = 1, 2, \ldots, s\}, \text{ where } Э^{B_j} \subseteq Э^{TC}$$

The elements belonging to the set $Д^{B_j}$ are called as generating elements of class B_j.

Elements $Э_i$ belonging to the set $Э^{TC_j}$ are called as generated elements accordingly.

For every element, there is a set of generating elements $Д^{Э_i} = \{d_k | k = 1, 2, \ldots, u\}$ determining this element $Д^{Э_i} \subseteq Д^{B_j}$, $Э = f(Д^{Э_i} M)$ where M—a set of transformations permitted for this technological conversion.

Every element $Э_i$ is characterized by a set of characteristics $P^Э = \{P_i | i = 1, 2, \ldots, p\}$, where $P^Э \in P$.

Every characteristic determines a set of values, the size of which is determined for every concrete parameter.

Specific competitiveness index of TC is defined as an additive function which takes into account complexities specified for a particular Parts Assembly Unit (PAU)

$$K_{TC} = \sum_{j=1}^{l} \left[\sum_{i=1}^{s} \left[\sum_{k=1}^{n_j} K_k^Э \right] \right] \tag{5.4}$$

where K_{TC}—specific competitiveness index of conversion applied to PAU;
l—number of classes of TC elements;
s—number of generated elements in *j-m* class;
n_j—number of the same elements corresponding to the *i*-th generated element;
$K_k^Э$—specific competitiveness index of the *k*-th element corresponding to the *i*-th generated element.
In turn, $K^Э$—is determined in the form of the functional dependence taking into account parameters of the element and corresponding output.

$$K^Э = f(Д^Э, P^Э P_{PAU} P) \tag{5.5}$$

where $Д^Э$—a set of generating elements determining this element;
$P^Э$—a set of parameters characterizing element $Э$;
P_{PAU}—a set of parameters characterizing concrete PAU;
P—a set of parameters characterizing production.

Formula (5.5) presented in general terms makes it possible to evaluate concrete specific indices of competitiveness K_{PAU} and K_{TC} of the matter under inquiry.

After we determine specific indices of competitiveness for a PAU (Parts Assembly Unit—production) and technological conversion (firm), there is a possibility to compare the matter under inquiry with other firms and products in the market, both domestic and external.

With this aim in view, we put in integrated competitiveness index which is equal to

$$K_{ИН_N} = \sum_{i=1}^{t} K_{N_i}^{П} \tag{5.6}$$

where N—number of the matters under inquiry (production, firms);
$K_{N_i}^{П}$—the i-th specific competitiveness index of the N-th matter under inquiry;
t—number of specific indices of competitiveness;

$$K_{N_i}^{П} = K_{N_i}^{П} n_i \tag{5.7}$$

где n_i—The Specific coefficient taking into account the significance of the i-th specific competitiveness index;
$K_{N_i}^{k}$—the classified i-th competitiveness index of the N-th matter under inquiry (production, firms).

In turn

$$K_{N_i}^{k} = \frac{K_{N_i}}{K_{N_i \ \max}} \tag{5.8}$$

where $K_{N_i \ \max}$—maximum value of the i-th specific index in set N of firms.

On can see from formula (5.8) that value $K_{N_i}^{k}$ will change within $K_{\min \ t}^{k} \leq K_{N_i}^{k} \leq 1$, where $K_{\min t}^{k}$—minimum value $K_{N_i}^{k}$ in a set of matters under inquiry N.

In calculating formula (5.8), it is necessary to take into account that those specific indices of competitiveness are considered to be the best in the analysis and have the minimum numerical values; it may be presented as

$$K_{N_i}^{\min} = \frac{1}{K_{N_i}} \tag{5.9}$$

Specific coefficient n_i in formula (5.7) should be calculated with allowances made for formula:

$$\sum_{i=1}^{t} n_i = 1, \tag{5.10}$$

it is obvious that $0 \leq n_i \leq 1$ where $i = 1, 2, \ldots, t$

Semantic meaning of specific coefficient consists in the fact that the more the share n_i the more the share of participation of the i-th index in the value of integrated competitiveness index $K_{ИН_N}$.

Value n_i is found from formula:

$$n_i = \frac{1}{1 + \sum_{j=1\ i \neq j}^{t} \frac{K_i^k}{K_j^k}} \tag{5.11}$$

From formula (5.11) one can see the following: the more the value of the classified i-th specific competitiveness index, the less its specific coefficient in the integrated competitiveness index.

Taking into account formulas (5.7) and (5.11), formula (5.6) will take on form as follows:

$$K_{ИH_N} = \sum_{i=1}^{t} K_{N_i}^{K} \cdot \left(\frac{1}{1 + \sum_{j=1\ i \neq j}^{t} \frac{K_{N_i}^k}{K_{N_j}^k}} \right) \tag{5.12}$$

The formula analysis shows that the best value $K_{ИH_N} = 1$, i.e., the more the value $K_{ИH}$, the better competitiveness of the matter under inquiry.

The integrated competitiveness index should be determined for a group of homogeneous items. Hence, the number of items is not limited.

Reliability of the integrated index will be higher than a great number of specific indices of competitiveness of subject matter K_{PAU} and K_{TC}.

The number of specific indices can be unlimited and their values should be positive, i.e., $K_{PAU} > 0$ and $K_{TC} > 0$.

The value of specific indices can be expressed in relative units.

So, for example, for evaluation of the output by method of expert assessment on a five-point scale, the evaluation of specific competitiveness index of a camera from the point of view of commissioning design solutions can be four points, i.e., $K_{PAU_{Ф}} = 4$.

For evaluation of a firm, for example, as specific competitiveness index, they use flexibility coefficient of this firm $K_Г$ which may be from 0 to 1.

Hence, suggested algorithm of determination of competitiveness indices being complex indices of the firm Capacity to produce competitive goods and a number of other indices (economic, technical, etc.) makes it possible to solve a number of industrial and economic problems arising at the various stages of life cycle of the products.

5.2 Methods In Order to Determine of Technical Level of Production

One of the major coefficients to determine competitiveness of a firm is its technical level of production.

The process of increasing technical level of production should be carried out on a permanent basis in order to provide competitiveness of the firm and its output in domestic and foreign markets. With this end in view, it is necessary to carry out periodic evaluation of technical level of production and on its the basis to modernize production and optimize the firm management by means of development and introduction of advanced innovative technologies.

It is important to formalize approaches to the comparative evaluation of technical levels available by various enterprises or this particular enterprise during the various periods of its activity.

On the basis of this comparison, it is possible to identify potential reserves of growth of production effectiveness and to develop technical policy aimed at realization of such reserves.

For assessment of the enterprise technical level, we offer the following simple mathematical model:

$$\text{Т}_{\text{УП}} = \text{Т}_{\text{И}} \times \text{К}_{\text{И}} + \text{Т}_{\text{Т}} \times \text{К}_{\text{Т}} + \text{Т}_{\text{o}} \times \text{К}_{\text{o}} + \text{Т}_{\text{i}} \times \text{К}_{\text{i}}, \tag{5.13}$$

where $\text{Т}_{\text{УП}}$—enterprise technical level (shop, site, division);
$\text{Т}_{\text{И}}$—product technical level;
Т_{o}—technical level of the management;
Т_{i}—technical level of the *i*-th index, for example, technical level of the PLC preoperating phase or technical level of project construction works automation;
$\text{К}_{\text{И}}$, $\text{К}_{\text{Т}}$, К_{o}, К_{i}—coefficients characterize significance from $\text{Т}_{\text{И}}$, $\text{Т}_{\text{Т}}$, Т_{o}, Т_{i} in the general evaluation and are determined by the experts.

Indices $\text{Т}_{\text{И}}$, $\text{Т}_{\text{Т}}$, Т_{o}, Т_{i} can be determined in general terms from the formula

$$T_i = \sum \Pi_i j_i. \tag{5.14}$$

As an example, we will show how the technical level of technologies is determined

$$T_T = \sum \Pi_T j_i, \tag{5.15}$$

where $\Pi_{\text{Т}}$—index of technical level of technologies;
j_i—weightiness of the index.
In order to determine technical level, it is possible to use the following indices:
Π^{Π_i}—labor intensity of the output;
Π^{H_i}—materials-output ratio;
$\Pi^{\text{Э}_i}$—output energy consumption;
Π^{a_i}—level of automation of technological processes.

Every enterprise in the market conditions determines the control indicators; therefore, a circle of indices can be expanded or reduced to the minimum.

Substituting values of these indices in the above-stated formula with make allowances made for j_i determined by experts, it is possible to receive the values characterizing technical level of technology.

For more accurate evaluation of technical level of the enterprise, an integrated performance measure which can be developed proceeding from the vector meeting a reference enterprise should be used. The vector is formed on the basis of optimum values of every index by sample.

For such evaluation they use a "method of distances" suggested for a group of the same enterprises. The principle of this method consists in determination of reference distance from a "reference point" of the matter under inquiry making the same uniform group of the enterprises.

As specific estimated figures are nonmeasurable quantities, they are standardized by their partition into optimum value for this type of indices, that is X_i by $X_{\text{опт}}$, and integrated index T is determined by formula:

$$T = \left[\sum_{i=1}^{t} \left(1 - \frac{X_i}{X_{onm}} \right)^2 \right]^{1/2} \tag{5.16}$$

where X_i—current value of the estimated characteristic;
X_{onm}—optimum value of the specific estimated characteristic in the series;
i—number of estimated figures.

Estimated figures may include production costs, export output, development of new types of competitive products, level of production automation and mechanization, application of progressive technologies, etc., which are used now to control or evaluate activity of industrial enterprises By means of substituting values of the specified estimated figures in formula (5.16), it is possible to receive a value of the index of technical level of production with confidence. The reliability will depend on the number of selected indices and correct accounting philosophy.

The above-stated methods of evaluation of technical level can be easily used by the firms with small nomenclature of the output products, number of personnel, and incomplete cycle of technological conversion.

The firms with big nomenclature (more than 30 item names) and with full cycle of technological conversion should apply mathematical model of evaluation of the technical level, developed on the basis of the general labor intensity of output with specific changes characterizing work of the enterprise in the market conditions.

In conditions of the market economy, the assessment of the enterprise technical level is the most effective on the basis of measurement of labor intensity of industrial output as this index possesses evident advantages in comparison with other possible criteria.

The basic and the most representative index of the enterprise technical level shall be current labor productivity with high quality output being competitive in the world market. In order to characterize available labor productivity level, it is worthwhile to use full ratio of labor to output which adequately reflects available labor productivity level and its dynamics, not only within the enterprise as a whole but also in all its structural divisions; it also depends on the enterprise technical level.

Full ratio of labor to output is subdivided into industrial labor intensity and management labor intensity. Industrial labor intensity ($T_{\text{пр}}$) consists of technological labor intensity and labor intensity of serviceability.

Full ratio of labor to output is the amount of all labor outlays for manufacturing a unit of output at this enterprise of all categories of industrial and production personnel. Industrial labor intensity is determined by the workers' labor costs of primary and auxiliary production:

$$T_{\text{пр}} = T_{\text{техн}} + T_{\text{об}}, \tag{5.17}$$

where $T_{\text{техн}}$—technological labor intensity, that is labor costs of the workers who are carrying out technological influence on subjects of labor (change of form, condition, physical and chemical properties etc.), for a unit of production;

$T_{\text{об}}$—labor intensity of serviceability, that is the labor costs of auxiliary workers of primary production and all workers of auxiliary production dealing with serviceability.

Labor intensity of production management ($_{\text{That}}$) is the labor costs of all other categories of the industrial and production personnel—technical and engineering employees, security.

Full labor intensity is determined from the formula:

$$T_{\text{п}} = T_{\text{техн}} + T_{\text{об}} + T_{\text{у}} = T_{\text{пр}} + T_{\text{у}}. \tag{5.18}$$

The labor-output ratio is subdivided into standard, actual, and scheduled labor intensity according to the character and designation of labor costs.

Standard labor intensity—normalized labor costs for product manufacturing, or for performance of a particular amount of work established for $T_{\text{техн}}$, $T_{\text{об}}$, $T_{\text{у}}$, proceeding from the standard hours per piece, norms of service, staff listing, and scheduled fund of working hours taking into account an enterprise operating schedule.

Actual labor intensity—real labor costs for a unit of product, scope of work.

Scheduled labor intensity—product manufacturing charges or costs for particular scope of work, established with allowance for their decrease in the scheduled period. Scheduled labor intensity is especially important during development of new production. Rates of drawdown in labor intensity in this case, as a rule, are higher 3–5 times in comparison with the rates of drawdown in labor intensity of the mastered production. From the point of view of evaluation of available labor productivity level, and therefore the technical level and production management, the special role belongs to the regulatory ratio of labor to output.

The concept of "regulatory ratio of labor to output," pari passu, can be referred to both full (industrial) and technological labor intensity of servicing production and its management. In general terms, the regulatory ratio of labor to output of this product is expressed as follows:

$$T_{нср} = \frac{\left[\sum_{i=1}^{n} T_{\phi j} V_j - \sum_{j=1}^{m} T_{\phi j} V_j\right]}{\left[\sum_{i=1}^{n-m} V_j\right]}, \tag{5.19}$$

where $T_{\phi j}$—actual ratio of labor to output of a unit of product on the j-th enterprise;
V_j—production volume of this product on the j-th the enterprise;
n—number of enterprises producing this item;
m—number of enterprises where the actual ratio of labor to output with respect to this product is higher than the average level in all the enterprises.

Analysis of the standard labor intensity makes it possible to solve a number of problems connected with comparative evaluations of available level, including technical level of separate enterprises.

In order to determine values of the target labor intensity values, it is necessary to determine a set of coefficients characterizing technical level of this division, and therefore, technological ratio of labor to output.

As the coefficients influencing technological labor intensity, it is worthwhile to choose the following indices:

X_1—Hour productivity of equipment;
X_2—Materials-output ratio by components of the unit of product;
X_3—Power consumption, that is consumption of electric energy per unit of product;
X_4—Level of saving in material resources consumption by components;
X_5—Ecological compatibility of production in this division, calculated in percentage of gases emission in atmosphere, wastewater treatment, etc.;
X_6—Relative share of machine tools and equipment with microchip technology in production of the process equipment;
X_7—Capacities of computer complexes on the basis of general purpose processors;
X_8—Availability and number of the flexible automated systems, automatic rotor lines and rotor conveyor lines, industrial robots, including “intelligent” robots;
X_9—Level of automation of design and construction work;
X_{10}—Relative share of competitive and export products in the total output;
X_{11}—Relative share of products with high degree of profitability at the expense of enhanced demand in the market in the total output;
X_{12}—Relative share of products with low profitability at the expense of reduction in demand in the market and reductions of price to the minimum level in the total output.

Every particular case of the enterprises grouping and calculation of technological labor intensity may have the above listed coefficients vary, and their number is either increased or reduced. Hence, it is important to bear in mind that it is worthwhile to be guided by statistically independent coefficients as they simplify the problem of process model building very much and raise the accuracy of calculating coefficient of the regression equation.

Then it is necessary to build functional dependences for every structural division:

$$T^{\alpha}_{mexн} = f_{\alpha}(X_1, X_2, X_3, X_4, X_5), \tag{5.20}$$

where $\alpha = I, \ldots, p$ determines concrete division in the technological chain from the beginning to the end of product manufacturing.

In practice, as a rule, these dependences are well approximated by the linear regression equation:

$$\acute{Y} = \alpha_0 + \sum_{\beta=1}^{n} \alpha_{\beta} X_{\beta} \tag{5.21}$$

where $\acute{Y}$—target value of the ratio of labor to output;
α_{β}—parameters of regression equation $\beta = I, \ldots, n$;
X_{β}—coefficients,

or by power functions

$$\acute{Y} = \alpha_0 + \prod_{\beta=1}^{n} X_{\beta} \alpha_{\beta} \tag{5.22}$$

Calculation of parameters of regression equations α_0и$\alpha_{\beta}$is carried out by standard methods of mathematical statistics.

Data about parameters α_0, $\alpha_{\beta}(\beta = 1, \ldots, n)$ make it possible to calculate labor outlays $T_{техн}$ in every given structural division of the enterprise according to actual values X_1, X_2, X_3, X_4, X_5.

The information on the estimated values of labor intensity makes it possible to group structural divisions or the entire enterprise and for every given group, and to determine either progressive average or the best progressive standard of labor intensity ($T^{\alpha}_{ср.\,прог.\,норм}$, $T^{\alpha}_{прог.\,норм}$).

Comparison of actual labor intensity of every given structural division with these specifications makes it possible to estimate available technical level and to identify available reserves. Computational analysis of the entire chain of work cycle of different enterprises-competitors with identical or homogeneous production provides a possibility to determine progressive technological standard for manufacturing of the j-th product:

$$T^{j}_{прог.норм} = \sum_{\alpha=1}^{n} min\ T^{i}_{aпрог.норм} \tag{5.23}$$

Comparison of $T^{j}_{факт}$ with $T^{j}_{прог.\,норм}$ makes it possible to estimate technical level of the enterprises in the form of indices:

$$\eta^{i}_{j} = \frac{T^{j}_{прог.норм}}{T^{j}_{факт}}. \tag{5.24}$$

If the i-th enterprise $(i = 1, \ldots, n)$ has value η^{i}_{j} by all types of products $(i = 1, \ldots, q)$ higher than all other enterprises $(j = 1, \ldots, n)$, then it is fair to say that the technical level of the i-th enterprise is Pareto, dominating in relation to the technical level of all other enterprises.

Provision of high technical level of production and competitive power of the enterprise in conditions of market and unstable environment should be connected with its stable development on the basis of high innovative activity and acceleration of alternating generations of output products, flexibility of production, and modernization on the basis of implementation of innovative technologies providing high technical level of production.

5.3 Methods for Evaluation of the Firm Competitiveness Level

Investigation of the firm competitiveness requires quantitative assessment, the results of which would be used in formation of the enterprise strategy in conditions of the market competition.

This book presents a model for evaluation of the level of enterprise competitiveness (Fig. 5.2), based on the groups of indices characterizing potential opportunities of a particular enterprise, results of its economic activities and customer satisfaction.

Such model can be applied in analysis of competitiveness of the market entity in order to identify disproportions between its potential opportunities and actual results of its activity, and to work out of organizational and economic measures aimed at rectification of the said disproportions.

Within the framework of the specified model, the task of evaluation of the enterprise competitiveness is formulated as follows: it is necessary to calculate values of integrated indices of competitiveness of comparable enterprises with the purpose of their ordering relative to the reference enterprise characteristics.

Procedure of implementation of the model operation consists of the following steps.

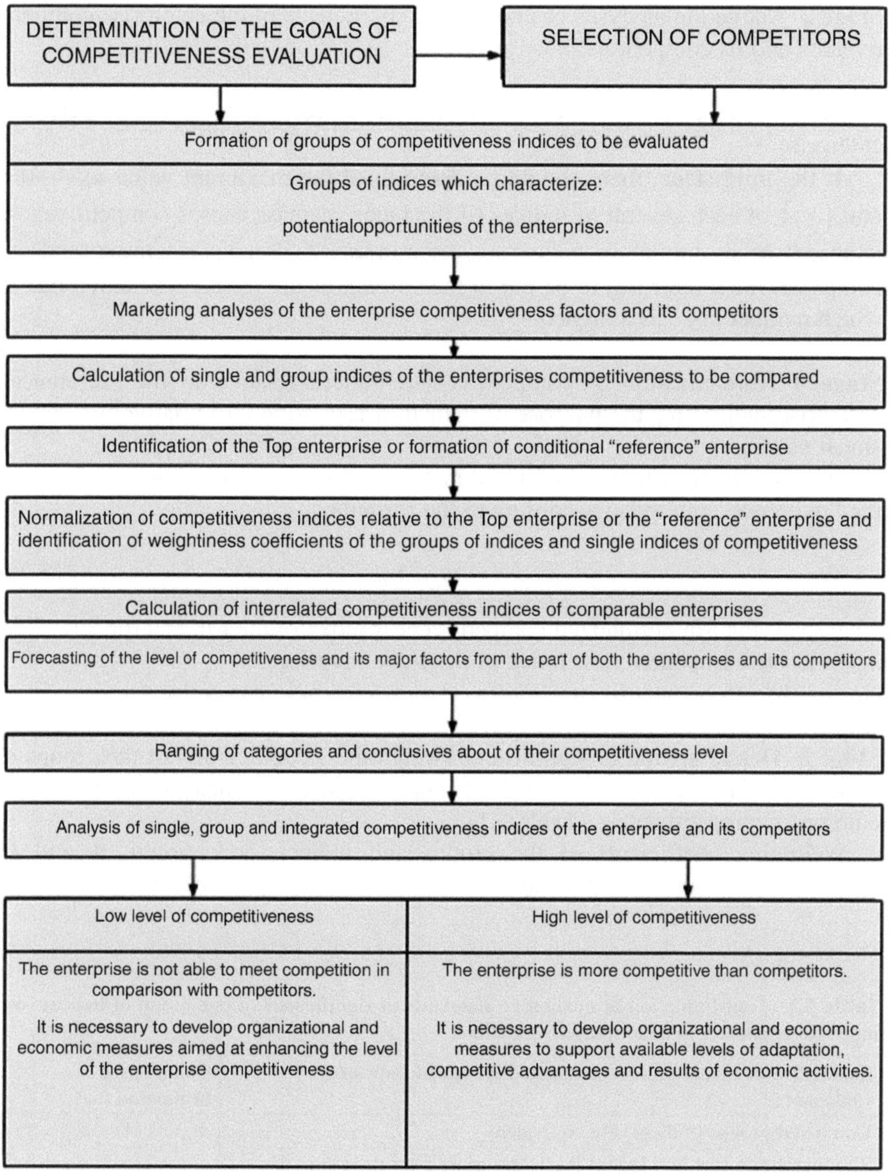

Fig. 5.2 Scheme of evaluation of the enterprise competitiveness level

Stage 1 Identification of the list of groups of the single indices characterizing competitiveness of the enterprise.

A set of comparable enterprises is represented by matrix $A = \{a_{ij}\}$ of single indices of their competitiveness, where i is the number of competitiveness index $(i = 1, 2, \ldots, n)$ of the j-th enterprises $(j = 1, 2, \ldots, m)$.

Stage 2 Marketing analyses of indices and coefficients of the enterprise competitiveness and its competitors.

Stage 3 Identification of the Top enterprise or formation of the "reference" enterprise.

At the third stage, there should be determined the maximum value $a_{im}+1=\max\{a_{ij}\}$ of each several of indices (if the index increase causes competitiveness increase) or its minimum value $a_{im+i}=\min\{a_{ij}\}$ (if index decrease leads to competitiveness increase) to be put in the column of the "reference" enterprise to which number $m+1$ is assigned.

Stage 4 Normalization of competitiveness indices relative to the "reference" enterprise indices for the purpose of their transformation into relative nondimensional values.

Indices of competitiveness of initial matrix And are normalized by each index of the "reference" enterprise according to the formula:

$$x_{ij} = a_{ij}/a_{im+1} \tag{5.25}$$

where x_{ij}—the i-th normalized competitiveness index of the j-th enterprise;
a_{ij}—the i-th competitiveness index of the j-th enterprise;
a_{im+1}—the i-th competitiveness index of the "reference" enterprise.

Stage 5 Determination of significance (weightiness coefficients) of the groups of indices and single indices in order to provide representative measure of the level of enterprise competitiveness (Table 5.1).

Weighting coefficients of the groups and indices, accordingly, β_j and k_i, ($j=1,2\ldots, l$, l—number of groups, $i=1,2\ldots, n$), meeting conditions:

Table 5.1 Transformation of qualitative standards of significance of one group of indices (one index) over another in quantitative evaluations

Qualitative evaluation of two compared groups of indicators (indicators)	Quantitative evaluation (a_{ji})	
Compared groups (indices) are equivalent	$a_{ij}=1/1$	$a_{ij}=1/1$
The first group (the first index) is slightly more important than the other one (another)	$a_{ij}=2/1$	$a_{ij}=1/2$
The first group (the first index) is much more important than the other one (another)	$a_{ij}=3/1$	$a_{ij}=1/3$
The first group (the first index) is much more important than the other one (another)	$a_{ij}=4/1$	$a_{ij}=1/4$

$$\sum_{i=1}^{n} k_i = 1 \text{ and } \sum_{i=1}^{n} \beta_j = 1$$

$$0 < k_i < 1, \quad 0 < k_j < 1,$$

There is provided to determine with the help of the expert method of pair-wise comparison with the use of scale of transformation of qualitative standards of significance of one group (one index) over another group (another index) in quantitative evaluations.

Hence *i*, *j*—numbers of comparable groups of indices, (*i*, *j* = *1*,*2*. . ., *k*, *k* = *1 or k* = *n*).

The algorithm of calculating weighting coefficients is presented in Table 5.2.

For purposes of calculation of weightiness coefficients of the groups of competitiveness indices β_j and k_i, it is possible to use also the scoring method in formula:

$$k_i = \sum_{j=1}^{d} \left(Б_{ij} \div Б_{cj}\right)/d \tag{5.26}$$

where k_i—weightiness coefficients of the i group (the *i*-th index) of the enterprise competitiveness;

i—number of the group (index);

j—number of the expert;

d—number of experts;

Table 5.2 Calculation of weighting coefficients of the groups of indices characterizing level of the firm competitiveness

Groups of indices	$П_1$	$П_2$	. . .	. . .	. . .	$П_K$
The first group (the first index) $П_1$	1	a_{21}	. . .	. . .	. . .	a_{k1}
The second group (the second index) $П_2$	a_{12}	1	. . .	. . .	. . .	a_{k2}
. . ...	. . .	. . .	1	. . .	. . .	. . .
. . ...	. . .	. . .	. . .	1	. . .	. . .
. . ...	. . .	. . .	. . .	. . .	1	. . .
k-th Group (*k*-th index)	a_{1k}	a_{2k}	. . .	. . .	. . .	1
The sum of by each group (each index) S_i	$S_1 = \sum_{i=1}^{k} a_{1i}$	$S_2 = \sum_{i=1}^{k} a_{1i}$	. . .	. . .	. . .	$S_k = \sum_{i=1}^{k} a_{1i}$
Calculation of weighting coefficients of the groups of indices of competitiveness relative to *i*	$K_1 = \frac{S_1}{S}$	$K_2 = \frac{S_2}{S}$	. . .	. . .	. . .	$K_k = \frac{S_k}{S}$

S—result of summing up of coefficients by all groups (all indices) $S = \sum_{i=1}^{k} S_i$

$Б_{ij}$—a score assigned to the i-th group (i-th index) by the j-th expert;
$Б_{cj}$—scores assigned by the j-th expert to all groups (all indices).

The number of indices and groups of indices depends on the task which is set to determine the enterprise competitiveness, special aspects of its activity, its market position in comparison with competitors, etc.

Stage 6 Determination of the group competitiveness indices of the comparable measures.

Before calculating integrated index of the enterprise competitiveness, it is necessary to calculate the group indices of competitiveness according to the formula:

$$П_i = \sum_{i=1}^{f} k_{ij} x_{ij}, \tag{5.27}$$

where k_{tj}—weighting coefficient of the j-th index in the i-th group of indices of the enterprise competitiveness;

$$\sum_{i=1}^{f} k_{ij} = 1,$$

where x_{ij}—the j-th normalized competitiveness index the i-th group;
f—number of indices in the group.

It is possible to use geometric middling of single indices as a group index of the enterprise competitiveness. It is possible to present the following arguments in favor of such approach.

First, multiplication of single indices is performed because all of them are closely interrelated, and a failure to take at least one of them into consideration is equal-zero index of the group of competitiveness which cannot be determined partially. Competitiveness determination makes meaning only in the event the entire spectrum of coefficients is adequately assessed.

Second, as follows from the general theory of statistics, the average geometric middling yields the most correct result of averaging, if the problem consists in finding a value being equidistant from the maximum and minimum values.

Hence, it is possible to present a group index of the enterprise competitiveness like this

$$П_i = \sqrt[f]{\prod_{j=1}^{f} k_{ij} x_{ij}}, \tag{5.28}$$

Stage 7 Determination of the integrated competitiveness index of every comparable enterprises according to the formula:

$$R_j = \sqrt{\sum_{i=1}^{l} \beta_i (1 - \Pi_{ij})^2}, \quad (j = 1, 2, \ldots m), \tag{5.29}$$

where R_j—integrated competitiveness index of the j-th enterprises;
β_i—weighting coefficient of the i-th group of indices of competitiveness;
Π_{ij}—i-th group competitiveness index of the j-th enterprise.

Stage 8 Forecasting of major coefficients of competitiveness and determination of forecast level of competitiveness of the comparable enterprises.

Stage 9 Ranging of the enterprises in descending order of the integrated index (i.e., growth of competitiveness) $R_1 \geq R_2 \geq \ \ldots \ \geq R_m \geq R_{m+1}$, where indexes $1, 2, \ldots, m$—new numbers of preferability of the enterprises in decreasing order of their integrated competitiveness index.

Stage 10 Analysis of the single, group, and integrated indices of the enterprise competitiveness.

In the modern market conditions, an enterprise while using its potential opportunities should work for improvement of results of its economic activities on the one hand and for the maximum satisfaction of the market requirements on the other hand. Therefore, it is natural to determine competitiveness of the enterprise following three major factors: potential opportunities of the enterprise, results of its economic activities, and satisfaction of the market requirements by means of competitive production (Fig. 5.3). High levels of every factor shall be a guarantee of high competitiveness of the enterprise as a whole.

As is known, the structure of Production System (PS) of any level of hierarchy traditionally includes the following resources as its elements: technical, technological, personnel, spatial, management organizational structure, information, and financial. A basic principle of identification of elements of the production system for the purposes of its strategic management is assessment of opportunities of achieving PS strategic objectives arising when this element is used. In other words, the system elements shall not be materialized resources; the said elements shall be the opportunities (PS strategic resources) to achieve PS strategic goals which are available when these resources are in use. Possibility frontiers of the enterprise strategic resources make its strategic potential. The approximate list of components of strategic potential which the enterprise should have in order to meet the challenges of external environment and to improve and expand possibility frontiers, on the basis of available resources, looks as follows:

Components of the enterprise strategic potential:

- Capacity for macroeconomic analysis of the situation in the country and outside its national territory

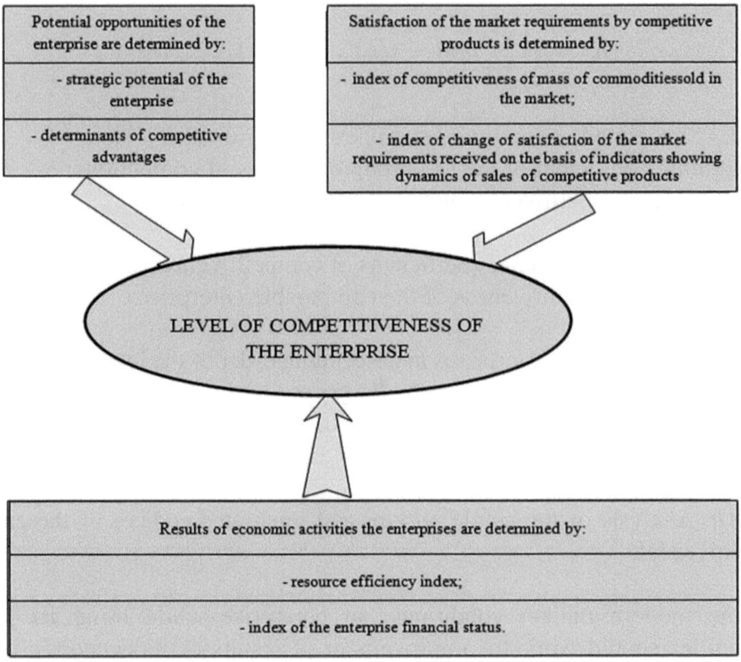

Fig. 5.3 Factors to determine competitiveness of the enterprise

- Capacity for timely identification of pressing needs, requirements, and demand of potential buyers
- Capacity for analysis of economic conjuncture of commodity markets which make it possible to satisfy available needs, requirement, and demand in effective and qualitative way in due time
- Capacity for analysis of economic condition of the markets, production factors, and activities of the groups of strategic influence
- Capacity for advancing competitive ideas in the field of designing, creation of technologies and production of best-selling goods in the commodity markets
- Capacity for implementation of competitive ideas in the course of production of goods, their promotion, organization of after-sales service
- Capacity for provision of the enterprise independence from changing of conjuncture of commodity, financial, and market factors of production at the expense of external PS flexibility
- Capacity for competitive status of the enterprise by means of management of strategic areas of economic activities
- Capacity for provision of internal PS flexibility by means of adaptive technological tools and equipment
- Capacity for provision of internal PS flexibility by means of fruitful technologies
- Capacity for provision of internal PS flexibility by means of adequate HR potential

- Capacity for change in architectural and planning solutions adequate to PS purposes
- Capacity for provision of competitive power required to become top in support and perspective segments of the market
- Capacity for output in the volumes corresponding to potential demand in specific segments of the market, with allowance for competitive status of the enterprise and a scheduled share of the market
- Capacity for high effectiveness of the enterprise functioning of by means of the most efficient use of its investment opportunities
- Capacity for effective development and implementation of strategic program of technical and social development of the enterprise

Components of strategic potential together with the enterprise resources form a set of its strategic resources and should be concretized in relation to every enterprise.

By definition, strategic potential determines one of potential opportunities of the enterprise—its adaptability. The second component of potential opportunities—competitive advantages characterized by determinants of competitive advantage of the country according to M. Porter's opinion.

Determinants, as a system, create environment in which the enterprises of this country operate, and they characterize:

- Availability of resources and skills required to achieve competitive advantage of the enterprise
- Information that specifies whether opportunities of competitive advantage will be taken or not
- Dimensions of application of resources and skills, available at the enterprises
- Enterprise goals;
- Factor forcing the enterprise to invest funds into one or another sphere of activity and to do business.

It follows from what has just been said above that Assessment of Potential Opportunities of the Enterprise (APOE) should take into account the significance of every determinant of competitive advantage of the country and the enterprise structure of strategic potential.

We take as a basis of APOE utilization factor of every element of strategic potential used for achievement of strategic goals at a particular stage of life cycle by the enterprise, its concrete resource. APOE procedure consists of a sequence of the following computing steps.

Step 1 Indices of aggregate influence of the determinants for every m-th stage of life cycle of enterprise $ДHP_m$ and for all cycle $ДHP$, accordingly, are determined under formulas:

$$ДНР_m = \sqrt[5]{\prod_{k=1}^{5} \alpha_{km} Q_{km}} \text{ and } ДНР = \sqrt[4]{\prod_{m=1}^{4} ДНР_m}$$

where Q_{km}—ratio of number of favorable factors relative to the general number of factors, formed by the *k*-th determinant (determinants are described above) in the *m*-th stage of the enterprise life cycle (there are four stages only: formation, growth, maturity, dilapidation);

a_{km}—coefficient of significance of the *k*-th determinant for the *m*-th stage

$$\left(\sum_{k=1}^{5} \alpha_{km} = 1 \right).$$

Step 2 Determining of indices $РЭ_{jim}$ making it possible to estimate resource endowment of every *i*-th element of strategic potential used for achievement of the goals, every *j*-th resource in every *m*-th stage of the life cycle according to formula:

$$РЭ_{jim} = КЭ_{jim} КСР_{jim}, \quad i = 1, 2, \ldots, s, \; j = 1, 2, \ldots 7, \; m = 1, 2, \ldots 4, \tag{5.30}$$

where $КЭ_{jim}$—coefficient of significance of the *j*-th resource in provision of the *i*-th element of strategic potential in the *m*-th stage of the life cycle;

$$\left(\sum_{j=1}^{7} КЭ_{jim} = 1 \right);$$

$КСР_{jim}$—utilization factor of the *i*-th element of strategic potential of the *j*-th resource in the *m*-th stage of the life cycle

s—number of elements of strategic potential of the enterprise (СПП).

Step 3 Determining of utilization factor $СП_{im}$ of every *i*-th element of strategic potential by all resources in every *m*-th stage of the life cycle from the formula:

$$СП_{im} = \sqrt[7]{\prod_{j=1}^{7} РЭ_{jim}}, \quad (i = 1, 2, \ldots, s), \quad (m = 1, \ldots, 4), \tag{5.31}$$

Step 4 Determining of utilization factor $ВСП_{jm}$ of the whole strategic potential by every *j*-th resource in every *m*-th stage of the life cycle according to

$$ВСП_{jm} = \sqrt[s]{\prod_{j=1}^{s} КЗЭ_{im}РЭ_{jim}}, \quad j = 1, 2, \ldots, 7; \quad m = 1, \ldots, 4 \qquad (5.32)$$

where $КЗЭ_{im}$—coefficient of significance of the i-th element of strategic potential in achieving strategic targets in the m-th stage of the life cycle.

Step 5 Determining of utilization factor $СПЦ_j$ of the whole strategic potential by every j-th resource for all life cycle from the formula:

$$СПЦ_j = \sqrt[4]{\prod_{m=1}^{4} ВСП_{jm}}, \quad j = 1, 2, \ldots, 7. \qquad (5.33)$$

Step 6 Determining of utilization factor $СПП_m$ of the whole strategic potential by all resources for every *m-th* stage of the life cycle from the formula:

$$СПП_m = \sqrt[s]{\prod_{j=1}^{s} СП_{im}КЗЭ_{im}}, \quad m = 1, 2, \ldots, 4. \qquad (5.34)$$

Step 7 Determining of utilization factor СПП of the whole strategic potential by all resources for the entire life cycle according to ratios

$$СПП = \sqrt[4]{\prod_{m=1}^{4} СПП_b} \qquad (5.35)$$

Step 8 Determining of generalized estimators of Assessment of Potential Opportunities of the Enterprise $\mathrm{СПВП_m}$ and СПВП for the m-th stage of the life cycle and for the entire life cycle under formulas

$$\mathrm{СПВП_m} = \sqrt{\mathrm{СПП_m} - \mathrm{ДНР_m}} \text{ and } \mathrm{СПВП} = \sqrt{\mathrm{СПП} - \mathrm{ДНР}}. \qquad (5.36)$$

The recommend sequence of calculations makes it possible to receive indices of quantitative assessment of the enterprise potential opportunities and to analyze them both for the entire life cycle and for a particular stage.

During evaluation of the second factor of competitiveness—satisfaction of the market requirements—it is necessary to determine what it means. First, there is always a demand for particular number of goods in the market. Second, a buyer as a market entity has a main objective—satisfaction of its requirements by means of acquisition of goods which have particular consumer properties characterizing its competitiveness. Goods purchased, while in service, carry out their specified functions ,on the one hand, and exhibit their particular qualitative properties on the other hand, capable to strengthen or weaken their competitiveness. Hence, the manufacturer of the goods should offer to the market a particular volume of competitive products with their particular consumer properties to satisfy requirements of the buyer.

In this connection, there is a necessity of choosing a number of indices permitting to assess satisfaction of the market requirements to the goods which would include parameter of the value of output and parameters to characterize competitiveness of the goods and their consumer properties. In our opinion satisfaction of the market requirements can be determined either by means of the index of competitive commodity weight sold by the enterprise in the market for a particular period or by means of the generalized index of variation in satisfaction of the market requirements received on the basis of indices reflecting the sales dynamics of competitive production.

We suggest to calculate the competitiveness index of commodity weight of the enterprises K_m as the weighted mean value of competitiveness indices for every product under the following formula:

$$K_m = \sum_{i=1}^{p} \beta_i \cdot n_i \cdot I_{ni} \tag{5.37}$$

where p—number of types of goods produced;
n_i—number of comparable goods of the i-th type sold by the enterprise;
β_i—coefficient of significance of the i-th type of the goods in the market competition;
I_{ni}—integrated competitiveness index of the i-th type of the goods.

Quantitative evaluation of the product competitiveness I_n can be performed from the formula taking into account quality of service and production, determined by its useful effect,

$$I_n = \sum_{i=1}^{2} \alpha_i \Pi_i \tag{5.38}$$

where Π_1—index of relative effectiveness of production;
Π_2—index of quality of the service;
α_i—weighting coefficients of these indices, $\sum_{i=1}^{2} \alpha_i = 1$

Index of relative effectiveness of production Π_1 is evaluated according to the formula

$$\Pi_1 = (E/E_э)k, \tag{5.39}$$

where E—effectiveness of the product sample in a particular market, unit of useful effect/monetary unit;

$E_э$—effectiveness of the best sample-leader used in this market;
k—adjusting factor making it possible to consider competitive advantages of the goods.

Effectiveness of a product is calculated from the formula:

$$E = П/З, \tag{5.40}$$

where П—useful effect of the product operation within the standard calendar life in the conditions of specific market (unit of useful effect);
З—aggregate expenses for the product life cycle in the conditions of specific market (monetary unit).

Total expenditures of the consumer for the PLC unit with respect to comparable goods (З) and "product-leader" ($З_0$) are determined according to formula:

$$З = З_{с.м} + З_{мНИОКР} + З_{отпп} + З_{изг} + З_{вн} + З_{серв} + \sum_{t=1}^{T} З_{эт} \pm З_{ликв}, \tag{5.41}$$

where $З_{с.м}$—expenses for strategic marketing;
$З_{мНИОКР}$—budget value of the marketing researches, Research & Development—НИОКР;
$З_{отпп}$—budget value of organizational and technological preoperating phase of a new product;
$З_{изг}$—product manufacturing cost (without amortization of the previous expenses);
$З_{вн}$—expenses for introduction of the product (transport expenses, budget cost of construction, and commissioning work);
$З_{серв}$—service cost;
T—product standard service life (industrial function products' life is equal to the amortization period);
$З_{эт}$—operation cost, service, and product repair in a year (t) (without amortization of the previous expenses);
$З_{ликв}$—expenses for dismantle and liquidation (realization) of the elements of the basic production assets (including the product), withdrawn due to introduction of a new product (if these expenses there is less than the income from realization of withdrawn elements, in formula (5.41) they should be with minus, if more—with plus).

The useful effect of a product is determined from the formula:

$$П = \sum_{t=1}^{T} П_ч \cdot Ф_г \cdot K_1 \cdot K_2 \ldots K_9, \tag{5.42}$$

where T—standard product life cycle, years;

$\Pi_ч$—hour technical passport capacity of the product;
$\Phi_г$—annual scheduled fund of the product operating time;
K_1—non-failure operation factor;
K_2—repairability factor;
K_3—storage coefficient;
K_4—environmental performance indicator;
K_5—ergonomics index;
K_6—index of aesthetics (design);
K_7—processability index;
K_8—standardization and unification index (factor of standardization of object);
K_9—compatibility and interchangeability index.

Coefficients and indices K_1, K_2..., K_9 characterize discrepancy of the quality indices of the product to consumer requirements, disadvantageousness of their performance, low organization of the product operation and repair resulting to reduction of its useful effect.

Product repairability factor is evaluated with its readiness use of factor which is calculated from the formula

$$K_2 = T_0/(T_0 + T_в), \tag{5.43}$$

where T_0—mean time between failures of the restored object, h;
$T_в$—mean time of restoration of the object after failure, h.

The integrated index of service quality of the product should be calculated according to the formula:

$$\Pi = \sum_{i=1}^{n} b_i \Pi_{Ci} \tag{5.44}$$

where Π—number of specific indices of service quality of the product;
b_i—weighting coefficient of the i-th index of the service quality,

$$\sum_{i=1}^{n} b_i = 1$$

Π_{Ci}—value of the i-th specific index of service quality of the product relative to the reference index.

The following are considered as the indices of service quality of the product: quality (reliability, conscientiousness, ethical feasibility) of advertising, points; the goods warranty period, years; quality of goods marking and packing, points; fullness coefficient, reliability and quality of accompanying documentation, unit fraction; image of the trade mark and shopping center, points; consumer experience, points; labor intensity of the goods preparation to their functioning, n/hour; quality of after-sale service, points;

It is possible to present the generalized index of variation of the market satisfaction $I_{утр}$ by means of the following formula:

$$I_{утр} = \sqrt{I_{обп} \cdot IK_{kc}} \tag{5.45}$$

where $I_{обп}$—index of variation of the sales volumes, $I_{обп} = R_k/R_n$;
R_n, R_k—sales volumes accordingly at the beginning and at the period's end;
IK_{kc}—an index of variation of the product competitiveness, determined as

$$IK_{kc} = I_{кск}/I_{ксн}$$

$IK_{кск}$, $IK_{ксн}$—competitive power accordingly at the period's end and at the beginning.

During evaluation of results of the enterprise economic activities, it is necessary to proceed from the basic principle—competitiveness of the enterprise reflects effectiveness of use of its resources. Therefore in order to provide competitiveness, the enterprise should continuously take care of the fullest and effective utilization of available resources. In this connection, there is a problem of choosing criteria of effectiveness of their use.

Effectiveness assumes the most effective output, the greatest result per unit of aggregate resources available at the enterprise. If the enterprise activity is connected with profit earning, and the aggregate resources are estimated in money terms, effectiveness can be evaluated by means of indices of output profitability.

Theoretically, it is possible to calculate a complex index of effective use of resources I_p of the enterprise, including a number of specific indices PR_j (relative to the reference index), calculated from the formula:

$$I_p = \sum_{j=1}^{k} \gamma_j \cdot PR_j \tag{5.46}$$

where γ_j—coefficient of significance of the j-th index of effectiveness;
k—number of indices of effectiveness.

This book suggests that results of the enterprise economic activities should account for its financial conditions. The complex index of the financial conditions Φ_c is calculated from the formula:

$$\Phi_c = \sum_{m=1}^{k} \mu_m \cdot Pf_m, \quad (5.47)$$

where μ_m—coefficient of significance of the m-th index of financial status of the enterprise;
k—number of indices;
Pf_m—value the m-th specific index of a financial status relative to the reference index.

The index of results of the enterprise economic activities, designated R_x, is calculated from the formula:

$$R_x = \delta_1 \cdot \Phi_c \pm \delta_2 \cdot I_p, \quad (5.48)$$

where δ_i—weighing coefficients of indices of the enterprise financial status and effectiveness of use of its resources.

Indices $K_м$, $I_{утр}$ and R_x can be calculated both according to the enterprise life cycle phase as a whole and according to its any internal interval.

The pressing problem of the enterprise competitiveness system is optimum distribution of limited financial resources for the purpose of strengthening effects of competitiveness and, as consequence, its increase.

This paragraph proposes to evaluate all the enterprise resources aimed at enhancing its competitiveness in money equivalent.

Distribution optimization of allocated funds consists in minimization of difference between the integrated index of enterprise competitiveness, received as a result of redistribution of funds, and integrated index of competitiveness of the standard enterprise. Minimized functional is considered as a function of financial cost aimed at strengthening of coefficients determining competitiveness of the enterprise.

The model of optimum distribution of financial resources allocated for enhancement of the enterprise competitiveness is as follows:

$$\left(\sqrt{\sum_{i=1}^{n} (R_i(f_i))^2} \right) - R_э \to min \quad (5.49)$$

under condition of limited financial resources of the enterprise

$$\sum_{i=1}^{n} f < F, \ \ f_i > 0, \ (i = 1, 2, \ldots, n), \quad (5.50)$$

where n—number of coefficients determining competitiveness of the enterprise;
f_i—volume of financial costs aimed at strengthening of the i-th factor of the enterprise competitiveness;

$R_i(f_i)$—level of the i-th factor of the enterprise competitiveness as a function of financial costs;
R—integrated competitiveness index of the reference enterprise under optimization;
F—volume of financial assets aimed at enhancing enterprise competitiveness.

Level R_i of the i-th factor of the enterprise competitiveness should be calculated according to formulas (5.1)–(5.4)

$$R_i = k_i(1 - x_i), \tag{5.51}$$

where k_i—weighting coefficient of the i-th, $i = 1, 2, \ldots, n$ factor of the enterprise competitiveness;
x_i—actual level the i-th factor of the enterprise competitiveness this time.

As the coefficients determining competitiveness of the enterprise within the framework of the model, the following groups of indices are offered:

- Group of potential opportunities of the enterprise [(5.29)–(5.36)]
- Group of satisfaction of the market requirements [(5.39)–(5.45)]
- Group of results of economic activities (4)

The basic one, according to this model, is the assumption of functional dependence of funds allocated by the enterprise in order to increase the levels of coefficients determining competitiveness of the enterprise depends and percentage variance of these levels.

In particular, investigation of dynamics of competitiveness coefficients levels has shown that there is quadratic functional dependence between financial costs aimed at the action enhancement of considered coefficients, and its percentage growth

$$f_i(P_i) = a_i P_i^2 \tag{5.52}$$

where a_i—proportionality factor;
P_i—percent amount by which the value of level of the i-th factor of competitiveness is increased.

Hence, proceeding from (5.52)

$$P_i(f_i) = \sqrt{f_i/\alpha_i} \tag{5.53}$$

where $P_i(f_i)$—percent amount (as a function of financial expenses) by which the value of level of the i-th factor of competitiveness is increased.

This implies that strengthening the action enhancement of such coefficients is connected with their growth. Then on the assumption of (5.51), new value of the level of the i-th factor of competitiveness as a result of investment of financial assets in the amount of f_i may be determined according to formula:

$$R_i = k_i \left(1 - \left(1 + \frac{P_i(f_i)}{100}\right) x_i\right). \tag{5.54}$$

After substitution (5.53) in (5.54) we receive

$$R_i = k_i \left(1 - \left(1 + \frac{\sqrt{f_i/\alpha_i}}{100}\right) x_i\right). \tag{5.55}$$

Definitely taking into account (5.55) the offered optimization model of distribution of financial resources (5.49)–(5.50) is as follows (5.56)–(5.57):

$$\left(\sqrt{\sum_{i=1}^{n} k_i \left(1 - \left(1 + \frac{\sqrt{f_i/\alpha_i}}{100}\right) x_i\right)^2} - R\right) \to \min \tag{5.56}$$

$$\sum_{i=1}^{n} f_i \le F, \quad f_i \ge 0, \quad \langle i = 1, 2, \ldots, n \rangle. \tag{5.57}$$

Model implementation (5.56)–(5.57) will make it possible for the enterprise to increase validity of managerial decisions concerning questions of optimum use of the limited industrial resources with a view of enhancing the enterprise competitiveness.

5.4 Methodology of Quantitative Assessment of the Firm Competitiveness

The modern world market of industrial products is an arena of competitive struggle of suppliers which has covered all spheres of their activity and insists on application of various forms and methods in order to attract buyers and provide competitive advantages of the goods. This is why the firms pay much attention to investigation of the product competitiveness in their development of the sale strategy which becomes a key factor in management of all economic activities and depends on the firm competitiveness.

Nowadays, enhancement of competitiveness of domestic-owned firms and production is one of the major problems, the solution of which determines effectiveness and survival of many machine-building and high technology industries of economy directly influencing well-being of people and their standard of living.

Competitiveness is understood to be an ability of corporation (firm) to support high rates of economic growth in the medium term and in the long run. In general terms, economy competitiveness is possession of the properties creating advantages to the agent of competitive struggle. As a rule, three approaches are used for evaluation of competitiveness:

- Value-for-cost approach
- Rating approach
- Approach based on implemented competitive advantages

The value-for-cost approach to competitiveness evaluation is based on the labor productivity index. However, in practice the low index of specific payment usually is not a result of progress of technologies and growth of labor productivity efficiency: it reflects only low payment and underestimated ruble purchasing-power ratios.

The rating approach to competitiveness evaluation gives a complex characteristic of competitive advantages of corporation on the basis of ratings of different groups of competitiveness coefficients.

Within the framework of the third approach, analysis of competitive advantages is performed on the basis of the data on volume and structure of export and import, as well as on change of a share of domestic production in internal goods turnover.

Competitiveness of the agent can differ considerably in the internal and external markets. It is explained by distinctions of the factors forming external and internal environment in the said markets, namely rate of demand creditworthiness, price spread between domestic and the world prices, character of the current foreign trade policy.

As mentioned earlier in Chap. 2 determination of takes into account the factors situated in three levels:

1. Micro-level (production, enterprises, corporations, holdings, concerns)
2. Meso-level (industry sectors)
3. Macro-level (state and specific economic complexes, countries, associations of the countries)

Undoubtedly, competitiveness indices on micro-, meso-, and macro-levels are in close interrelation with each other and make direct impact on the level of competitiveness of one or another economic agent.

Investigation of competitiveness of the meso-agent is impossible without analyses of competitiveness of the micro-agent, and investigation of competitiveness of the macro-agent is impossible without analyses of competitiveness of the meso-agent and vice versa.

It is important to evaluate competitiveness at all the levels and to determine their mutual influence. There are many recommendations in scientific literature concerning this issue. However, in order to work out a system of organization management responsible for competitiveness, there should be determined the indices arising at these levels, and their influence on competitiveness of the firm and its production.

It is possible to cite an example of the oil prices established by the OPEC countries. If the oil price fluctuates upwards or downwards, the export and internal prices for oil and energy products in Russia change at once, and there is a rippling effect concerning change of prices for the goods connected with the energy carriers, their manufacture, and sale. Continuation of this process is the change of competitiveness of goods, production, and firm. Therefore, it is important to forecast changes of indices of every level which particularly influence competitiveness of the firm. For example, for the European banks it is a dollar/euro ratio, as well as ratio of euro and any other national currency and forecast of their exchange rate. Critical for the metallurgical companies are compliance (superiority in some cases) with the quality world standards, as well as the level and tendencies of change in prices for metal and energy resources. Machine-building firms are interested in the technical level, quality, production price, its rates, and tendencies of its variation in time.

On the basis of the above-mentioned characteristics, a system of indices, which allows evaluating and reflecting completely the influence of external and internal environment factors on the firm activity, may be built.

This system of indices can be described with application of mathematical modeling. In the course of working out of concrete mathematical models, there is a danger of including description of too many indices making the mathematical model cumbersome, and the process of analysis—rather time-consuming. In order to avoid such situation while selecting indices, it is worthwhile to be guided by the following reasons:

- Not all factors of external and internal environment are equally necessary from the point of view of the goals it is facing
- If there is a specific number of indices important for this study, it is highly limited; according to Jane Aubert-Krier, the number of such most important indices should amount to 25–30 % of the general number.
- The more simple the indices are and the more they are traceable, the smaller influence their quantity has.

Specific indices make it possible to assess a possible influence of environmental factors on separate aspects of activity of a firm structural division. They represent a statistical basis for formation of consolidated and generalized indices and an initial basis in order to determine corresponding strategic and tactical measures in the firm activity.

Specific indices should be selected so that their contents would have specific rational value for examination of the firm status and tendencies of its development.

On the basis of specific indices, it is possible to receive the following generalizing indices:

- Indices of commodity output (TB)
- Indices of the basic production assets (BPA)
- Indices of the industrial and production personnel (PMD)
- Indices of material resources (MP) used in production
- Indices characterizing competitiveness of the firm's goods or services

The specified groups of production indices, as a rule, are considered for production systems of various levels. They can be holdings, concerns, firms, industrial shops, sites.

In order to determine the specified above indices and their connections with other internal indices in the integrated control system, the following methodology is offered.

Any of the specified groups of production indices can be presented like this

$$Q = \sum_{i=1}^{N} Q_i, \ R_i \tag{5.58}$$

where Q—composite index;
N—number of material elements making composite index;
Q_i—composite index of the i-th type element;
R_i—number of elements in the i-th

The element characteristics are directly connected with the composite index:

$$Q_i = \Psi(\Pi_i, \ \Delta_i, A_i, \Gamma_i),$$

where $\Pi_i, \ \Delta_i, A_i, \Gamma_i$ characteristics of productivity, accuracy, automation, geometrical dimensions.

Formula (5.58) reveals only the integral index value regardless of market conditions, using the competitiveness indices. Therefore, it is necessary to consider some indices that characterize the competitiveness of a set index. It becomes possible due to the following formula:

$$Q_1 = \sum_{i=1}^{N} Q_i R_i K_i \alpha_i \tag{5.59}$$

where Q_1 is the integral index value given the competitiveness of the index K_i and the weighting coefficient α_i.

The weighting coefficient of the i-th shows the importance of this factor in the functioning process of an organization and how noticeably it enhances the competitiveness of products of the organization. The weighting factor depends also on the level at which we analyze functioning of organization—micro-, meso-, macro-level. Obviously the values depend on the purpose and strategy of the organization, but the index will be always higher at the micro-level in comparison with the meso- and macro-levels, and it is always proportional to the importance of this indicator used to assess the level of competitiveness of production on any of the investigated level.

Formula (5.59) differs from formula (5.58) by availability of factor of competitiveness of the *i*-th type:

$$K_i = \frac{S_i}{S_{i0}}, \tag{5.60}$$

Где S_i—value of test parameter of the *i*-th type (S) to value of the basic sample index—the competitor of the *i*-th type (S_{i0}).

It is obvious that:

If $K_i = 0$, the *i*-th type does not possess competitiveness
If $0 \leq K_i < 1$, competitiveness of the *i*-th type is lower than the parameter of comparable competitor
If $K_i > 1$, competitiveness of the *i*-th type is higher than the parameter of comparable competitor
If $K_i = 1$ competitiveness of the *i*-th type is equal to the parameter of comparable competitor

It should be noted that in calculating, for example, of competitiveness index of the cost and the price, there is inverse dependence, i.e.,

$$K_i = \frac{S_{i0}}{S_i}. \tag{5.61}$$

In other words, it is possible to say that from among formulas (5.60) and (5.61), there should be taken the one according to which the index growth corresponds to improvement of the indices parameter. For example, if the level of our firm's costs is lower than the level of costs of the competitor, then according to this index our production is more competitive, and it should be calculated in the formula in the form of inverse dependence of parameters (5.61).

It is necessary to provide a possibility of timely replacement of equipment owing to its moral and/or physical deterioration. In order to determine wear rate of equipment, they use the following indices.

Depreciation coefficient of various types or groups of a fixed capital (in particular, the equipment)

$$S_u = \frac{З_u}{\Phi_n},$$

where $З_u$—deterioration cost of the fixed capital (equipment, in particular);
Φ_n—initial cost of all or separate types, groups of fixed capital (in particular, equipment).

This coefficient makes it possible to determine a share of the worn out equipment of the firm for the time being. The share of newly commissioned equipment is calculated from the formula

$$S_{обн} = \frac{\Phi_{введ}}{\Phi_{кг}},$$

where $S_{обн}$—coefficient of renewal of a fixed capital;
$\Phi_{введ}$—cost of new fixed capital for a particular period;
$\Phi_{кг}$—cost of fixed capital by the year end of the same period.

The share of retire fixed capital may be calculated by retirement rate

$$S_{выб} = \frac{\Phi_{выб}}{\Phi_{нач}},$$

where $\Phi_{выб}$—cost of retire fixed capital for a particular period;
$\Phi_{нач}$—cost of fixed capital for the beginning of the same period.

Owing to tough competition in the market and continuously growing requirements of the consumer, sooner or later, there is a question about launching new and more competitive production. The share of updated production in relation to earlier output may be calculated by the coefficient of renewal:

$$S_{оп} = \frac{\Pi_{введ}}{\Pi_{кг}},$$

where $\Pi_{введ}$ cost of new products for a particular period;
$\Pi_{кг}$—production cost by the year end of the same period.

Competitiveness of firm in line with the above indices can be calculated, comparing these coefficients with the similar coefficients of the competitor, using formula (5.60) or (5.61).

Value

$$W = \frac{Q_1}{Q}$$

shows a gap between annual volume of production made by the enterprise and the output which can be sold in the market under parameters of competitiveness established for this enterprise. Proceeding from these data it is possible to correct, for example, output or a volume of purchased raw materials and by means of factor K_i to determine a parameter influencing success of selling the products. It is obvious that parameter W always is less than 1, but the closer the parameter W to 1, the more competitive the enterprise is.

After these determinations, there comes direct work concerning Preproduction and Manpower Deployment (PMD).

It should be noted that formula (5.58) can be presented in a more complicated form when the nomenclature of material elements has hierarchy:

$$Q = \sum_{i_1=1}^{N_1} \cdots \sum_{i_2=1}^{N_2} \cdots \sum_{i_p=1}^{N_p} Q_{i_1, i_2, \ldots, i_p} \ R_{i_1, i_2, \ldots, i_p},$$

where p—number of levels in dividing material elements according to the nomenclature.

Analysis of the firm competitiveness can be performed quarterly.

For example, average annual value of the Basic Production Assets (BPA) can be divided into cost of machines and the equipment (active part BPA) and cost of buildings and constructions. In turn, the cost of machines and equipment can include the cost of blank production, processing, and assembly equipment. The cost of processing equipment can include the cost of machine tools: computerized mills, wiredrawing mills, turning machines, etc. Besides, the equipment can be classified according to automation and mechanization level.

As the test parameter of the *i*-th type S_i, there may be such parameters of competitiveness as production price, production quality, enterprise technical equipment and the enterprise production costs, etc.

Any production index (both volumetric and structural) can be evaluated according to absolute value and rate of change. At the evaluation of the rate of change of the index, there may be used the first derivative of the function of the change production index in time.

The analytical type of function of index change in time is usually unknown; therefore, in assessment of the index rate of change its growth rate is used

$$\alpha_\delta = \frac{Q_{\delta+1}}{Q_\delta},$$

where $Q_{\delta+1}$, Q_δ values of the index accordingly in (δ + 1) δ-th years.

In general, if it is required to estimate acceleration of the index change there can be considered rate of change of its growth rates:

$$\alpha_\delta = \frac{\alpha_{\delta+1}}{\alpha_\delta},$$

where $\alpha_{\delta+1}$, α_δ rates of growth of the index accordingly in (δ + 1) δ-th years.

The following direction of production indices formation is connected with their comparison which was already mentioned above. It can be made according to the principles of morphological analysis with material relations as the basis. Hence, there may be used both volumetric and structural indices and the firm competitiveness indices. There are 30 variants of the analyzed relations. Indices are compared during construction of the firm competitiveness management system owing to their close correlation and influence on the index of final profit.

Finally, the last direction of production indices formation is dynamics of their change because of updating. Any volumetric index changes with the course of time because one part of the nomenclature of material component retires and another part—appears. Hence, for every volumetric index, there is a volume of new nomenclature and retirement volume (formulas of calculation of these indices are specified above). In line with the above, it is possible to conclude that directions of forming basic technical and economic production indices are based on the following:

1. Material components of production: TB, BPA, PMD, MP.
2. Levels of production systems: workplace, line, site, production facility, enterprise, associations, corporation, holding.
3. Volumetric-structural characteristics: output, nomenclature, number of elements, volumetric index of an element, element characteristic.
4. Time characteristics of the index: absolute value and rates of growth.
5. The ratios of the indices, the total of which can be considered by 30 variants.
6. Dynamics of indices because of updating of material components of production.

Procedure of the index formation includes its consecutive consideration according to each of six specified directions.

In consideration of TB of production indices, first of all, it is necessary to note the basic volumetric indices: annual commodity output, revenues from sales, profit, its cost price, capital intensity, labor intensity, and materials–output ratio. Then, for TB indices there should be specified nomenclature of products, output and price of the products, profit per one product, cost price, capital intensity, labor intensity, and materials–output ratio.

Characteristic features of TB elements are the product technical characteristics directly influencing its price, structural and technical characteristics of the products directly influencing its cost price.

Rate of growth for TB indices is determined, as a rule, for annual commodity output, profit, and cost price, though it can be considered for other indices too.

By means of index W representing a divergence between annual output made of the enterprise and the volume of production which can be sold in the market, taking into account competitiveness of the basic volumetric indices, it is possible not only to correct the firm work under the market current conditions but also to observe dynamics of development of the enterprise during a long time.

The relative indices may include:

- Profitability as the ratio of commodity output to the cost price
- Coefficient of capital intensity productive fixed capital as the ratio of capital intensity of production to its labor intensity
- Capital productivity ratio
- Labor productivity

Indices of updating commodity output are:

- Annual production output of new commodity items
- Annual production output of retirement commodity items
- Nomenclature of new commodity output
- Nomenclature of retirement commodity items

Updating indices can be considered and in relative values. For example, a share of new commodity output in its general annual volume and a nomenclature share of new commodity output within the general nomenclature.

The BPA volumetric characteristics can be divided into the following components:

- Yearly average cost BPA
- Equipment cost (BPA active part)
- Cost of buildings and constructions

In turn, the cost of machines and equipment as the basic objects at BPA development can be divided by types of equipment depending on proximity to ready-made product.

Each of the specified types can be divided by levels of automation which include various types of industrial equipment.

The number of ratios determined for BPA, first of all, include capital-labor ratio and a share of BPA active part.

Finally, in determination of BPA updating it should be specified:

- Annual volume of new BPA
- Annual general capital investments
- Annual volume of new machines and equipment
- Annual capital investments for modernization
- Annual commissioning of buildings and constructions
- Annual capital investments for production reconstruction

Similar characteristics can be used for BPA too.

The same method, as for TB and BPA indices, can be used for consideration and formation of PMD and MP indices according to above six directions of formation of the basic production indices. Based upon accepted method, it is possible to generate considerable number of production indices reflecting various changes, taking place in it with the course of time. Hence, the part of indices can be estimated, and a part can be initial information.

The following requirements are made to the initial information:

- The volume of initial information should provide a possibility to calculate all other production indices, but in so doing there should be no indices which are not used in calculating.

- The information should be based on the accounting reporting of the enterprise which has no subjective interpretation and is closely connected with financial system of its activity.
- The information should be based on the stable indices. It means that their changes during the time are subject to the minimum casual fluctuations.

The volumetric indices of production meeting requirements specified above and regulated by means of change of competitiveness indices are as follows:

1. Annual volume of commodity output
2. Revenues from sales
3. Cost price of annual volume of commodity output
4. General annual wages fund of PMD including bonuses and compensations
5. BPA average annual value
6. MP annual volume
7. Annual volume of general capital investments
8. Annual BPA amortization for its renovation
9. Average annual BPA number
10. Average annual number of units of BPA industrial equipment
11. Average annual cost of machines and equipment
12. Annual cost of operation and maintenance of machines and equipment
13. Annual amortization of machines and equipment for sale

All listed (specific) indices of the firm competitiveness are quantitative and positive. It makes it possible, on their basis, to generate a uniform complex index which will permit to assess competitiveness of investigated firm in comparison with other firms operating in the same commodity market (works or services) in a quantitative automated way.

Let us result algorithm of calculation of a uniform complex competitiveness index. We designate through $x_{k,i}$—value of the i-th specific competitiveness index from the above list, $i = 1, \ldots, 13$, in relation to the k-th firm functioning in the commodity market (works or services). We assume that the number of such firms is equal to K, and the competitiveness of one of them is evaluated (Table 5.3).

Let us transform the value of indices $x_{k,i}$ to comparable units to compare them with each other and to make computing operations with them. We make it so: the value of indices, which should be maximized from the point of view of

Table 5.3 Indices of the firm competitiveness

Firms	Indices			
	i = 1	i = 2	...	i = 13
k = 1	$\overline{x}_{1,1}$	$\overline{x}_{1,2}$	...	$\overline{x}_{1,13}$
k = 2	$\overline{x}_{2,1}$	$\overline{x}_{2,2}$	...	$\overline{x}_{2,13}$
...	...	...	...	...
k = K	$\overline{x}_{K,1}$	$\overline{x}_{K,2}$	...	$\overline{x}_{K,13}$

competitiveness (for example, $i = 1,2$), we divide by their best value $\overline{x}_i$ which is available in aggregate with K of the firms under analysis:

$$x_{k,i}^{np} = \frac{x_{k,i}}{\overline{x}_i},$$

where $x_{k,i}^{np}$ transformation of value of the i-th index;

$$x_{k,i}^{np} = \max_{k=1,K} x_{k,i}.$$

It is obvious that value $x_{k,i}^{np}$ will change within limits

$$x_i^{np} \leq x_{k,i}^{np} \leq 1,$$

where x_i^{np} minimum value $x_{k,i}^{np}$ per totality of the firms K

$$x_i^{np} = \min_{k=\overline{1,K}} \frac{x_{k,i}}{\overline{x}_i}$$

The value of indices to be minimized (e.g., $i = 3, 6$), we transform in a different way. At first we make initial transformation $x_{k,i}^{np1}$

$$x_{k,i}^{np1} = \frac{1}{x_{k,i}^{np}}.$$

It is clear that with such transformation, minimization of $x_{k,i}^{np}$ will lead to maximization of $x_{k,i}^{np1}$.

Therefore, the best (minimum) value $\overline{x}_k$ corresponds to the maximum value $x_{k,i}^{np1}$:

$$x_i^{np1} = \frac{1}{\overline{x}_i}.$$

And further we operate according to the algorithm stated for competitiveness indices, the values of which should be maximized. That is

$$x_{k,i}^{np} = \frac{x_{k,i}^{np1}}{x_i^{np1}}.$$

It is obvious, that the maximum value of index $x_{k,i}^{np}$ in the set of firms K is equal to $\overline{x}_i^{np} = 1$, and the minimum value is determined from formula $x_i^{np} = \min_{k=\overline{1,K}} \frac{x_{k,i}}{\overline{x}_i}$.

Hence, in both cases we have a range of changed values $\left[1, 1 - x_i^{np}\right]$ for relative values of every i-th index. On the one hand, it adjoins the best value of index $x_{k,i}^{np}$ equal to 1, and on the other hand—to the minimum value x_i^{np}.

We use this minimum value for calculation of "scales" (priorities) of separate specific indices of competitiveness as a part of one complex index Y_k which looks like:

$$Y_k = \sum_{i=1}^{13} \pi_i x_{k,i}^{np},$$

where π_i—weighting coefficient characterizing significance (priority) of the i-th specific index.

This priority is suggested to be calculated as follows:

1. For convenience we input normalization requirement:

$$\sum_{i=1}^{13} \pi_i = 1, \quad 0 < \pi_i \leq 1, \quad i = 1, \ldots, 13\,.$$

   From this condition follows that the more the value π_i, the more the share ("weight") of participation of the i-th index in the value of complex index Y_K.
2. Values π_i are determined by means of ratios:

$$\frac{\pi_i}{\pi_j} = \frac{x_j}{\overline{x}_i}, \quad i, j = 1, \ldots, 13\,.$$

   The meaning of this ratio consists in the following: the closer the values of the i-th index to 1 (i.e., the closer the relative values $x_{k,i}^{np}$ are) the less they are unlike according to the i-th index of the firm competitiveness and the smaller is the "weight" of the i-th competitiveness index within the complex index.

The formula for calculation of priorities can be written down like this:

$$\pi_i = \frac{1}{1 + \sum\limits_{j=1,\, j\neq i}^{13} \frac{\underline{x}_i^{np}}{x_j}}.$$

Here value Y_K is calculated from formula:

$$Y_k = \sum_{i=1}^{13} \left(\frac{1}{1 + \sum\limits_{j=1,\, j\neq i}^{13} \frac{\underline{x}_i^{np}}{x_j}} \right) x_{k,i}^{np}.$$

The best value of the complex competitiveness index Y_k is 1. The worst is value Y_k, calculated from formula:

$$Y_k = \sum_{i=1}^{13} \left(\frac{1}{1 + \sum\limits_{j=1,\, j \neq i}^{13} \frac{x_i^{np}}{x_j}} \right) x_i^{np}.$$

The firms involved are arranged in order (registered) depending on value Y_k. The closer the value Y_k to 1, the more competitive is the firm in the commodity market (works or services).

If a firm, which is not included in the list of firms K, enters the market, its characteristics should be added in Table 5.3, and then the algorithm of calculation of priorities and value Y_k should be repeated.

For an express evaluation it is logical to take advantage of calculations for K operating firms. Hence, value Y_k for a new firm (if it is competitive to an adequate degree) can exceed 1.

Competitiveness of a firm is determined by its strategy. The problem of such strategy and ways of perfection of the current strategy of the firm competitiveness management in the economic science and practice is a multidimensional one, which requires the system &purposive approach. In particular, there should be development of analytical methods of competitiveness investigation and the organizational & economic methods composing a uniform Organizational & Economic Mechanism (OEM) to support the enterprise competitiveness management which unites administrative, technical, and technological activities of its enhancement.

In the scientific literature, the system is understood as a complex of the interrelated elements possessing general properties and united for the sake of specific purpose. The system approach means that all connections, elements, functions, and management problems are considered as a single whole. Specification of systems is carried out on the basis of five major coefficients, according to which the systems:

- Has a general purpose
- Consists of the interrelated elements forming its internal structure
- Together with internal elements has external environment forming its restrictions
- Possesses certain resources to provide its functioning
- Is guided by the operating center to provide its movement to intended objective

Hence, OEM of the firm competitiveness managements, and, hence, the complexes of corresponding technical, administrative, and technological activities should be developed proceeding from the target figure on the basis of integral philosophy. It is worthwhile to use the following seven groups of principles in this integral philosophy of competitiveness management:

- System-wide principles
- Development management principles
- Strategic principles
- Principle of knowledge and sufficiency of the management process participants
- Principle of using continuous monitoring
- Principle of diversification of competitiveness management strategies
- Feedback principle

System-wide principles:

- Integrated approach—separate links of OEM competitiveness management should be built in all the functional divisions of the enterprise.
- Systemacity—process of development and implementation of OEM competitiveness management should be based on methodology of the system analysis of developing systems.
- Dynamism—strategic decisions on competitiveness management should be based on dynamic numbers of evaluations of strategic opportunities and competitive positions of the enterprise.
- Continuity—work on competitiveness management strategy should be performed continuously, with tracing of spasmodic changes of its factors.
- Optimality—administrative choice is based on use of criterion basis reflecting principle of optimality proceeding from the system of value paradigms at the enterprise.
- Constructibility—OEM should formulate the strategy and tactics of competitiveness management to prove them and to develop ways of their implementation.

Principles of development management:

- Principles of the systems development
- Modeling principles
- Principles of managerial decision making
- Self-organization principle
- Principle of synergism

For adequate description of OEM competitiveness management, it is necessary to use the approach on the basis of self-organization and to be guided by the main principles of synergism as basic theory of self-organization.

Strategic principles mean concentration of efforts, balance of risks, and cooperation.

The principle of using continuous monitoring provides continuous supervision and control over implementation and dynamics of the life cycle of the enterprise competitiveness management process.

On the basis of the principle of diversification of the enterprise competitiveness management strategy, there is continuous monitoring and preparation of alternative variants of the management strategy.

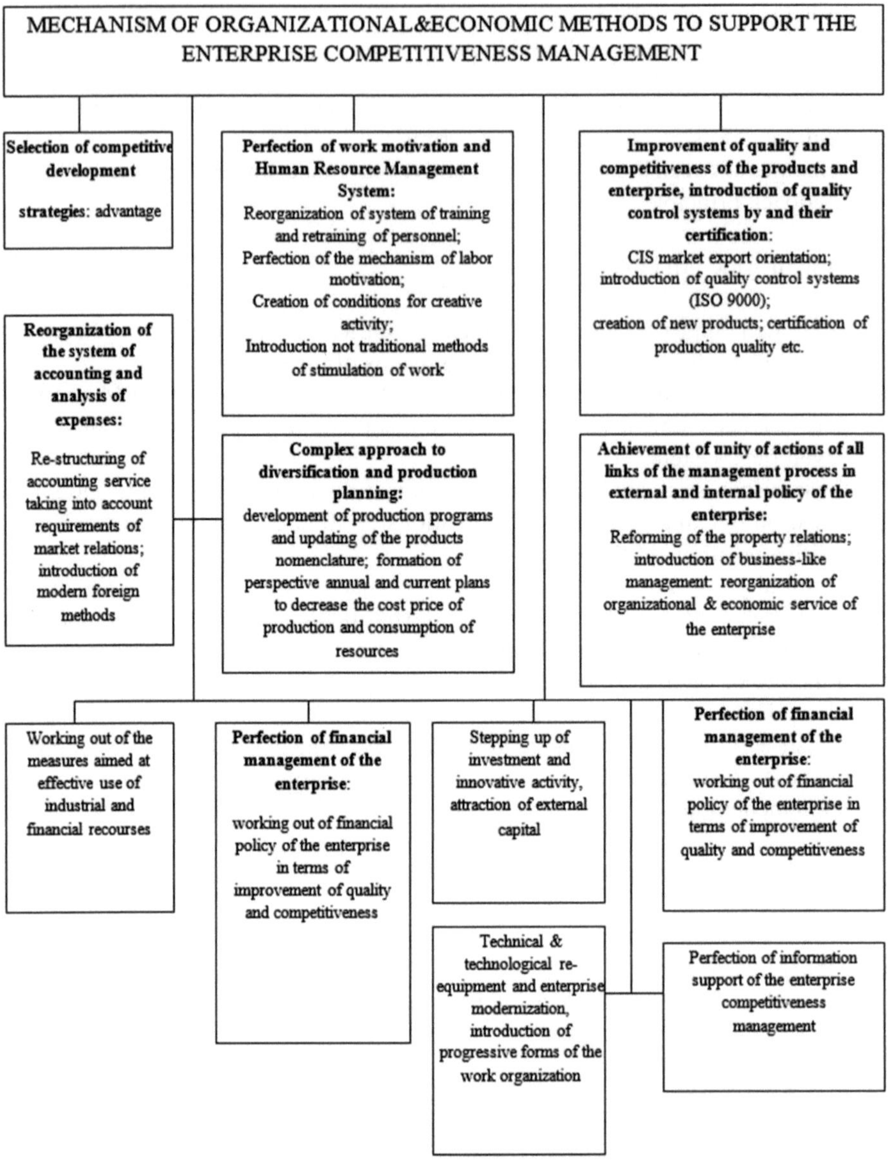

Fig. 5.4 Organizational and economic methods to support competitiveness management of the enterprise

The feedback principle makes it possible to make competitiveness management OEM adaptive in relation to the transformed market environment. The account of this principle makes it possible to make necessary structural, organizational, and resource changes at the enterprise resulting in affecting its interests and opportunities.

As may be inferred from Fig. 5.4, the structure of basic elements of competitiveness management OEM is formed by the program & target blocks reflecting the necessary measures, concrete organizational, economic, technical and technological activities in their interdependence, the implementation of which promotes productive managerial decisions in this field of activity.

The offered OEM includes the following blocks:

- Selection of competitive development strategy
- Reforming of work motivation and Human Resource Management System
- Improvement of quality and competitive power of products and enterprise, and introduction of quality control systems and their certification
- System approach to diversification and production planning
- Achievement of unity of actions of all links and managerial processes in external and internal policy of the enterprise
- Reorganization of the system of accounting and analysis
- Perfection of marketing orientation, strengthening of marketing service
- Activization of investment and innovative activity; attraction of external investments; perfection of information support of competitiveness management
- Perfection of financial management
- Working out of measures aimed at effective use of industrial and financial resources
- Technical and technological reequipment and enterprise modernization, introduction of progressive technological processes

All the specified blocks of OEM competitiveness management, being interrelated and, thereby, forming particular integrity, are united by a single principle.

Every block provides solution of enhancement of competitiveness and stability of the enterprise in internal and external markets at the expense of creation and support of competitive advantages and high adaptation to dynamically changing external market environment. Each block is considered as a system including diverse systemically important components.

Let us consider in detail the basic components of the offered competitiveness management OEM and the logic and structure of their formation.

Selection of Competitive Development Strategies Correctly chosen competitive strategy of the firm development, based on strategic analysis of its competitive positions and potential opportunities, makes it possible to be determined more accurately with the measures enhancing adequacy, dynamism, and inductive susceptiveness of in-house mechanism to the changes of market environment and strengthening scientific and technical and industrial potential of the firm. The management literature specifies the most widespread and verified various strategy classifications of the firms under conditions of tough competition. Possibility of wide maneuver by strategies under conditions of market economy makes the business motive power.

M. Porter has specified three strategies which have universal character and are applicable relative to any competitive force—advantage in costs, differentiation, and focusing. Such approach can be taken as a principle choice of long-term strategy of any firm development, for example:

- Minimization of expenses in the entire manufacturing composite lead time and its large-scale diversification
- Development and output in conformity with the world standards of quality
- Introduction of progressive technologies
- Expansion of zones of strategic economy management

With due account for the strategy and target of development, the firm mission can be determined as follows:

- Satisfaction of internal and external market requirements as the leading manufacturer of equipment at the expense of effective use of intellectual and technical opportunities
- Provision of stable growth of society well-being on the basis of highly professional work

Achievement of Unity of Actions of all Links and Management Processes in the Enterprise External and Internal Policy On the basis of unity of actions of all links, it is possible to reach an administrative synergy in system of management and, thereby, to ensure greater effect from combination of forces of all the personnel, to liquidate gaps in strategy and potential opportunities of the management system, and to create the necessary preconditions for business activity.

With this consideration in mind, composite components of this block are the following directions of activity:

- Optimum reforming of property relations
- Introduction of entrepreneurial internal management
- Cardinal reorganization of organizational & economic structure of management
- Creation of profit centers responsible for self-sustained results of activity
- Provision of complex approach to reorganization of the system and structure of the enterprise management

Various development strategies require essentially different systems and structures of management, the formation of which, in turn, is predetermined by corresponding organizational style of the enterprise behavior. The management literature describes incremental and entrepreneurial styles of organizational behavior.

Incremental style of the firm behavior is aimed at minimization of deviations from traditional behavior both in the firm and in relation with external environment. The changes are not welcomed, they should be limited or minimized.

Entrepreneurial style involves another relation to the changes. Such enterprises support continuous change of available condition and conduct entrepreneurial search of opportunities for growth at the expense of changes.

Non-prejudicial necessity of transition to the entrepreneurial type of management demands reorganization of the management organizational structure. All-pervasive structure of management at the domestic factories of mechanical engineering on the functional basis is not conducive to market conditions; it is focused on execution only, instead of the creative search. The purpose of organizational structure is to support the enterprise, to promote strengthening of the management role in implementation of its strategic goals and the mission, and to provide opportunities for implementation of the rapid response to the volatile environment and market conjuncture.

5.5 Calculation Example for the Firm Competitiveness

Objective assessment of the firm competitiveness is performed with the help of mathematical model. It is applied in the form of a system of functional dependences of specific indices, similar to model (3.4.) developed for evaluation of competitive power:

$$F(U) = \begin{cases} f_1 = f_1(u_{1,1}, \ldots, u_{1,\mathrm{N1}}) \\ \ldots \\ f_w = f_w(u_{w,1}, \ldots, u_{w,\mathrm{Nw}}) \end{cases} \tag{5.62}$$

where f_i—the i-th function reflecting interdependence N_i of specific indices of the firm competitiveness $(u_{i,1}, \ldots, u_{i,N_i})$ when $i = 1, \ldots, w$ and $u_{i,1} \in U, \ldots, u_{i,N_i} \in U$;

U—a set of all specific indices of the firm competitiveness (including specific scientific and technical indices of the firm competitiveness $u'i \in U' \subset U$ and the risk indices $u_{iR} \in U \subset U$)

w—number of functional dependences f_i in system $F(U)$.

By analogy with the generalized indices of the product competitiveness, the generalized indices of the firm competitiveness are formed; their number should be optimum. But the system of generalized indices of competitiveness will have more complicated hierarchy for a firm owing to complexity of organizational system, production, relations, and interaction of one index with the others.

By analogy with formula (3.5) hierarchy of the generalized indices, indices of the first level of generalization will consist of specific indices of the firm competitiveness taking into account their weight in the generalized index:

$$R_{1,j} = \sum_{i=1}^{m_{1,j}} H_i \beta_{0,i} + \sum_{i=m_{1,j}+1}^{M_{1,j}} H'_i \beta_{0,i}, \tag{5.63}$$

where $R_{1,j}$—j-th generalized competitiveness index of the first level of generalization;

$m_{1,j}$—number of specific indices of the firm competitiveness;

$(M_{1,j} - m_{1,j})$—number of specific scientific and technical indices of the firm competitiveness $R_{1,j}$;

$\beta_{0,i}$—weighting coefficient of the i-th specific index at the first level of generalization

$(i = 1, \ldots, M_{1,j})$ and is satisfied by a condition: $\sum_{i=1}^{M_{1,j}} \beta_{0,i} = 1$.

As well as in case of the generalized indices of the product competitiveness (Sect. 4.5), for any p-th level of generalization, the generalized indices will consist of generalized indices of the firm competitiveness of the previous (p-1) level of generalization with allowance for their weight in this generalized index:

$$R_{p,j} = \sum_{i=1}^{M_{p,j}} R_{p-1,i} \cdot \beta_{p-1,i}, \tag{5.64}$$

where $R_{p,j}$—j-th generalized index of the firm competitiveness of the p-th level of generalization;

$M_{p,j}$—number of generalized indices of the previous level $R_{p-1,i}$, making index $R_{p,j}$;

$\beta_{p-1,i}$—weighting coefficient of generalized index $R_{p-1,i}$, and condition $\sum_{i=1}^{M_{lj}} \beta_{p-1,i} = 1$ is met.

The top level of hierarchy (P) of the generalized indices of the firm competitiveness will have the generalized indices characterizing the firm competitiveness in all basic fields of its activity: designing, preproduction, manufacturing, supply, management of the basic production assets, management of HR, financial activity, production sales, transportation. The number of such indices will depend on structure of the organization and complexity of production. In each field of the firm activity, with formula (5.64), there should be generated a composite index of competitiveness reflecting influence of specific and generalized indices with their weightiness in a quantitative way, which influence competitiveness of the firm in this field of its activity.

The firm functioning in various fields of activity is unequally reflected in formation of its competitive advantages and aggregate competitiveness. So, design and industrial activity of machine-building firm influences its competitiveness very much, more than, for example, financial activity.

Priority of the fields of activity in formation of the firm general competitiveness should be taken into account in determining integrated competitiveness index of the firm, summarizing generalized indices of the top level of hierarchy taking weightiness into account

$$H_{I,op\varepsilon} = \frac{\sum_{i=1}^{M_P} R_{P,i} \cdot \beta_{P,i}}{\sum_{i=1}^{M_P} \beta_{P,i}}, \tag{5.65}$$

where $R_{P,i}$—generalized index of the firm competitiveness in the i-th field(direction) of its activity;

$\beta_{P,i}$—weighting coefficient of index $R_{P,\ i}$, reflecting a share of competitiveness formed in this direction of the firm activity;

M_P—number of competitiveness generalized indices of the highest level of hierarchy (the basic directions of the firm activities).

The integrated index of the firm competitiveness within the framework of its activity should increase in the course of the firm management, effective variation of the earlier defined generalized and specific indices of competitiveness, and their weightiness

$$H_{I,op\varepsilon} \to \max. \tag{5.66}$$

In the light of the above-mentioned there can be made the following mathematical model determining competitiveness of the firm taking into account optimality of the generalized indices of the firm competitiveness and existing correlation of specific indices of the firm competitiveness:

$$\begin{cases} f_{i_1} = f_{i_1}\left(u_{i_1,1}, \ldots, u_{i_1,N_{i_1}}\right), \quad (i_1 = 1, \ldots, I_f) \\ H_{i_2} > 0, \quad (i_2 = 1, \ldots, I_2) \\ H'_{i_3} > 0, \quad (i_3 = 1, \ldots, I_3) \\ R_{1,j_1} = \sum_{i=1}^{M_{1,j_1}} H_i \beta_{0,i} + \sum_{i=m_{11\,j_1}+1}^{M_{1,j_1}} H'_i \beta_{0,i}, \quad (j_1 = 1, \ldots, J_1) \\ R_{p,j_p} = \sum_{i=1}^{M_{p,j_p}} R_{p-1,i} \beta_{p-1,i}, \quad (p = 2, \ldots, P; \ \ j_p = 1, \ldots, J_p) \end{cases} \tag{5.67}$$

$$H_{I,op\varepsilon} = \frac{\sum_{i=1}^{M_P} R_{P,i} \cdot \beta_{P,i}}{\sum_{i=1}^{M_P} \beta_{P,i}} \to \max$$

where f_{i_1}—i_I-th function reflecting interdependence N_{i_1} of specific indices of the firm competitiveness $\left(u_{i_1,1}, \ldots, u_{i_1,N_{i_1}}\right)$, and $u_{i,1} \in U, \ldots, u_{i,N_i} \in U$;

U—a set of all specific indices of the firm competitiveness (including specific scientific and technical indices of the firm competitiveness $u' i \in U' \subset U$ and risk indices $u_{iR} \in U \subset U$);
I_f—number of such functional interdependences;
H_{i_2}—factor of competitiveness of the i_2 -th specific index of the firm which is not scientific and technical characteristic of the firm;
I_2—Number of coefficients H_{i_2};
H'_{i_3}—factor of competitiveness of the i_3-th specific scientific and technical index of the firm;
I_3—number of coefficients H'_{i_3};
R_{1,j_1}—J_1-th generalized competitiveness index of the first level of generalization;
m_{1,j_1} —Number of specific indices of competitiveness of the firm, not being scientific and technical characteristics of firm;
$(M_{1,j_1} - m_{1,j_1})$—number of specific scientific and technical indices of the firm competitiveness R_{p,j_p};
J_1—Number of indices R_{1,j_1} at the first level of generalization;
$\beta_{0,i}$—weighting coefficient of the i-th specific index at the first level of generalization $(i = 1, \ldots, M_{1,j_1})$, condition $\sum_{i=1}^{M_{1,j_1}} \beta_{0,i} = 1$ is met;
R_{p,j_p}—j_p-th generalized index of the firm competitiveness of the p-th level of generalization;
M_{p,j_p}—number of the generalized indices of the previous level $R_{p-1,j}$, being index R_{p,j_p};
J_p—number of indices R_{p,j_p} at the p-th level of generalization;
P—number of levels of generalization;
$\beta_{p-1,i}$—weighting coefficient of generalized index $R_{p-1,i}$. Condition is met: $\sum_{i=1}^{M_{p,j_p}} \beta_{p-1,i} = 1.$

Indices $R_{1,i}$, $R_{p,i}(p = 2, \ldots, P)$, and $H_{I,ope}$ can be repeatedly evaluated in the course of time, for example, in a year. Behavior of these indices in time will show dynamics of change of the firm competitiveness in all the fields of its activity that will help its managers or managing directors with decision-making on optimization of the firm work.

Within the framework of such system, it is necessary to provide a set of specific indices of the firm competitiveness U and achievements *HTΠU′* in time. Then the formula will be as follows:

$$U'(t) \subset U(t). \tag{5.68}$$

For mathematical model (5.67), all specific indices of the firm competitiveness, weighing coefficients of all (specific and generalized) indices of the firm competitiveness in forming competitive power are as follows:

$$\begin{aligned} &\beta_{i,j} = \beta_{i,j}(t), \quad (i = 0, \ldots, P); \\ &H_{i_2} = H_{i_2}(t); \\ &H'_{i_3} = H'_{i_3}(t), \end{aligned} \tag{5.69}$$

where t—time.

The generalized indices of the firm competitiveness from the first to the R-th level are as follows:

$$\begin{aligned} &R_{1,j_1} = R_{1,j_1}(t), \\ &R_{p,j_p} = R_{p,j_p}(t). \end{aligned} \tag{5.70}$$

The integrated index of the firm competitiveness will look like

$$H_{I,opz} = H_{I,opz}(t). \tag{5.71}$$

Mathematical model (5.67) is as follows

$$\begin{cases} f_{i_1}(t) = f_{i_1}\left(u_{i_1,1}(t), \ldots, u_{i_1,N_{i_1}}(t)\right), \quad (i_1 = 1, \ldots, I_f) \\ H_{i_2}(t) > 0, \quad (i_2 = 1, \ldots, I_2) \\ H'_{i_3}(t) > 0, \quad (i_3 = 1, \ldots, I_3) \\ R_{1,j_1}(t) = \sum_{i=1}^{m_1,j_1} H_i(t) \cdot \beta_{0,i}(t) + \sum_{i=m_{11}j_1+1}^{M_1,j_1} H'_i(t) \cdot \beta_{0,i}(t), \quad (j_1 = 1, \ldots, J_1) \\ R_{p,j_p} = \sum_{i=1}^{M_{p,j_p}} R_{p-1,i}(t) \cdot \beta_{p-1,i}(t), \quad (p = 2, \ldots, \mathrm{P}; \quad j_p = 1, \ldots, J_p) \end{cases} \tag{5.72}$$

$$H_{I,opz}(t) = \frac{\sum_{i=1}^{M_P} R_{P,i}(t) \cdot \beta_{P,i}(t)}{\sum_{i=1}^{M_P} \beta_{P,i}(t)} \to \max$$

With the help of such mathematical model within the framework of the firm competitiveness management system, the integrated index of the firm competitiveness is calculated; forecasting of changes of the firm competitiveness takes place with due account for all coefficients it is influenced by, including introduction of innovative technologies providing automation, mechanization of production. It will make it possible for the firm management to have timely information on variation of

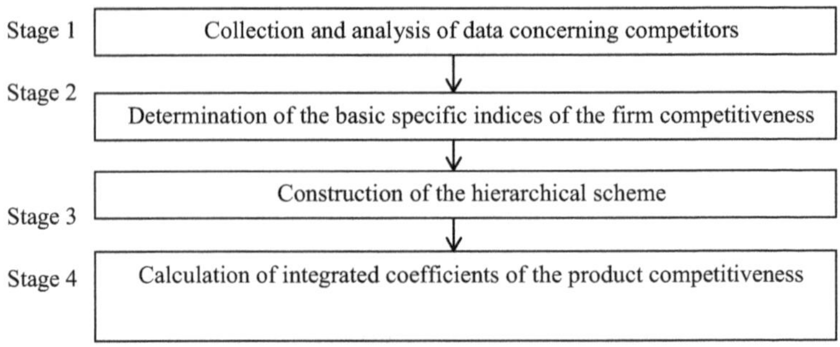

Fig. 5.5 Computation algorithm for integrated coefficient of the firm competitiveness

the firm competitiveness at any stage and in any direction of its functioning. The similar information will give a chance to make in due time a non-prejudicial decision on competitiveness regulation, perfection of the output competitive advantages, and the firm as a whole: replacement of concrete type of equipment, technical opportunities; change of materials applied in production and accessories with competitive advantages; search and replacement of "know-how" providing in advance particular terms and quality.

The basis of calculation methodology of integrated coefficients of the firm competitiveness is founded on the computation scheme presented in Fig. 5.5.

Let us consider effectiveness of this technique by the example of determination of competitiveness of three enterprises producing identical items, the statistical data of which we model.

Stage 1–2 Collection and analysis of statistical data of three enterprises. Identification of the basic specific indices to characterize the firms, presented in Table 5.4.

Stage 3 In building the firm hierarchical structure with complicated scientific and technical production, it is thought that determining indices of the firm competitiveness of the similar enterprises are scientific and technical, industrial, and innovative indicators, besides the structure includes financial and management activity. The hierarchical structure of the firm competitiveness presented in Fig. 5.6 is constructed on the basis of this approach.

Stage 4 Calculation of integrated coefficients of the product competitiveness is performed with due account for the above offered calculation model of integrated indices of the product competitiveness.

Step 1 We transform values of indices $X_{k,i}$ to comparable units so that we could compare them with each other and to make arithmetic operations with them. With that end in view, we divide the firm competitiveness indices, which should be increased, into their corresponding maximum values—$x_{i,k} = X_{i,k}/X_{i\ \max}$ (e.g., we

Table 5.4 Collection of statistical data concerning specific indices of the firm competitiveness

Basic fields of the firm activities	Specific indices	Enterprises 1	2	3
I. Scientific and technical.	1. Labor productivity (q per day)	610	650	600
	2. Capital productivity ratio per unit of equipment (rbl.)	30	38	26
	3. Automation level	0,8	0,65	0,7
	4. Power consumption (th.kw/h)	10	12	9
II. Industrial	1. Cost price of unit of production (rbl.)	300	70	60
	2. Output volume	1.2	1.5	1.8
	3. Production nomenclature	6	5	7
III. Innovative	1. Innovations implementation scope (million rbl.)	7	6,5	6
	2. Amount of financing of scientific researches (million rbl.)			
	3. Amount of financing of purchasing and introduction of patents (million rbl.)	0.6	0.65	0.55
IV. Financial	1. Profitability (rbl.)	15	20	16
	2. Volume of in-house financial resources	430	450	480
	3. Amount of credit exposure (million rbl.)	14	15	13
	4. Financial risks	0,1	0,2	0,15
V. Administrative	1. Automation of the management process, (%)	100	80	90

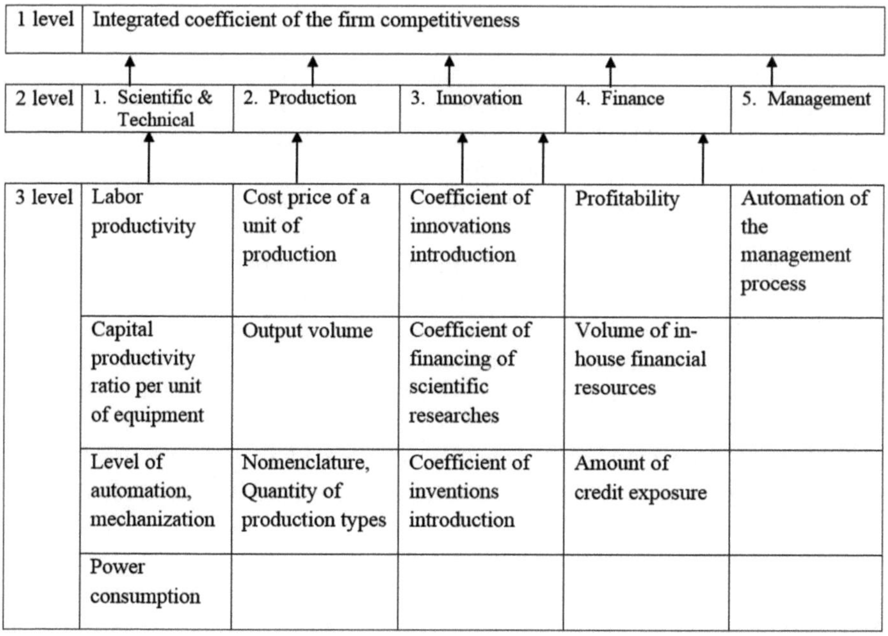

Fig. 5.6 Hierarchical structure of the firm competitiveness

Table 5.5 Standardized specific indices of the firm competitiveness

	Firms		
Specific indices of the competitiveness	1	2	3
I.1. Labor productivity	0.9385	1	0.9231
II.1. Cost price of unit of production	0.8667	0.9630	1
III.1. Volume of innovations introduction	1	0.9286	0.8571
IV.1. Profitability	0.75	1	0.8
V.1. Management process automation	1	0.8	0.9
I.2. Capital productivity ratio per unit of equipment	0.7895	1	0.9211
II.2. Output volume	0.6667	0.8333	1
III.2. Amount of financing of scientific researches	1	0.75	0.5
IV.2. Volume of in-house resources	0.8958	0.9375	1
I.3. Automation level	1	0.8125	0.875
II.3. Nomenclature (scope of output)	0.8571	0.7143	1
III.3. Expenses for acquisition and introduction of patents	0.9231	1	0.8462
IV.3. Amount of credit exposure	0.9286	0.8667	1
I.4. Power consumption	0.7857	0.8571	1
3.4. Financial risks	1	0.5	0.6667

divide all indices characterizing labor productivity by 650). In case of indices, which should be reduced, their "standardized" values are found from formula

$$x_{j,k} = X_{j\,\min}/X_{j,k}. \tag{5.73}$$

For example, in case of indices characterizing the cost price of a unit of production, 260 is divided by the indices of every firm. By means of the functional diagram presented in Fig. 5.6, we receive the standardized table of specific indices of the firm competitiveness (Table 5.5).

Please note that the firm competitiveness indices should be reduced—$X_{j,k}$.

Step 2 Calculation of integrated coefficient of the firm competitiveness was performed according to the functional diagram presented in Figs. 5.7 and 5.8. Calculation should be performed from the first level, rising step by step to the next level where the generalized indices were calculated from formula (5.76). Please note that in identification of the vector of priorities β, the Analytic Hierarchy Process has been used.

Within the framework of this method, considered is $\{D_i\}$—a set of ranged objects (alternatives). Quantitative statements about pairs of objects (D_i, D_j) are represented by matrix $n \times n$; $A = \left(a_{ij}\right)$, $(i, j = 1, 2, \ldots, n)$. Elements a_{ij} are determined by rules:

Rule 1 If $a_{ij} = b$, $a_{ji} = 1/b$, $b \neq 0$;

Rule 2 If properties D_i and D_j are equally important, $a_{ij} = 1$, $a_{ji} = 1$; in particular, $a_{ii} = 1$ for all i.

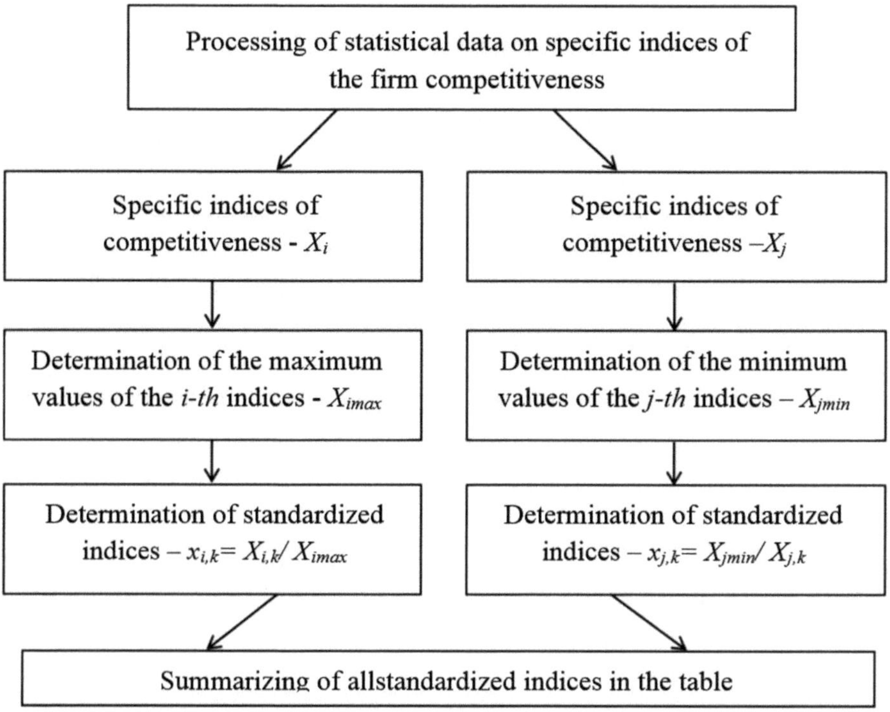

Fig. 5.7 Computation scheme for standardized specific indices of the firm competitiveness

Hence, matrix A looks like

$$A = \begin{bmatrix} 1 & a_{12} & \dots & a_{1n} \\ 1/a_{12} & 1 & \dots & a_{2n} \\ 1/a_{1n} & 1/a_{2n} & \dots & a_{2n} \end{bmatrix} \tag{5.74}$$

Quantitative statements about pairs (D_i, D_j) shall not be set on binary scale $(b = 0, 1)$; they should be set on the multidimensional scale reflecting resolution opportunities of a person in psychophysical measurements. The scale is determined by the following rules:

Rule 3 If D_i is slightly more important than D_j, then $a_{ij} = 3$;

Rule 4 If D_i is more important than D_j, then $a_{ij} = 5$;

Rule 5 If D_i is clearly important than D_j, then $a_{ij} = 7$;

Rule 6 If D_i is absolutely important than D_j, then $a_{ij} = 9$;

Rule 7 Value $a_{ij} = 2, 4, 6, 8$ and their inverse values are used for simplification of the compromises between statements slightly differing from the basic numbers;

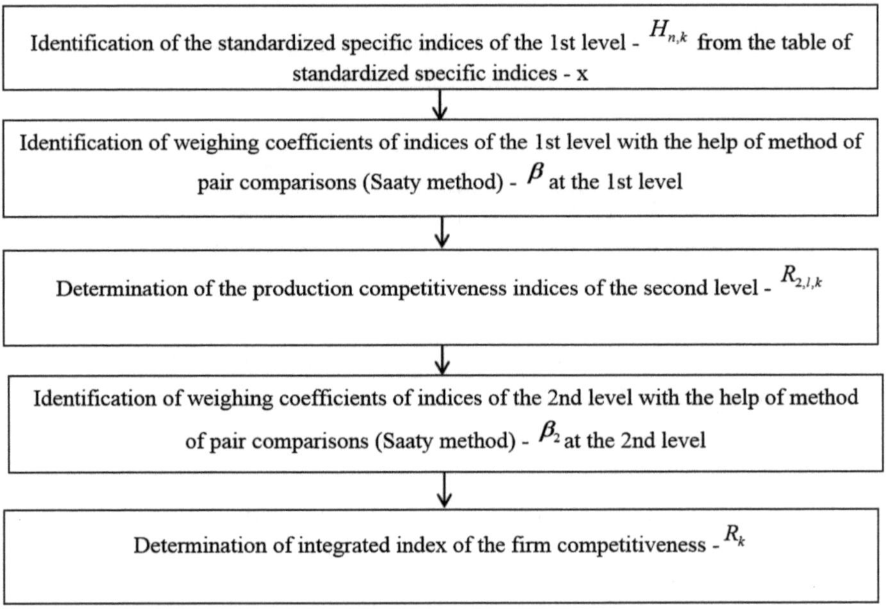

Fig. 5.8 Computation scheme for integrated indices of the firm competitiveness

Rule 8 By convention, comparison of degree of significance is always made for the object in the left column relative to the object in the top line.

After presentation of quantitative statements about pairs (D_i, D_j) in numerical formula through a_{ij}, the task is reduced to assigning a set of numerical indices of significance, which would correspond to the stated statements about pair comparisons to the set of objects $D_1, D_2, \ldots, D_n$.

This problem is solved by calculation of the vector of priorities on matrix A, formula (5.74). In mathematical terms, this is a calculation of the main own vector which after standardization becomes a vector of priorities. Assessments of this vector are carried out by one of four ways which are presented below in increasing accuracy of evaluations.

Way 1 To summarize elements of every line and to normalize by division of every sum into the amount of all elements. The amount of results received will be equal to unity element. The first element of resultant vector will be a priority of the first object, the second one will be a priority of the second object, etc.

Way 2 To summarize elements of every column and to receive inverse values of these sums, to normalize them so that their sum it was equaled to unity element, to divide each inverse value by the amount of all inverse values.

Way 3 To divide elements of every column by the sum of elements of this column, that is to normalize the column, then to combine elements of every line received and to divide this sum by number of elements of the line. It is an averaging process by the normalized columns.

Way 4 To increase n elements of every line and to take root of n-th degree. To normalize the numbers received.

All four ways provide identical vectors of priorities if the matrix is coordinated. It is common knowledge that coordination of positive antisymmetric matrix A is equivalent to requirement $\lambda_{\max} = n$, where $\lambda_{\max}$—maximum characteristic value of the matrix.

The departure from coordination is determined by coordination index:

$$ИС = \frac{\lambda_{\max} - n}{n - 1}. \tag{5.75}$$

Coordination index generated in a random way on the T. Saaty scale of antisymmetric matrix with corresponding inverse values is called casual index (CI).

Average CI for matrixes of the order from 1 to 15 received on the basis of 100 sample taken at random are presented in the standard form in Table 5.6.

Ratio of IS to the average CI for the matrix of the same order is called Conformity Relation (CR). Value of CR smaller or equal to 0,10 is considered comprehensible.

Advantage of the Analytic Hierarchy Process over other methods of determination of weighing coefficients consists in simplicity and visualization of solution of multicriteria problems in challenging environment with hierarchical structures including the model of the firm competitiveness evaluation. Further we will use way 4 for calculation of the vector of priorities β.

Determination of Scientific and Technical Indices at the First and the Second Levels

With due account for the standardized data presented in Table 5.5 and according to the functional diagram presented in Fig. 5.4, we have received specified normalized specific scientific and technical indices of the firm competitiveness of the first level—$H_{1,l}$, presented in Table 5.7.

Then with application of the Analytic Hierarchy Process, we determined the vector of priorities for specific scientific and technical indices of the firm competitiveness of the first level, presented below in Table 5.8.

Value of CR of =1 %.

Taking into account formula (3.39), by multiplication of the transposed matrix from Table 5.8 and vector β_1, we receive specific scientific and technical indices of the firm competitiveness of the second level $R_{2,l}$, presented in Table 5.9.

As may be inferred from analysis of Table 5.9, the first firm has the worst scientific and technical index.

Determination of Industrial Indices at the First and the Second Levels

With due account for the data presented in Table 5.5 and according to the functional diagram presented in Fig. 5.7, we have received specified normalized specific

Table 5.6 Standard table of average casual indexes (CI) for n = [1,15]

N	1	2	3	4	5	6	7	8	9	10	11	12	13	14	15
C	0.0	0.0	0.5	0.9	1.1	1.2	1.3	1.4	1.4	1.4	1.5	1.4	1.5	1.5	1.5
I	0	0	8	0	2	4	2	1	5	9	1	8	6	7	9

Table 5.7 Normalized specific scientific and technical indices of the firm competitiveness of the first level—$H'_{1,l}$

	Firms		
Scientific and technical indices—$H'_{1,l}$	1	2	3
1. Labor productivity	0.9385	1	0.9231
2. Capital productivity ratio per unit of equipment	0.7895	1	0.9211
3. Automation level	1	0.8125	0.8750
4. Power consumption	0.7857	0.8571	1

Table 5.8 Matrix of binary comparisons by Analytic Hierarchy Process and the vector of priorities for specific scientific and technical indices of the firm competitiveness of the first level

Ranged objects	1	2	3	4	β_1
1. Labor productivity	1	2	2	3	0.4
2. Capital productivity ratio per unit of equipment	0.5	1	1	2	0.2274
3. Automation level	0.5	1	1	2	0.2274
4. Power consumption	0.3333	0.5	1/2	1	0.1222

Table 5.9 Scientific and technical indices of the second level

	Firms	Scientific and technical indices
2 level	1	0.8999
	2	0.9399
	3	0.9211

Table 5.10 Normalized specific industrial indices of the firm competitiveness of the first level—$H_{1,l,k}$

	Firms		
Industrial indices	1	2	3
1. Cost price of unit of production	0.866667	0.962963	1
2. Output volume	0.666667	0.833333	1
3. Nomenclature	0.857143	0.714286	1

industrial indices of competitiveness of organizations of the first level, presented in Table 5.10.

With application of Analytic Hierarchy Process, we determined the vector of priorities for specific industrial indices of the firm competitiveness of the first level, presented in Table 5.11.

Taking into account formula (5.9) by multiplication of transposed matrix of Table. 5.11 and the vector, we receive specific industrial indices of the firm competitiveness of the second level, presented below in Table 5.12.

From analysis of Table 5.12 follows that the first firm has the worst industrial indices.

Table 5.11 Matrix of binary comparisons by a Analytic Hierarchy Process and the vector of weightiness for specific industrial indices of the firm competitiveness of the first level

Ranged objects	1	2	3	β_1
1. Cost price of unit of production	1	1	3	0.4286
2. Output volume	1	1	3	0.4286
3. Nomenclature	0.333333	0.333333	1	0.1429

Table 5.12 Industrial indices of the second level

	Firms	Industrial indices
2 level	1	0.77959184
	2	0.87188209
	3	1

Table 5.13 Normalized specific innovative indices of the firm competitiveness of the first level

	Firms		
Innovations	1	2	3
1. Volume of mastered innovation	1	0.928571	0.85714
2. Amount of financing of scientific researches	1	0.75	0.5
3. Expenses for acquisition and introduction of patents	0.923077	1	0.84615

Table 5.14 Matrix of binary comparisons by the Analytic Hierarchy Process and the vector of weightiness for specific innovative indices of the firm competitiveness of the first level

Ranged objects	1	2	3	β_1
1. Volume of mastered innovation	1	1	3	0.4286
2. Amount of financing of scientific researches	1	1	3	0.4286
3. Expenses for acquisition and introduction of patents	0.333333	0.333333	1	0.1428

Determination of Innovative Indices at the First and the Second Levels

With allowances made for the data presented in Table 5.5 and following the functional diagram presented in Fig. 5.7, we have received normalized specific innovative indices of the firm competitiveness of the first level, presented in Table 5.13.

With application of the Analytic Hierarchy Process, we determined the vector of weightiness for specific innovative indices of the firm competitiveness of the first level, presented in Table 5.14.

With allowances made for the formula (5.9) and by multiplication of the transposed matrix of Table 5.14 and the weightiness vector, we receive specific innovative indices of the firm competitiveness of the second level, presented in Table 5.15.

From analysis of Table 5.16 follows that the third firm has the worst innovative indices.

Table 5.15 Innovative indices of the second level

	Firms	Innovative indices
2 level	1	0.9890
	2	0.8622
	3	0.7025

Table 5.16 Normalized specific financial indices of the firm competitiveness of the first level

	Firms		
Financial indices	1	2	3
1. Profitability	0.75	1	0.8
2. Volume of in-house resources	0.895833	0.9375	1
3. Amount of credit exposure	0.928571	0.866667	1
4. Financial risks	1	0.5	0.66667

Table 5.17 Matrix of binary comparisons by the Analytic Hierarchy Process and the vector of priorities for specific financial indices of the firm competitiveness of the first level

Ranged objects	1	2	3	4	β_1
1. Profitability	1	1	2	3	0.351187
2. Volume of in-house resources	1	1	2	3	0.351187
3. Amount of credit exposure	0.5	0.5	1	2	0.188687
4. Financial risks	1/3	1/3	0,5	1	0.108939

Table 5.18 Financial indices of the second level

	Firms	Financial indices
2 level	1	0.8621
	2	0.8984
	3	0.8934

Determination of Financial Indices at the First and the Second Levels

With allowances made for the data presented in Table 5.5 and following the functional diagram presented in Fig. 5.7, we have received normalized specific financial indices of the firm competitiveness of the first level, presented in Table 5.16.

With application of the Analytic Hierarchy Process, the vector of priorities for specific financial indices of the firm competitiveness of the first level, presented in Table 5.17, has been determined.

With allowances made for the formula (5.67) by multiplication of the transposed matrix of Table 5.17 and the vector, we receive specific financial indices of the firm competitiveness of the second level, presented in Table 5.18.

From the analysis of Table 5.18 follows that the first firm has the worst financial indices.

Table 5.19 Normalized specific indices of the firm competitiveness management of the first level

Management	Firms		
	1	2	3
Automation of the management process	1	0.8	0.9

Table 5.20 The firm management indices of the second level of competitiveness

	Firms	Management indices
2 level	1	1
	2	0.8
	3	0.9

Table 5.21 Generalized indices of the firm competitiveness of the second level

Scientific and technical	Production	Innovation	Finance	Firm	Management
0.8999	0.7796	0.9890	0.8621	1	1
0.9399	0.8719	0.8622	0.8984	0.8	2
0.9211	1	0.7025	0.8934	0.9	3

Determination of the Management Indices at the First and the Second Levels With allowances made for the data presented in Table 5.5 and following the functional diagram presented in Fig. 5.7, we received normalized specific management indices of the firm competitiveness of the first level, presented in Table 5.19.

As the said index is the only one in Table 5.19, it defines the firm management index at the second level, presented in Table 5.20.

From analysis of Table 5.20 follows that the second firm has the worst administrative indices.

Stage 4. Determination of the Firm Integrated Index (the Third Level) Calculation results concerning specific indices of the second level presented in Table 5.4 should be reduced to a single Table 5.21.

With application of the Analytic Hierarchy Process, the vector of weightiness for specific financial indices of the firm competitiveness of the first level presented in Table 5.22 has been defined.

With allowances made for the formula (5.67), by multiplication of the matrix of Table 5.22 and the vector of priorities, we receive integrated indices of the firm competitiveness, presented in Table 5.23.

As follows from Table 5.23, the least competitive is the third firm. It should strengthen its innovative component to enhance competitiveness.

Conclusions This chapter shows that competitiveness of a firm is one of the basic indicators of its activity to determine its competitive position in the market. Competitiveness of a firm depends on various external and internal factors. External factors are caused by development tendencies of the markets where the firm acts

Table 5.22 Matrix of binary comparisons by the Analytic Hierarchy Process and the vector of priorities for specific indices of the firm competitiveness of the second level

Indices	1	2	3	4	5	β_1
1. Scientific and technical	1	1	1	2	3	0.260125
2. Production	1	1	1	2	3	0.260125
3. Innovation	1	1	1	2	3	0.260125
4. Finance	0.5	0.5	0.5	1	2	0.137765
5. Firm	1/3	1/3	1/3	0.5	1	0.08186

Table 5.23 Integrated indices of the firm competitiveness

Firms	Integrated indices
1	0.895
2	0.885
3	0.879

and purchases raw materials and accessories, as well as scientific and technical, economic and political trends. The specified factors create conditions for the firm development and have direct and indirect effect on its internal factors (availability of the human capital, financial capital, status of fixed capital, etc.) which the firm can control by means of its organizational management toolkit.

Versatility of conditions of the firm development provides for necessity of calculation of competitiveness integrated index on the basis of mathematical modeling that will make it possible to consider influence of the said factors on the firm development. Taking into account the fact that one of the basic internal factors determining competitiveness of a firm is its production technological level, there is provided to make its assessment. On the basis of assessment of the technological level of production, the firm can make a decision concerning measures either to maintain or increase production on the basis of modernization and optimization of the firm management processes by introduction of modern innovative technologies. There upon, provision of high technological level of production and hence competitiveness should be carried out with the help of innovative activity, fast alternation of generations of products, and at the expense of flexibility and production modernization.

Calculation of integrated index of the firm competitiveness is offered to be carried out with application of appropriate methodology based on economic-mathematical model which on the one hand takes into account the influence of factors on the firm development and on the other hand takes into account potential possibilities and results of economic activities, etc. The offered model of assessment of the firm competitiveness takes into account the optimality of the firm competitiveness indices and current interrelation of the firm competitiveness specific indices. By means of such model, it is possible to determine an integrated index of the firm competitiveness, to construct the dynamics forecast of the firm competitiveness with allowances made for influence exercised by various factors. Such forecast will permit the firm executive to receive timely information on changes in level of the firm competitiveness in the short-run and on a mid-term horizon; as a result the CEO will be able make a decision in due time concerning competitiveness managements and enhancement of the products competitive advantages. For example, this chapter verifies competitiveness assessment model, making it possible to put the firms in order of competitiveness level.

Theoretical Approaches to Assessment of Productive Industry Competitiveness 6

6.1 Theoretical Approaches to Assessment of Productive Industry Competitiveness

Purposeful transformation of competitiveness development of productive industries considered as a complex system of economic entities and the objects they create (products, goods, and services) requires effective methods to control competitive advantages and, as a consequence, enhance their competitiveness.

Enhancement of competitiveness of any productive industry, as well as any other object—evolutionary process, defined by not only a possibility of acceptance of effective management decisions on the basis of previous experience but also a necessity of creating specific models and mechanisms of mobilization of scientific and technical, industrial and technological, financial and economic, and social and organizational potential of productive industry.

As a consequence, enhancement of the industry competitiveness requires working out and substantiation of effective tools, methods of the industry competitiveness management, and providing optimum management decisions on the basis of quantitative assessment of indices of productive industry competitiveness in real time.

There are several definitions of concepts of productive industry competitiveness in the economic theory. Each of these definitions reflects one or another side of this economic category or an attempt of its complex characteristic.

From our point of view, the concept of "productive industry competitiveness" is the most representative in the following definition:

Competitiveness of productive industry is a complex comparative characteristic reflecting level of advantages of a set of estimation figures of productive industry functioning which determine its success within particular framework for a particular time interval with respect to a set of indices of competitive industries in this context.

It should be noted that competitiveness of national economy is formed on the basis of competitive power of production, firms, and productive industries in the

A. Chursin, Y. Makarov, *Management of Competitiveness*,
DOI 10.1007/978-3-319-16244-7_6

international markets. The economy of the high-technology industries has a global character; accordingly, competitiveness of national economy consists of competitiveness of productive industries.

Competitiveness of a firm is shown in two aspects. On the one hand, it is a characteristic of the firm itself, and it is determined by assignment level of its innovative, scientific and technical, industrial, personnel potential, and potential of marketing services. On the other hand, competitiveness of a firm depends on external social & economic and organizational factors making it possible for the firm to create production which is more attractive to consumers according to its price and non-price characteristics as compared with competitors. Hence, res ipsa loquitur, the firm competitiveness is a wider category as compared with competitive power.

In the course of working out of technique for evaluation of productive industry competitiveness, it is worthwhile to take into consideration availability of competitive advantages of the firms. In this connection, we put forward the following assumptions:

- Competitive industry is a relative category, that is, the way particular values of indices are harmonized with the similar indices of competitors is more important than the values of the said indices.
- Competitiveness of productive industry is interrelated with both competitiveness of separate firms and competitiveness of national economy as a whole.
- Competitive industry has a developed structure and includes a group of highly competitive firms; it possesses developed design and experimental and industrial and technological basis and applies flexible system of innovative, scientific and technical, industrial, material, and commercial cooperation both within the industry and with other industries in the country and abroad.

On the assumption of these hypotheses, we receive definition of productive industry competitiveness on which basis this monograph presents evaluation method and builds the mathematical model.

Competitiveness of productive industry is a category of national economy, which:

- Is determined by indices of productive industry performance effectiveness in the national market and in the international markets;
- Represents a set of internal and external characteristics of the industry and its firms which make it possible for the productive industry to act in the markets effectively in comparison with competitors and to receive a possibility for further development of productive industry.

This definition of competitive power takes into consideration competitiveness of the firms within this productive industry, possibilities of competitors, and availability of potential for further development of productive industry.

Table 6.1 Hierarchy of concepts of competitiveness of the market entities

Level of hierarchy	Concept of competitiveness
Competitiveness of productive industry	Ability of productive industry to make the goods and services, which meet requirements of the national and international markets, and to create conditions of growth of innovative potential of the firms within the productive industry
Competitiveness of a firm	Ability of a firm to make competitive production and to create conditions of growth of competitiveness potential on the basis of innovative factors of development
Competitiveness of production	Ability of production to meet requirements of this market in comparison with the analogue competitor

In the course of building the model of evaluation and competitiveness management of productive industry, we proceed from the premise that hierarchy of concepts of competitiveness of the market entities is determined according to Table 6.1.

The model of competitiveness management of the high-technology industries has its own hierarchical structure and includes three levels, shown in Fig. 6.1:

- Competitiveness management of the high-technology industries;
- Competitiveness management of the enterprises within the high-technology industries;
- Product competitiveness management within high-technology industries.

Within the framework of above assumptions for formalization of the competitiveness model of the high-technology industries, it is possible to introduce the following system of designations:

Set P of types of production $(P = |P|)$;

Set E of firms, organizations, enterprises $(E = |E|)$;

Set P_e of types of products of enterprise e, meeting conditions

$$\left(P_e \subseteq P;\ P_{ei} \cap P_{ej} \neq \varnothing;\ P_e = |P_e|,\ e \in E\right);$$

Set of I indices of development of productive industry $I = |I|$;

Set I_p of production indices of type p, meeting conditions

$$\left(I_p \subseteq I; I_{pi} \cap P_{pj} \neq \varnothing;\ I_p = |I_p|, p \in P\right)$$

Set I_e or the indices of enterprise e, meeting condition $(I_e \subseteq I),\ e \in E$.

Integrated index ICI of the industry competitiveness, meeting a condition $(0 \leq ICI \leq 1)$;

Set M of production markets of the industry $(M = |M|)$;

Vector α of the market industry strategy

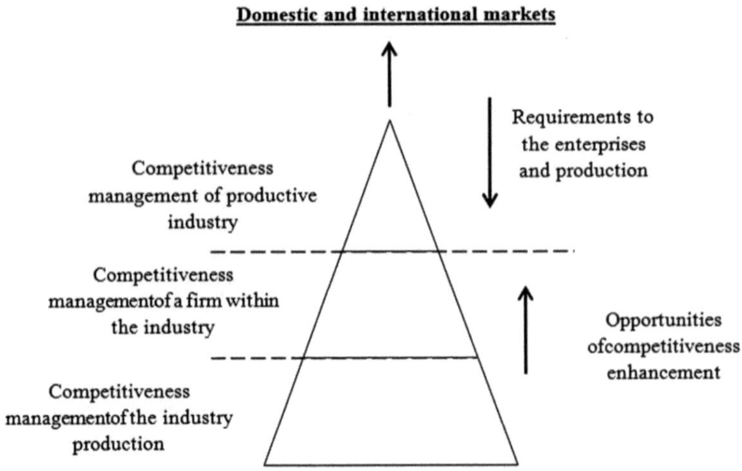

Fig. 6.1 Pyramid of competitiveness management of productive industry

$$\left(\alpha(\alpha_m)_{m\in M}, 0 \le \alpha_m \le 1, \sum_{m\in M} \alpha_m = 1\right);$$

Matrix B of the enterprise of strategies within productive industry

$$\left(B\left(\beta_e^m\right)_{e\in E}^{m\in M}, 0 \le \beta_e^m \le 1, \sum_{e\in E} \beta_e^m = 1\right);$$

Strategy β_e of the enterprise within productive industry, $\beta_e = \left(\beta_e^m\right)_{m\in M}$;
Competitiveness index of e-enterprises in the market M_m;
Competitiveness index of p-production in the market M_m.

Taking into consideration the introduced designations, index ICI of productive industry competitiveness is determined by the weighted values of competitiveness indices of the enterprise in productive industry with respect to the market strategy of productive industry:

$$ICI = \sum_{m\in M} \alpha_m \sum_{e\in E} \beta_e^m ICE_e^m.$$

It should be noted that the above indices are of nondimensional character. Use of nondimensional values is natural in the course of building estimation models as it is instrumental in quantitative assessment of these values on the unified scales. Particular economic meaning of these values will be provided in the technique described in Sect. 6.3.

The generalized model of productive industry competitiveness is represented in the form of a matrix shown in Fig. 6.2.

E \ M	M_1	…	M_m	…	M_M	
e_1						β_{e_1}
⋮						
e_i			$ICE_{e_i}^m$			β_{e_i}
⋮						
e_E						β_{e_E}
	α_1		α_m		α_M	

Fig. 6.2 Matrix model of productive industry competitiveness

Now we give the formalized description of the management process of the enterprise and industry competitiveness.

In what follows, it is assumed that (see TOC method described in Sect. 6.3) there are a number of methods of evaluation and/or calculation of the firm competitiveness indices $\{ICE\} = \{ICE_e\}_{e \in E}$ and production $\left\{ICP_p\right\}_{p \in P}$.

Hence, it is possible to take into consideration that there are methods to calculate functional

$$ICE_e^m = F(ICE^m, |_e), \quad m \in M, \quad e \in E, \tag{6.1}$$

and vector α

$$m \in M \tag{6.2}$$

Direct problem of evaluation of productive industry competitiveness consists in the fact that under the known values of the enterprise competitiveness indices $\{ICE\} = \{ICE_e\}_{e \in E}$, we should find such strategy (α, B) of productive industry in the markets, when its competitiveness index takes on the maximum value:

$$\max_{\{ICE\}} ICI = \sum_{m \in M} \alpha_m \sum_{e \in E} \beta_e^m ICE_e^m \partial, \tag{6.3}$$

$$\sum_{m \in M} \alpha_m = 1, \quad \sum_{e \in E} \beta_e^m = 1, \quad m \in M. \tag{6.4}$$

The inverse problem of evaluation of productive industry competitiveness consists in the fact that for the set strategy of productive industry (α, B), we should find such values of competitiveness indices of the enterprise and production when the index of industry competitiveness takes on the maximum value:

$$\max_{(\alpha,B)} ICI = \sum_{m \in M} \alpha_m \sum_{e \in E} \beta_e^m ICE_e^m, \tag{6.5}$$

$$ICE_e^m = F\left(ICP^m, |_e\right), \quad m \in M, \quad e \in E. \tag{6.6}$$

Competitiveness management of the high-technology industries is suggested to be carried out on assumption of the concept of the balanced strategy of productive industry competitiveness which consists in the following.

Let us assume that $\{ICE\}$ is solution of the inverse problem, and $\{ICE\}*$ is index of the enterprise competitiveness, corresponding to the optimum strategy $(\alpha, B)*$ found in the solution of direct problem. Strategy $(\alpha, B)*$ is in balance (according to the current indices $\{ICE\}*$ of the enterprise competitiveness) if small value ε is set in advance, which determines acceptable level of difference between solution of direct and inverse problems. Fulfillment of this condition means that as a result of efficient management, there is a balance (conformity) between competitiveness opportunities of the enterprise and production and requirements to the industry by competitors in the national and international markets.

6.2 Approaches to Quantitative Assessment of Competitiveness of the High-Technology Industry

In order to reach the primary goal of competitiveness management of the high-technology industries, it is necessary to have mathematical models that make it possible to compute quantitative indices of competitiveness of the high-technology industry. The specified methods and models, on the one hand, should be based upon a modern mathematical apparatus, and on the other hand, they should be rather simple for application in practical calculations.

Calculation of quantitative indices of competitiveness of the high-technology industry can be made in the following sequence:

Calculation of the product competitiveness

$\Downarrow$

Calculation of the enterprise competitiveness

$\Downarrow$

Calculation of productive industry competitiveness

Such sequence of calculations makes it possible to consider to the fullest extent possible the information on the status of the high-technology industry in assessment of competitiveness according to the approach described in Sect. 6.1.

By virtue of the fact that many enterprises are integrated and go hand in hand in the high-technology industries, in order to analyze competitiveness of the high-technology industries, we shall use analysis of hierarchical arrangements based on the theory of loaded graphs. Such an approach makes it possible to compute integrated quantitative indices of competitiveness of the high-technology industry.

On the other hand, indices of competitiveness of the high-technology industry should reflect statistic data on the industry status in the past and objective data about its current condition. It will make it possible to take into consideration the integrated quantitative index of competitiveness of the high-technology industry and its nonprejudicial economic condition for the time being and in the future.

As the basic method for calculation of quantitative indices, we will use economic and mathematical method Time—Object—Compare (TOC), presented by the authors in this monograph. This approach makes it possible to compute indices of competitiveness of the high-technology industry on the basis of analysis of the last condition of the industries (statistics), a current condition (objective indices), and the future condition (estimated figures).

Let us prove this approach.

It is obvious that potential of the high-technology industry cannot be evaluated without investigation of its last condition. It follows from the fact that scientific and technical potential includes design and engineering experience, qualification (often unique) HR, and specialized industrial and scientific organizations and enterprises.

The current condition of the high-technology industry and, accordingly, indices of the current condition take the central place in the calculation of integrated indices of its competitiveness. As these indices have objective character, they can be used as the primary figures.

Quantitative indices of competitiveness, as a rule, are used thereafter in managerial decision-making aimed at development of productive industry in the future. In this context of special value are the indices of competitiveness reflecting projected characteristics. Owing to high research intensity, many projects concerning development of hi-tech industry, especially innovative, have a long-term character. Therefore, in evaluation of competitiveness of the high-technology industry, it is necessary to use without fail the industry indices which reflect projected characteristics of its development.

Besides evaluating competitiveness quantitative indices relating to the past, present, and future condition of this high-technology industry, it is necessary to use comparative approach for analysis of production, enterprises, and productive industry as a whole.

For correct comparison of multifactor and multi-criteria conditions of objects (production, enterprises, and productive industries), it is necessary to use adequate mathematical methods.

The mathematical model, developed by the authors, uses methods of comparison based on special comparation functionals which are applied to various indices of competitiveness; and integrated quantitative indices of competitiveness are calculated on the basis of their values.

Special functionals of competitiveness comparation represent nonlinear comparative function. Use of nonlinear comparison is justified by the fact that it is possible to specify three areas while comparing characteristics of the objects.

The first area of comparison is used when normalized values of the indices are close. In this case, functional comparison will give close values too. In what follows, it is necessary to take into consideration the area when the indices values are different, but they are at the same level of competitiveness. In this case, functionals of competitiveness comparisons show the greatest values, as there is a superiority of one object over another. Finally, by comparison of objects, there may be the third area when comparable characteristics of the objects differ very much. There is a situation in this case when comparable objects are at different levels; therefore, the functional of competitiveness comparison will show small value.

In building aggregated quantitative economic and mathematical models, there is an important problem of nonequilibrium aggregation of parameters. The problem is that it is necessary to express a set of various numeric parameters by one number. Hence it is necessary to take into consideration that these parameters can have various nature and have various units of measure and can be expressed on various scales too.

Let us describe in short a method which we use for calculations on nonequilibrium scales.

For solution of this problem, we use nonequilibrium aggregation of parameters by means of the scalar product generated by positively determined matrix.

Let us assume that it is necessary to aggregate a vector of numeric parameters into a single numeric parameter:

$$x = \begin{pmatrix} x_1 \\ x_2 \\ \vdots \\ x_N \end{pmatrix},$$

With this end in view, we consider square matrix A of dimensionality $N \times N$. Let us assume that this matrix is symmetric. We will often assume that matrix A is nonnegative. The matrix is called nonnegative if this matrix is symmetric and for every vector $x \in R^N$ inequality

$$(Ax, x) \geq 0$$

is executed

(Here scalar product in space R^N is designated through $(\cdot, \cdot)$).

Usually, as matrix A, they select a diagonal matrix consisting of nonnegative numbers on the main diagonal.

The aggregated index $[x]$ of vector x will be calculated as scalar product by the following formula:

$$[x] = (Ax, \mathrm{I}_N)_{R_N}$$

where through I_N, we designate N-dimensional vector consisting of unity elements.

In what follows, in order to compare multifactor and multidimensional objects, we use the following method of introduction of a partial order on the sets of any nature.

Let us consider a set M of any nature. In our mathematical model, as a rule, we use vector Euclidean space as set M.

Let us say, that in this set, there is a partial order, if there is binary relation for a number of pairs of elements of set M:

$a < b, b \in M$ meeting axioms of reflectivity, transitivity, and antisymmetry which are written down as follows:

Reflectivity:

$$a < a, \forall a \in M;$$

Transitivity:

$$a < b, b < c \rightarrow a < c, a, b, c \in M;$$

Antisymmetry:

$$a < b, b < a \rightarrow a = b, a, b \in M.$$

The partial order which can be introduced for all elements of a set M is called the linear order. However, in practice, the partial order cannot always be introduced for all elements of a set M. Therefore, we will use a partial order on multidimensional sets which will be used in the model of quantitative assessment of competitiveness of the high-technology industry and when it is impossible to introduce a linear order.

In Sections 6.3 and 6.4, we will deal with particular algorithms and examples of calculation of quantitative assessments of integrated indices of competitiveness of the high-technology industries according to the above approaches to evaluation of competitive power of production, enterprises, and productive industries.

6.3 Technique for Quantitative Assessment of Competitiveness of the High-Technology Industry

For sustainable development of the high-technology industry, it is necessary to make a periodic evaluation of its competitiveness, and on this basis, in order to make decisions concerning maintenance of productive industry competitiveness or its enhancement in the commodity markets.

By virtue of the fact that the quantitative methods of assessment of competitiveness of the high-technology industry become increasingly important in recent times, the following technique is offered for solution of this problem.

As shown above, assessment of productive industry competitiveness is composed of characteristics of hi-tech industry, analysis of competitiveness of the enterprises in this industry, and production created by the said enterprises.

Analysis of competitiveness of various entities should be made by means of the single method making it possible to receive numeric characteristics of competitiveness for separate entities. Accordingly, in the analysis of competitiveness of complicated objects possessing particular hierarchy such as the enterprises and productive industries, there will be applied methods of analysis of hierarchical arrangements. These methods make it possible to construct an integrated quantitative assessment of competitiveness of complicated objects.

The principle of TOC method of competitiveness comparative analysis consists in the fact that the object under analyses is considered from two sides:

1. Analysis in time.
2. Analysis relative to competitive objects.

Each of these analyses, in turn, is carried out according to two coefficients.

The analysis in time is subdivided into two directions:

1. Analysis of statistic characteristics (“analysis relative to the past”).
2. Analysis of estimated characteristics (“analysis relative to the future”).

The analysis relative to competitive objects is subdivided into two directions too:

1. Analysis of objective characteristics (“internal analysis”).
2. Analysis of comparative characteristics (“external analysis”).

Hence, TOC method makes it possible to receive a four-dimensional vector of quantitative indices of competitiveness and on this basis to calculate an integrated weighed competitiveness index of the object.

The purpose of this technique of quantitative assessment of competitiveness of the high-technology industry is to receive nonprejudicial information making it possible to identify tendencies of development and to plan further actions for development of the high-technology industry. Indices used here should be calculated on the basis of objective computed data including a high-grade description of the high-technology industry status.

Competitiveness evaluation of a particular industry is calculated on the basis of competitiveness evaluations of the products and enterprises of this industry.

This Section specifies in detail the TOC method of quantitative assessment of competitiveness on the basis of analysis of hierarchical arrangements which makes it possible to evaluate competitiveness of separate objects and to receive an integrated assessment of productive industry competitiveness as a whole.

Calculations of quantitative assessment of productive industry competitiveness according to the TOC method will result in the four-dimensional vector of quantitative indices of competitiveness:

$$TOC = \begin{pmatrix} T_P \\ T_F \\ O \\ C \end{pmatrix},$$

where

T_P—quantitative index of statistic characteristics;
T_F—quantitative index estimated characteristics;
O—quantitative index of objective characteristics;
C—quantitative index of comparative characteristics.

For effective implementation of the TOC method, it is necessary to have a corresponding databank. Accuracy of competitiveness indices calculated according to the TOC method depends on the amount and quality of initial data.

Let us describe the initial data required for calculations according to the TOC method.

It is necessary to set the information according to four groups for every input parameter:

1. Statistic group of indices.
2. Objective group of indices.
3. Estimated group of indices.
4. Comparative group of indices.

Statistic characteristics of the object are described by the following initial data:

Vector of statistic characteristics:

$$x = \begin{pmatrix} x_1 \\ x_2 \\ \vdots \\ x_N \end{pmatrix}; \tag{6.7}$$

Vector of average values of statistic characteristics:

$$\overline{x} = \begin{pmatrix} \overline{x}_1 \\ \overline{x}_2 \\ \vdots \\ \overline{x}_N \end{pmatrix}; \tag{6.8}$$

Vector of normalized time values:

$$\tau = \begin{pmatrix} \tau_1 \\ \tau_2 \\ \vdots \\ \tau_N \end{pmatrix}; \tag{6.9}$$

and nonequilibrium matrix:

$$A = \begin{pmatrix} a_{11} & \cdots & a_{1N} \\ \vdots & \ddots & \vdots \\ a_{N1} & \cdots & a_{NN} \end{pmatrix}. \tag{6.10}$$

Estimated figures of the object characteristics are described by the following initial data:

Vector of indices of the matter under inquiry for which estimated figures are known:

$$y = \begin{pmatrix} y_1 \\ y_2 \\ \vdots \\ y_N \end{pmatrix} \tag{6.11}$$

Vector of average values estimated characteristics

$$\overline{y} = \begin{pmatrix} \overline{y}_1 \\ \overline{y}_2 \\ \vdots \\ \overline{y}_N \end{pmatrix} \tag{6.12}$$

Vector of normalized time values:

$$\tau = \begin{pmatrix} \tau_1 \\ \tau_2 \\ \vdots \\ \tau_N \end{pmatrix} \tag{6.13}$$

Probability vector (estimated data credibility):

$$p = \begin{pmatrix} p_1 \\ p_2 \\ \vdots \\ p_N \end{pmatrix}. \tag{6.14}$$

and nonequilibrium matrix:

$$A = \begin{pmatrix} a_{11} & \cdots & a_{1N} \\ \vdots & \ddots & \vdots \\ a_{N1} & \cdots & a_{NN} \end{pmatrix} \tag{6.15}$$

Objective characteristics are described by the following initial data:
Vector of objective indices:

$$z = \begin{pmatrix} z_1 \\ z_2 \\ \vdots \\ z_N \end{pmatrix}. \tag{6.16}$$

and nonequilibrium matrix

$$A = \begin{pmatrix} a_{11} & \cdots & a_{1N} \\ \vdots & \ddots & \vdots \\ a_{N1} & \cdots & a_{NN} \end{pmatrix}. \tag{6.17}$$

Comparative characteristics are described by the following initial data:
Vector of objective indices of competitive objects

$$q = \begin{pmatrix} q_1 \\ q_2 \\ \vdots \\ q_N \end{pmatrix}, \tag{6.18}$$

Vector of characteristics of the j-th competitive object

$$q^j = \begin{pmatrix} q_1^j \\ q_2^j \\ \vdots \\ q_N^j \end{pmatrix} \tag{6.19}$$

Nonequilibrium matrix:

$$A = \begin{pmatrix} a_{11} & \cdots & a_{1N} \\ \vdots & \ddots & \vdots \\ a_{N1} & \cdots & a_{NN} \end{pmatrix} \tag{6.20}$$

and the function of competitive comparison determined on a set of real number R

$$\varphi : R \rightarrow R_+, \quad R_+ = \{x \in R : x \geq 0\}. \tag{6.21}$$

where R_+ a set of nonnegative real numbers.

For construction of integrated quantitative assessment of competitiveness of productive industry, it is necessary to describe its hierarchical structure in the formalized form. For this purpose, it is necessary to set the following loaded graph:

1. Tree-type graph.
2. Selected.
3. TOC indices for every headmost.
4. Vector of connection multipliers for each edge.
5. Every edge incident matrix.

The selected headmost will always have number 1.

TOC indices will be computed in the form of $4 \times N$ dimension matrix:

$$TOC^A = \begin{pmatrix} TOC_1 \\ TOC_2 \\ \vdots \\ TOC_N \end{pmatrix}.$$

For each j-th edge of the graph, we set a vector of connection multipliers:

$$p^j = \begin{pmatrix} p_1^j \\ p_2^j \\ p_3^j \\ p_4^j \end{pmatrix}.$$

The specified below methodical approaches to calculation of quantitative assessment of competitiveness and analysis of competitiveness of productive industries with the hierarchical structure we used earlier introduced designations of indices and initial data, describing statistic and objective values, estimated figures and comparative characteristics of the object, and formalized description of productive industry in the form of the focused loaded graph.

6.3.1 Computation Algorithm and Technique for Quantitative Assessment of the Industry Competitiveness According to the TOC Method

Specified below is the formalized description of the basic procedures of the TOC method of comparative analysis of competitiveness with reference to calculation of quantitative assessments of productive industry competitiveness, including analysis procedures of statistic, estimated, objective, and comparative characteristics.

6.3.1.1 Analysis of Statistic Characteristics

On the basis of initial data on the selected indices with known values, their average values and corresponding normalized time values (vectors of type 6.7, 6.8, 6.9), and nonequilibrium matrices (type 6.10) generated as a result of significance analysis of parameters contribution in competitiveness, we compute competitiveness index according to statistic characteristics by formula:

$$T_p = (A\chi(x - \overline{x}), e),$$

where function χ is determined as follows:

$$\chi(x) = \begin{pmatrix} \dfrac{x_1}{1+\tau_1} \\ \dfrac{x_2}{1+\tau_2} \\ \vdots \\ \dfrac{x_N}{1+\tau_N} \end{pmatrix}$$

The economic meaning of function χconsists in the fact that the characteristics which belong to rather along-term period of time have smaller contribution to the general index of competitiveness.

6.3.1.2 Analysis of Estimated Characteristics

Similarly, on the basis of initial data according to the selected indices with known estimated figures, their average values and corresponding normalized time values (vectors of type 6.11, 6.12, 6.13, 6.14), and nonequilibrium matrix (type 6.15) generated on the basis of significance analysis of parameters contribution in competitiveness, we compute competitiveness index of estimated characteristics by formula:

$$T_F = (A\chi(y - \overline{y}), p), \tag{6.22}$$

where function χ is determined as follows:

$$\chi(x) = \begin{pmatrix} \frac{x_1}{1+\tau_1} \\ \frac{x_2}{1+\tau_2} \\ \vdots \\ \frac{x_N}{1+\tau_N} \end{pmatrix}. \tag{6.23}$$

The meaning of function χ consists in the fact that the characteristics which belong to rather along-term predicted period of time have smaller contribution to the general index of competitiveness.

6.3.1.3 Analysis of Objective Characteristics

The objective characteristics of the object under investigation are the basic contribution to competitiveness.

On the basis of initial data on the selected objective indices (vector type 6.16) and nonequilibrium matrices (type 6.15) generated on the basis of significance analysis of parameters contribution in competitiveness, we compute competitiveness index of estimated characteristics by formula:

$$O = (Az, e) \tag{6.24}$$

where z—vector of objective characteristics

6.3.1.4 Analysis of Comparative Characteristics

Analysis of comparative characteristics of investigated and competitive objects is the most complicated in the TOC method; therefore, we will consider this question in detail.

Let us assume that objective indices of the object under investigation (type 6.18) are selected, that is, the vector is known:

$$q = \begin{pmatrix} q_1 \\ q_2 \\ \vdots \\ q_N \end{pmatrix}.$$

On the basis of the significance analysis of the contribution of these indices in competitiveness, nonequilibrium matrix is formed:

$$A = \begin{pmatrix} a_{11} & \cdots & a_{1N} \\ \vdots & \ddots & \vdots \\ a_{N1} & \cdots & a_{NN} \end{pmatrix}.$$

Let us compare object being analyzed with M competitive objects which we designate:

$C_1, C_2, \ldots, C_M$—a set of competitive objects.

Let us assume that for each competitive entity, there are objective indices similar to corresponding components of vector q.

Let's designate vector q^j particular characteristics of the j-th competitive object:

$$q^j = \begin{pmatrix} q_1^j \\ q_2^j \\ \vdots \\ q_N^j \end{pmatrix}.$$

The comparative analysis is made by consecutive (paired) comparison of indices of object under analyses with corresponding indices of competitive objects. For fulfillment of paired comparison of separate characteristics, we use special functions of competitive comparison:

$$\varphi : R \to R_+, \quad R_+ = \lfloor x \in R : x \geq 0 \rbrace,$$

possessing the following properties:

$$\varphi(0) = 0;$$

$$\lim_{x \to \infty} \varphi(x) = 0;$$

there is one point where $x_m > 0$, so that:

$$\begin{array}{ll} \frac{d\varphi}{dx}(x) > 0, & 0 \leq x < x_m; \\ \frac{d\varphi}{dx}(x_m) = 0; & ; \\ \frac{d\varphi}{dx}(x) < 0, & x > x_m. \end{array}$$

$$\varphi(-x) = -\varphi(x).$$

The first condition means that if two objects have identical values of any characteristic, from this follows that the object under analyses has no competitive advantages, and simultaneously, the competitive object has no competitive advantages over the object under analyses.

The second condition means that the competitive object in this parameter is far away from the object under analyses; hence, comparison is incorrect and should be practically excluded from calculation of competitiveness index.

The fourth condition means symmetry of comparison of two competitive objects.

The third condition means that during comparison of parameters of competitive objects, there are three cases:

1. Parameters of competitive objects are very close; in this case, the value of competitive comparison function is not enough—both objects in this parameter equipoise each other;
2. Parameters of competitive objects differ but still are comparable; in this case, function of competitive comparison has the greatest value. It means that in this parameter, one of the objects has considerable competitive advantage;
3. Parameters of competitive objects considerably differ, and it is important to underline, in this case, value of competitive comparison function is not enough—the objects are practically noncomparable in this parameter.

The index of competitiveness relative to comparative characteristics is calculated from the formula:

$$C = \frac{1}{M}\sum_{m=1}^{M} (A\varphi(q - q^m), e) \tag{6.25}$$

6.3.2 Method of Analysis of Competitiveness of Hierarchical Arrangements

With a view of quantitative assessment of competitiveness at various levels (for example, at the level of enterprise or industry) for formalized description of the objects with hierarchical structure, we will use the theory of graphs.

Let us consider the loaded graphs which describe hierarchy in considered structures and relations between its components.

For hierarchical arrangements, as a rule, it makes meaning to take into consideration the graphs which are trees, that is, graphs in which do not have cycles.

Also we will consider graphs with the chief vertex.

Let us calculate competitiveness of hierarchical structure relative to the chief vertex.

The enterprise which is producing a set of production can be an example of hierarchical structure. Then the chief vertex is the enterprise, and the subordinated vertex describes output.

Another example of hierarchical structure which can be described by means of loaded graphs is the industry consisting of various enterprises which in turn produce various types of items. It is possible to consider an industry including many enterprises, which have hierarchical connection among themselves.

The loaded graphs make it possible to compare a particular number or a vector to each edge. We will also consider the functions set by both on the edges and graph vertexes. Hence, we will attribute values (scalar or vector) to the edges and graph vertexes.

Formal presentation of the graph consists in the following:

1. Sets of vertexes V.
2. A set of edges G.

3. Function set at the vertexes.
4. Function set on the edges.

Let us designate a set of vertexes through $K_i = \frac{S_{i0}}{S_i}$; hence a set of edges represents a set of pair vertexes :

$$G \in V \times V$$

Often for modeling of graphs, vertexes should be described with the help of, so-called, matrices of incidence. If number of vertexes is equal to N, then the matrix of incidence represents a square matrix of dimension $N \times N$ where element:

$a_{ij} = 1$, if there is an edge connecting i-th vertex with j-th top;

$a_{ij} = 0$, if there is no edge connecting i-th vertex with j-th top.

Let us attribute to each vertex a four-dimensional vector describing competitiveness according to the TOC method.

Accordingly, the four-dimensional vector of multipliers for connection of the hierarchical structure elements is attributed to each edge:

$$p^j = \begin{pmatrix} p_1^j \\ p_2^j \\ p_3^j \\ p_4^j \end{pmatrix}.$$

Components of the vector of multipliers for connection of hierarchical structure elements correspond to the vector elements describing competitiveness according to the TOC method.

6.3.2.1 Method of Inverse Calculation of Competitiveness in the Hierarchical Structure

Let us assume that the loaded graph which represents the hierarchical structure is set. We will also believe that this graph is a tree with the chief vertex for calculation. We will describe recursive procedure of competitiveness calculation for the hierarchical structure.

6.3.2.2 Algorithm of Calculation of Competitiveness of Hierarchical Structure

Step 1. If the tree consists of one chief vertex, procedure is finished, and competitiveness coincides with the value of TOC vector of this vertex. If the graph contains leaves, we pass to step 2.

Step 2. We designate through V_i—a set of vertexes of the graph, each of which has leaves. For every vertex through V_{ij}, we designate a set of leaves incidental to vertex V_i. For TOC vector of vertex V_i, we make transformation under the following formula:

$$V_i^{TOC} := V_i^{TOC} + \sum_{V_{ij}} (pI) V_{ij}^{TOC}$$

Step 3. We delete all leaves and corresponding edges in the graph.

Step 4. We pass to a step 1.

Hence, this technique makes it possible to receive a quantitative assessment of productive industry competitiveness. Hence, this evaluation will meet the principles of diversity and objectivity of competitiveness analysis.

Diversity of quantitative assessment of productive industry competitiveness means that the calculations use the maximum available information about the industry status. This information includes statistics data, current (objective) indices, and estimated figures which make essential impact on competitiveness of productive industry.

6.4 Example of Calculation of the High-Technology Industry Competitiveness

The previous Sections of this Chapter present the general problems of quantitative competitiveness assessment of productive industry, enterprises, and their production.

According to the approach we offer, competitiveness of productive industry is composed of the enterprise competitiveness within this industry and competitive power of the products they manufacture.

This Section presents two computing experiments concerning competitiveness of the high-technology industries which use the following methods:

- TOC method of a multivector assessment of competitiveness of various entities;
- Method of analysis of hierarchical structures competitiveness.

Theoretical basis of these methods is specified in Sects. 6.2 and 6.3; for this reason, this Section will present a practical use of these formulas.

As the specified methods are computationally intensive for assessment of competitiveness of the high-technology industries, enterprises, and production, we use specially developed software here.

For convenience of the reader, we repeat formulas (6.7–6.24) to be used in calculating of quantitative indices of statistic, estimated, objective, and comparative characteristics.

So, the calculations results according to the TOC method of quantitative assessment of productive industry competitiveness should have calculated four-dimensional vector of quantitative indices of competitiveness (see 6.7) which characterizes competitiveness of productive industry on the basis of all available information about the status of productive industry up to the present time, estimated figures about the future of productive industry, and the data concerning comparison with competitors:

$$TOC = \begin{pmatrix} T_P \\ T_F \\ O \\ C \end{pmatrix},$$

where

T_P—quantitative index of statistic characteristics;
T_F—quantitative index of estimated characteristics;
O—quantitative index of objective characteristics;
C—quantitative index of comparative characteristics.

Calculation of quantitative index of statistic characteristics of productive industry is performed from formula (see 6.19):

$$T_p = (A\chi(x - \overline{x}), e),$$

where

x—vector of statistic characteristics,
A—nonequilibrium matrix,
e is N—measured unit vector,

multidimensional function χ is set by the following formula:

$$\chi(x) = \begin{pmatrix} \frac{x_1}{1+\tau_1} \\ \frac{x_2}{1+\tau_2} \\ \vdots \\ \frac{x_N}{1+\tau_N} \end{pmatrix}.$$

Calculation of competitiveness index according to estimated characteristics is performed from formula:

$$T_F = (A\chi(y - \overline{y}), p),$$

where

y—vector of estimated characteristics,
A—nonequilibrium matrix,
p—probability (estimated figures reliance),
χ—multidimensional function set by formula:

$$\chi(x) = \begin{pmatrix} \frac{y_1}{1+\tau_1} \\ \frac{y_2}{1+\tau_2} \\ \vdots \\ \frac{y_N}{1+\tau_N} \end{pmatrix}.$$

Competitiveness index according to objective characteristics is calculated from formula:

$$O = (Az, e),$$

where

Z—vector of objective characteristics,
A—nonequilibrium matrix,
e is N—measured unit vector.

Competitiveness index according to comparative characteristics is calculated from formula:

$$C = \frac{1}{M}\sum_{m=1}^{M}(A\varphi(q - q^m), e),$$

where

φ—function of competitive comparison,
q and q^m—vectors of objective indices of the estimated and m-th competitive objects, accordingly,
A—nonequilibrium matrix,
M—number of competitive objects,
e is M-dimensional unit vector.

Initial Data
As the initial data for index of statistic characteristics of productive industry are:

vector $\boldsymbol{x}$ of the indices for which values are known (see 6.7),
vector $\bar{x}$of average values, (see 6.8),
vector τ of normalized time (see 6.9).

Initial data for calculation of competitiveness index of the industry estimated characteristics are:

vector $\boldsymbol{y}$ of the indices of the entity under inquiry with known estimated values (6.11),

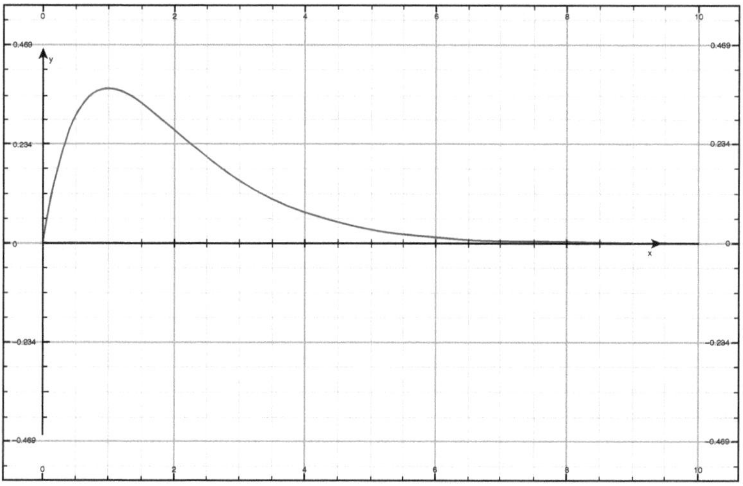

Fig. 6.3 Function graph of competitive comparison of type $y = xe^{-\alpha x}$

vector $\overline{y}$ of average values of estimated indices (see 6.12) and
vector τ of normalized time (see 6.13).

Besides, as a part of initial data, we set probability vector p (6.14) reflecting estimated figures reliance for predicted indices of productive industry competitiveness

$$p = \begin{pmatrix} p_1 \\ p_2 \\ \vdots \\ p_N \end{pmatrix}.$$

And components of a vector of probability satisfy to natural property
$0 < p_i \leq 1, \quad i = 1, 2, \ldots, N.$

Initial data for calculation of competitiveness index of <u>objective characteristics</u> are vector z of objective indices of productive industry.

Initial data for calculation of competitiveness index relative to <u>comparative characteristics</u> are vector $\boldsymbol{q}$ of the corresponding selected objective indices of productive industry (6.25) and nonequilibrium matrix $\boldsymbol{A}$ (6.25).

According to the technique of quantitative assessment of the high-technology industry competitiveness presented in Sect. 6.3, we will perform comparison of the object under analyses with the objects

$C_1, C_2, \ldots, C_M$, within a set of competitive objects, and characteristics of j-th competitive object to be used for comparison are set by vector q^j.

As a modeling example of competitive comparison function (6.3.-17), we use function:

$\varphi(x) = xe^{-\alpha x}, \quad \alpha > 0$, which approximate type is specified in Fig. 6.3.

Calculation of competitiveness of the high-technology industry on a particular example is implemented in compliance with the methods of competitiveness analysis of hierarchical arrangements presented in Sect. 6.3 in which frameworks

Table 6.2 Initial parameters and values for calculation of competitiveness of the high-technology industry

	Productive industry	Enterprise	Production
	RSI	RSI enterprise	Launch vehicle
1	*Statistic characteristics*		
	Index of industrial potential	Index of industrial potential	Launch success rate
	Index of financial performance	Index of financial performance	
2	*Characteristics of estimated figures*		
	Index of scheduled state financing	Index of scheduled state financing	Index of estimated sales
	Index of scheduled contracts with foreign partners	Index of scheduled contracts with foreign partners	
3	*Objective characteristics*		
	Index of products quality	Index of products quality	Performance characteristics index
	Index of the current financial status	Index of the current financial status	Value index of products
4	*Comparative characteristics*		
	Product performance characteristics index	Product performance characteristics index	Product performance characteristics index
	Value index of products	Value index of products	Value index of products

this industry is presented by a set of vertexes V and a set of edges $\boldsymbol{G}$, which represents a set of vertex pairs $G \in V \times V$, as well as the functions set on these vertexes and edges.

Each vertex has a four-dimensional vector describing competitiveness according to the TOC method, and each edge has a four-dimensional vector of multipliers for connection of hierarchical structure elements.

For competitiveness calculation of the industry having a hierarchical structure, a recursive procedure of calculation consisting of 4 formalized steps was used, also described in Sect. 6.3.

Below we consider two computing experiments of demonstration character when, as a high-technology industry, there acts a Space–Rocket Industry (RSI) and initial parameters and values according to scheme "*Industry—Enterprise—Production*" (Table 6.2).

All initial data about parameters and values specified in Table 6.2 represent nondimensional indices for which calculation should be made separately in each particular case.

Table 6.3 presents initial data calculated for nondimensional indices, selected for two computing experiments, differing by number of the enterprises and products selected for competitive comparison; the of calculations are presented in below table.

Table 6.3 Initial data for computing experiments according to the TOC method

	Computing experiment 1: 1 industry, 1 enterprise, 1 product	Computing experiment 2: 1 industry, 2 enterprises, 2 products
Initial data on the industry		
Statistic characteristics		
Dimension of the vector	2	2
Values of the vector component	(0.7 0.3)	(0.7 0.3)
Average values of the vector component	(0.5 0.2)	(0.5 0.2)
Normalized times	(2 1)	(2 1)
Nonequilibrium matrix	$\begin{pmatrix} 1 & 0 \\ 0 & 1 \end{pmatrix}$	$\begin{pmatrix} 1 & 0 \\ 0 & 1 \end{pmatrix}$
Estimated characteristics		
Dimension of the vector	2	2
Values of the vector component	(0.7 0.4)	(0.7 0.4)
Average values of the vector component	(0.5 0.1)	(0.5 0.1)
Normalized times	(2 1)	(2 1)
Reliance vector	(0.7 08)	(0.7 08)
Nonequilibrium matrix		
Objective characteristics		
Dimension of the vector	2	2
Values of the vector component	(0.2 0.3)	(0.2 0.3)
Nonequilibrium matrix		
Comparative characteristics		
Dimension of the vector	2	2
Values of the vector component	(0.5 0.7)	(0.5 0.7)
Nonequilibrium matrix	$\begin{pmatrix} 1 & 0 \\ 0 & 1 \end{pmatrix}$	$\begin{pmatrix} 1 & 0 \\ 0 & 1 \end{pmatrix}$
Number of competitive objects	1	1
Values of competitive comparison function	(0.2 0.4)	(0.2 0.4)
Initial data on the enterprise		
Statistic characteristics		
Dimension of the vector	2	2
Values of the vector component	(0.7 0.6)	(0.7 0.6)
Average values of the vector component	(0.5 0.5)	(0.5 0.5)
Normalized times	(2 1)	(2 1)
Nonequilibrium matrix	$\begin{pmatrix} 1 & 0 \\ 0 & 1 \end{pmatrix}$	$\begin{pmatrix} 1 & 0 \\ 0 & 1 \end{pmatrix}$
Estimated characteristics		
Dimension of the vector	2	2
Values of the vector component	(0.7 0.8)	(0.7 0.8)

(continued)

Table 6.3 (continued)

	Computing experiment 1: 1 industry, 1 enterprise, 1 product	Computing experiment 2: 1 industry, 2 enterprises, 2 products
Average values of the vector component	(0.5 0.5)	(0.5 0.5)
Normalized times	(2 1)	(2 1)
Reliance vector	(0.7 0.8)	(0.7 0.8)
Nonequilibrium matrix	$\begin{pmatrix} 1 & 0 \\ 0 & 1 \end{pmatrix}$	$\begin{pmatrix} 1 & 0 \\ 0 & 1 \end{pmatrix}$
Objective characteristics		
Dimension of the vector	2	2
Values of the vector component	(0.2 0.3)	(0.2 0.3)
Nonequilibrium matrix		
Comparative characteristics		
Dimension of the vector	2	2
Values of the vector component	(0.5 0.7)	(0.5 0.7)
Nonequilibrium matrix	$\begin{pmatrix} 1 & 0 \\ 0 & 1 \end{pmatrix}$	$\begin{pmatrix} 1 & 0 \\ 0 & 1 \end{pmatrix}$
Number of competitive objects	1	2
Values of competitive comparison function	(0.2 0.4)	(0.2 0.4)
		(0.7 1)
Initial data on the product		
Statistic characteristics		
Dimension of the vector	1	1
Values of the vector component	(0.7)	(0.7)
Average values of the vector component	(0.5)	(0.5)
Normalized times	2	2
Nonequilibrium matrix	$\begin{pmatrix} 1 & 0 \\ 0 & 1 \end{pmatrix}$	$\begin{pmatrix} 1 & 0 \\ 0 & 1 \end{pmatrix}$
Estimated characteristics		
Dimension of the vector	1	1
Values of the vector component	(0.7)	(0.7)
Average values of the vector component	(0.5)	(0.5)
Normalized times	2	2
Reliance vector	(0.7)	(0.7)
Nonequilibrium matrix	$\begin{pmatrix} 1 & 0 \\ 0 & 1 \end{pmatrix}$	$\begin{pmatrix} 1 & 0 \\ 0 & 1 \end{pmatrix}$
Objective characteristics		
Dimension of the vector	2	2
Values of the vector component	(0.2 0.3)	(0.2 0.3)
Nonequilibrium matrix	$\begin{pmatrix} 1 & 0 \\ 0 & 1 \end{pmatrix}$	$\begin{pmatrix} 1 & 0 \\ 0 & 1 \end{pmatrix}$

(continued)

Table 6.3 (continued)

	Computing experiment 1: 1 industry, 1 enterprise, 1 product	Computing experiment 2: 1 industry, 2 enterprises, 2 products
Comparative characteristics		
Dimension of the vector	2	2
Values of the vector component	(0.5 0.7)	(0.5 0.7)
Nonequilibrium matrix	$\begin{pmatrix} 1 & 0 \\ 0 & 1 \end{pmatrix}$	$\begin{pmatrix} 1 & 0 \\ 0 & 1 \end{pmatrix}$
Number of competitive objects	1	2
Values of competitive comparison function	(0.2 0.4)	(0.2 0.4)
		(0.6 0.8)

Results of calculations statistic, evaluated, objective, and comparative indices of competitiveness according to the TOC method

	Computing experiment 1		Computing experiment 2	
	RSI	RSI Enterprise	RSI	RSI Enterprise
Statistic index	0.3	0.183	0.3	0.183
Estimated index	0.38	0.213	0.38	0.213
Objective index	1.5	1	1.5	1
Comparative index	1.333	0.889	0.454	0.009

Computing experiment 1 within the framework of one industry and one estimation enterprise includes one competitor firm and one competitive product. Moreover, comparative parameters of the competitor firm and the product were worse than behavior of the enterprise.

Computing experiment 2 has one more competitor firm and one more product with characteristics superior to the behavior of the enterprise and characteristic features of comparable product.

In accordance with the findings of computing experiment 2, one can see that comparative indices of competitiveness of the industry and the enterprise have sharply decreased. It reflects the fact that the market entry of a competitor firm and a competitive product with superior characteristics reduces competitiveness of the entire industry and the enterprises within its structure.

Conclusions This Chapter presents theoretical approaches to assessment of competitiveness of productive industry. It has been established that purposeful transformation of development process of competitiveness of productive industries considered as a complex system of economic entities and their objects (products, goods, and services) requires effective management methods to create competitive advantages and, as a consequence, increase of their competitiveness.

It is established that competitiveness management and assessment can and should be made on micro-, meso-,and macro level, in other words, at the level of organization, productive industry, and the state. We offer an appropriate technique and calculation example according to the said technique for assessment of competitiveness of productive industry. This technique is based upon the TOC method of quantitative assessment of competitiveness in reliance on analysis of hierarchical arrangements, which makes it possible to evaluate competitiveness of separate entities and receive an integrated assessment of competitiveness of productive industry as a whole.

Economic and mathematical TOC method ("Time—Object—Compare") used in this technique makes it possible to compute competitiveness indices of the high-technology productive industry on the basis of analysis of the past condition of productive industry (statistical values), current status (objective indices), and the future condition (estimated figures). Technique application makes it possible to receive the nonprejudicial information to identify tendencies of development and to plan further actions to develop productive industry depending on estimated figures.

The assessments of productive industry competitiveness following the calculations can be the basis for more objective managerial decision-making, working out of the strategy to enhance competitiveness of productive industry, and its implementation program.

7 Formation of the Firm Competitiveness MIS Systems

7.1 Managing Resource Center as an Element of Enhancing the Firm Competitiveness

Efficient management of big concerns, corporations, and companies and their achievement of particular advantages in all the cycle of designing, production, and sale are possible with application of big organizational and economic automated systems. These systems should unite all fields of activity of the integrated structure, including the Managing Resource Centers influencing over efficient competitiveness management of the firm on the basis of creation and conducting common databases with application of modern information technologies.

To generate an object of management means to determine the number and structure of its units and relations between them. It is always possible to distinguish an object and a subject of management in the management system. There is an interconnection and interaction between the object (managed system) and the subject (management system). The correlation consists in the fact that managed and management systems cannot exist independently and function separately as one of them, as a rule, represents a certain technological and production process, and another one—management process and decision-making.

Interaction becomes apparent in the following:

(a) Changes in the object structure cannot be carried out without consent or direct participation of its subject (subjects) in order to avoid conflict situations.
(b) Rearrangement of the object structure or its parameters requires directed influence of the subject of management—according to the available algorithm.
(c) Changes in the structure of management's objects triggered by change of the number of managed objects require adequate response of the entire system as a whole for the purpose of its rational functioning.

A. Chursin, Y. Makarov, *Management of Competitiveness*,
DOI 10.1007/978-3-319-16244-7_7

(d) The changed system should remain flexible and should be alert to the influences in external and internal environments, arising in real time, thus keeping all communications, connections, and information flows between the system and its elements.

Role of the Management Structure in Implementation of Programs and Strategies on Micro-and Macro-levels Management structure is one of the key concepts of management, closely connected with the goals, functions, management process, and distribution of powers between the economic agents being objects of management (i.e., the entities we can control). The whole management process (movement of information flows and managerial decision-making) with participation of managers of all levels takes place within the framework of this structure. The structure can be compared to the building skeleton of the management system, so that all the processes in this system could be carried out in due time and qualitatively without fail, and most importantly—in an effective way.

The firm structure can be determined as a simple set of ways, through which the labor process, at first, is divided into separate operating task, and then comes coordination of actions inorder to challenge the problems. As a matter of fact, organizational structure determines distribution of responsibility and powers within the firm. As a rule, it is displayed in the form of the graphic scheme where its elements are hierarchically ordered organizational units (divisions, official positions).

An organizational structure is built on distribution of powers, responsibilities, and accountabilities. The powers can be subdivided into linear and functional. In the first case, the managers have a formal right to control activities of their subordinates and to supervise them, and in the second case, the manager can give advice, recommendations, and consultations to the linear managers.

In each firm, as far as micro-level is concerned, powers are distributed in different ways. They can be delegated, i.e., when the manager powers are transferred to the employees in the lower positions, including executors. Responsibility is understood as a duty assignment for solution of problems or fulfillment of certain types of activity. The accountability consists in the fact that the authorized managers are obliged to report and discuss fulfillment of operating tasks with senior managers.

The management structure is considered as a necessary form of implementation of the management functions. Key concepts of the management structures are elements, connections (relation), levels, and powers. Elements of the management organizational structure can be both individual workers (heads, experts, or employees) and services or managerial apparatus in the executive offices. There is another definition of elements in the management too. They are levels of management, management links and divisions, and management connections.

A management level is understood as a set of control links on a certain step in the management systems of the firm. Management steps are in vertical dependence and submit to each other in the order of hierarchy: managers of the higher level of management make decisions which are concretized and forwarded to subordinate links. So a pyramidal structure of the firm management appeared.

Management link is an element, unit of management, representing a structural division or separate workers. Management links are structural divisions and separate experts who are carrying out specific functions of management. Management links should also include managers who perform regulation functions and coordinate activities of several structural divisions.

Performance of certain management function by a department is at the heart of the management link. Connections established between departments have horizontal character.

Management connection is shown in the process of management interaction. The point is that one of the subjects of management is interested in certain type of functioning of the second subject and generates management teams to set desirable behavior, and the second subject, owing to certain reasons, behaves according to the management teams of the first one.

Development of designing methods for the structures of management makes it possible to improve management and to raise production efficiency for the following reasons:

- Firstly, in new conditions in a variety of cases, it is impossible to operate with old organizational forms which do not meet requirements of the market relations and create danger of deformation of the very problems of management.
- Secondly, it is impossible to transfer the laws of technical systems management into the economic sphere. Creation of the automated management systems is often considered separate from the improvement of the management structure.
- Thirdly, creation of the structure should be based on scientific methods of organizational design in addition to experience, analogy, and habitual schemes.
- Fourthly, the complicated mechanism of management should be projected by the experts owning methodology of formation of organizational systems.

In working out the principles and techniques of management structures design, it is important to withdraw from representation of the structure as a frozen set of management bodies corresponding to each specialized control function.

Methods of construction of organizational management structures applied until recently possessed certain drawbacks: they had a standard character and used typical solutions and were insufficiently various. It led to mechanical transfer of organizational forms applied in the past to the modern conditions. Initial factors of formation of structures were considered in a very narrow way:

- Number of personnel instead of the firm purposes;
- Permanent set of managements bodies instead of change in their structure and combination in different conditions;
- Out-of-date schemes and manpower structures as the average indices of existing firms without analysis of their negative attributes and suitability grade.

Today in creation of organizational structures, they use a system approach which in practice leads to more effective utilization of all the firm resources—material, financial, and labor. It creates economic advantages for the firm activities, which in modern conditions are the basis for success. Identification and analysis of emergent problems of the firm construction and development are of special value now. The given approach assumes initial definition of the firm's system of purposes which give rise to the task structure and the contents of functions of the managerial apparatus.

It should also be taken into account that the organizational structure is a complex characteristic of the management system relative to implementation of the system's principles of formation of internal structure of personnel management. The uniform system should consider various methods of formation of organizational structures of management, many of which have appeared just recently. These methods have different nature; each of them separately cannot solve all practically important problems of construction of organizational structure of managerial apparatus and should be applied in organic combination with the other methods.

Final criterion of efficiency in comparison of various variants of organizational structure is the fullest and steady achievement of the purposes in the field of production, economy, technical progress, and social development. It is worthwhile to use a set of standard characteristics of managerial apparatus:

- Productivity in the process of information processing;
- Efficiency of managerial decision-making;
- Reliability of managerial apparatus expressed in implementation of decisions within the framework of target dates and resources;
- Adaptability and flexibility characterized by ability of timely identification of organizational problems and corresponding reorganization of work.

The said definitions make it possible to determine organizational effectiveness of management. The approach to assess the efficiency of various options of organizational structure is determined by its role as a characteristic feature of the management system.

The set of effectiveness criteria of the management system is formed with provision for two directions of assessment of its functioning according to:

- level of compliance of available results with the established purposes of industrial and economic firm (from the level of fulfillment of target Figures);
- level of compliance of the process of the system functioning with objective requirements to its contents, organization, and results.

As a criterion of efficiency in comparison of various variants of organizational structure, there is a possibility of the fullest and steady achievement of ultimate goals of the management system with rather smaller cost for its functioning.

As a criterion of efficiency of actions for perfection of organizational structure, there is a possibility of fuller and more stable achievement of the established purposes or reduction of costs for management, and effect from solution of the target problems within the standard term should exceed industrial expenses.

The principal value for assessments of the management effectiveness system is the selection of the basis for comparison or definition of efficiency level to be assumed as the standard.

The indices used in assessments of efficiency of managerial apparatus and its organizational structure can be divided into interconnected groups.

For assessment of the management efficiency, it is important to determine compliance of the management system and its organizational structure with the object of management. It is expressed in equation of the functions structure and the purposes of management, substantial completeness and integrity of the management processes, compliance of the number and structure of workers with the scope and complexity of works, completeness of information required for industrial-technological processes, and provision of the management processes with technological means with due account for consideration of their nomenclature, capacity, and fast response

The modern management system is a man–machine system; in other words, it is an organizational system for which effective functioning requires such essential factors of interaction of people with technical systems as electronic computing complexes, information & analytical and flexible industrial systems, as well as managerial apparatus with the people to serve these systems, collect and process information being the basis for managerial decision-makings.

Management systems of large firms, corporations, and holdings can be constructed as adaptive systems, and in this case, they should have corresponding mechanisms of adaptation to changing conditions. The necessary elements of the management system are subsystems of information processing and subsystems to regulate the processes aimed at optimization of the whole management system. Relative to the industrial systems specified above, it means provision of their competitiveness and economic benefit (in particular, high profit). Availability of the above-specified adaptable mechanisms in system makes it possible to achieve optimum (the best, from the point of view of the criterion) results in case of unforeseen or casual change of external and internal environment.

It is obvious that for effective functioning of the big adaptive system, it is necessary for each of the subsystems to be qualitatively designed and coordinated with all subsystems according to parameters and functions. From here follows that in designing big adaptive management systems, it is necessary to use the complex approach covering all the activities of the firm. The firm activity is controlled by separate structural divisions being elements of the management system.

Each element of the management system operates according to the established rule specific to its nature, but at the same time, it corresponds to development of the system's components as a whole. In spite of the fact that each element plays an independent role in implementation of the system purposes, their autonomy is relative as they inevitably are parts of this system and can function only in this guise, interacting on the basis of the organized connections. The precondition of connections between the elements is their functions thanks to which they get the ability to integrate and interact. The more effectively the system functions, the more logical and accurate are the communication channels of its elements. Hence, a set of connections between them, resources and possibilities has essential value in studying of the management system elements and their interaction.

The firm resources are financial, scientific, information, human, technical, and industrial resources which can be used in aggregate or separately during the functioning of the firm management system.

Differentiation of the elements and dispose of resources can be formulated as follows:

(a) Concept of the primary element of the firm management system should comprise connection of the basic conditions for implementation of the system functions.
(b) Correlations of primary elements should be considered with due account for general distribution of the purposeful behavior property.
(c) Parameters distinguishing primary elements require invariant property of volume and variety of requirements which the system should meet.
(d) Parameters of connections between primary elements should provide comparison between various options of structures.
(e) The structure and the firm management system (consisting of buildings, constructions, various types of equipment, computer complexes, and personnel united in the big adaptive integrated management system of the firm) should be designed so that they could function as a uniform harmonious mechanism providing solution for problems of purposeful development. The personnel in this case, expressly or by implication, become the manager of all resources of the firm. The structure of the firm and personnel recruitment are carried out according to the mission of the firm.

Depending on structure of the firm management where the personnel works, HR implement a function of distribution of resources by types and fields of the firm activities. This is the only way the human resources are structurally separated from each other. From here, it is possible to introduce a concept of the primary element of economic structure which unites technical, computing or financial, and other means which the personnel of this element dispose of. We will name such primary element a "Management Center" (MC). During each particular moment of time, MC is in a certain condition from which it can pass to another state. Stimulus to such transition can be a decision of the manager only, i.e., conscious selection of direction and way of transformation of the resources at his disposal.

In the firm system, every M Cimplements a number of useful results. They are products and services, production process which are elements of output from the system or the elements to enter other MCs.

For useful results, it is possible to determine a cycle of their formation in time—frequency of occurrence. From this point of view, MC resources can be classified into three categories:

1. Resources, for which the character of transformation can be changed within smaller time interval, than the cycle of formation and the frequency of occurrence of the useful results.
2. Resources for which the corresponding interval of preservation in the selected mode of transformation is between frequency and the cycle.
3. Resources for which the mode of their transformation to the useful results, selected by the manager, cannot be changed during longer time, than the frequency and cycle.

From here, it is clear that the freedom in choosing the manager is decreasing with the increase of the period of time during which the manager, owing to particular material conditions of management, cannot change the previous decision.

Accordingly, with the increase of this period of time, influence of decisions on implementation of the basic function of economy is growing and aggravates the process of choice.

Here we see the role of the whole structural policy of the firm: change of connection of resources and managers can render influence and influences results of effective functioning of the firm and its management system as a whole.

MC resources can consist of many isolated components, but MC manager should always be one person only. If there is a situation in the management system when one MC has a number of managers and every manager makes a decision which is not coordinated with other managers, it will testify to low level of this system of management.

Managers of different MC differ from each other by values and motives, possibilities and knowledge. This is why they learn about their MC status and other MC systems according to vertical and horizontal connections. In what follows, the managers differ in knowledge which determines a difference of those areas of choice which are open for them; at the same time, they differ in technical and economic level of MC management—it determines their resource abilities. Finally, they differ in the ways which help to compare possible decisions in order to understand what result will follow implementation of the said decisions.

Taking into consideration the above-resulted reasons, it is possible to make the following definition: a structure of the firm management is the sound in space and in time distribution of decisions and appropriate resources expressed in isolation and interaction of MC structural divisions.

A variety and placing of properties by structure elements can be considered as display of complexity of the organization. Extremely simple system (minimum complicated) consists of absolutely identical primary elements. As soon as the system differentiates properties of at least two elements, immediately there is a material and technical basis for connection between them.

In economy, actual connection means the moving of energy, matter, or information. Hence, its implementation changes complexity of business and can lead to two results: to increase in number of new potentially possible connections or to their decrease, i.e., increase or reduction of complexity of business.

Thus, there are two constant processes in business: change of complexity and change of actual quantitative connections within it.

Formation of actual connections is a result of activity of all managers of this system. By virtue of considerable variability of character and duration of coexistence of connections and their big number, it is worthwhile to assume that for additional connection, expected level of expenses is a constant value. Then dynamics of a number of actual connections becomes "expenditure side" in a variety of the met requirements.

Hence, in advancing growth of complexity relative to the number of actual connections, the system functions more effectively. The choice of the managers generates decreasing volume of potential connections within the system and increasing volume of connections at the output. As a result, the system requires rather fewer resources for its functioning. In this case, owing to finiteness of the total resources, the system can forward the greater part of resources for increase in a variety of satisfaction of consumer requirements.

If complexity grows more slowly than the numbers of actual connections, the choice of the system managers increases the number of potential connections in the business and reduces it at the output. As a result, the system is less effective.

As a rule, each TC functional division comprises other processes (divisions) or subprocesses. They, in turn, can be a uniting link of subprocesses of the lower level. And so to the bottom hierarchical level of indivisible elements which are functions.

Hence, in designing structure of the firm management, it is important not only to identify the processes in TC structural divisions but to analyze structures of subprocesses and their hierarchical dependence. In so doing, it is important to take into consideration that complexity of the said process is measured exclusively on the assumption of level of complexity of the structure itself and a number of interacting functions, instead of the people who operate the process. As can be seen from the above, ten persons who perform one function cannot be considered as ten functional elements.

Subprocesses of any hierarchical level should contain description of the product of activity, structure of functions, and consumption. The structure of subprocesses is built in the form of a tree. As a matter of fact, subprocess is a structural formation within the said process and represents informal organization of the subordinate functional elements.

In the company management structure, subprocesses are not accounted; they are used as internal control facilities for the business process. The specified breakdown is necessary for accounting of consumption of resources and coordination of the team work.

Description of correlations of subprocesses is another major characteristic of the process properties. There are two types of connections—consecutive and parallel. Consecutive connections are related to the group of dependent consumption where a product of activity of internal subprocess is used in the capacity of raw materials for production of the end product (Fig. 7.1).

In-line assembly of various products can be an example of dependent hierarchy.

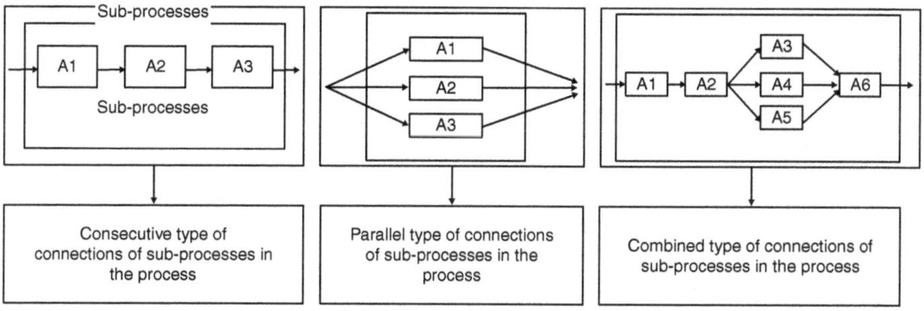

Fig. 7.1 Types of connections of subprocesses in the process

Parallel connections are such relations of subprocesses where activity of one division does not directly influence performance of other divisions.

Absence of hierarchy can be observed by the example of the team process of performing supply services where groups of subprocesses (divisions) are conditionally divided by types of delivered raw materials. In this case, the product of consumption and product of activity are combined.

In complex and multilevel processes, most often there is a combined type of connections where consecutive and parallel connection of subprocesses takes place simultaneously.

Most often, it occurs in the firms with high level of differentiation of the same type of production or multivariant approach of its complete set.

Understanding of the processes structure will make it possible for designer to avoid errors in model construction where level of complexity of each process should be optimized and meet the system task of the firm.

In our case, the key system task of the firm is a problem of enhancing its competitiveness. The approach to solution of this problem should be a complex one, when all the processes and subprocesses should be interconnected, which requires, first, that every MC should function effectively (accumulated resources and distributed them in the optimum way in the problems preference manner with a view of enhancing competitiveness of production with minimization of expenses), and secondly, as a result of the measures provided with MC resources, there should be an escalating of competitive advantages of the firm at the expense of growth of efficiency, reduction of the cost price, and, hence, the final price of the ready-made products which determines competitiveness of production and the firm in the market to a certain degree under all other equal conditions.

It is obvious that the easier correlation between processes and subprocesses, the higher the maneuverability of management and transparency of accounting of economic activities. The study concerning the structure of production and conclusions make it possible to specify a system of criteria characters the new process teams should comply with. But, first of all, it is necessary to take into consideration certain rules of the business processes designing.

First, the analysis of the current production structure makes it possible to specify two basic categories of the process teams, one of which has product of its activity focused on external consumer, another one—on domestic.

External consumer is a person who is not connected with the company but is a consumer of its goods and services. Internal consumer is a direct managing subject in the set structure of the company and uses the product of activity of other process teams as a raw material.

The algorithm of sequence of designing consists in the fact that the first step within the project should be reconstruction of the processes which are focused on external consumer and engaged in direct production of the goods and services. It is important to note that the process teams realizing services in sale of the goods are not taken into consideration, as according to the set properties, they are focused on satisfaction of internal consumer in the name of the process teams making external product of consumption.

It is exactly through external consumer they receive funds for settlement with other teams of the processes and financing of all other production costs. It is not mere chance that the company activity is characterized by its successes in sales of goods and services with allowance for their quantitative and qualitative levels. Thus, the process teams focused on external consumer are the basis of construction of the whole business structure.

Secondly, reengineering of the teams making a product of domestic consumption is carried out stage by stage. Mission of the process teams consists in creation of environment for the industrial and marketing activity providing reception of the maximum income and minimization of costs. The team's task includes accounting, management, analysis, consulting, strategic planning, management, etc.

As can be seen from the above, it is possible to make a conclusion that ability of economic system to regulate its own complexity can be considered as its organized nature. The rate of increment of complexity to the increment of a number of actual connections within the system becomes an organization measure.

In order to characterize the system, they usually specify its elements, levels of organization, structure and functions, and indices.

The system should monitor changes of indices of external and internal environment and provide information according to multivariant offers being the basis for the management to make online an objective assessment of occurring processes and to choose the optimum decision on the firm development for the time being.

The system should receive information from two sources:

- Initial external environment including an input and an output of the system, connection with environment, and a feedback (an inward glance);
- Secondary internal structure—a set of interconnected components providing process of influence of the subject of management on the object, transformation of input into output, and achievement of the system purposes (an outward glance).

The system description characterizes not only the system indices but also ways of their connection and the data on the system possibilities, which could provide meeting a goal objective (or the purposes if it is a multipurpose system) and strategy of perspective development.

By means of analysis of external and internal environment, we establish the indices. Its evaluation and regulation lead to progressive advance of the firm. In identification of possible influences of external and internal environment, there are certain boundary conditions formed, the violation of which may trigger termination of the firm development, and in some cases—its bankruptcy.

The principal indices for competitiveness management system are the firm's competitiveness index as a whole and indirectly indices of competitiveness of production providing technical and economic advantages.

Influencing these indices by means of one or another management methods, by introduction of innovations, acceleration of the products modernization (output with high competitive advantages), organization of production updating etc., it is possible to achieve high competitiveness in the commodity markets.

7.2 Methodological Basis for Designing a System of the Firm Competitiveness Management

Proceeding to description of the main principles of building automated organizational economic management systems of competitiveness, we provide some well-known concepts required for development of such systems.

In consideration of the automated management systems, it is important to define concept "management." A management assumes availability of a managed object or a group of objects: a live organism, mechanism, organization, etc. Except the managed object, there should be a managerial body which influences the managed object, changing its condition in a desirable way. Management represents a set of influences aimed at maintaining or improving the functioning of the managed object according to the available program or the purpose of management.

Optimum management consists in choosing the best management actions from the set of possible actions according to specific criterion of efficiency and established purpose of management, with provision for some restrictions and on the basis of information on the status of the managed object and environment, as the actual systems always have limited possibilities.

In implementation of the optimum management, the most significant is the criterion of efficiency. There is an often error—they fail to do distinctions between the purpose of the system and criterion of efficiency. It is important to emphasize that the purpose of the system determines its designation, its meaning of functioning. This purpose expresses our point of view concerning what the system is created for, what it should do, and what we expect it to do. By contrast, criterion of efficiency is an assessment of how the system operates, reflects what we expect it to do. As can be seen from the above, the purpose and criterion of efficiency are important for both the system and its environment and for the higher system to which this system is subordinated to. They are laid down at the stage of creating Management Information System (MIS) and mostly formed in the course of implementation of scientific results in particular systems.

In creation of such systems, they consider and use social and business factors at different levels of management, possibilities of computer complex, technological level of production, possibilities to quickly readjust production on the assumption of the market requirements, and highly effective technologies making it possible to make low-cost products; it provides stability of the system, reliability of data, and efficiency of management.

Basically, in every industrial enterprise, its management system represents a hierarchical structure where each level is a closed contour of management with all inherent functions (planning, accounting, management, analysis, and regulation). Each management contour is a part of the higher contour: the higher the management level, the bigger the integrated functional problems it solves.

It is important to underline that management functions are different at various levels, and they are subordinated to each other but do not duplicate each other, and between the management contours, there is a change and analysis of data formed at one or another hierarchical level of the system.

From here, there is a hierarchical structure of data on the basis of which the indices of enterprise performance are determined in the system as a result of mathematical processing. These indices are changed depending on influences of external environment and changes in internal structure of the firm. The information database is a multilevel structure.

It is easy to draw a parallel between methodology of the MIS creation by the firm and creation of competitiveness management system. However, the organizational and economic management system of the enterprise is a system of higher level than the MIS. It unites majority of the MIS systems working in the firm, and competitiveness of output directly depends on result of performance.

In development of the basis for designing the firm competitiveness management system, it is possible to come to conclusion that, as a matter of fact, it is a complex big organizational and economic system consisting of various functional management systems of the enterprise, connected in a single whole for the purpose of creation of the firm's competitive advantages in order to have profit at various stages of its life cycle.

In order to support this thesis, Table 7.1 presents principal types of the firm management systems, their functional designation and influence on competitiveness, and creation of competitive advantages of the firm. This list is far from being complete; it specifies only the basic management systems. Depending on the firm's activity, it can be added.

Like all other management information systems of the enterprise, the firm competitiveness management system has:

- Connections within the system of firm competitiveness with external environment—they are information and documentary flows in the system between its components for acceptance and coordination of implementation of the

Table 7.1 Types of the firm management system

SNo.	System's name	System's designation	Influence on creation of competitive advantages
1	2	3	4
1	System of automated production design	Product development	Creation of competitive advantages at the development stage
2	Enterprise assets management system	Production	Creation of competitive advantages at the expense of high level of production process, enhancement of production profitability
3	Material resources management system	Planning and management of material resources	Creation of competitive advantages at the expense of optimization of warehouse stocks, minimization of taxes, elimination of inefficient use of circulating assets, provision of stock required for production, raw materials, and components
4	Finance management system	Financial planning of the firm's assets	Creation of competitive advantages at the expense of management of financial activity and implementation of financial processes
5	HR management system	HR management	Creation of competitive advantages at the expense of high qualification and intellectual possibilities of workers
6	Quality control system	Manufacturing quality control	Creation of competitive advantages at the stage of production, providing appropriate requirements of the market quality
7	Transport system	Products delivery	Creation of competitive advantages at the expense of effective methods of delivery
8	Sales management system	Sales management	Creation of competitive advantages at the stage of receiving and processing of orders, completing and preparations of products for the buyers, shipments and transportation to the place of sale, and organization of settlements
9	Service system	Before-sale services and warranty service	Creation of competitive advantages at the sales stage and work with consumers
10	Marketing management system	Assessment of the enterprise potential, forecast of tendencies of the enterprise development	Creation of competitive advantages at the expense of market researches and product portfolio policy management, formation of demand, sales promotion

management decision. The information should be in required amount and quality on demand.

- Industrial resources are people, tools of trade, internal information, and innovations.
- Feedback—requirements, claims of consumers, offers of consumers concerning introduction of innovations, and other information from the sphere of consumption to the manufacturer.

Efficiency criterion here is online level of competitiveness of the goods.

In so much as owing to dynamic character of the situation in the market, sharp and unforeseen change of competitiveness parameters of output, there is a necessity of online adjustment of the firm's performance. That is, the firm competitiveness management system should possess properties of automatic adaptation to the changing parameters of competitiveness, providing the most effective mode of functioning from the point of view of the system goals. Hence, the firm competitiveness management system should be flexible and easily adaptive to the changes of environment.

Organizational and economic competitiveness information system of the firm management, including all Computer-Aided Management Systems in the firm (technical CAMS), integrating them in a uniform computer-aided complex, should take into consideration influence of external factors on competitiveness of every such CAMS and supervise not only their separate functioning but take into consideration their correlations too.

For every technical CAMS available at the firm in the process of its integration, it is necessary to determine:

- Basic characteristics of technical CAMS which will make it possible to carry out their integration into the firm's CAMS.
- Features of correlations between technical CAMS in integrated CAMS of the firm.

It is necessary to expand functional tasks of every technical CAMS, so that, along with fulfillment of their basic functions of automated service of technical and economic processes of the organization, it could evaluate competitiveness of output and the firm within the framework of the functional purpose.

At the same time, characteristics of every technical CAMS being a subsystem for the firm should be adapted for the firm characteristics.

Such characteristics are stability, high-speed response, accuracy, sensitivity, adaptability, flexibility, hierarchy, ability to forecasting, and multivariant approach to managerial decisions. These characteristics can be determined by means of the method of modeling or other economic and mathematical methods with the use of predetermined specific and generalized competitiveness indices of production or the firm.

It is obvious that the basic characteristics of every CAMS are closely connected with each other. Therefore, within the framework of the firm, there should be established for each technical CAMS correlation of the listed characteristics in the form of functional dependences between them:

$$F_j\left\{f_{ji}(D_j, T_j, \varepsilon_j, fc_j, \lambda_j); \quad (j = 1, \ldots, n_j)\right\},$$

where F_j—system of functional dependences of the basic characteristics for the j-th a technical CAMS.
f_{ji}—functional dependence between characteristics for the j-th technical CAMS.
i—index of functional dependence in the j-th CAMS $(j = 1, \ldots, n_j)$.
n_j—number of dependences in the j-th technical CAMS.

Functioning of the firm when its CAMS possesses a set of all characteristics (see Table 7.2) can be demonstrated by means of the known management approach named "management by weak signals."

The optimality of decisions connected with functioning and development of the firm is considerably determined by degree of awareness of its management about existing and imminent risks to lose competitive advantages both from within and outside. Management by weak signals means ability of the CAMS to find out negative situations beforehand. This provides more time to respond to negative situations, and there is a possibility to make managerial decisions to adapt to such changes and to avoid the risk of decrease in the firm competitiveness and/or production in due time. For implementation of such possibility, it is necessary to change the approach to collection, analysis, and use of strategic information. At the early stage of potential danger, when there is not enough information, reciprocal measures will have a general character and are aimed at preservation of strategic flexibility, i.e., the firm's possibilities to adapt to time and/or constant changes of the external and internal environment without losing competitive advantages and lowering the level of competitiveness. In process of receiving particular information, there will be concretized the firm's reciprocal measures, the ultimate goal of which is either danger elimination (e.g., change of supplier) or use of available possibilities (adaptation to a new political situation). Such approach in a context of strategic management is called "gradual strengthening of reciprocal measures" and "response to weak signals."

For every technical CAMS functioning within the firm, with an allowance for its division into management and managed subsystems (Fig. 7.2), it is necessary to determine the characteristic features of the basic data flows for implementation of their integration in further. After fulfillment of these actions, it would be possible to say that entire system of the firm competitiveness management (hereinafter referred to as "CMS"—Competitiveness Management System) is completely formed.

For every CAMS, it is possible to present a flow of input signals as

$$X_u = \{X_{uc}, X_{uf}\},$$

where Xuc—decisions on management of local functions of the CAMS, for

Table 7.2 Basic characteristics of technical CAMSof the firm

SN	Characteristic	Functions determining characteristic[a]
1	Stability	Mean square deviation (MSD): $D = f_D(s_{D,1}, \ldots, s_{D,N_D})$, where $s_{D,i}$—parameters characterizing MSDCKO; N_D—quantity of parameters $s_{D,i}$ $(i = 1, \ldots, N_D)$
2	High-speed response	Time from the moment of change of the system condition until the moment the CEO of the firm (or division) receives analyzed information on this change, $T = f_T(s_{T,1}, \ldots, s_{T,N_T})$, where $s_{T,i}$—parameters characterizing system performance; N_T—number of parameters $s_{T,i}$ $(i = 1, \ldots, N_T)$
3	Accuracy	Operational margin $\varepsilon = f_\varepsilon(s_{\varepsilon,1}, \ldots, s_{\varepsilon,N_\varepsilon})$, where $s_{\varepsilon,i}$—parameters characterizing accuracy of the system; N_ε – number of parameters $s_{\varepsilon,i}$ $(i = 1, \ldots, N_\varepsilon)$
4	Sensitivity	Sensitivity function $fc = f_{fc}\left(s_{fc,1}, \ldots, s_{fc,N_{fc}}\right)$, where $s_{fc,i}$—parameters characterizing sensitivity of the system; N_{fc}—number of parameters $s_{fc,i}\left(i = 1, \ldots, N_{fc}\right)$
5	Adaptability	Parameters characterizing ability to adapt to changing environment.
6	Flexibility	Flexibility $\lambda = f_\lambda(s_{\alpha,1}, \ldots, s_{\alpha,N_\alpha})$, where $s_{a,i}$—parameters characterizing flexibility of the system; N_α – number of parameters $s_{a,i}(i = 1, \ldots, N_\alpha)$
7	Hierarchy	Generalized indices of the firm's competitiveness taking into account the firm's structure and hierarchy
8	Ability to forecasting	Changes in time of specific s(t) and generalized competitiveness indices of the products Q(t) and the firm R(t), competitiveness coefficients K(t) and their weightiness α(t), and time interval Δt for measurement of these indices
9	Multivariant approach	A number of specific and generalized indices of the system describing its condition and changes, influencing competitiveness of production and the firm, as well as specific, generalized, and integrated competitiveness indices of production and the firm. Multivariant approach to the management decisions should include measures to increase the values of integrated indices.

[a]As an example

example, on change of structure of the basic production assets or professional and numeric strength of the shop workers.

X_{uf}—management decisions connected with the CAMS competitiveness management, for example, instructions on replacement of the used material on the assumption of forecasts concerning more modern and qualitative material or introduction of the new production methods.

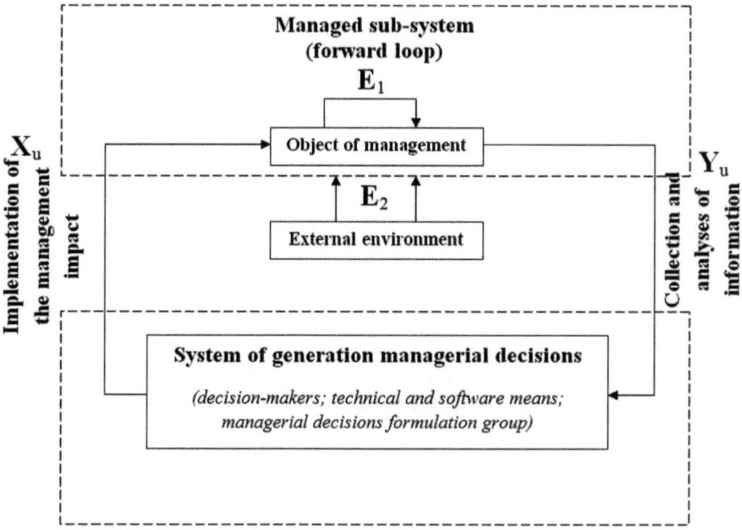

Fig. 7.2 CAMS structural components and connections

Generally the input object of the system consists of a set of management impacts X_u and influences of environment E_2:

$$X = \{X_u; E_2\}.$$

Environment influences are change in prices for similar production of competitors and resources as well as new methods of materials processing.

Flow of output influences for every Computer-Aided Management System (CAMS):

$$Y_u = \{Y_{uc}, Y_{uf}\},$$

where Y_{uc}—information on changes of the CAMS local functions, for example, about reduction of a number of workers, change of the reject rate in the lot quality, failure of equipment, etc.

Y_{uf}—information on changes of the CAMS competitiveness indices, for example, about a possibility of introduction of new modern equipment, results of application of new policy of discounts, and service changes.

The optimum solution of the system of criterion functions of every CAMS is provided at the expense of self-management mechanism E_1.

For every CAMS, it is necessary to determine Cs—a set (family) of global conditions of the object of management representing value for all of its internal parameters for the time being: number of workers, profit, losses, and schedule of materials deliveries.

Key problem in modeling of the automated object of management is creation of the mechanism of influence of its inputs on the outputs, named a processor (operator) of the object. Thus, processor of the object of management provides display P when

$$P\{X_u, E_1, E_2, Cs\} \to Y_u,$$

and the processor of management system-

$$P_u\{Y_u\} \to X_u.$$

In order to improve efficiency within enhancement of the firm competitiveness by every technical CAMS, there should be formed a system of criterion functions, for which optimum solution is provided by every CAMS only in coordination with management subsystem.

Generally, for the i-th CAMS, such system of criterion functions will look like:

$$Fu_i : \begin{cases} fu_{i1} \to opt_1; \\ fu_{i2} \to opt_2; \\ \ldots, \\ fu_{in} \to opt_n; \end{cases}$$

where Fu_i—schematic symbol of the system of criterion functions of the i-th CAMS.

fu_{ij}—j-th criterion function of the i-th CAMS, the solution of which is aimed at enhancement of the firm competitiveness within the framework of the CAMS functioning and achievement of purpose of Zf_i.

opt_j—optimum value for the j-th functions.

$$\text{If } fu_{ij} \to \max, \text{ then } fu_{ij} > fu_{ijadd};$$

$$\text{If } fu_{ij} \to \min, \text{ then } fu_{ij} < fu_{ijadd},$$

where fu_{ijadd}—acceptable value of function fu_{ij}.

From this, it follows that the management system of the firm competitiveness in general has structure $\{P, X, Yu, Cs, R, Q\}$, and the i-th CAMS being a part of the management system of the firm competitiveness has structure $\{P_i, X_i, Yu_i, Cs_i, \varphi_i, Q_i, Fu_i\}$,where φ_i—state transition function of the i-th CAMS. Thus, each of such CAMS is subordinated to the global purpose of enhancing the firm competitiveness in addition to the system of local purposes.

For all technical CAMS functioning in the firm, it is necessary to establish correlations and interdependence between them.

For every CAMS, besides input and output flows of information, there should be determined sets X_{ij}—data flow from the i-th CAMS in the j-th, and there may be several such flows for every CAMS (correlations of one system with the other systems).

Generally, when CY_i and CY_j are not directly coordinated in their work, i.e., they have various information and analytical organization, data flow X_{ij} is a family of functions transforming the output data flow CY_i forwarded by CY_j into the input data flow CY_j (generally speaking, time dependent):

$$X_{ij} : Y_{i(ij)} \rightarrow X_{j(ij)},$$

where $Y_{i(ij)} = \left\{ y_{i(ij)} \right\}$—the output data flow CY_i directed by CY_j; $X_{j(ij)} = \left\{ x_{j(ij)} \right\}$—input data flow CY_j arriving from CY_i.

Self-regulation of the i-th CAMSis governed by data flows $E1_i$ which include states of the i-th system (time dependent) Cs_{ti} and the state transition function $\varphi_{ti}$of the i-th system (also time dependent):

$$E1_i = \{Cs_{ti}, \varphi_{ti}\}.$$

Then for every CAMS, a set of input data will be broken into flows

$$X_j = \left\{ Xu_j, X_{ij}, i = 1, \ldots, n \right\},$$

where n—number of CAMS with which the j-th system is connected. Accordingly, the set of output data (flows) for the j-th will look like:

$$Y_j = \left\{ Yu_j, X_{ji}, i = 1, \ldots, n \right\}.$$

Thus, it is possible to note that for interconnected CY_i and CY_j, the following statements are true:

1) $X_i \cap X_j = X_{ji} \cup X_{ij}$, i.e., For two interconnected CAMS, the common data flows between their input flows will be the flows from the j-th systems into the i-th system.
2) $X_i \cap X_j = X_{ji}$, i.e., For two interconnected CAMS, the common data flows between the input data flow of the i-th CAMS and the output data flow of the j-th CAMS is data flow X_{ji}.

After definition of correlations and interdependences between technical CAMS, there is stage-by-stage integration of such systems into a uniform intellectual, management, organizational, and economic complex based on application of information technologies, which meets the specified requirements to resource intensiveness, high-speed response, accuracy, universality, adaptability, and openness, as well as supervision of the implementation.

Integration is required for the following:

- to determine for every firm's CAMS input Xu_i and output Yu_i data flows, and the local goals of each system Yu_i, indices of environment influences E_2, and a set of global states of the system Cs_i.
- to develop and introduce in every CAMS additional input X_{ufi} and output Y_{ufi} data flows (indices and functions), concerning enhancement of the firm competitiveness, and to create a system of criterion functions Zf_i within the framework of every CAMS aimed at enhancement of the firm competitiveness within the framework of CAMS functioning.
- to set terms for the input and output information and parameters of the firm's status for every technical CAMS separately and to determine priority ranking of such information.
- to determine an optimum flow of information between various CAMS and to develop a functional information block connecting these CAMS, necessary for increasing efficiency of the firm functioning.
- to develop within the framework of every CAMS indices and the functions to assess separate characteristics of the products and the firm, degree of their influence on the firm competitiveness, and for each technical CAMS to determine functions of increasing the firm competitiveness at the stage of functioning of such CAMS.
- to determine priority ranking (weightiness) of every CAMS within the framework of the main task of this mechanism—enhancement of the firm competitiveness as a whole.
- to carry out integration of such systems within a uniform complex.
- to collect information on the status and level of the firm competitiveness from the various technical CAMS functioning in the firm in order to provide it to the firm CEO (or to decision-maker).

The systems integration into a uniform complex can be done by means of the firm parametrical scheme presented in Fig. 7.3.

This scheme has the following designations:

K_{i_1}—index of competitiveness of production according to i_1-specific indicator.

K'_{i_2}—index of competitiveness of production according to i_2-specific scientific and technical indicator.

Q_{i_3}—i_3-generalized index of competitiveness of production.

α_i—weight number of index of competitiveness of production K_i (or K'_i).

K_I—integrated index of competitiveness of production.

$f_{i_1} - i_1$—the function reflecting interdependence of N_{i_1}-specific indices of competitiveness of the firm $u_{i_1,1}, \ldots, u_{i_1,N_{i_1}}$, moreover, $u_{i_1,1} \in U, \ldots, u_{i_1,N_{i_1}} \in U$.

H_{i_1}—competitiveness coefficient according to the i_2-th specific index of the firm, which is not scientific and technical characteristic of the firm.

H_{i_3}—competitiveness coefficient according to the i_3 -th specific scientific and technical indicator of the firm.

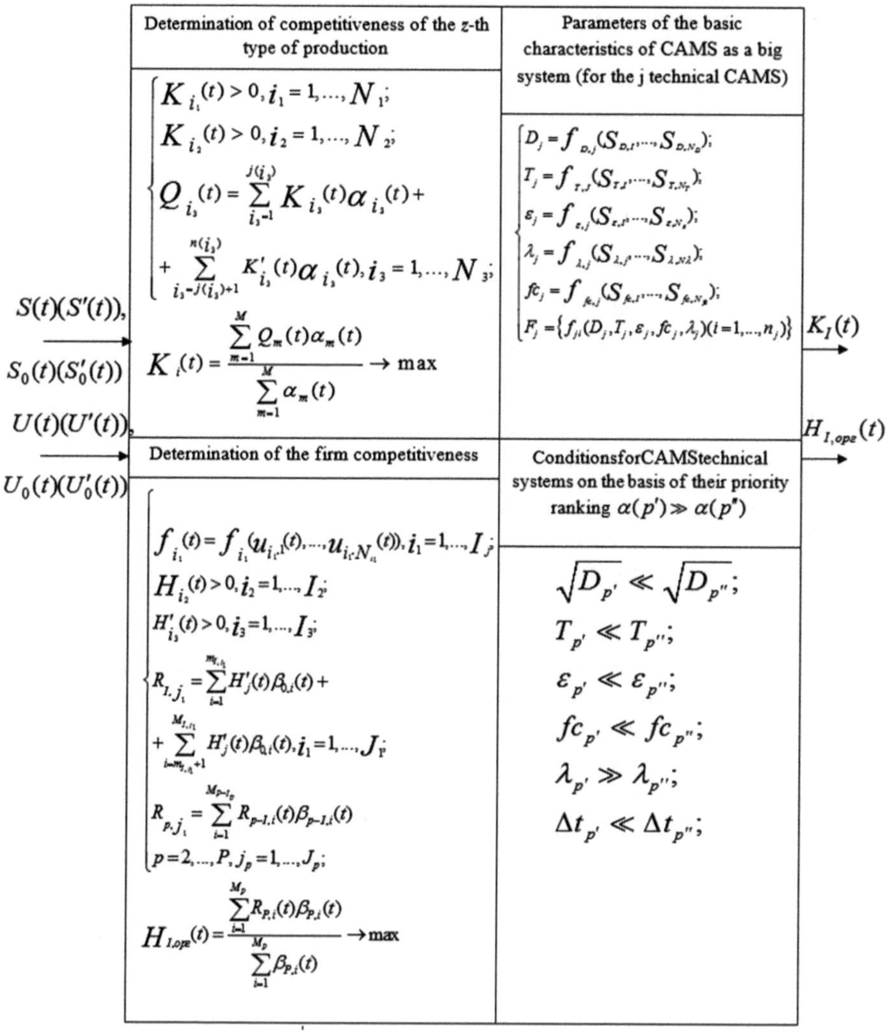

Fig. 7.3 Parametrical scheme of the firm

R_{1,j_1} —i_1 -th generalized index of competitiveness of the first level of generalization.

R_{p,j_p}—j_p -th generalized index of the firm competitiveness of the p-th level of generalization.

P—number of levels of generalization.

$H_{I,opz}$—integrated factor of the firm competitiveness.

β_0—weighing coefficient of the generalized index of the first level of generalization.

$\beta_{p-1,i}$—weighing coefficient of generalized index $R_{p-1,i}$.

$\alpha(p'), \alpha(p'')$ – weighing coefficients of more or less prioritized technical systems, accordingly.

$\Delta t_{p'}$, $\Delta t_{p''}$—periods of measurement of competitiveness parameters of more or less prioritized technical systems, accordingly.

At the system input: resource, technical, cost indices of production S, and production of competitor (sample) S_0; indices of external and internal environment of the firm U and the firm-competitor (sample) U_0; scientific and technical characteristics of production S' and the firm U'; indices of scientific and technical achievements in the field of creation of this type of production (sample) S_0' and automation, mechanization, and technologies developed for the firms of this type of industrial activity (sample) U_0'.

Within the framework of the system functioning carried out are the following activities:

- calculation of coefficients of competitiveness of production and the firm by comparison of the listed indices of production and the firm with the indices of the corresponding sample with due account for change in time of these coefficients;
- formation on the basis of the said coefficients of competitiveness of production and the firm of the generalized competitiveness indices of production and the firm taking into consideration their change in time;
- calculation of the integrated coefficients of competitiveness of production and the firm taking into consideration their change in time;
- formation (on the basis of the indices received at the input of the organization of) of the basic characteristics of every technical CAMS functioning in the firm with provision for priority ranking of these systems in formation of the firm competitive advantages.

At the system output: data about level of competitiveness of production K_I and firm $H_{I,\ opr}$; their estimated figures; and management decisions concerning regulation of competitiveness of production and the firm in case of achieving critical assessments by any specific or generalized competitiveness indices of production or the firm or by parameters of the basic characteristics of the firm.

With the help of the said indices and their functional dependences, the firm can assess its competitiveness and each type of production in the current and estimated period of time with an allowance for dynamics of external and internal environment. On the basis of this assessment, the firm can have a basis for timely making of management decision on competitiveness regulation.

Designing of the management system of the firm competitiveness may be performed on the basis of the graph relevance tree. The relevance tree is built on the assumption of tasks to be solved by the firm competitiveness management. The breadboard model of the relevance tree of the firm competitiveness management system is presented in Fig. 7.4.

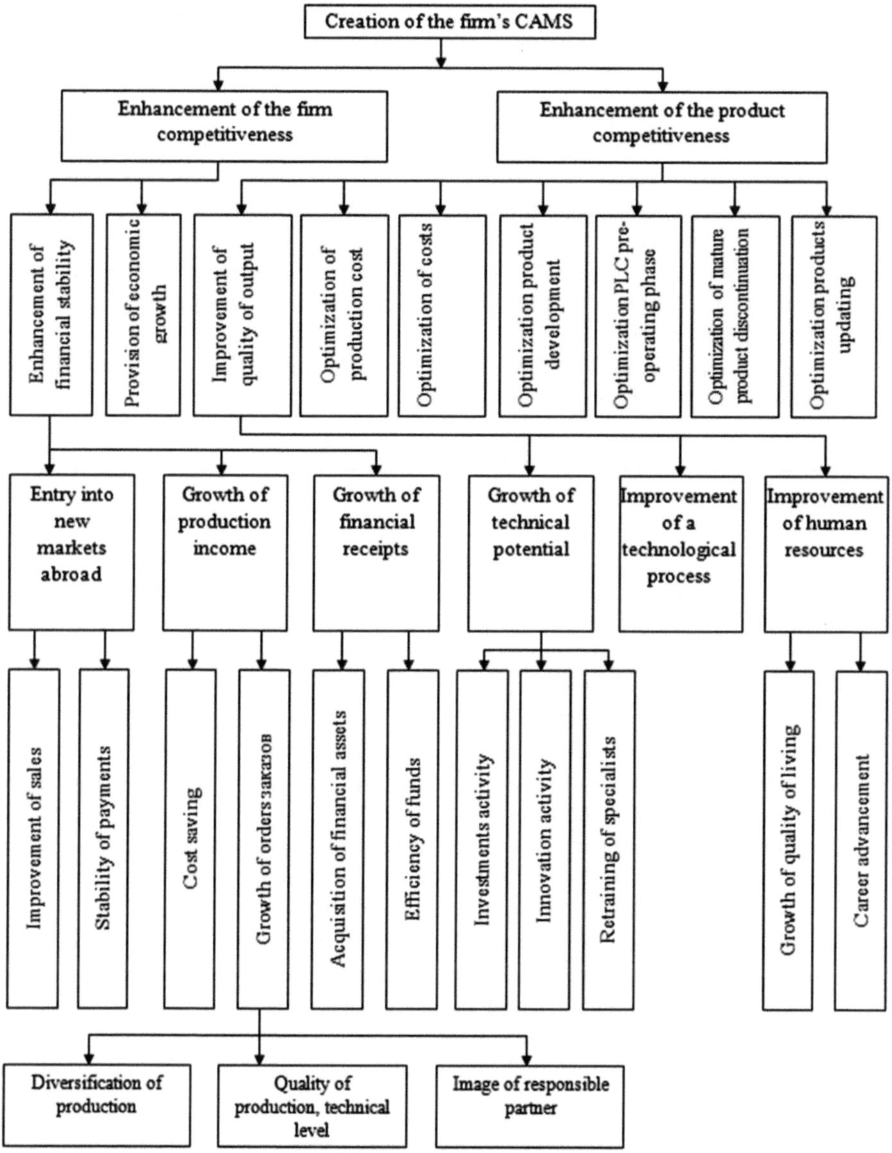

Fig. 7.4 Relevance tree of the firm competitiveness management

From the relevance tree, it is clear what priorities should be laid down in the technical project at designing. On the assumption of the said priorities, it is possible to formulate the following main principles of designing of the firm competitiveness management system:

- Design of organizational system should be started and based on modeling of the firm processes. Such models are called standard models, that is, they determine general principles of construction and the system functioning which we should comply with as much as possible.
- Design of organizational system should take into account characteristic features and specificity of technology of the basic and auxiliary production, as well as manufacturing preparation and functioning of all the factors which influence the firm's performance.
- Organizational system should be mobile and self-regulated so that it could support required rate of approach of actual results to the planned figures as much as possible.
- Organizational system should be structured according to the management levels and links. The lower we go down, the more detailed should be its expansion.

It is necessary to pay attention to characteristic features of the firm CMS designing:

- Evaluating of specific indices of competitiveness of output and the firm given their economic and technical characteristics change in time. On the basis of these indices with provision for their weightiness in creation of competitive advantages of production and the firm, the generalized indices reflecting state of competitiveness of output and the firm are generated taking into consideration the complexity of their hierarchy;
- Establishment of correlations of specific and generalized indices of the firm competitiveness and, on this basis, selection of parameters of assessment of the basic characteristics of the firm.
- Assignment of special purpose—competitiveness management of the firm at the stage of functioning of this technical CAMS at the stage of the firm design for every technical CAMS in the firm, in addition to the local purpose.
- Definition of significance of every technical CAMS within the framework of solution of the general problem of the firm competitiveness management.
- Calculation of parameters of the basic characteristics and definition of their correlations for every technical CAMS.
- Working out of integration conditions of all technical CAMS within the uniform integrated system.

Thus, in the process of creating management system, the following should be done:

1. Establish a range of tasks to be supported, analyze its structure and determine the technical CAMS within this structure and the functions which are performed by these systems. It is important to identify correlations and interdependence between these systems too.
2. Take into consideration that the system should conceive the changes of external and internal environment, expressly or by implication, influencing its

functioning, and to distinguish them and to provide corresponding adaptation of the firm economic activities on the basis of modern technologies.

3. Identify control loop of objectives definition functions and planning of activity, diagnosing, analysis of the current and forecasting of the future industrial situation, and assessment of consequences of the firm's decisions concerning competitiveness and its development. It is also necessary to determine input and output parameters of the system, parameters of technical CAMS responding to change of input and output parameters of the system.
4. Analyze the system structure of the firm. Establish conditions of coherence of technical CAMS with each other and with the firm. In so doing, it is necessary to do the following:

   - provide accurate coordination of the purposes (tasks) at the level of technical CAMS with each other and with the system as a whole. For this purpose, it is necessary to carry out coordination of problems of technical CAMS. Besides, the specified CAMS should possess properties of compatibility according to the modes of functioning, required efficiency (time indices) in fulfillment of the main functions according to their assignment, and requirements for functioning of the firm and as a whole;
   - provide passage of information flows (availability of connections) between technical CAMS, efficiency of reception, processing, and transfer of information into the next links if the information of one CAMS is required for effective functioning of another CAMS within the framework of the increase of the firm competitiveness as a whole.

5. A provision must be included that the firm competitiveness management should be carried out on the basis of creation and conducting of uniform databases in all aspects of the firm activities with application of modern information technologies. The information required for work of every CAMS should always be available. The output information of every CAMS should be built on the basis of the single information space convenient for subsequent decision-making on the firm competitiveness management as a whole.

In the course of designing the firm competitiveness management system, there should be picked up technical means and there should be performed their interface among themselves and technological means providing the whole process from creation of production up to service of the products, purchased by the consumer.

In the course of development of ideas of the first point of stage-by-stage creation of the management system, it is necessary to determine the primary goals and their correlations and to evaluate efficiency of the systems performance as a whole. Figure 7.5 presents the scheme of correlation of primary goals to be achieved in the course of the system designing.

Problem 1 Determination of the purposes of creation or perfection of the firm management system.

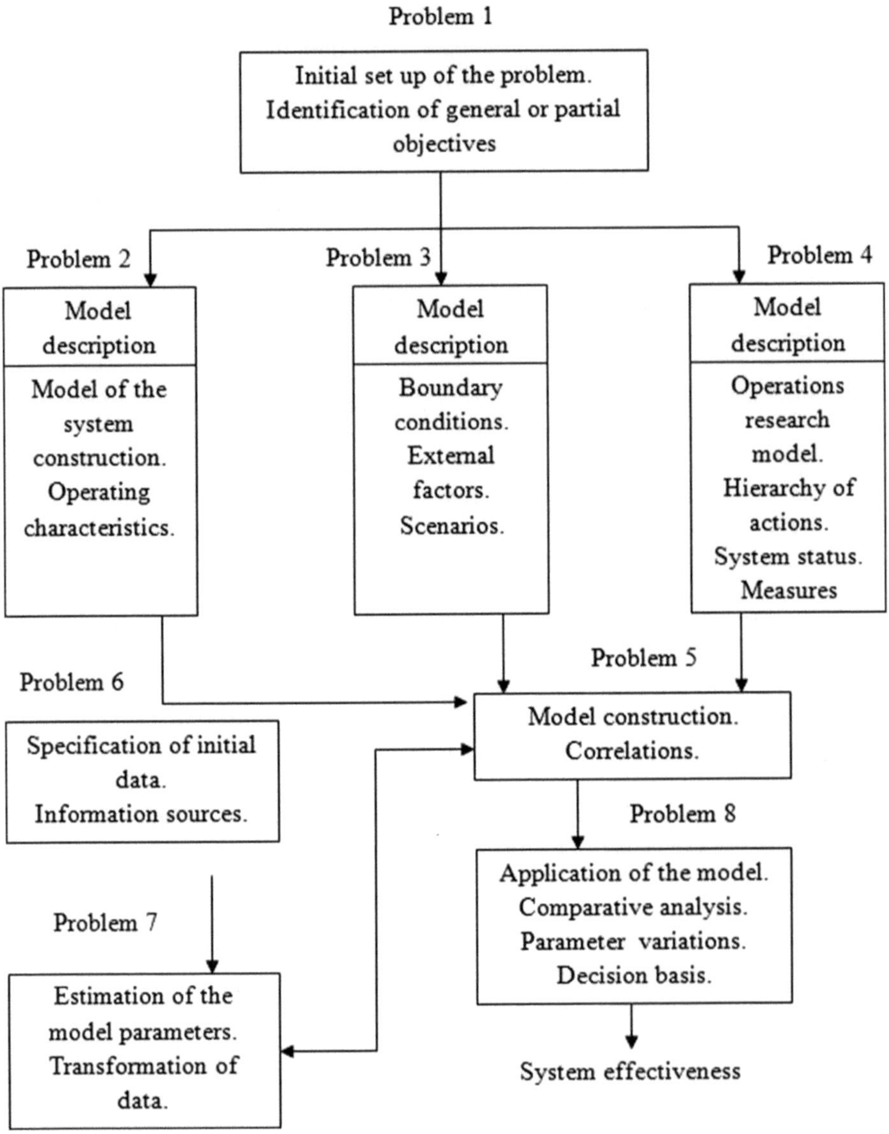

Fig. 7.5 Correlations of the primary goals to be achieved in the course of the system competitiveness management

This process begins with definition of the purpose of the system creation including strategy of development and the firm's basic characteristics.

Problem 2 Description of the system.

The system description should contain not only description of the particular system and its indices but also the functional diagram showing correlation of the said system with subsystems intended for fulfillment of the system tasks.

Thus, the system description will also contain data on the systems' hierarchy which could provide a roadmap (or end of purpose in case system is multipurpose) and a strategy of perspective development too.

Problem 3 Identification of the external and internal factors operating on the system which can be taken into consideration.

This problem includes not only assumptions and boundary conditions for the system but also assumptions concerning external environment, in particular, scenarios or descriptions of various influences of outside environment the system is expected to work in. If it is necessary to consider more than one scenario, all of them should be listed.

Problem 4 Online description.

On the basis of the set hierarchy and the basic characteristics of the systems, we build a mathematical model which has to be used as a basis for efficiency assessment of the decisions made at the previous stages of work, including various events which can take place, hierarchy of actions and various indices of the system and characteristics of external environment connected with every submodel.

Problem 5 Development of mathematical model.

It is a two-stage problem. Its first stage consists in model development of the system construction and an operational model.

The second stage—definition of quantitative relations which are set by a number of mathematical and (or) logic equations connecting various factors in each of the operational submodels.

For accurate definition of parametrical correlations between the factors and the data required for receiving quantitative results, the analysis executor should choose the scenario describing one of the said systems and to study interaction of the system with outside environment. Then he brings to a sharper focus each of the events in the general operations, displayed in the operational model built in advance for stage-by-stage determination of specific factors and their correlations. It will be better if the analysis maker builds so-called "test hypotheses" which are determined by correlation of the said events and expressed in the parametrical form. This correlation is based on the fact that the analysis maker knows the type of operation as a result of his power of observation and experience.

Problem 6 Specification of initial data following the modeling results.

This task makes it possible to correct initial data (for example, to increase amount of financing or to change qualitative structure of equipment or computer facilities) on the assumption of this mathematical analysis of the factors influencing the system of management.

Problem 7 Assessment of the model parameters of.

In the course of exploitation of available data or the information with allowances made for restrictions in time and resources, there should be quantitative assessments of corresponding parameters. Assessment process may assume exploitation of the known equations connecting corresponding factors, statistic methods, or subjective evaluation based on the expert's opinion. This way of assessment makes it possible to determine value of the error assumed in the input data. Upon solution of this problem, it is necessary to specify the method which can be used for extrapolation of the data in assessment of the model parameters.

Problem 8 Use of the model.

This problem consists in association (joining) of submodels within the operational model, in receiving qualitative assessments for output data at the set input data. It is expected that various economic and mathematical methods including the system simulation modeling can be applied. The choice of particular method is a function of quantity and accuracy of available data, accuracy of desirable results, and quantity of resources assigned for carrying out the analysis.

Solution of the said problems makes it possible to generate a competitiveness management system which provides trustworthy information about activity of the firm and its competitiveness to the decision-makers.

As a reference mathematical model of the firm's functioning, it is possible to use average assessments of efficiency indices of the group of firms successfully operating in this sector of the market. It is obvious that the firms with different profile will correspond to various models; therefore, the functional diagram of the model building (Fig. 7.6) should contain a basic package where every firm would have its own reference model.

Obligatory property of this functional diagram is its ability of "self-training." "Self-training" consists in the fact that after every diagnostic examination of the firm, there is not only correction of the reference model, but there are amendments made to the system of assessments of significance of efficiency criteria.

The offered approach makes it possible to take into consideration the changes of internal and external environment within a long period of time; thereby the results of performed diagnostic examination can be used not only for procedures of online correction but also for assessment of the firm's ability to respond to changes of the general market conditions of strategic nature. In case of sharp changes in economic situation (for example, in case of crisis in economy), available integrated assessments will make it possible to forecast the process of correcting the firm management system for new conditions.

Degree of impact of external factors (social and economic, scientific and technical, legal, political, international, natural, etc.) on activity of every particular firm is evaluated by expert methods. The block of increasing reliability of expert

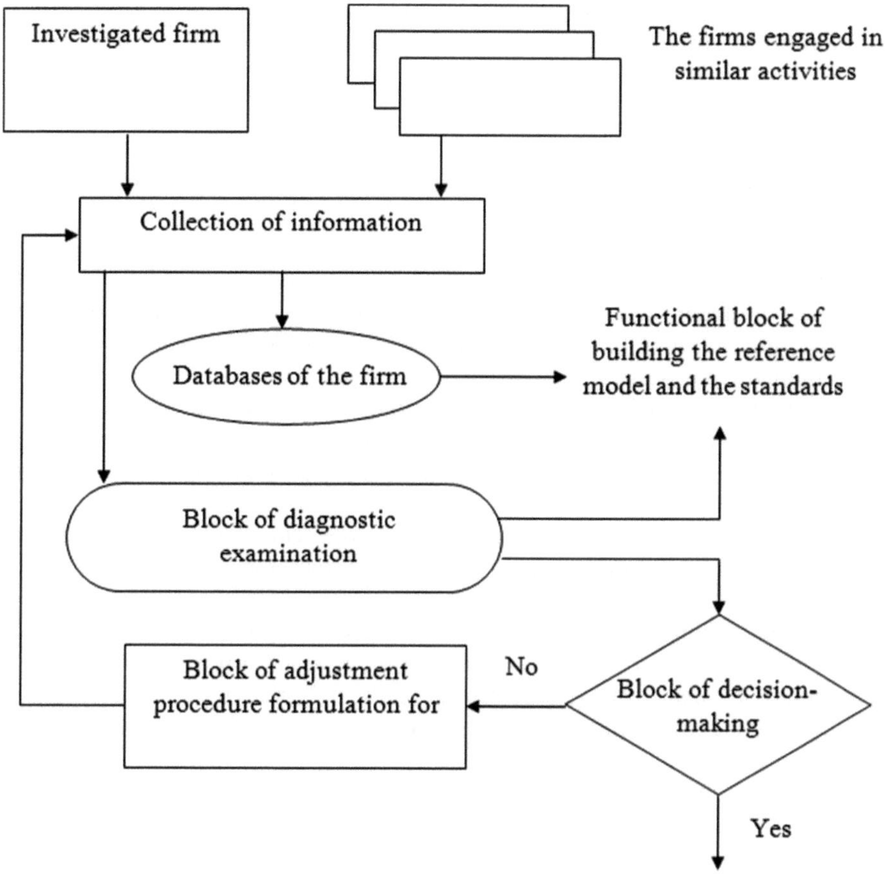

Fig. 7.6 Functional diagram of the system of online management correction

assessments makes it possible to evaluate coordination of experts' opinions in the course of ranging the factors influencing the CMS work of the firm according to their significance.

It is noteworthy to pay attention to availability of the special block of online correction of decisions in the system intended for processing of information. It is based on control over the level of deviation of the said assessment from the figures of the reference model for each criterion taken into account. The functional block helps to calculate the norm of deviation from the reference model indices or the set indices. If it is established, that discrepancy surpasses threshold value in any criterion, then the system of online correction of the firm management system will be activated. The data on the received results enter the database, and decision-making procedure is doubled given the said changes.

Development of the big organizational and economic management system may be considered successful if it contributes to achieve competitive advantages in various spheres of the firm activities.

7.3 Information Support of the Firm Competitiveness Management

Market conditions require common sense and experience of the firm's CEO, attraction of modern tools of analysis of great volumes of information, modeling, and computerization of the management processes for efficient management of the firm competitiveness.

The organization of competitiveness management should promote growth of financial and economic activities of the firm, encouragement of saving of all types of resources on the basis of their effective utilization, and satisfaction of increasing requirements of consumers.

Information support of competitiveness management should meet the general requirements of information support of marketing studies and general principles of design of the enterprise information system.

Decision-making in competitiveness management is based on the processes which are, as a matter of fact, information processes. Correctness and value of managerial decisions considerably depend on the information support.

Stages of the firm competitiveness management process in information context are shown in Fig. 7.7

Qualitative implementation of the management functions requires the following:

- Information about the managed object and its environment;
- Display means;
- Connections between the user activities and response of the managed object;
- Possibilities of unequivocal implementation of management action;
- Feedback;
- Management objectives.

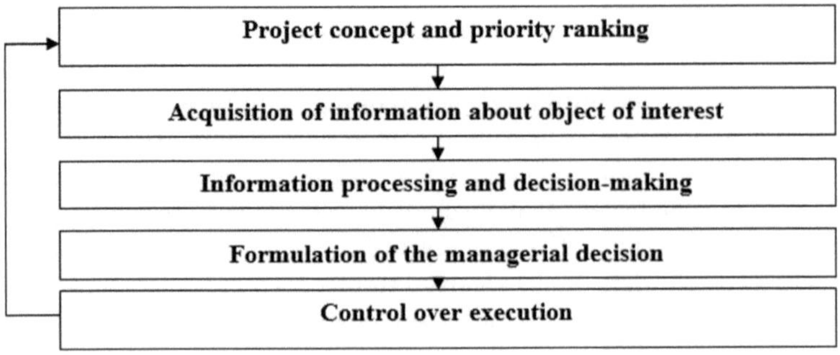

Fig. 7.7 Stages of the firm competitiveness management

Fulfillment of these conditions in the course of development of information system for competitiveness management predetermines designing of qualitative human–computer interface. The important condition to identify the elements of such system is necessity of full satisfaction of the user information requirements for the purpose of his rational decision-making.

From the perspective of the data processing technology, designation of information system is determined as set of processes of formation of primary messages (collection, registration, data transmission), their transformation, selection, and delivery of information to the users of all levels of management.

Top-priority goal of the information support of the firm competitiveness management is creation of the information system in order to:

- Process, filter, and pack information quickly and rationally;
- Forward the information as needed at the right time and place in a proper way;
- Identify the sources of information and the users' rights at every level.

The functional diagram of the information system for competitiveness management is presented in Fig. 7.8.

Development of information system for the firm competitiveness management includes three stages:

- Development of methodology for collection of the necessary information about the object or process of interest;
- Creation of the information file;
- Transformation of available data.

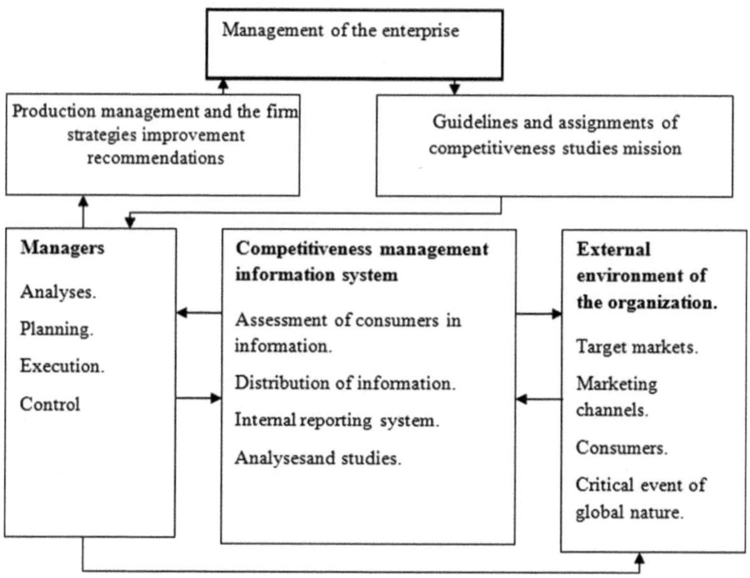

Fig. 7.8 Information system for competitiveness management

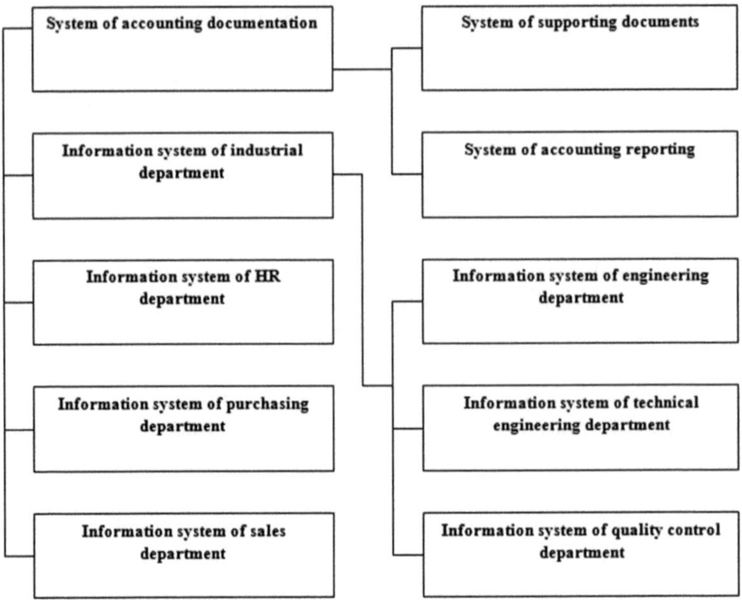

Fig. 7.9 Structure of the system of internal information

The system of internal reporting contains the enterprise data in the form of accounting and statistic reporting, and the online industrial, scientific, and technical information (Fig. 7.9).

Besides, it is necessary to organize monitoring of external environment which considerably influences decision-making processes concerning competitiveness management of the firm. Competitiveness monitoring system brings together data on the enterprise external environment concerning:

- Market and its infrastructure;
- Behavior of buyers, suppliers, and competitors;
- Measures of state regulation of the market mechanisms;
- Exchange rate;
- Market shares of the enterprise and its competitors, etc.

This information is accumulated in published periodic and special editions, statistics collections, and market reviews of commercial research organizations. The similar information is also collected by experts in the field of competitiveness management or from allied areas of competence by means of visiting exhibitions and conferences, carrying out of negotiations and business meetings, etc.

Research stages of the firm competitiveness are formed on the basis of this information (Fig. 7.10).

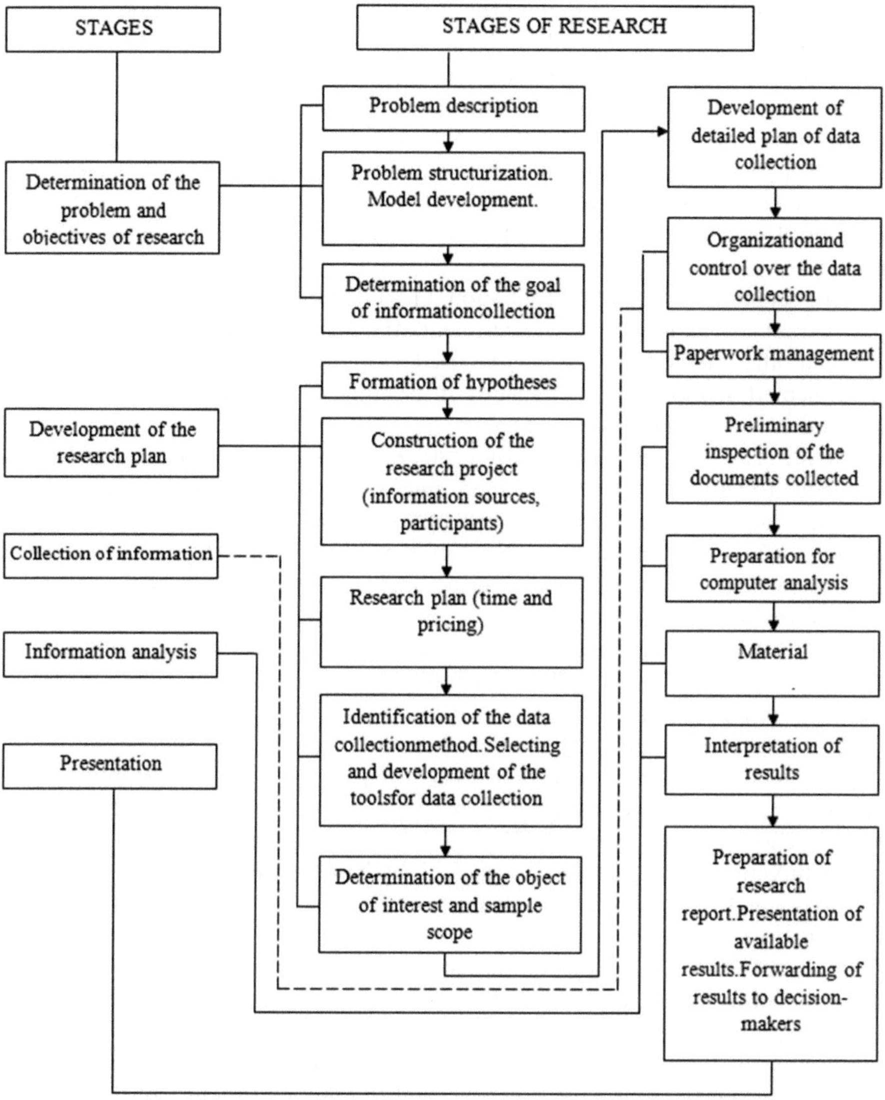

Fig. 7.10 Research process of the firm competitiveness

The basic elements of the research plan are development and pilot test of theoretical hypotheses, and identification and substantiation of their cause-and-effect links. Hypotheses and models describing the situation predetermine possible sources of information; however, in order to receive full and reliable information, it is necessary to have well-thought concept and detailed plan of the data collection.

In the course of development of the data collection plan, it is essential to decide upon many questions with alternative answers: full or selective, disposable or reusable, single-purpose or multipurpose research, and data collection forms and tools. Besides, there is a need to decide upon the source information—already available data or new information. At this phase of research, it is necessary to specify required time and cost of works for the manager to make a decision on the research in the field of competitiveness and consideration of organizational questions. The change of quantitative and qualitative correlations between separate phenomena of activities of industrial object managed should not be more expensive than the effect received from consideration of these correlations in the management process.

For reception of required information, the following methods are used: opinion poll, expert advice, monitoring, experiment, trial marketing, automatic data recording, and other methods. There may be used a closed system of receiving information, named marketing intelligence. It is important to prevent violation of legislation and commercial ethics too.

At the stage of data analysis, it is necessary to have them compressed for convenient analysis. In so doing, there may be used the following functions of data transformation: generalization, conceptualization, communication, and extrapolation. Afterward, statistical analysis of the data with the help of descriptive, derivation, forecast analysis and also the analysis of distinctions and ties should be performed.

At the stage of presentation, there is a preparation of research report and its handover to decision-makers. The structure of research report should correspond to customer requirements.

The systems of internal accounts and monitoring of competitiveness level are implemented by means of the databases covering all available current information, and system of researches in the field of competitiveness—by means of banks of models and banks of methods. Thus, the basic components of the information competitiveness management system are databases, banks of models, banks of methods, and the system of technical means of communication for their coordination.

As stated above, designing of information support of researches in the field of the firm competitiveness should be carried out on the basis of the general principles of designing information system based on the model of business, i.e., on schematic description of the enterprise activity without minor details, so that it could be possible to formalize business functions and to regulate structure of the business processes within the enterprise; to determine acceptable and inacceptable sequence of actions of executors working with this information system; and to fix logic correlations of data according to causing sequence of coordinated changes as a result of any information alteration.

The enterprise information system as a business model exists in two forms. In the course of creation and verification of the competitiveness management information system, it is convenient to present it in the form of schemes and verbal descriptions, and in practice—in the form of semantic equivalent set of program modules. Equivalence of both forms guarantees the use of modeling tools which make it possible, based upon time-proved methodology of developing models, to reflect the problem logic in a graphic way and to receive ready schemes of the databases and the model program code at the output. Discrepancies in model presentations are unacceptable neither in the course of creation of information system nor in the course of alteration. Therefore, the instrument of modeling should be the only tool of influence on the program code during the entire life cycle of the information system.

Personal information systems form a basis of automation of the management functions on the basis of the primary information about the object, methods of preparation, making of optimum decisions, and experience of the employees. Thus, the user is an element of this information system thanks to advance interface and supports of intellectual functions. While working in the management system the user plays a role of the subject of conscious activity integrating the process of functioning of the information system elements with a view of management of the economic object. Therefore, a matter of principle during designing of the specified interaction shall be an approach when a person becomes the main point both from the point of view of implementation of the purposes and designation of the management system and from the point of view of activity of this person within its framework. Allowance must be made for the leading and creative role of the human being in the course of work and, in particular, in the course of formation and making of managerial decision. The human being processes information, makes decisions, and manipulates management bodies showing his personal properties (experience, intuition, qualification).

A special place in designing of the enterprise information management system should be taken by the software being the basis of interface of interaction of a human being and personal computer (PC). The software should expand possibilities of projected system and eliminate their negative attributes. Therefore, in the course of the software development, a special role of the human factor should be taken into account in the management system.

In the course of creation of automated workplaces, a task should be set for the development of the personal system, making it possible for the user to do the work which cannot be executed by the system (data input, analysis, decision-making). The projected system should provide support for the user, expressing the fact that the latter while receiving the final information should not normalize it, interpret, or select required data.

The process of development of the information system intended to solve a set of management problems at the industrial enterprise includes the following stages:

- identification of the future users of the information and their rank in the management system;
- research and the analysis of the users information requirements for the purpose of allocation of the necessary and sufficient volume of information for the enterprise management and its resources;
- selection of methods for meeting the users information requirements, i.e., definition of contours of the information system with allowances made for the terms of delivery of the information to users;

- determination of contents and structure of the databases for the enterprise management, research of correlation of separate files, periodicity of their formation, and updating;
- designing of technological process of the data processing providing the necessary information to a particular user on demand;
- development of materials (guidelines, methodical instructions, dictionaries, catalogues, etc.), and regulating the users' work in the course of their interaction with the information management system.

The information system requires considerable accuracy of measurements of parameters and high reliability of data processing. Besides, rather tough restrictions are caused by the nature of technological processes, forms of documentation, and document circulation established at the enterprise. The problem of information support of the enterprise competitiveness management should be solved with allowances made for the following aspects: organizational (principles of organization of the information system and interaction of its elements); technological (methods of the information processing and technology of implementation of these methods); and technical (possibilities of computer engineering and organizational techniques). An important problem for the users of all levels is the enterprise resource management aimed at enhancing its competitiveness and to its regulation in case of divergency from the estimated parameters. Therefore, the optimum organization of the information support is one of the major factors to determine efficiency of competitiveness management as a whole. The volume of information required by the user for execution of the specified work and for managerial decision-making characterizes its information requirement.

There should be different information in the system competitiveness management at different levels of managerial decision-making. The most complicated stage in the course of the information support designing is identification of information requirements of every user participating in the managerial decision-making. For implementation of the specified stage, it is necessary to carry out detailed elaboration of process of the enterprise use of resources; identification of the market segments and a circle of competitors and their possibilities; assessment of competitiveness level of the enterprise and production; identification of the circle of users engaged in planning, assessment and analysis of competitiveness, their rights, duties, and area of responsibility; assessment of information requirement of every user for solution of specific problems, i.e., development of documents forms and definition of terms of their representation to a particular user; and formation of information to be provided to the user on demand.

Assessment of the user requirements in information on the level of enterprise competitiveness should be based on in-depth study of external and internal environment and the processes of the enterprise use of resources aimed at enhancing competitiveness, as well as on consideration of management particularities of the said processes. Correctness of determination of the information requirement to the full extent specifies designing of automated workplace; technological process of information transformation; formation of resulting information; methods and terms of its use; and designing mathematical and software support for every automated workplace and information support as a whole.

The process of information system designing can be implemented in three stages. At the first stage, it is necessary to investigate processes of the primary data formation, to describe characteristics of their movement, to form quantitative assessments of documents flows, and to determine possibilities for automation of registration processes and collection and transmission of data. There is a need to examine all divisions of the enterprise engaged in assessment of information concerning analysis, forecasting of the enterprise competitiveness level, and use of resources aimed at competitiveness increase. This stage is intended to specify sufficient aggregates of the primary data necessary for the enterprise competitiveness management.

At the second stage, technological processes of the information transformation on the basis of the databases and messages of the basic level are projected; algorithms of assessment and forecast of the enterprise competitiveness, as well as optimum distribution of assets aimed at competitiveness increase, are developed; corresponding databases are formed; and modes of the information provision for the users are determined. This stage characterizes procedural level of the information system which is directly connected with the basic level and a complex of technical means.

At the third stage, methods of providing transformed data to the functional divisions of the enterprise are considered, and a possibility of meeting requirements of the users of all levels in the following information is determined by assessments of the enterprise competitiveness level reflecting quantitative and qualitative comparative characteristics relative to the enterprises' competitors; forecast results of competitiveness standards; data on the optimum distribution of the enterprise assets; data on the complex of organizational and economic measures, and decisions on competitiveness management for the purpose of its enhancement. On the basis of the said requirements to the information and the principle of competitiveness management, information system developed is the concept of information support of the enterprise competitiveness management (Fig. 7.11). The primary goal is creation of conditions for information rational processing and its provision to the user on demand with definition of the rights to use it. As may be seen from Fig. 7.11, a set of methods of processing external and internal information is required for the enterprise competitiveness management.

The external information enters into the enterprise information databases from various sources: periodicals, statistic collections, announcements of presentations, information databases, advertizing brochures, Internet, e-mail, laws and governmental decrees, questionnaires of experts, etc. The internal information is a result of functioning of the automated workplaces providing book keeping, marketing researches, technical preproduction, basic production management, management of inventory, finance, sales, etc.

As the process of automation of formulation and managerial decision-making cannot be provided by computer aids to the full extent, this work envisages human–computer interface technologies of information support in the processes of

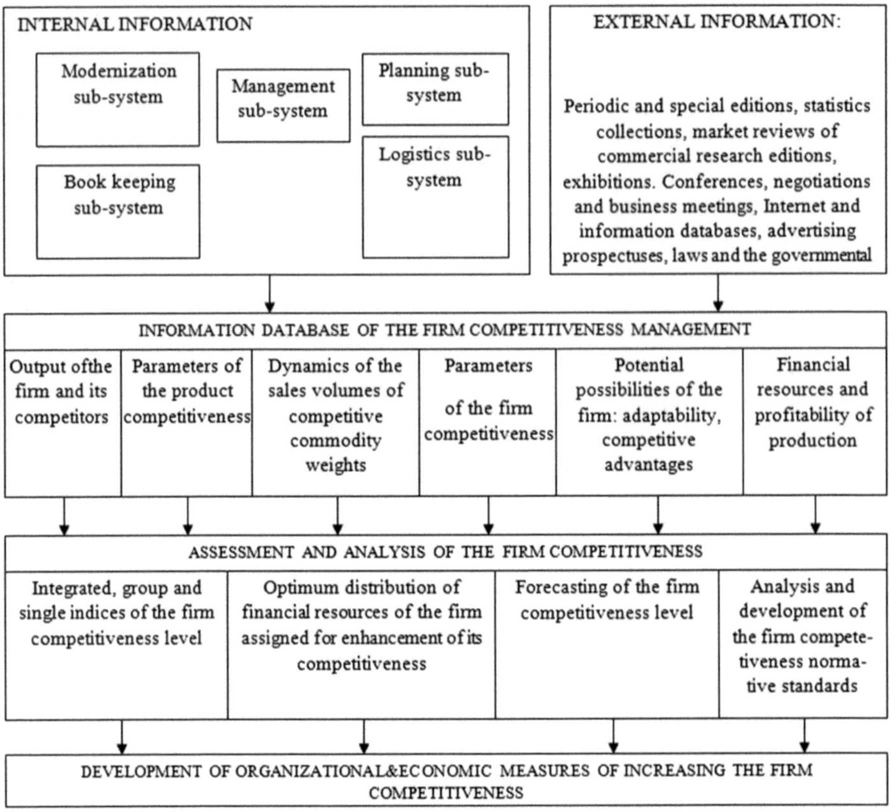

Fig. 7.11 Information support of the firm competitiveness management

managerial decision-making. This technology provides a combination of possibilities of a human being and computer in the information processing.

In other words, the computer techniques provide high efficiency of the information processing, its reliable storage in required volumes, fast access to the data, various ways of their display, and a convenient user interface with personal computer for executives and experts of the enterprise. All intellectual operations concerning information processing are carried out by the experts and decision-makers.

Technical aspect of information support is implemented in the form of local computer network of various orientations providing information support to the administration and experts, including their interaction among themselves. As a result, it is possible to reach high quality of information support of the enterprise competitiveness management. The software has high degree of adaptability giving a chance to adjust it for any industrial enterprise in the short-run.

At the automated workplace, the expert can carry out the following operations: to enter and correct the information; to evaluate quality of the input information; to make a decision on reception of additional information; to receive results of calculation of levels of the enterprise competitiveness and its factors; to forecast and identify tendencies of behavior of the enterprise competitiveness and its factors; and to make conclusions and decision on the basis of available information.

Preliminary information analysis makes it possible for the experts or administration to identify its incompleteness or discrepancy and make a decision to make up the deficiency. Organization of feedback is required in the course of preparation of decisions on elimination of discrepancy, incompleteness, and inauthenticity. In the course of amalgamation and storing of the saved information redundancy, elimination is carried out; and at the stage of generalization of data during their analysis and comparison, the expert makes a decision on sufficiency of the available information for further functioning of the system.

Process of designing the databases for information support of the enterprise competitiveness management includes the following stages: definition of the subject domain; creation of conceptual model of the subject domain; formation of the databases logic model; and development of its physical model. At the first stage, determined are borders of the problem, objects and information flows between them, and the structure of output reports of information support. As a result of analysis of the subject domain, a number of the basic objects are specified with their particular quantitative properties.

Within the framework of the stage of development of conceptual model established are all the objects of subject domain, their attributes, and correlations. The data elements, their correlations, and key elements are determined on the basis of conceptual requirements.

The next design of the databases stage is creation of its logic model and display of conceptual model onto one of the logic data models: relational, network, hierarchical, or combined. In the course of its development, it is necessary to decide upon which model is the best one for display of particular conceptual model of the subject domain. For designing of logic model of the databases, the relational data model which consists of a number of relations (tables) has been selected. This choice has been made because display of conceptual data model onto the relational model is rather simple.

The final stage of designing databases is creation of the physical model which is its "skeleton" and subject to filing. At this stage, we determine database physical parameters: distribution of records in the data storage, amount of the information blocks, characteristics of input–output, etc. The main criteria of the physical model are the memory required for storage of information and access time to the databases records.

Process of formation of the generalized analytical materials is intended for informing decision-makers on the state condition of the enterprise competitiveness in the form of special forms which are the basic information product.

The stage of information support of analysis and assessment of situation is intended for identification of correlations between the primary information and the generalized analytical material. At this stage, dynamics of the enterprise basic competitiveness indices is investigated, and recommendations concerning implementation of the said situations are provided.

Process of formation of the statistic database provides accumulation of results received at every stage of solution of this problem. After analyses of the current situation, department responsible for competitiveness management, from the whole set of primary information, specifies the data which will be suitable for the further identification of dynamics of the enterprise competitiveness and reception of its estimation levels. Process of forecasting the levels of enterprise competitiveness on the basis of the saved retrospective data is intended for their online use in analysis and assessment of the current situation for the purpose of identification of ways of perfection of the enterprise competitiveness management.

All the above processes are implemented by the experts according to Fig. 7.12 and make it possible to build a general functional scheme of the subject domain of the information support characterizing information flows in the course of preparation of managerial decisions according to competitiveness and stability of the enterprise. The system, on the basis of above-described processes, organizes continuous monitoring of primary information while it is analyzed, generalized, and estimated at the various stages of its life cycle.

Application in information support of the described methods of assessment, analysis, and forecasting of the enterprise competitiveness makes it possible to receive online qualitatively new information characterizing actual status of the enterprise and its competitors under conditions of market relations within the framework of transitional economy.

7.4 Construction of Economic and Mathematical Model of Competitiveness Assessment of the High-Technology Productive Industries

In this section, we build economic and mathematical model of competitiveness management of the high-technology productive industries. At the first stage, we consider a model of overlapping generations.

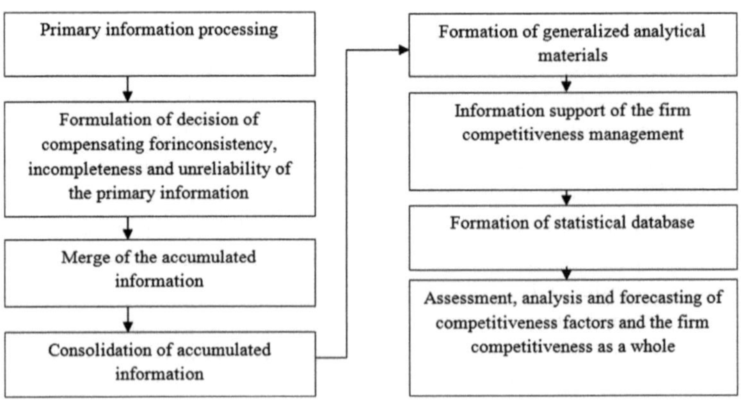

Fig. 7.12 Functional diagram of information formation for the firm competitiveness management

Let us assume that two generations of individuals both young and elderly live in each country at any time.

At the initial stage, the elderly generation lives only during one period and pays for its consumption from inherited capital. The young individual possesses one unit of labor. We receive that the youth period of the individual lasts one period of time during which he accumulates a part of his wages in order to purchase capital and finance his old age lasting one period of time too.

Let us consider n of the countries manufacturing two types of products under the same "know-how."

There is fixed number L^j of individuals of each generation in j country. The capital at the point of time t amounts to K_t^j. The first sector of economy makes consumption items; the second—means of production. By virtue of the fact, each sector consists of a set of goods, both imported to the country and exported from the country. Aggregate consumption unites all end products being useful for the individuals. Output of consumption items in j country at the time t is described

$$Q_{t,1}^j = \left(K_{t,1}^j\right)^{\theta}\left(L_{t,1}^j\right)^{1-\theta}, \tag{7.1}$$

where $K_{t,1}^j$—amount of capital and $L_{t,1}^j$—volume of labor. Total investments represent intermediate goods increasing the capital. Output of intermediate goods looks like

$$Q_{t,2}^j = \Gamma K_{t,2}^j, \tag{7.2}$$

where $K_{t,2}^j$—capital amount.

All goods and production factors are competitive, providing employment condition in each j country:

$$L_{t,1} \leq L^j \text{ and } k_{t,1}^j + k_{t,2}^j \leq k_t^j. \tag{7.3}$$

The capital amount in j country meets transition equation

$$k_{t,1}^j = Q_{t,2}^j + Z_t^j, \tag{7.4}$$

where Z_t^j—volume of imported means of production in j country at the moment t. We assume that the capital is completely depreciated, and it corresponds to the fact that one period of time corresponds to employment history of the individual. Nevertheless, we believe that the reproduced production factor is the physical accumulated capital, in which individual and public levels of the income coincide.

The individual of j country born at the point of time 0 has preferences

$$u^{j,0}\left(c_1^{j,0}\right) = \log c_1^{j,0} \tag{7.5}$$

And the individual born at the point of time $t \geq 1$—utility function

$$u^{j,t}\left(c_1^{j,t}, c_{t+1}^{j,t}\right) = (1 - \sigma^j)\log c_t^{j,t} + \sigma^j \log c_{t+1}^{j,t}, \tag{7.6}$$

where $c_t^{j,s}$—consumption at the moment t of the individual born at the point of time s in j country, σ^j—maximum inclination to savings. As may be inferred from (7.6), the norm of savings does not depend on the actual interest rate.

Let us designate $P_{t,i}$ maximum cost i of goods in t period and τ_i^j total tariff rate from declared price of i goods in j country. Then $\tau_i^j P_{t,i}$—price of i goods in the home market.

Let $P_{1,1} \equiv 1$, $p_t \equiv \frac{P_{t,1}}{P_{t,2}}$—relative world price for the consumption goods in t периоде, $1 + i_{t+1} \equiv \frac{P_{t,1}}{P_{t+1,1}}$—actual world interest rate in transition from t period to $(t+1)$ period.

Every enterprise in sector $i = \{1, 2\}$ seeks to maximize its income in every period, choosing the volumes of invested capital and labor. We will designate W_t^j and R_t^j rates of wages and rent accordingly in j country in t period, $k_{t,1}^j$—relation of capital to labor in the first sector. Under conditions of the market equilibrium, we have production factor

$$\tau_1^j P_{t,1} \theta \left(k_{t,1}^j\right)^{\theta - 1} \leq R_t^j \quad \text{and} \quad \tau_2^j P_{t,2} \Gamma \leq R_t^j. \tag{7.7}$$

Inequalities (7.7) are turned into equalities if the output is strictly positive. Inequality is met:

$$\tau_1^j P_{t,1}(1 - \theta)\left(k_{t,1}^j\right)^{\theta} \leq W_t^j, \tag{7.8}$$

which is also turned into equality if the output of consumption items is strictly positive. If outputs of consumption items and means of production are strictly positive, then from (7.7) it follows that

$$k_{t,1}^j = \left(\frac{\theta \tau^j p_t}{\Gamma}\right)^{\overline{\theta - 1}}, \tag{7.9}$$

where $\tau^j \equiv \frac{\tau_1^j}{\tau_2^j}$— relative level of protection of the first sector in j country. We notice that (7.9) is a standard connection between domestic relative prices and accumulation of resources between the sectors.

Let us describe preferences of individuals. The elderly individual in j country in the 1st period chooses $c_1^{j,0}$ to maximize (7.5) with allowances made for budgetary restriction

$$\tau_1^j c_1^{j,0} \leq R_1^j k_1^j, \tag{7.10}$$

where k_1^j—amount of capital per one worker in j country. Inequality (7.10) may be explained as follows: the elderly individual during the 1st period gets consumption goods under the local price, and he receives income from rent. Each young individual possessing one unit of labor, chooses such pair $\left(c_t^{j,t}, c_{t+1}^{j,t}\right)$ to maximize (7.6) with allowances made for restriction

$$\left(\tau_1^j P_{t,1} c_t^{j,t} + P_{t+1,1} c_{t+1}^{j,t}\right) \leq W_t^j. \tag{7.11}$$

During each period, the young individual gets production means to provide his old age.

From utility function (7.5) and budgetary restriction follows

$$c_1^{j,0} = \frac{R_1^j k_1^j}{\tau_1^j}, \tag{7.12}$$

And from (7.6) and (7.11)

$$\left(c_t^{j,t}, c_{t+1}^{j,t}\right) = \left(\frac{(1-\sigma^j)W_t^j}{\tau_1^j P_{t,1}}, \frac{\sigma^j W_t^j}{\tau_1^j P_{t,1}}\right). \tag{7.13}$$

7.4.1 Balanced Ways of Growth

Let us designate $W_t = \left(W_t^1, \ldots, W_t^n\right)$ and $R_t = \left(R_t^1, \ldots, R_t^n\right)$ of the vector of rates of wage and a rent accordingly for all the countries during t period, $\lambda^j = \frac{L^j}{\sum_{i=1}^{n} L^i}$ a population share in j country. Then consumption and investments into economy in all the countries per one worker look like accordingly $c_t = \sum_{i=1}^{n} \lambda^j \left(c_t^{j,t-1} + c_t^{j,t}\right)$ and $q_t = \sum_{i=1}^{n} \lambda^j \frac{Q_{t,2}^j}{L^j}$.

Let us assume that provision of goods requires fiscal tariffs which are small enough relative to the national income in the majority of the modern industrial countries and practically do not influence financial and monetary policy. We also believe that redistribution of fiscal tariffs does not break consumption but influences savings and rates of growth.

Let us designate $\tau = \left(\tau_1^1, \tau_2^1, \ldots, \tau_1^n, \tau_2^n\right)$ vector of consumption and investments tariffs. Then an equilibrium condition of world economy will correspond to a set of prices $\{(P_{t,1}, P_{t,2}, W_t, R_t)\}_{t=1}^{\infty}$ and total volumes $\{(c_t, q_t)\}_{t=1}^{\infty}$, such that:

formulas (7.1), (7.2), and (7.3) describe restrictions on production and resources for each of the countries ;
formulas (7.12) and (7.13) characterize preferences in consumption of each individual;
formulas (7.7) and (7.8) connect the price and intensity of production factors;
formula (7.4) describes the law of capital movement in each of the countries under the set initial capital $(K_1^1, \ldots, k_1^n)$.

The balanced way of growth will be considered as equilibrium for world economy if the rate of growth of gross national product of all the countries is identical. Then $k_t = \sum_{j=1}^{n} \lambda^j k_t^j$—capital per one worker in t period. Under the balanced way of capital, growth per each worker does not depend on time.

As tariffs are constant in time,

$$P_{t,2} = \Gamma P_{t+1,2}, \tag{7.14}$$

where Γ—marginal efficiency of investments. Thus, decrease in the current price for production means is determined by maximum change of the capital amount between periods t and $t+1$.

Connection between savings and investments can be written down in the following way:

$$\sum_{j=1}^{n} \lambda^j \sigma^j W_t^j = \sum_{j=1}^{n} \lambda^j \tau_2^j P_{t,2} k_{t+1}^j. \tag{7.15}$$

From this equation, one can see that the individual who was born in t period spends share σ^j of the income for purchase of capital. From formulas (7.7), (7.8), (7.9), and (7.14) it follows, that the formula (7.15) can be turn into the following ratios between the rate of capital growth G and the interest rate:

$$G \equiv \frac{k_{t+1}}{k_t} = \left(\frac{p_t}{p_{t-1}}\right)^{\frac{1}{1-\theta}} = \left(\frac{\Gamma}{1+i_t}\right)^{\frac{1}{1-\theta}}, \tag{7.16}$$

As the marginal efficiency of investments is invariable and equal to Γ, the growth can be achieved only in case of reduction of the interest rate and absorption of increasing outflow of the capital by the enterprises.

From formulas (7.8), (7.9), (7.13), and (7.16), it is possible to write down the volume of consumption items m_t^j imported by j country:

$$m_t^j = \left(\frac{p_t \tau^j \theta}{}\right)^{\frac{1}{1-\theta}} \left((1-\theta)\sigma^j \frac{\Gamma}{G} - \Phi^j\right), \tag{7.17}$$

Where $\Phi^j \equiv (1-\sigma^j)(1-\theta) > 0$. We designate $M_t(\tau, G) \equiv \sum_{j=1}^{n} \lambda^j m_t^j$ superfluous demand for imported goods. Then condition of the market balance relative to consumption goods in t period will be

$$M_t(\tau, G) = \left(\frac{p_t \theta}{\Gamma}\right)^{\frac{1}{1-\theta}} \sum_{j=1}^{n} \lambda^j (\tau^j)^{\frac{1}{1-\theta}} \left((1-\theta)\sigma^j \frac{}{G} - \Phi^j\right) = 0. \tag{7.18}$$

It is important to note that the equation (7.18) does not depend on P_t—relative world price for consumption products, i.e., the market will be balanced at any value of P_t, and the tariffs will not depend on trade conditions. On the contrary, from formula (7.16), one can see that change of conditions of trade leads to essential growth of the capital. Having solved (7.18) relative to rate of growth:

$$G = \frac{(1-\theta)\sum_{j=1}^{n} \lambda^j (\tau^j)^{\frac{\theta}{1-\theta}} \sigma^j}{\sum_{j=1}^{n} \lambda^j (\tau^j)^{\frac{\theta}{1-\theta}} \Phi^j}, \tag{7.19}$$

Let us notice that G is increasing relative to marginal efficiency of investments function and smooth function relative to any tariff of the country. We receive that tariffs for consumption goods are equivalent to the export rate of production means.

In conclusion of this section, we notice that $1 + i_t = \frac{}{G^{1-\theta}}$, i.e., under the balanced mode of growth, the actual interest rate is constant and is more than the rate of the growth of consumption in the world G^θ.

7.4.2 Dynamics of Output Growth

We investigate the connection between output of high-technology production and savings process in a separate country.

Let us substitute (7.19) in (7.17):

$$m_t^j = \frac{\sum_{j=1}^{n} \lambda^i (\tau^i)^{\frac{\theta}{1-\theta}} (\sigma^j \Phi^i - \sigma^i \Phi^j)}{\sum_{j=1}^{n} \lambda^i (\tau^i)^{\frac{\theta}{1-\theta}} \sigma^i} \left(k_{t,1}^j\right)^{\theta}. \tag{7.20}$$

Let us consider a balance case under free trade. Then $\tau^i = 1, \Phi^j \equiv \theta + \sigma^j (1 - \theta)$ for all j. We designate $\widetilde{\sigma} = \sum_{i=1}^{n} \lambda^i \sigma^i$ an average norm of savings. Then the equation (7.20) will become $m_t^j = \theta \left(k_{t,1}^j\right)^{\theta} \frac{\sigma^i - \tilde{\sigma}}{\tilde{\sigma}}$.

Let us make definition of static and dynamic creation of trade. As the import of j country depends on its tariffs and rate of the capital growth in the world, we differentiate (7.17) and receive

$$\frac{dm^j/m^j}{d\tau^j/\tau^j} = \frac{dm^j/m^j}{d\tau^j/\tau^j} + \frac{dm^j/m^j}{dG/G} \frac{dG/G}{d\tau^j/\tau^j} \tag{7.21}$$

The first composed in the left part determines static creation of trade, whereas the second—dynamic.

7.4.3 Model of Endogenous Growth

Let us consider the model describing behavior N_t of household and N_t of the enterprises, the number of which depends on period t as $N_{t+1} = nN_t$ where $n \geq 1$ —constant speed of increasing number of subjects and N_0 is set. Household will be designated by index h, and the enterprise—index f.

7.4.3.1 Household

Function of utility of housekeeping h is separable in time and looks like

$$E_0 \sum_{t=0}^{\infty} \beta^t U\left(C_t^h\right), \quad h = 1, \ldots, N_t, \tag{7.22}$$

where E_0—conditional mathematical expectation, C_t^h—consumption of housekeeping h during t, $0 < \beta < 1$—interest rate. Utility function is increasing and bent, and it meets Inada condition. We write down function of utility in the form of CRRA (Constant Relative Risk Aversion)

$$U_t = \frac{\left(C_t^h\right)^{1-\sigma}}{1-\sigma}, \quad h = 1, \ldots, N_t, t = 0, 1, \ldots, \tag{7.23}$$

Где $1/\sigma$ $(\sigma > 1)$—marking time elasticity of replacement.

Each household h during period t makes savings I_t^h and receives income from interest rate $r_t K_t^h$, where r_t—income per capital and K_t^h—private capital at the beginning of period t. In each period t, there is one unit allocated for work u_t^h and education e_t^h:

$$u_t^h + e_t^h = 1,\ h = 1, \ldots, N_t, t = 0, 1, \ldots \tag{7.24}$$

Household h also possesses human capital H_t^h for which it receives wages $\omega_t u_t^h H_t^h$ where ω_t—wage rate, and $u_t^h H_t^h$—effective work. Finally, household h receives dividends Π_t^h from the enterprises. Thus, budgetary restriction can be written down in the form of

$$C_t^h + I_t^h = r_t K_t^h + \omega_t u_t^h H_t^h + \Pi_t^h, \quad h = 1, \ldots, N_t, t = 0, 1, \ldots \tag{7.25}$$

The value of private physical and human capital at the beginning of the next period is calculated under formulas

$$K_{t+1}^h = \left(1 - \sigma^k\right) K_t^h + I_t^h, \quad h = 1, \ldots, N_t, t = 0, 1, \ldots \tag{7.26}$$

$$H_{t+1}^h = \left(1 - \sigma^k\right) H_t^h + B_t \left(e_t^h H_t^h\right)^\theta \left(\overline{H}_t\right)^{1-\theta}, \quad h = 1, \ldots, N_t, t = 0, 1, \ldots \tag{7.27}$$

where $0 \le \sigma^k,\ \sigma^k \le 1$—constant norms of amortization of private physical and human capital accordingly. The second summand on the right side of equality (7.27) can be interpreted as a volume of "new" human capital created during t period: B_t—capital productivity ratio, $e_t^h H_t^h$—household effective human capital h, $\overline{H}_t$—value of the human capital averaged by households, θ—parameter of efficiency of the human capital.

Let us consider that the market prices and cumulative results are set, and households are in the competitive environment. Thus, it is necessary to find such $\left\{C_t^h, u_t^h, e_t^h, I_t^h, K_{t+1}^h, H_{t+1}^h\right\}_{t=0}^{\infty}$ for each household to maximize (7.22) with allowances made for restrictions (7.24)–(7.27) and initial conditions for two markets and two conditions of productivity.

Condition of optimum consumption looks like

$$\Lambda_t^a = \left(K_t^h\right)^{-\sigma}, \quad h = 1, \ldots, N_t, t = 0, 1, \ldots \tag{7.28}$$

because latent cost Λ_t^a connected with (7.25) is equal to the maximum value of consumption during period t.

Euler equation for private physical capital K_{t+1}^h

$$\Lambda_t^a = \beta E\left[\Lambda_{t+1}^a \left(r_{t+1} + 1 - \delta^k\right)\right], \quad h = 1, \ldots, N_t, t = 0, 1, \ldots \tag{7.29}$$

reflects equality of the maximum values of the missed consumption during period

t and expected profit during period $t+1$ in case of investments into one unit of the physical capital during period t.

The equilibrium condition of the optimum time for education e_t^h looks as follows:

$$\Lambda_t^b = \frac{\Lambda_t^a \omega_t H_t^h}{B_t \theta \left(e_t^h\right)^{\theta-1} \left(H_t^h\right)^{\theta} \left(\overline{H}_t\right)^{\theta-1}}, \quad h = 1, \ldots, N_t, t = 0, 1, \ldots \tag{7.30}$$

and shows that latent cost Λ_t^b connected with (7.27) is equal to the maximum volume of education during t. In other words, this value is equal to the ratio of the maximum cost to the maximum income for the time of education.

From Euler equation for the private human capital,

$$\Lambda_t^b = E_t \beta \Lambda_{t+1}^a \omega_{t+1} \left(1 - e_{t+1}^h\right) + E_t \beta \Lambda_{t+1}^b \left[1 - \delta^h + B_{t+1} \theta \left(e_{t+1}^h\right)^{\theta-1} \left(H_{t+1}^h\right)^{\theta} \left(\overline{H}_{t+1}\right)^{\theta-1}\right],$$
$$h = 1, \ldots, N_t, t = 0, 1, \ldots \tag{7.31}$$

One can see that maximum cost of non-realized labor productivity during t amounts to the maximum wages during $t+1$, and the maximum income from investments during $t+1$ reduced to one unit of the human capital during period t.

7.4.3.2 Firms

Each enterprise f produces Y_t^f units of homogeneous end product, thus using K_t^f units of the private physical capital and $u_t^f H_t^f$ units of effective productive force. Thus, production function for enterprise f can be written down in the form of

$$Y_t^f = A_t \left(K_t^f\right)^{\alpha} \left(u_t^f H_t^f\right)^{1-\alpha}, \quad f = 1, \ldots, N_t, t = 0, 1, \ldots \tag{7.32}$$

where A_t—level used by all the enterprises of neutral technology according to Hicks, $0 < \alpha < 1$—efficiency index of the private capital, and $(1 - \alpha)$—efficiency index of labor productivity.

Let us have a case of fixed prices and total output of each of the enterprises. Then for (7.32), maximization enterprise f should choose such K_t^f and $u_t^f H_t^f$ to maximize profit function

$$\Pi_t^f = Y_t^f - r_t K_t^f - \omega_t u_t^f H_t^f, \quad f = 1, \ldots, N_t, t = 0, 1, \ldots \tag{7.33}$$

From corresponding conditions of the first order it follows that the enterprise will continue to employ workers and to increase its capital until it reaches rate of wages ω_t and rate of rent r_t accordingly:

$$\frac{(1-\alpha)Y_t^f}{u_t^f H_t^f} = \omega_t, \quad f = 1, \ldots, N_t, t = 0, 1, \ldots \tag{7.34}$$

and

$$\frac{\alpha Y_t^f}{K_t^f} = r_t, \quad f = 1, \ldots, N_t, t = 0, 1, \ldots \tag{7.35}$$

In conclusion, we point out that in the assumption of constant scale of production, the costs of production factors completely "eat" profit from output—$Y_t^f = r_t K_t^f + \omega_t u_t^f H_t^f$.

7.4.3.3 Decentralized Competitive Balance

Decentralized competitive balance is reached, if:

- Households and enterprises maximize above production functions taking into consideration that the prices and output aggregate volume are set;
- All boundary conditions are met;
- $$\sum K_t^h = \sum K_t^f, \quad \sum (1-e_t^h)H_t^h = \sum u_t^f H^f, \quad \sum \Pi_t^h = \sum \Pi_t^f = 0.$$

Let us designate $X_t = N_t H_t^h = N_t H_t^f$, where N_t—the number of households and the number of enterprises in period t, and $\overline{X}_t = X_t / N_t$—the value of one subject where $X_t \equiv (Y_t, C_t, I_t, K_t, H_t)$. Then we reduce the values to one unit of the human capital, for example, $x_t \equiv \overline{X}_t / \overline{H}_t$ and may also $y_t \equiv \overline{X}_{t+1} / \overline{H}_t$—speed of the human capital growth. With allowances made for the introduced designations and known $\{r_t, \omega_t\}_{t=0}^{\infty}$, we receive the following decentralized competitive balance:

$$\begin{aligned}
&y_t = c_t + n\gamma_t k_{t+1} - (1-\delta^k)k_t, \; t=0,1,\ldots,\\
&y_t = A_t(k_t)^\alpha (1-e_t)^{1-\alpha}, \; t=0,1,\ldots,\\
&n\gamma_t = 1-\delta^h + B_t(e_t)^\theta, \; h=1,\ldots,N_t, t=0,1,\ldots,\\
&\lambda_t^a = (e_t)^{-\sigma}, \; t=0,1,\ldots,\\
&\lambda_t^a = \beta(\gamma_t)^{-\sigma} E_t\left[\lambda_{t+1}^a\left(\alpha\frac{y_{t+1}}{k_{t+1}}\right) + 1 - \delta^k\right], \; t=0,1,\ldots,\\
&\lambda_t^b = \frac{(1-\alpha)y_t}{B_t(1-e_t)\theta(e_t)^{\theta-1}}, \; t=0,1,\ldots,\\
&\lambda_t^b = \beta(\gamma_t)^{-\sigma}\left\{E_t\left[(c_{t+1})^{-\sigma}(1-\alpha)y_{t+1}\right] + E_t\lambda_{t+1}^b\left[1-\delta^h + B_{t+1}\theta(e_{t+1})^\theta\right]\right\}, \; t=0,1,\ldots,
\end{aligned} \tag{7.36}$$

where λ_t^a and λ_t^b—modified latent costs. The system (7.36) containing 7 equations with 7 unknowns $(\gamma_t, y_t, c_t, e_t, k_{t+1}, \lambda_t^a, \lambda_t^b)$ describes autoregressive process under analyses.

7.4.3.4 High-Technology Production Efficiency

Under the said initial data, neutral productivity A_t according to Hicks and productivity of human capital B_t are casual processes which meet the following relations:

$$\begin{aligned} A_t &= A^{(1-p^a)} A_{t-1}^{p^a} e^{\varepsilon_t^a}, \quad t = 0, 1, \ldots, \\ B_t &= B^{(1-p^b)} B_{t-1}^{p^b} e^{\varepsilon_t^b}, \quad t = 0, 1, \ldots, \end{aligned} \tag{7.37}$$

where $A, B > 0$—constants, $0 < p^a, p^b < 1$—parameters of autoregressive process, ε_t^a and ε_t^b—independent values, equally distributed casual economic shocks with zero average and dispersions σ_a^2 and σ_b^2 accordingly.

It is worthwhile to note that introduction of innovations into the index of cumulative factorial productivity influences efficiency of both the labor productivity and the capital, while occurrence of shocks in the human capital leads to the changes only, namely to the growth of labor productivity.

7.4.3.5 Model Solution

Let us write down the solution of linear stationary model of the decentralized competitive balance in the matrix form

$$y_t = \widetilde{Z}_t \delta_t, \quad t = 0, 1, \ldots, \quad \delta_{t+1} = \widetilde{T} \delta_t + \widetilde{R} \varepsilon_{t+1}, \quad t = 0, 1, \ldots, \tag{7.38}$$

where $y_t = [\hat{y}_t\ \hat{c}_t\ \hat{u}_t]$, $\delta_t = [\hat{k}_t\ \hat{a}_t\ \hat{b}_t]$, $\hat{x}_t = \ln(x_t/x)$, x—steady value x_t, $\hat{y}_t$—variable parameter, $\hat{c}_t$ and $\hat{u}_t$—variables for which values vary in steps, $\hat{a}_t$ and $\hat{b}_t$—exogenous processes, $\widetilde{z}_t$ and $\widetilde{T}$—matrices containing convolutions of various parameters of the model, and $\widetilde{R}$—matrix consisting of zero and one; it supervises behavior of productivity shocks set by vector ε_{t+1}.

Let us continue research of the model we constructed and add in (7.38) errors VAR (1) (autoregressive vector), and we calculate likelihood function, using Kalman filter to the model, provided the human and physical capital, both types of technologies, and possible measurements errors are unobservable variables.

Let us add errors VAR (1)—a vector of dimension n to system (7.38)

$$\mu_{t+1} = A\mu_t + \nu_{t+1}, \quad \nu_{t+1} \sim N(0, \textstyle\sum), \quad t = 0, 1, \ldots, \tag{7.39}$$

Then we receive

$$y_t = \begin{pmatrix} \widetilde{Z} & I_n \end{pmatrix} \begin{pmatrix} \delta_t \\ \mu_t \end{pmatrix} = Z\alpha_t, \quad t = 0, 1, \ldots,$$
$$\alpha_{t+1} = \begin{pmatrix} \widetilde{T} & 0_{n\times n} \\ 0_{n\times n} & A \end{pmatrix} \alpha_t + \begin{pmatrix} \widetilde{R} & 0_{n\times n} \\ 0_{n\times 2} & I_n \end{pmatrix} \begin{pmatrix} \varepsilon_{t+1} \\ v_{t+1} \end{pmatrix} = T\alpha_t + R\eta_{t+1}, \quad t = 0, 1, \ldots, \tag{7.40}$$

where

$$\eta_{t+1} \sim N(0, Q), \ Q = \begin{pmatrix} \sigma_a^2 & 0 & 0_{1\times n} \\ 0 & \sigma_b^2 & 0_{1\times n} \\ 0_{n\times 1} & 0_{n\times 1} & \sum \end{pmatrix}, \quad t = 0, 1, \ldots, \tag{7.41}$$

7.4.3.6 Kalman Filter

Kalman filter should be applied in two steps:

Step one

$$\begin{aligned} a_{t|t-1} &= Ta_{t-1}, \quad t = 0, 1, \ldots, \\ P_{t|t-1} &= TP_{t-1}T' + RQR', \quad t = 0, 1, \ldots \end{aligned} \tag{7.42}$$

Step two

$$\begin{aligned} v_t &= y_t - Za_{t|t-1}, \quad t = 0, 1, \ldots, \\ F_t &= ZP_{t|t-1}Z', \quad t = 0, 1, \ldots, \\ K_t &= TP_{t|t-1}Z'F_t^{-1}, \quad t = 0, 1, \ldots, \\ a_t &= Ta_{t|t-1} + K_t v_t, \quad t = 0, 1, \ldots, \\ P_t &= (T - K_t Z)P_{t|t-1}(T - K_t Z)' + RQR', \quad t = 0, 1, \ldots \end{aligned} \tag{7.43}$$

where $a_0 = E(a_0)$ and P_0—initial parameters and v_t—forecast errors.

7.4.3.7 Function of Maximum Likelihood and Algorithm of Assessment

Let us write down the maximum likelihood function in the form of

$$p(y_{t,t=1,\ldots,T}|\psi) = \prod_{t=1}^{T} (2\pi)^{-0.5n} |F_t|^{-0.5} \exp\left(-0.5 v_t' F_t^{-1} v_t\right), \tag{7.44}$$

where ψ—vector of parameters to be estimated. For assessment of ψ, we use Metropolis-Hastings algorithm. New implementation ψ will be built on the assumption that

$$\psi_1 = \psi_0 + \xi, \quad \xi \sim N(0, \Xi), \tag{7.45}$$

where Ξ—covariance matrix.

It is worthwhile to note that conditions should be met:

$$\alpha \geq u, \quad u \sim U(0,1),$$

$$\alpha(\psi_1, \psi_0) = \min\left(\frac{p(y_{t,t=1,\dots,T}|\psi_1)\, p(\psi_1)}{p(y_{t,t=1,\dots,T}|\psi_0)\, p(\psi_0)}, 1\right), \tag{7.46}$$

where $p(\psi)$—aprioristic distribution is shown in Table 7.3.

Calculated values of parameter ψ are specified in Table 7.4.

This economic and mathematical model for assessment of hi-tech industries competitiveness makes it possible to evaluate quantitative parameters for particular high-technology industries. However, taking into consideration characteristic features of the high-technology industries, it is possible to formulate economic and mathematical model for qualitative competitiveness assessment of hi-tech industries on the basis of this model.

As it has already been noted, the basic feature of hi-tech production is a big share of financing of Research &Development. In turn, specificity of R&D financing consists in the fact that there is a certain delay in enhancement of the enterprise (firms) competitiveness. It is possible to use the following economic and mathematical model as a generalized qualitative model for competitiveness assessment of the high-technology industries. For qualitative competitiveness assessment of the said high-technology industry, we will use an integrated assessment of competitiveness index which is designated by C. This will assume numerical values. As we consider qualitative behavior of competitiveness indices in the model, this scale is nondimensional. Its economic meaning consists in the fact that negative values mean decrease in competitiveness of productive industry, and positive values—its increase. Functional dependence of integrated assessment of competitiveness indices looks like as follows:

$$C = \frac{\Phi^{-1}\left(\sum_{n=1}^{N} \Phi(\phi_n(C_1, C_2, \dots, C_M))(1-\tau_n)^{\gamma}\right)}{\sum_{n=1}^{N}\sum_{k=1}^{K(n)} F_k^n}$$

In this formula, we use the following designations of parameters:

N—number of enterprises in the industry.
$K(n)$—number of R&D for n-th enterprise.
F_k^n—financing of k-th measure for n-th enterprise of productive industry.
τ_n—nondimensional parameter characterizing delay of influence on competitiveness of R&D financing of n-th enterprise.
$\gamma > 0$—model parameter estimating influence of delay in the mathematical model.
C_n—particular characteristics of competitiveness of production and the enterprises of productive industry.

Table 7.3 Aprioristic values of parameters

Factor	Parameter	Limitation
Capital amount	α	(0.25, 0.5)
Interest rate	β	(0.965,0999)
K amortization rate	δ^k	(0.0114,0.0126)
H amortization rate	δ^h	(0.0043,0.0047)
Parameter of utility function	σ	(1,3)
Shock root-mean-square deviation A	σ^a	(0,0.05)
Shock root-mean-square deviation B	σ^b	(0,0.05)
External parameter	$(1-\theta)$	(0,1)
Parameter AR (1) for the process A_t	p_a	(0,1)
Parameter AR (1) for the process a B_t	p_b	(0,1)
Constant for process A_t	A	(0.238,0.263)
Constant for process B_t	B	(0.029, 0.032)
Growth in production N	n	(1,1.0042)
Characteristic values (VAR)	$\lambda_{\{i=1,2,3\}}$	$\max\lvert\lambda_i\rvert < 1$
Covariance	• Σ_{cc} Σ_{kk} • Σ_{yc} Σ_{yh} Σ_{ck}	
Model decision	There is a steady-state situation	
Growth in production H	γ (steady-state conditions)	(1.0037,1.0074)

ϕ_n—functional dependences of integrated index of competitiveness of n-th enterprise on production characteristics.

Φ—averaging function of competitiveness indices of separate enterprises.

This assessment of competitiveness of the high-technology industry can be used for qualitative assessment of productive industry competitiveness and for assessment of economic efficiency of the enterprises of this productive industry and a number of other applied economic problems.

Conclusions This chapter presents the elements of the firm competitiveness management system. One of the basic elements of the firm competitiveness management system is a management center integrating technical, computing or financial, and other resources at the firm's disposal.

This system of competitiveness management should take into consideration the functions and possibilities of the said management centers and a range of tasks concerning identification of the technical management systems with the structure of the system we build, and carry out functions of assessment and forecast of competitiveness on the basis of the simulation modeling, in order to consider various options of its dynamics in the short-run and medium-term periods. This system should be sufficiently flexible for online response to the changes of external and internal environment, expressly or by implication influencing its functioning and make allowances for the firm features: its organizational structure, productive industry where it functions, features of national legislation. Methodical toolkit

Table 7.4 Calculated values of parameter ψ

ψ_j	Average value	Dispersion	$\frac{Root-mean-square\ error}{\psi_j}$ %
α	0.41775	0.00341	0.00008
A	0.24634	0.00287	0.00012
B	0.03092	0.00058	0.00019
β	0.97028	0.00219	0.00002
δ^k	0.01179	0.00027	0.00023
δ^h	0.00449	0.00013	0.00029
n	1.00121	0.00096	0.00001
σ	1.99150	0.00470	0.00002
θ	0.51216	0.00280	0.00005
p_a	0.99425	0.00165	0.00002
p_b	0.99949	0.00041	0.00000
σ^a	0.00500	0.00007	0.00014
σ^b	0.01000	0.00000	0.00029
a_{yy}	– 0.09240	0.00251	0.00027
a_{cy}	– 0.12444	0.00245	0.00020
a_{yc}	0.16814	0.00401	0.00024
a_{cc}	– 0.14867	0.00184	0.00012
a_{uc}	– 0.17121	0.00474	0.00028
a_{yu}	– 0.12401	0.00183	0.00015
a_{uu}	– 0.00974	0.00040	0.00041
Σ_{yy}	0.00113	0.00014	0.00123
Σ_{cy}	0.00091	0.00027	0.00303
Σ_{uy}	– 0.00353	0.00019	0.00055
Σ_{cc}	0.00391	0.00062	0.00158
Σ_{cu}	– 0.00677	0.00035	0.00052
Σ_{uu}	0.02915	0.00093	0.00032

should be developed for effective work of competitiveness management system in order to perform monitoring of the firm development on the basis of multilevel system of indices, to plan economic activities, to forecast the basic indices of the firm activities, to operate the firm by weak signals and to diagnose online an adverse phenomena and events, etc. Multilevel system of indices should have input and output parameters of the system, parameters of the technical systems responding to change of input and output parameters of the system. It should also be taken into account that efficiency of the firm activities monitoring is determined by availability of the automated system including integrated databases on all aspects of the firm activities with application of modern information technologies. The information required for work by every Computer-Aided Management System (CAMS) should always be available online. The output information of every CAMS should be formed on the basis of integrated information space.

It is worthwhile to note that the information support of the firm competitiveness management system should meet general requirements to the information support of marketing researches and general principles of designing of the enterprise information system. Application of the methods of assessment, analysis, and forecast of the firm competitiveness in information support, described in this section, makes it possible to receive online qualitatively new information characterizing actual status of the firm and its competitors under conditions of market relations. Received information can be used in the economic and mathematical model of enhancing competitiveness of hi-tech productive industries present in this section.

8 Theoretical Approaches to Formation of the Systems of High-tech Industries Competitiveness Management

8.1 Structure of Competitiveness Management of the High-technology Industries

High-tech industry as well as any another productive industry represents a complex system of economic relations, and this system is characterized by various quantitative and qualitative parameters.

On the basis of current and forecast assessments of these parameters, management of the enterprises of hi-tech industries makes managerial decisions with a view of achievement of one or another of indices provided by strategic documents on development of these productive industries. Thus, assessment and influence on these parameters are carried out by means of various regulation tools.

Competitiveness is the basic economic category to characterize effectiveness of productive industry management system according to the said researches. Competitive power of enterprises determines their positions in domestic and foreign markets, creates image of the state, and as the final result, provides national safety of the state.

The most acute problems now are the issues arising from analysis of alternative solutions in the course of management of the complex objects.

The objects for consideration in this section are the firms (enterprises) of the hi-tech industry and their aggregate (productive industry, in our case—hi-tech industries).

Operations management of the specified objects is carried out at three levels (Fig. 8.1):

- State level
- Productive industry level
- Enterprise level.

The result of competitiveness management realized at the lower levels indirectly influences the higher levels, namely:

A. Chursin, Y. Makarov, *Management of Competitiveness*,
DOI 10.1007/978-3-319-16244-7_8

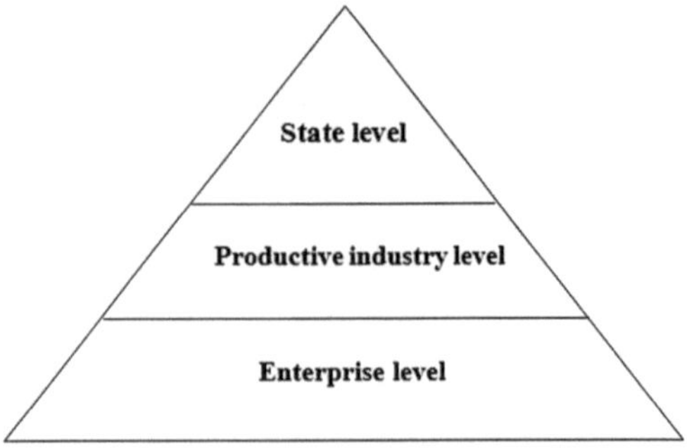

Fig. 8.1 Functional scheme of multilevel competitiveness management

- Productive industry is influenced not only by competitiveness management at the level of productive industry but also by competitiveness management at the level of separate enterprises;
- State standing is influenced not only by competitiveness management at the state level but also by competitiveness management at the level of separate productive industries and, hence, the separate enterprises.

At every level, each enterprise, each productive industry, and the state are influenced by external environment.

External influences include:

- For particular enterprise—activities of other enterprises, including the entities within the framework of competitiveness management;
- For particular productive industry—activities of other productive industries, including the branches within the framework of competitiveness management;
- For particular state—activities of other states, including the countries within the framework of competitiveness management.

Thus, there is an acute problem of development and implementation of such mechanisms of competitiveness management in volume sufficient enough for the level of competitiveness being under any possible external influences.

It is worthwhile to note that the setting of competitiveness management problem described above can be formulated within the framework of terminology of the general theory of large and complex dynamic systems.

We formalize a model by introducing required designations in Table 8.1.

Table 8.1 presents functional scheme describing activities of the state in the field of competitiveness management as a large and complex dynamic system; allowance must be made for the said designations.

Taking into consideration the question of creation of the competitiveness management system of productive industry, let us apply construction of criteria matrix for this multi-objective model.

Criteria matrix has columns—management loops—and lines—management levels.

Table 8.1 Designations for description of innovative activity of the state as a large and complex dynamic system

Designation	Description
	Level of enterprises
$N_{пред}$	Number of enterprises in productive industry
$X_n^{пред}$	$X_n^{пред}$ Number of quantitative parameters to evaluate activity within the framework of competitiveness management of *n*enterprise, $n = 1, \ldots, N_{пред}$
$x_n^{пред} = \left(x_{n_1}^{пред}, \ldots, x_{n,X_n^{пред}}^{пред}\right)$	Quantitative parameters to evaluate activities within the framework of competitiveness management of *n* enterprise, $n = 1, \ldots, N_{пред}$
$F_n^{пред}$	Number of quantitative parameters to evaluate external influences on *n* enterprise, $n = 1, \ldots, N_{пред}$
$f_n^{пред} = \left(f_{n_1}^{пред}, \ldots, f_{n,F_n^{пред}}^{пред}\right)$	Quantitative parameters to evaluate external influences on *n* enterprise, $n = 1, \ldots, N_{пред}$
$Y_n^{пред}$	Number of quantitative parameters to evaluate results of activities within the framework of competitiveness management of *n* enterprise, $n = 1, \ldots, N_{пред}$
$y_n^{пред} = \left(y_{n_1}^{пред}, \ldots, y_{n,Y_n^{пред}}^{пред}\right)$	Quantitative parameters to evaluate results of activity within the framework of competitiveness management of *n* enterprise, $n = 1, \ldots, N_{пред}$
	Level of productive industries
$N_{отр}$	Number of enterprises in productive industry
$X_n^{отр}$	Number of quantitative parameters to evaluate activity within the framework of competitiveness management of *n* industry, $n = 1, \ldots, N_{отр}$
$x_n^{отр} = \left(x_{n_1}^{отр}, \ldots, x_{n,X_n^{отр}}^{отр}\right)$	Quantitative parameters to evaluate activities within the framework of competitiveness management of *n* industry, $n = 1, \ldots, N_{отр}$
$F_n^{отр}$	Number of quantitative parameters to evaluate external influences on *n* industry, $n = 1, \ldots, N_{отр}$
$f_n^{отр} = \left(f_{n_1}^{отр}, \ldots, f_{n,F_n^{отр}}^{отр}\right)$	Quantitative parameters to evaluate external influences on *n* industry, $n = 1, \ldots, N_{отр}$
$Y_n^{отр}$	Number of quantitative parameters to evaluate results of activities within the framework of competitiveness management of *n* industry, $n = 1, \ldots, N_{отр}$
$y_n^{отр} = \left(y_{n_1}^{отр}, \ldots, y_{n,Y_n^{отр}}^{отр}\right)$	Quantitative parameters to evaluate results of activity within the framework of competitiveness management of *n* industry, $n = 1, \ldots, N_{отр}$
	Level of state
$X_n^{гос}$	Number of quantitative parameters to evaluate activity within the framework of the state competitiveness management
$x_n^{гос} = \left(x_{n_1}^{гос}, \ldots, x_{n,X_n^{гос}}^{гос}\right)$	Quantitative parameters to evaluate activities within the framework of the state competitiveness management
$F_n^{гос}$	Number of quantitative parameters to evaluate external influences on the state
$f_n^{гос} = \left(f_{n_1}^{гос}, \ldots, f_{n,F_n^{гос}}^{гос}\right)$	Quantitative parameters to evaluate external influences on the state
$Y_n^{гос}$	Quantitative parameters to evaluate the level of competitiveness management of the state

Taking into consideration that time factor in creation of the organizational and economic system plays rather essential role, the search of approaches to formation of criteria according to loops is supposed to be natural.

Accordingly, we proceed from the fact that there are three loops of management $U_i(i = 1, 2, 3)$ and three levels of management $V_i(i = 1,2,3)$.

Loops of competitiveness management:

U_1—Target long-term tasks of productive industry in the major directions of development;
U_2—Intermediate tasks within the framework of implementation of the long-term programs of innovative development;
U_3—Current plans providing achievement of the maximum target efficiency.

Levels of competitiveness management (Fig. 8.2):

V_1—Macro-level (level of productive industry management by the state);
V_2—Meso-level (program level of the enterprises industrial management);
V_3—Micro-level (competitiveness of the firm, production, and goods).

Managed vectors (according to the management levels):

X_1—complex of various classes with various types and generations of the systems;
X_2—various types and generations of the systems;
X_3—various generations of the systems.

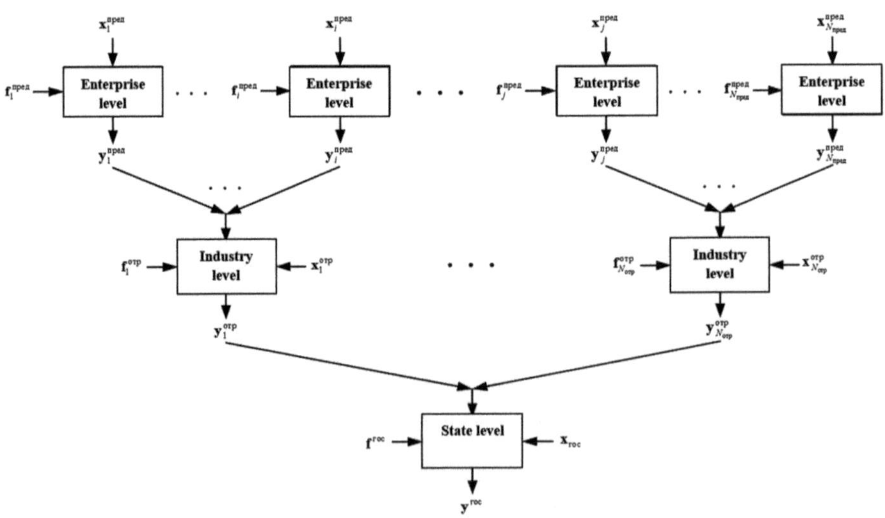

Fig. 8.2 Functional scheme describing innovative activity of the state as a large and complex dynamic system

This matrix of competitiveness management of production, enterprises, and high-technology productive industry shows a feedback process between competitiveness management and implementation of decisions and programs. Namely, the information collected during activities already carried out within the framework of the programs and strategy on development of productive industries is used in the course of strategy determination for the next stage and the program of development of competitiveness of production, enterprises, and productive industry as a whole.

Effective collection and analysis of the data during stage-by-stage fulfillment of competitiveness management program needs a developed and fast system of monitoring of innovative processes occurring in hi-tech industries.

A number of efficiency indices relative to activities in the field of innovations should be established to achieve accuracy of assessment of execution of declared purposes.

Selection criterions of such indices are:

- Maximum generality of the index and a possibility to monitor in dynamics the greatest changes of the index in the industry innovative sphere;
- Degree of approximation to the world experience of competitiveness assessment;
- Degree of correlation of indices among themselves;
- Compliance with the purposes of development of hi-tech industry;
- Availability of statistics concerning the selected indices of competitiveness assessment.

It should be noted that there are a number of parameters of competitiveness management of objects of all levels, which influence the whole system. The result of influence on the said parameters becomes known, thanks to the monitoring system, namely, change of a number of target integrated indices. Thus, it is possible to regard the system "Production—Firm—Industry" as a single object with inputs (adjustable parameters) and outputs (integrated indices). Such vision gives the right to pass over to cybernetic nature of competitiveness space and review its ability to self-regulation.

8.2 Application of Mathematical Simulation Modeling in the Course of Distribution of Resources Allocated for Development of Hi-tech Industries

In considering competitiveness of the system "Production—Enterprise—Industry" as a mathematical object, the organizational and economic system is regarded as a self-adjusted object of dynamic nature under the influence of external environment and domestic processes that make it possible to pass over to considering criterion models of competitiveness system.

Features Criterion Models in Distribution of Resources

Initial methodical basis for formation of models to develop organizational and economic system is the strategy on the basis of analysis of economic, technical, and other concepts of planning development of these systems.

As is known, there are a number of strategies of planning development of organizational and economic system:

- Strategy of permanent superiority over the level of requirement;
- Strategy of balance relative to the level of requirement;
- Strategy of rampant (spasmodic) development on the basis of intensive resource and information support;
- Flexible (combined) strategy providing superiority in development, balance and spasmodic development depending on the type of systems.

Criterion models of development of any system are subdivided according to the nature of resources distribution as follows:

Direct—to provide achievement of the maximum level of target efficiency (resources and development period are set; it is required to determine the plan for development of organizational and economic system X (t));

Inverse—to provide the minimum consumption of resources (target efficiency and the period of development of organizational and economic system are set; it is required to determine the plan of resources distribution C (t));

Intensive (spasmodic) development to provide anticipatory achievement of the maximum target efficiency (at the initial stage, the system effectiveness is lower than the set level).

While modeling various situations, it is possible to use statistic or dynamic models.

In statistic models, development of the optimum plan is fixed in one of the points of the planned segment (usually in the end of period T).

In dynamic models, indices of the optimum plan of development are fixed in a number of time interval points that makes it possible to determine plans for development of organizational and economic system more thoroughly.

In connection with strong influence of external environment factors and a variety of versions of development of industrial systems, it is possible to assert that consideration of ambiguous problems is pressing in this situation. But it should be noted that in connection with social and economic orientation of the most problems of single innovative system, unambiguous problems of development of organizational and economic system will be claimed too.

Specified problems and their value in control of development of organizational and economic system have the following features.

For statistic models of development, it is possible to specify four alternate versions of mathematical statement of the problem.

- Statistic unambiguous direct problem;
- Statistic ambiguous direct problem;
- Statistic unambiguous inverse problem;
- Statistic ambiguous inverse problem.

The ambiguous system can be demonstrated by means of the game-theoretical approach, which takes into consideration the interests of various players (parties).

The setting of statistic unambiguous direct problem should determine:

resources $C_x(T)$ allocated for planned development of organizational and economic system of parties x and for the period of T;
form and dimensionality of forecasting vector $Y(t)$;
such vector $X(T)$ which provides peak efficiency of the system in solution of typical operation

$$maxE(x),\ C_x =\ C_x(T).$$

In such statement of the problem, the criterion of efficiency is selected either for typical operation in the main situation or for full enumeration of situations of the basic plan, or for artificial limited set of situations, characteristic of the active plan. Additionally, there may be restrictions imposed on production possibilities, operational characteristics of organizational and economic system, etc. The indices of target efficiency of organizational and economic system are assumed to be known.

Statistic ambiguous direct problem is formulated as follows:

unlike conditions of the previous problem, vector $Y(t)$ is known, and resources $C_y(T)$, allocated by party y, are not known (they are estimated);
optimum vectors $X(T)$ and $Y\ (t)$ are determined; they provide $max_x min_y[E(x,\ y)]$ under restrictions $R(x) \leq\ 0$.

It should be pointed out that in two problems, the resources are set without their distribution according to the planned period, and optimization of solutions does not reflect consumption of resources; in this connection, the available solution cannot be regarded as optimum by economic criterion.

In statistic unambiguous inverse problem:

There should be selected criterion of target efficiency $E(x,\ y)$, and should be set its required value

$$E(x, y)\ = E_{set};$$

to set (forecasted) vector $Y(t)$;
to determine vector $X(T)$ providing optimum consumption with allowances made for distribution of certain shares for development, batch production, and operation of the systems by the time point T;

to determine minimum $C_x(T)$, and with allowances made for restriction $R(x) \leq 0$, results of this solution can be regarded as optimum.

Statistic ambiguous inverse problem unlike the previous problem:

determines both vector $Y(t)$ and vector $X(T)$, providing $min_y max_x(C_{Y(T)} – C_{X(T)})$ under additional restrictions $R(x) \leq 0$ и $R(y) \leq 0$;
sets criterion of target efficiency $E(x, y) = E_{set}$;
imposes some additional requirements to the system effectiveness (according to criteria of quality K_0);
uses criterion $\Delta C(T) = [C_y(T) - C_x(T)]$ which makes it possible to determine excess expenses resulted (to point $t = T$) according to the selected strategy in comparison with other alternate versions.

It should be pointed out that mathematical models of the last two alternate versions are formulated without accounting expenses of the parties by the end of the planned period and in this meaning, evidently, do not make it possible to receive optimum solution according to economic criterion.

As far as dynamic models are concerned, it is necessary to be limited to three alternate versions of mathematical setting of the problem:

Dynamic unambiguous direct problem;
Dynamic ambiguous direct problem;
Dynamic inverse problem (unambiguous or ambiguous).

The dynamic unambiguous direct problem has the following formulation:

to set (0, T) in the range of time and to set plan $Y(t)$ of the system development of the party and resources $C_x(T)$ for development of the system of party x);
to regard technical characteristics and economic indices of the system as known;
to determine optimum plan of development $X(T)$ with the system of differential or discrete equations of development

$$dX_i/dt = Q_i(X_i, U_i);$$

to determine optimum vector function of management $a(t) = \{U_i(t)\}$ and a corresponding optimum plan $X(T)$ providing the maximum value of efficiency criterion at the moment of time T,

$$maxE[X(T), Y(T)]$$

In this statement, the problem is alternative.

Dynamic ambiguous direct problem unlike dynamic unambiguous problem has the following features:

Vector $Y(t)$ is unknown and, hence, this vector should be determined along with $X(T)$:

Resources $[C_X(t); C_Y(t)]$ of parties x and y, allocated for the systems development, are set in the interval (0, T);

Differential (or discrete) equations of development are made

$$dX_i/d_t = Q_i(X_i, U_i),$$
$$dY_j/d_t = G_j(Y_j, v_j)$$

with corresponding initial conditions (where U_i, v_j —managing functions of the parties x and y, being changed in the closed areas);

optimum vector functions of management $U(t)$ and corresponding optimum values of development $x(t)$; $y(0)$, providing

$$max_u min_v E(T).$$

In two above types of dynamic problems, the resources are set in the form of time functions. It gives the chance to determine consumption (and distribution) of resources in period T of the system development and, hence, to receive the optimum solution according to economic criteria.

Dynamic inverse problem (unambiguous or ambiguous) unlike direct dynamic problems in general can be formulated in discrete alternate version only, as the requirement of support of the set efficiency in any point of interval [0; T] can lead to necessity of spasmodic change of the target efficiency index.

Back to the specified criteria matrix of development management of the organizational and economic system (Table 8.2), it is worthwhile to pay attention to the features of using the said models depending on the accepted strategy of development planning of organizational and economic system, a loop and level of management.

The strategy of permanent superiority of available potential over requirement level can use Maximin models for the most part largely.

The balance strategy concerning the level of requirement may need the use of compromise models of planned backlog from the set level of requirement with allowances made for necessity of periodic increase in the planned rates of development of organizational and economic system providing in achievement of the set level of requirement.

Direct models (with the set resources) and models of intensive development of organizational and economic system are the principal models in the strategy of rampant (spasmodic) development.

The combined strategy of planning may require the whole set of models.

Requirements to accuracy of the problems solution are formulated depending on the management loop where modeling results for managerial decision-making are used.

These requirements appear to be growing in sequence of management loops: $U_1 \rightarrow U_2 \rightarrow U_3$. In the same sequence, the time interval (covering managerial decisions) is shortened, and accuracy of initial data is enhanced.

Table 8.2 Matrix of hi-tech industry competitiveness management

	Competitiveness management loop of the high-technology industries		
Levels of competitiveness management	Decisions of the state leadership (forecast U_1) T>10 years	Intermediate tasks within the framework of implementation of long-term programs of innovative development (long-term and perspective planning U_2) 5> T> 3 years	Amendment of the current annual plans (routine planning U_3) T =1 year
Macro-level V_1	K_{11} Maximization of the target effect of organizational and economic system within possible alternate versions, budgetary appropriations according to assessment results with the use of the following criteria: a) rank (significance) b) resource support c) settlement results according to interindustry balance. Method: regulatory forecasting	K_{12} Optimum compliance with the intermediate tasks in terms of interindustry balance and criterion of significance, rank. Method: cost forecast; long-term planning.	K_{13} Optimization of predicted annual task in terms of resource support according to characteristics of the tasks of the previous stages (years), change of environment, and change of forecast. Method: the same
Meso-level V_2	K_{21} ↑ Maximization of the target effect within the framework of the budgetary appropriations for the selected types of the systems to solve the problem. Method: research forecast.	K_{22} ↑ Maximization of the target effect within the framework of allocated budgetary funds for the systems under condition of fulfillment of works within the medium-term intermediate frameworks. Method: cost forecast according to the shape of this type systems, long-term planning.	K_{23} ↑ Maximization of the target efficiency in the course of typical operation with the use of possible alternate versions of creation of organizational and economic systems within the framework of selected resources. Method: planning and optimization according to criterion of fulfillment of typical operation.

(continued)

Table 8.2 (continued)

Levels of competitiveness management	Competitiveness management loop of the high-technology industries		
	Decisions of the state leadership (forecast U_1) T>10 years	Intermediate tasks within the framework of implementation of long-term programs of innovative development (long-term and perspective planning U_2) 5> T> 3 years	Amendment of the current annual plans (routine planning U_3) T =1 year
	K_{21} ↓ Cost minimization with a view of optimization of distribution of results. Method: research forecast.	K_{22} ↓ Cost minimization for development of the systems in the intermediate stage with a view of optimization of resource distribution of the between executors (associations) Method: forecast of technical and economic parameters, forward planning.	K_{23} ↓ Cost minimization for fulfillment of typical operation for the same conditions. Method: the same.
Macro-level V_1	K_{31} Optimization according to the rates of development of new or modernization of existing systems, optimization according to the elements of innovative system. Method: forecast and long-term planning	K_{32} Optimization of the rates of creating the systems and output depending on the accepted strategy of development. Method: optimization of terms of fulfillment of works for creation of organizational and economic systems with certain shape with the use of forward planning and system designing.	K_{33} Qualitative and quantitative design and technological criteria of the system shape (types, dimensions) Method: optimization of the system shape

It is worthwhile to be guided by the following models depending on this loop of management:

– In management loop U_1—dynamic unambiguous models which make it possible to monitor a trajectory of development of organizational and economic system in various points of the planned period with allowances made for distribution of resources in time;

- In management loop U_2—dynamic ambiguous models, which provide the most exact trajectories of the planned development of organizational and economic system (with allowances made for optimum strategy of development of competitive party) under optimum distribution of resources in time (to verify decision concerning sensitivity to change in strategy of competitive party, it is expedient to use unambiguous dynamic models too);
- In management loop U_3—statistic unambiguous models (to verify decision concerning sensitivity to change in strategy of competitive party, it is recommended to use statistic ambiguous models).

In analyses of possibilities and expediency of use of one or another model of planned development of organizational and economic system according to levels of management of criteria matrix, it is necessary to proceed from distinctions in the purposes and strategies of management.

The management objective at macro-level V_1—distribution of resources according to classes of the systems in order to achieve the set level of target efficiency under minimum of required resources.

The management objective at meso-level V_2—achievement of the maximum level of efficiency within allocated resources and their distribution under programs' processes.

The management objective at micro-level V_3—achievement of maximum level of efficiency within the selected resources and their distribution according to regional subsystems.

Inverse models at levels V_2, V_3—direct models are used according to objectives and conditions of scheduled development of organizational and economic system at level V_1.

Thus, at macro-level V_1, the effect is in the form of the preset value $[E(x) = E_{set}]$. Resources $[C(T) \rightarrow min]$ are distributed at this level according to the set effect.

In transition to meso-level V_2, these resources are already regarded as set $[C(T) = C_{set}]$. At this level, the problem is divided into two stages: in the beginning according to scheduled resources effect $[C(T) = C_{set}]$ is maximized under $E(x, y) \rightarrow E_{max}$ and then the system is divided into a number of subsystems for further use in associations when the effect maximized at the first stage is regarded as the scheduled one. Resources $[E(x, y) = E_{set}; C(T) \rightarrow min]$ are maximized, and further distribution of resources by enterprises is made level according to the said effect.

At micro-level V_3, these resources are regarded as already set. On them, the effect $[C(T) = C_{set}; E(x, y) \rightarrow max]$ is maximized according to the said resources.

Hence, in analysis of the matrix criteria model, the most important for the solution of specific planning tasks of creating organizational and economic system should take into account level V_2, and the most accurate—loop U_2.

In case of assessment of all resources of hi-tech industry enterprise in money terms aimed at enhancement of its competitiveness, distribution optimization of allocated funds should consist in minimization of difference between the integrated index of the enterprise competitiveness, received as a result of redistribution of assets, and the integrated index of competitiveness of the standard enterprise. Minimized functional is regarded as function of financial expenses for strengthening of factors determining the enterprise competitiveness.

The model of optimum distribution of financial resources allocated for enhancement of the enterprise competitiveness appears as follows:

$$\left(\sqrt{\sum_{i=1}^{n}(R_i(f_i))^2}\right) - R_э \rightarrow min \tag{8.1}$$

(8.1)

under condition of limitation of the enterprise financial resources

$$\sum_{i=1}^{n} f_i < F, f_i > 0,\ (i = 1, 2, \ldots n) \tag{8.2}$$

where

n—number of factors determining the enterprise competitiveness;
f_i—amount of financial expenses for strengthening of i-th index of the enterprise competitiveness of hi-tech industries;
$R_i(f_i)$—value of the i-th index of the enterprise competitiveness as a functional of financial expenses;
R—integrated index of competitiveness of the standard enterprise which is optimized;
F—amount of financial assets for enhancing enterprise competitiveness.

Levels of R_i—coefficients of the enterprise competitiveness should be calculated as follows:

$$R_i = k_i(1 - x_i), \tag{8.3}$$

where k_i—weighing coefficient of i-th, $i = 1, 2, \ldots n$ of the index of enterprise competitiveness;
x_i—actual level of i-th index of enterprise competitiveness at this point in time.

As the factors determining the enterprise competitiveness within the framework of this model, following groups of indices are offered:

- Potential enterprise possibilities;
- Customer satisfaction;
- Results of economic activities.

According to this model, there is a basic assumption of functional dependence of assets allocated by the enterprise in order to increase the levels of factors which the enterprise competitiveness of hi-tech industries depends on, and percent change of these levels. In particular, analyses of dynamics of competitiveness coefficients levels made it clear that there is quadratic functional dependence between financial expenses for action enhancement of the said factors and its percentage growth

$$f_i(P_i) = a_i P_i^2 \tag{8.4}$$

where a_i—proportionality factor;

P_i—percent value to increase the level of i-th index of competitiveness.

Thus, proceeding from (8.4),

$$P_i(f_i) = \sqrt{\frac{f_i}{a_i}} \tag{8.5}$$

where$P_i(f_i)$—percent value (as a function of financial expenses) to increase the level of i-th index of the enterprise competitiveness.

From the economic rational level of the said coefficients it follows that strengthening of action of such coefficient is connected with their growth; then with this consideration in mind, new level value of i-th index of competitiveness as a result of investing financial assets in amount of f_i can be determined according to expression:

$$R_i = k_i \left(1 - \left(1 + \frac{P_i(f_i)}{100}\right) x_i\right) \tag{8.6}$$

after substitution of (8.5) in (8.6)

$$R_i = k_i \left(1 - \left(1 + \frac{\sqrt{\frac{f_i}{a_i}}}{100}\right) x_i\right) \tag{8.7}$$

Finally, with allowances made for (8.7), this optimizing model of distribution of financial resources (8.1)–(8.2) will become (8.8)–(8.9)

$$\left(\sqrt{\sum_{i=1}^{n} k_i \left(1 - \left(1 + \frac{\sqrt{f/a_i}}{100}\right) x_i\right)^2 - R}\right) \to \min \tag{8.8}$$

$$\sum_{i=1}^{n} f_i \le F, f_i \ge 0, \langle i = 1, 2, \ldots n \rangle \tag{8.9}$$

Implementation of model (8.8)–(8.9) will make it possible for the enterprise of hi-tech industry to increase justification of the managerial decisions, concerning optimum use of limited industrial and financial resources in order to enhance competitiveness.

8.3 System of Competitiveness Indices as a Basis for Monitoring of Its Management in Hi-tech Industries

Mathematical interpretation of organizational and economic system of hi-tech industries is a complex dynamic object, the elements of which represent small dynamic systems.

Component wise description and modeling of all the processes within innovative system and its subsystems are very clunky, resource-intensive, and unreadable tool of innovative system management, despite its possible efficiency. Therefore, they widely used in practice the setting of aggregate problems in addition to concretized problems of the management system of organizational and economic system.

Because of the fact that solution of such concretized problems can be achieved by different ways, it is common practice to supervise implementation of such problems by means of control and monitoring systems as in such top companies of the space industry as Boeing, Airbus, and Lockheed Martin. They develop and improve their control systems and monitoring of competitiveness level of national high-technology industries.

Such systems have the following primary objectives:

- Identification of problems in the field of competitiveness management for their subsequent solution;
- Determination of economically feasible optimum measures in the field of the government competitiveness management.

According to the world experience, the indicators of competitiveness level of hi-tech industries should meet, whenever possible, the following criteria:

- They should be clear and have an unequivocal interpretation for decision-makers;
- have quantitative expression;
- They should be based upon available system of national statistics and do not require considerable costs for collection of information and calculations;
- They should provide a possibility of assessment in time dynamics;
- They should provide a possibility of thorough representation by levels and sectors, if necessary;
- They should meet specific features of decision-making;
- They should be representative for the international comparisons;
- The number of the said indices is limited, etc.

Information basis for development of indices of hi-tech industries development and their subsequent use in decision-making process at the regional or federal levels may include:

- international statistic information;
- state statistic information;
- departmental information;
- guidance paper, documents determining strategic development of hi-tech industries.

With a view of monitoring of the system competitiveness level of hi-tech industry enterprises, there should be developed a system of indices and indicators.

There are a considerable number of various integration indices for assessment of competitiveness level in the modern world practice.

So, for example, experts of the World Economic Forum (WEF) in assessment of competitiveness and calculation of the World Competitiveness Index take an approach when all the indices are divided into 12 blocks reflecting:

- Basis requirements to the countries' economic systems institutional system, infrastructure development, indices of macroeconomic stability, health situation, and elementary education status;
- Factors of efficiency enhancement: higher education and vocational training, efficiency of commodity markets and labor markets, improvement of financial markets, availability for acceptance of technologies, and scope of the market;
- Factors of innovations and economy modernization: improvement of conditions for doing business and innovations.

In the Global Competitiveness Report, the countries are diversified depending on what stage of competitiveness they are: factorial, effective, or innovative.

The index is a synthetic aggregated indicator; its one-third consists of statistic data and two-thirds—expert's assessments. However, as far as this index is concerned, as well as other indices of competitiveness assessment of a country, there is a large variety of critical comments, such as weakness of theoretical preconditions and sometimes uncertainty of applied statistic methods; validity criterion of economic growth and competitiveness is attributable to a greater extent to competitive vision and opinions of the authors than strong scientific approach; frequent changes of these criteria; and duplication of available macroeconomic indices.

WEF experts have also developed an index of scientific and technical potential as one of the components of integrated index of assessment of a country competitiveness level. According to this technique, a possibility of achieving steady economic growth in the medium term and long term equally depends on three categories of variables: macroeconomic environment, state institutes, and technology. In the long-term period, economy growth is impossible without innovative development. For "innovator" countries (including the USA, Japan, Korea, Canada,

Singapore, etc.), the share of innovative component in arriving at the index of competitiveness enhancement is 1/2, whereas the other countries—1/3 only. The index of scientific and technical potential is calculated on the basis of such data, as number of patents per 1 million population; country position according to the level of technological development; contribution of foreign investments to innovative activities of the local firms; number of Internet users per 10,000 persons; etc.

One more composite index used to evaluate competitiveness is the Global innovative index developed by international school of business INSEAD as a certain formal model for assessment of degree of conformity of separate countries and regions with modern innovative challenges. The index is based on eight blocks of indices, including five so-called "inputs": institutes and policy, human resources, infrastructure, technological level, business markets, and capital, and three "outputs": knowledge, competitiveness, and well-being. The "inputs" characterize the directions where the country can make attempts to increase efficiency of innovations, abilities to generate ideas, and to embody them in particular innovative products and services. The "outputs" reflect unconditional benefits from innovations for the country, enhancement of competitiveness, economic growth, and improvement of level and quality of life. As a matter of fact, this index is based on association of considerable number of quantitative and quality indices.

The European commission calculates ratings of the EU countries relative to various indices and summarizes them in the table, named European Innovation Union Scoreboard (EUS). EUS indices are divided into groups to display key criteria of innovative process, and they are in process of continual improvement, and they differ by years. In 2014, 25 indices were used and were divided into 3 large groups by 8 criteria which are presented in Table 8.3.

Experts of the Organization for Economic Cooperation and Development (OECD) recommend taking into consideration the following indices characterizing level and dynamics of development of innovative potential influencing competitiveness level:

- Share of hi-tech sector of economy in the output of manufacturing industry and services;
- Innovative activities;
- Amount of investments into knowledge sector (public and private), including higher education expenditures, Research &Development, and software development;
- Development and output of information and communication equipment, software product, and services;
- Employment volume in the sphere of science and high technologies, etc.

The World Bank offers its own assessment of innovative potential of the state and implements the program "Knowledge for Development," which uses one of the most complex and elaborated systems of qualitative and quantitative characteristic of scientific-technical and innovative potential of the state (region)—"Knowledge Assessment Methodology" (KAM) designed to measure and compare countries'

Table 8.3 Criteria, indices, and EIS data sources

№	Innovation dimension/Indicator	Data source
Enablers		
1.	Human resources:	
1.1	New doctorate graduates per 1,000 population aged 25–34	Eurostat
1.2	Percentage population aged 30–34 having completed tertiary education	Eurostat
1.3	Percentage youth aged 20–24 having attained at least upper secondary level education	Eurostat
2.	Open, excellent, and attractive research systems:	
2.1	International scientific co-publications per million population	Science-Metrix (Scopus)
2.2	Scientific publications among the top 10 % most cited publications worldwide as % of total scientific publications of the country	Science-Metrix (Scopus), Eurostat
2.3	Non-EU doctorate students as a % of all doctorate students	Eurostat
3.	Finance and support:	
3.1	R&D expenditure in the public sector as % of GDP	Eurostat
3.2	Venture capital investment as % of GDP	Eurostat
Firm activities		
4.	Firm investments:	
4.1	R&D expenditure in the business sector as % of GDP	Eurostat
4.2	Non-R&D innovation expenditures as % of turnover	Eurostat
5.	Linkages & entrepreneurship:	
5.1	SMEs innovating in-house as % of SMEs	Eurostat
5.2	Innovative SMEs collaborating with others as % of SMEs	Eurostat
5.3	Public–private co-publications per million population	CWTS (Thomson Reuters)
6.	Intellectual assets	
6.1	PCT patents applications per billion GDP	OECD
6.2	PCT patent applications in societal challenges per billion GDP (environment-related technologies; health)	OECD
6.3	Community trademarks per billion GDP	Office for Harmonization in the Internal Market
6.4	Community designs per billion GDP	Office for Harmonization in the Internal Market
Outputs		
7.	Innovators:	
7.1	SMEs introducing product or process innovations as % of SMEs	Eurostat
7.2	SMEs introducing market in organizational innovations as % of SMEs	Eurostat
7.3	Employment in fast-growing firms of innovative sectors	Eurostat

(continued)

Table 8.3 (continued)

№	Innovation dimension/Indicator	Data source
8.	Economic effects:	
8.1	Employment in knowledge-intensive activities (manufacturing and services) as % of total employment	Eurostat
8.2	Contribution of medium- and high-tech product exports to the trade balance	United Nations
8.3	Knowledge-intensive services exports as % total service exports	Eurostat
8.4	Sales of new to market and new to firm innovations as % of turnover	Eurostat
8.5	License and patent revenues from abroad as % of GDP	Eurostat

readiness for transition to the knowledge-based economy. KAM is used for calculation of two indices—Knowledge Index (KI) and Knowledge Economy Index (KEI).

Each of the said indices includes specific indices characterizing innovative and technological development, scientific and technical capacities, innovative and investment potential of productive industry, development of information and communication technologies, etc. Analysis of these indices made it possible to specify a number of basic indices characterizing competitiveness, including quantity of patents, inventions created, and embodied technologies, etc., to be the basis of multilevel system of indices and competitiveness indices. Based upon this system of indices, we suggest to monitor the level of enterprise competitiveness of hi-tech industries. We shall group the said indices according to three signs: primary indices, indices, and composite indices.

1. Primary Indices

Primary indices can be received on the basis of statistic information of the state and statistic services of productive industries. The basis of primary indices provides background for preparation of estimated figures.

Taken as a whole, the system of primary indices reflects a state of innovative development and competitiveness of economy of the state and productive industry, and it is in their best interests since hi-tech industries are 90 % financed from the state budget resources.

The system of primary indices should be divided into the following groups:

1.1. Indices to characterize raw materials potential, capacities of scientific and technical (technological) in-house developments, and acquired developments and inventions. There should be taken into consideration ability of enterprises of hi-tech industries to find and acquire the rights to use the necessary developments and a possibility to order new Research and Development concerning the subjects of interest.

Such indices are:

- Number of scientific and technical reports;
- Number of laboratory (development models) prototypes;
- Number of industrial prototypes;
- Number of patents;
- Number of computer programs;
- Number of inventions;
- Indices characterizing condition and potential of the intellectual capital (number of researchers, preparation of scientific personnel, participation of young scientists in innovative developments, preparation of innovative managers and their advanced professional training, creation of educational and consulting innovative centers, availability of educational and information materials in the sphere of innovative activity, and number and structure of personnel engaged in innovative activity);
- Indices of amount and structure of production assets used in innovative activity;
- Indices of amount and structure of innovation costs.

The values of indices specified above characterize the current level of competitiveness and resource status relative to innovative development of hi-tech industries.

1.2 Indices to characterize infrastructural abilities of the enterprises of hi-tech industries and their cluster-based innovative potential. This is an availability of departments at the enterprise responsible for:

- Solution of problems concerning protection of intellectual property in the state;
- Patent search and patenting of intellectual property abroad;
- Project appraisal;
- Certification of products;
- Information support of innovative development;
- Research of innovative production market (marketing).

This group of indices also includes:

- Share of small enterprises in innovative sphere;
- Number of acquired technologies;
- Number of transferred technologies.

These indices disclose cause-and-effect aspect of development problems of innovative development.

1.3 The third group of indices is formed by the functional indices reflecting key competitiveness coefficient of hi-tech industries, in particular:

Performance indicators of industrial and economic activities of enterprises of hi-tech industries:

- Indices of volume, structure, and dynamics of production, sales, and services in the hi-tech industry;
- Indices of innovations influence on results of activity of hi-tech industry enterprises;
- Indices of industrial resources saving as a result of commissioning innovations;
- Indices of profit from implementation of innovative production and services in hi-tech industries;
- Indices of innovative activity of hi-tech industry enterprises;
- Indices characterizing influence of innovations on activity of hi-tech industry enterprises;
- Indices of technological structure of hi-tech industries;
- Indices of export and import of products and services by the enterprises of high-technology industries.

The above groups of indices, as a whole, provide a complex assessment of the current competitive situation in the hi-tech industry.

They characterize rationality, performance efficiency of innovative and industrial systems of hi-tech industries relative to utilization of resources, and investment potential (productivity of research studies and development).

They reflect connections between various components of the industry competitiveness and characterize the capacity for interaction of these elements in order to evaluate performance efficiency of hi-tech industries.

1.4. The fourth group of indices includes dynamic indices to characterize orientation of tendencies and dynamic pattern of major parameters of competitiveness of hi-tech industries.

Measurement of competitiveness level of hi-tech industries assumes determination of order relation of comparable objects on the basis of the rating method. The set of indices for measurement of various characteristics of competitiveness level is determined depending on particular objectives and research tasks, transaction costs for reception of indices with provision for availability of information bases at the enterprises.

2. Indices

Indices are rather simple specific and structural figures received by calculation from the primary indicators. A part of indices is already available in official statistic materials, and another part represents new specially developed indices and figures.

Index of innovative activity is a descriptor within a set of indices to characterize results of introduction of new or advanced products and technological processes at the enterprises of hi-tech industries. It consists of the following:

2.1. Indices of share of innovative production and services in the hi-tech industry as a whole, including export:

- A share of new (newly introduced) products and services in the hi-tech industry;
- A share of advanced products and services in the hi-tech industry;
- A share of other innovative products and services in the hi-tech industry.

In the course of calculation of the specified indices, there should be considered all the innovations introduced within the last three years.

2.2. Indices to characterize influence of innovations on results of the enterprise activities within the hi-tech industry in so far as it refers to the growth of profits in the course of implementation of innovative products and services in the field of hi-tech industry and its share in the total amount of profit:

- Volume of sales of innovative products and services in the hi-tech industry in domestic and foreign markets and their share in total amount of sales;
- Access to new segments of the market;
- A share in the market's traditional segment;
- Production cost reduction as a result of innovations introduction (labor costs, expenditures for materials, energy, etc.);
- Improvement of capital productivity ratio, etc.

2.3. Index of innovative activity level of the enterprise of hi-tech industries is a relative index to characterize degree of participation of the enterprise of hi-tech industries in implementation of innovative activities during a certain period of time. It is determined as a ratio of quantity of innovative active enterprises of hi-tech industries to the total number of enterprises examined for a certain period of time in the country, productive industry, region, etc.

2.4. Index of competitiveness of products and services in the hi-tech industry is a set of criteria for quantitative assessment of the level of competitiveness of production and services in the hi-tech industry (single-unit, group, and integrated). A single-unit index is a percentage ratio of value of any technical or economic parameter to the value of the same parameter when requirement element is theoretically met in full.

3. Composite Indices

Composite indexes—a small number of complex indices to characterize complex parameters, such as quality of life, performance of the economy, development of human resources as a result of implementation of programs, and strategies of development of hi-tech industries.

This system of indices makes it possible to receive online reliable information about the level of competitiveness of hi-tech industries in order to apply methods of planning, modeling, and management based on resulting data. As a matter of fact, this indication system will be a starting point in search and approbation of optimum macroeconomic situations in hi-tech industries.

It is worthwhile to note that there are a number of parameters of hi-tech industries which impact on the whole system, if we influence on them. Accordingly, the result of influence on the said parameters comes to light, thanks to the monitoring system, namely, change of a number of target integrated indices. Thus, we can consider hi-tech industries as an integral object with inputs (adjustable parameters) and outputs (integrated indices). Such adduction enables us to proceed to the cybernetic nature of hi-tech industries and to consider its ability of self-regulation.

In consideration of the system of enterprises of hi-tech industries, as a mathematical object, the organizational and economic system appears as a self-adaptable object of the dynamic nature being under the influence of external environment and internal processes.

Thereupon, it is worthwhile to take into consideration the basic formula of automatic regulation being the basis of cybernetic interpretation of organizational and economic systems.

There are two systems: managed S_{Aij} and managing R_{aij} working on the principle of feedback.

State y_j of the output of system S_{Aij} is transferred to the input of regulator R_{aij}, rearranging it into state of the output which, in turn, is added to the input signal x_i. Thus, input S_{Aij} is $x_i + \Delta xy$. And Δxy depends on how much y_j differs from preset value of the fixed norm $|y|$ of the system output.

Corresponding adjustment of regulator R_{aij} means that amendment Δxy should led to $y_j = |y|$.

Let us assume that transformations in the system consist of input multiplication by actual number S_{Aij} (it is equal to a certain fluctuation caused by instability of external environment of hi-tech industries in a number of countries). Then $y_j = S_{Aij}x_i$, where $S_{Aij} = y_j/x_i$—proportional ability of the system.

There are the same transformations in the regulator with throughput capacity R_{aij}. Then the regulator amendment $\Delta xy = Ry_j$

$$y_j = S_{Aij}(x_i + \Delta x_j) = S_{Aij}\left(x_i + R_{aij}y_j\right) = S_{Aij}x_i + S_{Aij}R_{aij}y_j$$

From here, we have

$$y_j = \frac{S_{Aij}}{1 - S_{Aij}R_{aij}}x_i$$

This ratio is regarded as the basic formula of the management theory of development in hi-tech industries.

Let us consider some types of regulation and management, bearing in mind, that management of the hi-tech industries development consists in achievement of such activity of the system when all abnormalities of the output state of the system are equalized.

Solutions, where preset value is a constant number, are connected with direct regulation. If y_j is a variable, the regulation system is combined with the management being a definition of every value of variable y_j. In this case, regulation consists of deviation adjustment of the state of output y_j of the systems from a certain variable norm determined by management.

In general, there may be used various types of management, i.e., ways of definition Δxy.

If Δxy is a time function t, i.e., $\Delta xy = f(t)$, the programmed management takes place, making it possible, for example, to optimize the program of output $P(T)$ or service in the field of hi-tech industry by the organizational and economic system of hi-tech industries for a certain period of time. Naturally, there is a resource problem of distribution of required capital investments allocated for development of hi-tech industries, which was described in detail in the previous paragraph.

If Δxy is a function of certain energy and material value $\Delta x_j = f(\omega)$, then value ω is the leader, and Δxy—follower, i.e., the problem is reduced to the solution of the follow-up system.

The management system of hi-tech industries should establish preset number Δxy (norm of the system operation) on the basis of parameters of the previous management process. Hence, Δxy is a function of state in the preceding periods or points of time t. This case should be referred to adaptable management or self-training process (accumulation and generalization of conclusions on the basis of past experience).

Thus, the value $\Delta xy(t)$ set on moment t is a function of the condition of an output of system during the moments $t_1 = \theta_1$, $t_2 = \theta_2$, etc., i.e.,

$$\Delta xy(t) = f\,[y\,(t - \theta_1),\ y\,(t - \theta_2)\ \ldots].$$

Thus, the system of self-regulation of organizational and economic system of hi-tech industry enterprises makes it possible to respond in due time to changes in the system's performance and to restore a normal state of innovative space by means of changing adjustable parameters.

Besides the ability of self-regulation, the systems of enterprises of hi-tech industries should also be regarded as mathematical models which can be more or less used for optimization of planning and forecasting of development of hi-tech industry of these countries.

For this task, it is worthwhile to take into consideration criteria matrix of management and, on the assumption of multi-loop system and multilevel competitiveness management of hi-tech industries, to consider every criterion separately.

Criteria K_{11} and K_{12} are determinant for elaboration of development strategy on the national level, i.e., in order to determine the state strategic policy of development of hi-tech industries.

On the assumption of the principle of criterion (maximization of target effect within the framework of funds allocation and involving a number of other constraints), it seems possible to express criterion in the form of the linear function maximum:

$$K_1 = C_1X_1 + C_2X_2 + \ldots + C_nX_n = \sum_{i=1}^{n} C_iX_i = M$$

while meeting the constraints in the form of

$$\begin{array}{l}
g_1X_1 \ldots \qquad\qquad\qquad\qquad \geq 0, \\
\qquad g_2X_2 \ldots \qquad\qquad\qquad \geq 0, \\
\qquad\qquad g_3X_3 \ldots \qquad\quad \geq 0, \\
a_{11}X_1 + a_{12}X_2 + \ \ldots\ a_{1n}X_n = b_1 \\
a_{21}X_1 + a_{22}X_2 + \ \ldots a2nXn = b_2 \\
\ldots \ \ldots \ \ldots \ \ldots \ \ldots \ \ldots \ \ldots \ \ldots \ \ldots \ \ldots \ \ldots \ \ldots \ \ldots \\
a_{m1}X_1 + a_{m2}X_2 + \ \ldots\ a_{mn}X_n = b_m
\end{array}$$

where a_{ij}, g_i, b_j—constants;

C_i—cost coefficient.

It means that analytical expression of the basic criterion K_{11} can be reduced to the classical problem of dynamic programming.

For long-term forecast of development of hi-tech industries as a single system while meeting resource constraints, this feature is the most important. It is worthwhile to specify that the forms of the task and quantitative expression of coefficient C_i and constants a_{ij} and b_j are determined by the strategy (and by specific strategic criteria), assessment of significance of this system of hi-tech industries, as well a sevening-out of the system development within this time interval in respect of the aspect of providing optimum types of development (with due account for dynamics of problems of the high management level of organizational and economic system according to the hierarchy). In particular, in the system of indices, described above, quantitative expressions of constants a_{ij} and b_j are determined on the assumption of corresponding data of monitoring of external and internal environment of the system, while quantitative expressions of coefficient C_i are characterized on the assumption of structure of integrated indices.

Suggested multilevel system of indices presents a practical tool of monitoring competitiveness dynamics and the firm development as a whole. Designing of monitoring as an element of competitiveness management system is its integral part at all the levels of management.

At the macro-level, the monitoring system includes state authorities (departments, agencies, etc.) engaged in collecting, processing, and analysing of primary indices by productive industries and organizations. At the meso-level, the monitoring system is carried out by the industry ministries and departments. At the micro-level, it is carried out by the firms for which the source of primary indices is their book-keeping and financial accounting and quarterly and annual reports for investors and shareholders. Certainly, top management of any management level first of all is interested in the composite indicators reflecting development of economic agents to the fullest extent possible. At the same time, on frequent occasions, it is necessary to carry out analysis and identify "weak" points of the organization.

In this case, hierarchy of the system of indices gives a chance to identify "weak," or so-called "bottlenecks" of the organization, to take measures online on optimization of the business processes, to solve local problems of the firm, that would finally result into positive dynamics of both specific indices and the said indicators, and consequently to the growth of competitiveness target composite indicators.

With a view of increasing efficiency of performance of the system of monitoring, there is provided to use, firstly, management information system of the firms, secondly, on the regular basis to update single information databases so that the user could enter updated primary indices with their further automatic processing and calculation of indices concerning simple specific and structural indices received by calculation from the primary indices, as well as the composite indices characterizing complex parameters. Use of the automated management systems in the course of monitoring increases objectivity and accuracy of received assessments of competitiveness raises data processing rate and gives a chance to receive online the information on competitiveness dynamics and development of the firm, its competitive status in the market.

Conclusions This chapter contains generalization of theoretical approaches to formation of hi-tech industries' competitiveness management systems. This section presents structured information about the levels and structure of hi-tech industries competitiveness management, the indices characterizing the firm competitiveness and productive industries according to the mathematical point of view.

Taking into consideration the fact that one of the factors providing for implementation of measures to enhance competitiveness shall be financial capacities of the firm and productive industry as a whole; the section presents a mathematical simulation model for solution of problems of resources distribution allocated for development of hi-tech industries.

In furtherance of the ideas put in this monograph, a research was carried out of integrated indices characterizing level of competitiveness at the macro-level from the point of view of a set of characteristics and indicators they accumulate, and their calculation. On the basis of this research, there formed a multilevel hierarchical system of competitiveness indices of productive industry which can be used in designing of the information management system and a single database of the firm. There is provided the use of these indices in the course of management and monitoring of development and dynamics of the firm competitiveness within hi-tech industries.

Conclusion

9

This monograph presents various aspects of the developing theory of competitiveness management widely enough and in detail: framework of categories and concepts and methodical bases of quantitative assessment of competitiveness of production, firm, and productive industry; it provides approaches for construction of the firm competitiveness management system.

At the same time, this monograph presents a study of nature and degree of influence of separate classical economic laws on the process of competitiveness management, which is of great interest from the perspective of those who are setting the basis for competitiveness management theory. In this monograph, the authors draw the conclusion that the basic economic laws, either expressly or by implication, influence the processes defining the product competitiveness and creation of competitive advantages, in particular in the course of price-based competition. These laws should be taken into consideration in order to evaluate their impact on development of measures aimed at enhancement of the product competitiveness and creation of competitiveness management system of various economic entities.

The monograph presents analysis of economic laws and development of ideas concerning the issues of competitiveness, innovative activities, and economic cycle, which made it possible to formulate and describe from a mathematical standpoint the postulates and hypotheses of competitiveness management theory, which define conditions for stepping up competitiveness management processes and contribution of innovative activities in this process, as well as creation of new goods and commodity markets.

Based upon the postulates and hypotheses that the authors formulated, they have come to the logical conclusion of the competitiveness management law making and its mathematical demonstration. In furtherance of the postulates and laws, the monograph presents the mathematical models to describe competitiveness of high-technology products, firms and industries being the basis of this investigation of performance indicators dynamics of competitive products.

Proceeding from the position that competitiveness is determined by the process technical level and internal and external factors influencing the firm, there were

A. Chursin, Y. Makarov, *Management of Competitiveness*,
DOI 10.1007/978-3-319-16244-7_9

developed theoretical approaches for evaluation of the firm and products competitiveness and influence of the products updating on enhancement of competitiveness.

On the basis of mathematical models, there were developed theoretical approaches for formation of the firm competitiveness management systems including the firm competitiveness management structure and methodical bases of their designing. In the course of their practical application, they make it possible to take into consideration their particular features which depend on specificity of the firm and productive industry, their economic status, and degree of influence of various internal and external factors.

As is known, a set of the firms with the similarity of production within a certain sector of economy represents productive industry for which assessment of competitiveness is specified in the monograph too. In order to provide more clear representation about practical application of the said techniques, the monograph presents examples of calculating quantitative assessment of competitiveness of the products, firm, and productive industry. On the assumption of such calculations, business managers can implement measures concerning competitiveness management, innovative development, and creation of essentially new products capable to enter new commodity markets.

For a holistic view of competitiveness levels ratio on a worldwide scale, there is provided, to familiarize with the most popular on the market indicators (indices) of competitiveness and innovative development of the states, ways of their calculation and proposals concerning competitiveness regulatory system at the macro-level, which is a highly topical problem for all the countries now. The theoretical bases of competitiveness management of organization presented in this monograph with the use of modern mathematical methods make it possible to build simulation model and to demonstrate feasibility of development scenarios for an organization depending on its features and influence of internal and external factors under crisis and postcrisis conditions, as well as to formulate further tenets in development of the competitiveness management theory which meet the challenges of the twenty-first century.

Bibliography

Auktsionek SP (2003) Problems of measuring business struggle and competitiveness at micro-level. SP Aukutsionek. Competitiveness of Russia in global economy. [AA Dynkin, and colleagues]; Russian Academy of Sciences, Institute of World Economy and Int. Relations. M

Avdasheva SB, Rozanova NM (1998) Theory of industry-specific markets' organization. M: SP Publishing house Magistr

Bolt GD (1991) Hands-on sales management. M: Economy

Chernega OB. Structural competitiveness: some pressing issues. Economic problems and perspectives of stabilization of Ukrainian economy

Chursin AA (1982a) Concerning an issue of definition of technical and economic indicators of the VC enterprise. Article.—"Problems of defense technology". Scientific and technical collection. Series XVIII, publication 149. M. Central Scientific-Research Institution of Information

Chursin AA (1982b) Enhancement of efficiency of the enterprise Management Information and Control System department. Article. "Problems of defense technology". Scientific and technical collection. Series 17, publication149. M, Central Scientific-Research Institution of Information

Chursin AA (1983a) Problems of efficiency in implementation of the enterprise Management Information System. Monograph. M, Central Scientific-Research Institution of Information

Chursin AA (1983b) Application of "normative-clear production" under establishment of planned targets. Manual. Karaganda, Ministry of Higher Education Institutions. Kaz. Soviet Socialist Republic

Chursin AA (1984) Information-computer in engineering and economic calculations. Monograph. Karaganda, Ministry of Higher Education Institutions. Kaz. Soviet Socialist Republic.

Chursin AA (1987a) Problems of enhancing technological level and quality of economic production. Article. The best practices, Special issue. S.31–35

Chursin AA (1987b) Organizational and methodological issues of scientific and technical progress management. Article. "Problems of defense technology". The Scientific and technical collection. Series III, publication 5(202). M, Central Scientific-Research Institution of Information

Chursin AA (1987c) Principal directions of the social and economic development plan for 1998 and problems of the industry enterprises in technical re-equipment under new management conditions. Article. "Problems of defense technology". The Scientific and technical collection. Series III, publication 11(208). M, Central Scientific-Research Institution of Information

Chursin AA (1988a) Ways of management of scientific and technical progress and development of industrial production under new conditions of economic management. Monograph. M, Central Scientific-Research Institution of Information

Chursin AA (1988b) R&D economic management methods, article "Problems of defense technology". The Scientific and technical collection. Series III, publication 5 (213). M, Central Scientific-Research Institution of Information

Chursin AA (1988c) Complex assessment of economic efficiency of an effort to accelerate scientific and technical progress, "Problems of defense technology". The Scientific and

A. Chursin, Y. Makarov, *Management of Competitiveness*,
DOI 10.1007/978-3-319-16244-7

technical collection. Series III, publication 7(215). M, Central Scientific-Research Institution of Information

Chursin AA (1988d) Enhancement of technological level of production on the basis of complex automation, article “Problems of defense technology”. The Scientific and technical collection. Series III, publication 2 (210). M, Central Scientific-Research Institution of Information

Chursin AA (1988e) Indicators and incentives for enhanced technological level of output under conditions of self-financing. “The best practices”, № 7, M, Central Scientific-Research Institution of Information

Chursin AA (1989a) Development of flexible industrial systems and economic assessment of their development and functioning. Manual. M, Moscow State Technical University (MGTU)

Chursin AA (1989b) Cardinal economic reform and management of scientific and technical progress in the region. Article. Kaz. Research and Development Establishment “Scientific and Technical Information”, Alma-Ata

Chursin AA (1989c) Efficiency of management systems and the problem of interest coordination of various levels of management of industrial enterprises and production associations, article, Central Scientific-Research Institution of Information, the Scientific and technical collection. Series 3, publication 2 (221), M

Chursin AA (1989d) Economic management methods for scientific and technological progress, article Central Scientific-Research Institution of Information, the Scientific and technical collection. Series 3, publication 5 (213), M

Chursin AA (1990a) Substantiation of the concept and mechanism of scientific and technical progress management in the defense industry under new conditions of economic management and production conversion. The author’s abstract. M, Central Scientific-Research Institution of Information

Chursin AA (1990b) Basic methodologies for management of scientific and technical progress in defense industry. Monograph. M, Central Scientific-Research Institution of Information

Chursin AA (1990c) Conversion—basis for cooperation. Article. Economy and Technology, № 4, M

Chursin AA (1990d) Industry problems of scientific and technological progress management under conditions of economic reform. Article. Central Scientific-Research Institution of Information, the Best practices, M, № 5

Chursin AA (1990e) Basis of management of scientific and technical progress in a defense industry under new conditions of economic management. Manual. Bauman Moscow State Technical University, Industrial Advanced Training Faculty, M.

Chursin AA (2004) Innovation and the market. Manual. M: Mechanical engineering

Chursin AA (2005) Foreign trade activities of organizations. Manual. M: Academy of Labor and Social Relations

Chursin AA (2006) Organization competitiveness management. Monograph. Federal State Unitary Enterprise “Scientific and technological centre “Informtechnika”. Magazine editorship “Defense technology”

Chursin AA (2007) Corporate management. Study guide. Peoples’ Friendship University of Russia

Chursin AA (2008) Investigation of prerequisites to creation of the theory of competitiveness management of economic agents, article: Socialno ekonomicka revue FSEV. Slovakia: Trencianskej university Alexandra Dubceka 6(1);87–101.

Chursin AA (2013) Competitiveness management problems in the rocket-space industry under modern economic conditions. Defense technology M: Federal State Unitary Enterprise “Scientific and technical centre” Informtechnika №1

Chursin AA, Afanasyev MV (2014) Reform and development of the rocket-space industry of Russia (methods, concepts and models): Monograph. M: Publishing house “Spectrum”, p 451

Chursin AA, Baymuratov UB (2010a) Global economic management and competitiveness problems of developing national economies. Reports of the National Academy of Sciences of Kazakhstan 1:73–80

Chursin AA, Baymuratov UB (2010b) Modern economic crisis and post crisis development in terms of some world tendencies. Bulletin of the National Academy of Sciences of Kazakhstan 1; S.68–74

Chursin AA, Danilyk AY (2014) Fundamentals for creation of competitiveness management system in the high technology industry: Monograph. M: Publishing house "Spectrum" 405

Chursin AA, Davidov VA (2014) Competitiveness and the human capital in highly technological industries. Magazine "RISK: Resources, Information, Supply, Competitiveness", Publishing house: Institute ITKOR 3;65–70

Chursin AA, Dranayeva AA (2010) Quantitative assessment of the organization competitiveness level. Defense complex—to scientific and technical progress of Russia. 2;95–100

Chursin AA, Gusakova EA (2010a) Assessment of the goods competitiveness. Defense complex—to scientific and technical progress of Russia 2;89–95

Chursin AA, Gusakova EA (2010b) Competitiveness of the high technology products and their life cycle. Defense complex—to scientific and technical progress of Russia 2;118–120

Chursin AA, Ivankova MA (2008a) Solution of one problem from the theory of organizations competitiveness management. Socialno ekonomicka revue FSEV. Slovakia: Trencianskej university Alexandra Dubceka 6(1);87–101

Chursin AA, Ivankova MA (2008b) Designing of competitiveness management system for an organization. Article. "Defense technology", Federal State Unitary Enterprise "Scientific and Technological Centre "Informtehnika" 6;87–95

Chursin AA, Ivanov AS (2008) Efficiency of the management systems and a problem of the interest coordination of various levels of divisions and enterprises within the framework of financial and industrial group. Integral 4(42):96–97

Chursin AA, Ivanov AS (2009) Effective price policy as a factor of success in competitive struggle, article. Prob Mod Econ 1(29):132–137

Chursin AA, Ivanov AA (2010) Recommendation on creation of the concept of stable innovative development of structures with consolidated capital. Defense complex—to scientific and technical progress of Russia 3;110–117

Chursin AA, Kokuyseva TV (2011) Competitiveness management law. Problems of modern economy. St. Petersburg 1;43–45

Chursin AA, Milkovsky AG (2014) Contribution of information and communication technologies in the enterprise management. Business in law, Publishing house "Yur—Vak", 4;123–127

Chursin AA, Okatyev NA (2008a) Price-based competition and production cost price, article, Directory. Engineering magazine № 3; 48–55

Chursin AA, Okatyev NA (2008b) Approaches to optimization of resources for creation and manufacture of competitive products. Article. Directory. Engineering magazine 5;35–39

Chursin AA, Sergeev SA (2009a) Concerning the problem of management mechanism in the big Russian corporations by the example of an Air Company of the holding type. Defense Technol 4–5:59–68

Chursin AA, Sergeev SA (2009b) Technological level of production: a basis of corporation competitiveness. Defense Technol 4–5:79–90

Chursin AA, Shamin RV (2011) Investments and innovations and their role in enhancement of the organization competitiveness. Defensive complex—to scientific and technical progress of Russia 2;83–87

Chursin AA, Shamin RV (2012) Mathematical model of quantitative assessment of competitiveness of the RSI. System analysis, management and navigation: Collection of theses of reports. M: Publishing house MAI. p 135

Chursin AA, Shmakov EV (2014) Economic and mathematical model of optimum distribution of investments in modernization of the high technology enterprises. Business in law, Publishing house "Yur—Vak", 3;239–243

Chursin AA, Solovyev VP (2013) Innovations impact on competitiveness management mechanisms. Magazine "Innovation" 3(173); 60–66

Chursin AA, Trifonov SA (2003) Social and economic aspects of scientific and technical progress, Manual (Part I). Study guide. M: Academy of Labor and Social Relations

Chursin AA, Trifonov SA (2004) Social and economic aspects of scientific and technical progress, Manual (Part II). Study guide. M: Academy of Labor and Social Relations

Chursin AA, Trifonov SA (2005) Social and economic aspects of scientific and technical progress (Part III). Study guide. Part III. M: Academy of Labor and Social Relations

Chursin AA, Vasilyev SA (2011) Competitiveness, innovations and investments (nonlinear synthesis). M: Mechanical engineering. p 480

Chursin AA, Volkov VA (2012) Some theoretical approaches to competitiveness assessment of enterprises of the rocket-space industry in implementation of innovative technologies. System analysis, management and navigation: Collection of theses of reports. M: Publishing house MAI, p 133

Chursin AA, Sokolov HA, Geldman ID, Frantsev DG (1992) Definition of economic efficiency of scientific and technical process under conditions of new economic management. Article. M: Scientific and Technological Centre "Computer science"

Chursin AA, Skubachevsky AL, Solorukha OV (2010) Dynamic model of production of competitive items. Defense complex—to scientific and technical progress of Russia 2;100–107

Chursin AA, Makarov YN, Baymuratov UB (2011) Investment with innovations: synergy in economy competitiveness. Under general scientific editorship of AA Chursin. M.: Publishing house «MAKD»: Mechanical engineering. p 496

Chursin AA, Shamin RV, Kokuyseva TV (2012a) Method of quantitative assessment of the high technology industry competitiveness. Economy and management in mechanical engineering. M: Technology of mechanical engineering. № 3–12, pp 41–47

Chursin AA, Davidov VA, Ojiganov EN (2012b) Models of decision-making by non-government investors in terms of investment appeal of enterprises of the rocket-space complex. Defense technology. M: Federal State Unitary Enterprise "Scientific and technical centre "Informtechnika". № 6–7; pp 36–44

Chursin AA, Davidov VA, Ojiganov EN (2012c) Factors and indicators of investment appeal of enterprises of the rocket-space complex under modern economic conditions. Defense technology, M: Federal State Unitary Enterprise "Scientific and technical centre "Informtechnika", № 6–7. pp 36–44

Chursin AA, Makarov YN, Davidov VA, Kovkov DV (2013a) Foreign trade activities/Under general scientific editorship of AA Chursin: Manual. M: Printing house Federal State Unitary Enterprise "Central Engineering Research Institute of Russia TsNIIMash", p 650

Chursin AA, Kovkov DV, Shamin RV (2013b) Approaches to assessment of external and internal factors impact on competitiveness of production of the rocket-space industry. "Publishing house Yur-VaK" "Business in law" Magazine 1;127–131

Chursin AA, Kovkov DV, Shamin RV (2013c) Approaches to development of selection technique for innovative technologies promoting competitiveness enhancement in the RSI. Defense technology M: Federal State Unitary Enterprise "Scientific and technical centre "Informtechnika", № 3–4;77–81

Chursin AA, Danilyuk RA, Ostrovsky AA (2014) Efficiency assessment of the projects implemented in the high technology industries. Business in law, Publishing house "Yur—Vak", 4;148–151

Chursin AA, Кокуйцева TV (2010) Innovative economy as a strategic goal of development under crisis and post crisis conditions. The bulletin of National Academy of sciences of Kazakhstan. Almaty: National Academy of Sciences 4;80–88

Chursin AA, Мечар MV (2009) Foreign economic policy of an organization. Practical and theoretical aspects. Monograph. M: Federal State Unitary Enterprise "Scientific and Technological Centre "Informtehnika"; Slovakia: Mercury

Edrenkina EV. Quality as a factor of competitiveness enhancement. http://www.marketing.spb.ru/-conf/9/42.htm.

Fathutdinov RA (2000) Competitiveness: economy, strategy, management. M: INFRA-M. p 312

Fathutdinov RA (2005) Strategic competitiveness: textbook. M: Economy, p 504 (Higher education)
Gelvanovsky M, Zhukovskaya V (1998) Competitiveness within the global axes. Inst. of World Economy and Int. Relations. 7;146–152.
Gelvanovsky M, Zhukovskaya V, Trofimova I (1998) Competitiveness at micro-, meso- and macro-levels of measurement. Russ Econ Mag 3:67–71
Glazyev SY (1993) Theory of long-term technical and economic development. Int Fund of ND Kondratyev. M: VlaDar
Golubkov EP (1999) Study of competitors and achievement of advantages in competitive rivalry. Marketing in Russia and Abroad 2; 27–43
Kondratyev ND (1993) Big conjuncture cycles. ND Kondratyev. Selected compositions. ND Kondratyev; [originator: VM Bondarenko and colleagues] M
Kondratyev N, Yakovets Y, Abalkin L (2002) Big cycles of conjuncture and foresight theory. Selected works. M: Economy
Kulik II, Kazakov AF (1991) Marketing study of commodity markets: method, developed by Republican Interindustry Inst. of in-service training of executives and experts of productive industries. Minsk: RMIPK
Kurenkov Y, Popov V (2001) Competitiveness of Russia in the World economy. Economic Matters 6:36–49
Lebedev VV (1997) Mathematic modeling of social and economic processes. M: Isograph
Makarov YN (2010a) Methods of study and efficiency assessments of the space activity of Russia. Models and methods of innovative economy. M: IASS—Publication 2.
Makarov YN (2010b) Russian cosmonautics in the world market: competition, problems, perspectives—World financial and economic crisis and its particularities in Russia. Reports of the Round table. M: Central Economic and Mathematical Institute of the Russian Academy of Sciences
Makarov YN (2010c) Organization of efficient management of industrial corporations. Izhevsk: Publishing house "Association MODAORYu "Mitra"
Makarov YN (2011) Russian cosmonautics in the world market: competition, problems, perspectives. M: Economy and mathematical methods 47(3)
Makarov YN, Khrustalyov EY (2010a) Financial and economic analysis of the rocket-space industry of Russia. Audit and financial analysis. M, № 2
Makarov YN, Khrustalyov EY (2010b) Status and perspectives of development of the rocket-space industry of Russia—Preprint WP/2010/01. M: IASS
Makarov YN, Khrustalyov EY (2011a) Organizational and economic mechanisms of implementation of development plans and programs in the high technology fields of activity. Audit and financial analysis. M, № 1
Makarov YN, Khrustalyov EY (2011b) Fundamentals of economic analysis of the Russian space activity. Economic analysis: theory and practice. M, 29(236)
Makarov YN, Khrustalyov EY (2012) Methods of analysis and elaboration of development strategy of enterprises of the rocket and space industry. National interests. Priorities and security. M, 31(172).
Makarov YN, Kolchin SV (2008) Innovative technology of the 21st century and enhancement of competitiveness of space services. MR: State Scientific and Production Missile Space Center named after KE Tsiolkovsky
Makarov YN, Hrustalev EY, Khrustalyov YE (2012a) System approach to investigation of space activity. Economic analysis: theory and practice—M, 23(278)
Makarov YN, Hrustalev EY, Khrustalyov YE (2012b) System approach to investigation of space activity. Digests-Finances L: M 7(211)
Makarov YN, Butsenko EB, Lyalin VE, Yuakupov VI, Khrustalyov EY (2012c) Economic and mathematical modeling and intellectual information technologies for industrial corporations management. Ekaterinburg-Izhevsk: Publishing house of the Institute of Economy, Urals Branch of the Russian Academy of Sciences.

Makarov YN,Chursin AA, Vanyurikhin GI, Davidov VA, Kovkov GB, Pyeson LB (2013) Economy of space activity. Under the editorship of G.G. Raykunov. M: FIZMAT-LIT
Makarov YN, Davydov VA, Lyalin VE (2014) "Modeling of production optimum management of the rocket-space industry corporations". In the collection of materials of the First All-Russia Scientific and Practical Conference "Problems and perspectives of economic development of the rocket-space industry for the period until 2030 and its resource support" in the Peoples' Friendship University of Russia (PFUR–RUDN), November 21–23, 2013. T 1. M: Publishing house "MKD"
Marshall A (1993) Principles of Economics: [in 3 v.]: –M: Progress. University. T. 2. 310 Pages (Economic thought of the West)
Milgrom DA (1999) Competitiveness assessment of economic technologies. Marketing in Russia and abroad 2; 44–57
Pechenkin AN, Fomin VN (1995) Competitiveness of production and the manufacturer. Reliability and Quality Control·10
Pelikh SA, Davidov VA, Ivanov FF, Chursin AA, Sidorov IP (2011) Theoretical foundations of the enterprise competitiveness management under conditions of economic globalization. M: "Publishing house LLC. Spectrum"
Porter ME (1993) International competitiveness The Competitive Advantage of Nations: competitor, advantages of the countries. M. Porter; translation from English by I. V. Kavsyuk [and colleagues]; under the editorship of V. D. Schetinin. M: Int. Relations, p 896
Porter ME (2005) Competitiveness: M: Publishing house "Williams", p 588
Shapiro AD, Poznyakova TV (1999) Macroeconomic aspect of new technologies development by the enterprise for provision of competitiveness of production. Problems of technology, management and economy/under general editorship of Ph.D. in Economics Pankova V.A. 4.1.-Kramatorsk
Solovyev VP (2006) Competitiveness under conditions of innovative model of economy development. Under sci. editorship of Doctor of Economics B. A. Malitsky—Kiev: Phoenix. p 93
Streltsov NA (2004) Competitiveness of the national economy. N. A. Streltsov. Science and Innovations 7:62–65
Turina A (2003) Costs and competitiveness. Director. Minsk, № 5, pp 8–9
Varfolomeyev VP (2009) Hi-Tech production management. M: Economy
Volontsevich EF (2003) Competitiveness of the firms. Byelorussian State Econ. Uty. Minsk: BGEU
Voronov AA (2000) Concerning assessment of competitiveness level of machine-building enterprises. AA Voronov, Machinist 12;27–29
Zagorodsky A, Kara N (1997) Enterprise response to environment changes. Business-Inform 23;45–47
Zaharchenko VI (1999) Assessment and analysis of the enterprises competitiveness. Machinist 11:13–17

MIX
Papier aus verantwortungsvollen Quellen
Paper from responsible sources
FSC® C105338

If you have any concerns about our products,
you can contact us on
ProductSafety@springernature.com

In case Publisher is established outside the EU,
the EU authorized representative is:
Springer Nature Customer Service Center GmbH
Europaplatz 3, 69115 Heidelberg, Germany

Printed by Libri Plureos GmbH
in Hamburg, Germany